CHRISTIAN BUSINESS ALMANAC

The Ultimate Daily Guide for
Kingdom-Driven Entrepreneurs and Leaders

Books by Jacquelyn Lynn

Words to Work By: 31 devotions for the workplace based on the Book of Proverbs

Finding Joy in the Morning: You can make it through the night

Seven Day Anger Free Challenge: Be the Peace

The Simple Facts About Self-Publishing: What indie publishers need to know to produce a great book

Work as Worship: How Your Labor Becomes Your Legacy (a Conversations book)

How to Survive an Active Shooter: What You do Before, During, and After an Attack Could Save Your Life (a Conversations book)

Faith Words: Color the Words that Inspire You Every Day (a Christian coloring book for adults)

Christian Meditations (a Christian coloring book for adults)

Choices (a Joyful Cup story)

CHRISTIAN BUSINESS ALMANAC

The Ultimate Daily Guide for
Kingdom-Driven Entrepreneurs and Leaders

Jacquelyn Lynn

Christian Business Almanac
The Ultimate Daily Guide for Kingdom-Driven Entrepreneurs and Leaders
© 2024 Jacquelyn Lynn

All rights reserved. No portion of this book may be reproduced in any form without written permission from the publisher or author, except as permitted by U.S. copyright law. Send permission requests to info@contacttcs.com.

For bulk orders, contact info@createteachinspire.com.

Cover design: Jerry D. Clement
Photography: Jerry D. Clement
Illustrations: Jerry D. Clement
Interior design and production: Tuscawilla Creative Services, LLC

ISBN: 978-1-941826-48-5 *(hardback)*
978-1-941826-49-2 *(paperback)*
978-1-941826-50-8 *(ebook)*

Library of Congress Control Number: 2024909728

This publication is designed to provide accurate and authoritative information in regard to the subject matter covered. It is sold with the understanding that neither the author nor the publisher is engaged in rendering legal, investment, accounting or other professional services. While the publisher and author have used their best efforts in preparing this book, they make no representations or warranties with respect to the accuracy or completeness of the contents of this book and specifically disclaim any implied warranties of merchantability or fitness for a particular purpose. No warranty may be created or extended by sales representatives or written sales materials. The advice and strategies contained herein may not be suitable for your situation. You should consult with a professional when appropriate. Neither the publisher nor the author shall be liable for any loss of profit or any other commercial damages, including but not limited to special, incidental, consequential, personal, or other damages.

Published under the Create! Teach! Inspire! imprint
Tuscawilla Creative Services, LLC, Winter Springs, FL, USA
CreateTeachInspire.com.

Scripture quotations marked ESV are from ESV® Bible (The Holy Bible, English Standard Version®), copyright © 2001 by Crossway Bibles, a publishing ministry of Good News Publishers. Used by permission. All rights reserved.

Scripture quotations marked HCSB are taken from the Holman Christian Standard Bible®, Used by Permission HCSB ©1999,2000,2002,2003,2009 Holman Bible Publishers. Holman Christian Standard Bible®, Holman CSB®, and HCSB® are federally registered trademarks of Holman Bible Publishers.

Scripture quotations marked LSB are taken from the Legacy Standard Bible®, Copyright © 2021 by The Lockman Foundation. Used by permission. All rights reserved. Managed in partnership with Three Sixteen Publishing Inc. LSBible.org and 316publishing.com.

Scripture quotations marked NASB are taken from the New American Standard Bible®, Copyright © 1960, 1971, 1977, 1995, 2020 by The Lockman Foundation. Used by permission. All rights reserved. lockman.org

Scripture quotations marked NCV are taken from the New Century Version®. Copyright © 2005 by Thomas Nelson. Used by permission. All rights reserved.

Scripture quotations marked NKJV are taken from the New King James Version®. Copyright © 1982 by Thomas Nelson. Used by permission. All rights reserved.

Scripture quotations marked ICB are taken from the Holy Bible, International Children's Bible® Copyright© 1986, 1988, 1999, 2015 by Thomas Nelson. Used by permission. All rights reserved.

Quotations designated NET are from the NET Bible® copyright ©1996, 2019 by Biblical Studies Press, L.L.C. netbible.com. Scripture quoted by permission. All rights reserved.

Scripture quotations marked NIV are taken from the Holy Bible, New International Version®, NIV®. Copyright © 1973, 1978, 1984, 2011 by Biblica, Inc.® Used by permission of Zondervan. All rights reserved worldwide. www.zondervan.com The "NIV" and "New International Version" are trademarks registered in the United States Patent and Trademark Office by Biblica, Inc.®.

Scripture quotations marked NLT are taken from the *Holy Bible*, New Living Translation, copyright ©1996, 2004, 2015 by Tyndale House Foundation. Used by permission of Tyndale House Publishers, Carol Stream, Illinois 60188. All rights reserved."

Scripture quotations marked NLV are taken from the *New Life Version*, Copyright © 1969 and 2003. Used by permission of Barbour Publishing, Inc., Uhrichsville, Ohio 44683. All rights reserved.

Scripture quotations marked RSV are from Revised Standard Version of the Bible, copyright © 1946, 1952, and 1971 National Council of the Churches of Christ in the United States of America. Used by permission. All rights reserved worldwide.

Scripture quotations marked NRSV are from New Revised Standard Version Bible, copyright © 1989 National Council of the Churches of Christ in the United States of America. Used by permission. All rights reserved worldwide.

Scripture quotations marked NRSVue are taken from the New Revised Standard Version Updated Edition. Copyright © 2021 National Council of Churches of Christ in the United States of America. Used by permission. All rights reserved worldwide.

The steadfast love of the Lord never ceases;
his mercies never come to an end;
they are new every morning;
great is your faithfulness.

Lamentations 3:22-23, ESV

Welcome

There has never been a more challenging and rewarding time to be a Christian in business. And there has also never been a time when a resource like *Christian Business Almanac* was more needed.

Use *Christian Business Almanac* as a supplement to your daily prayer time. Read it with your breakfast. Keep it by your desk when you need a break, are on hold, or waiting for a meeting to start. Leave it on your nightstand to read before going to sleep. Put a copy on the coffee table of your office reception area or in the breakroom. Use it to spark family conversations. Or even put it in the bathroom. 😊

Each page includes a scripture, thought for the day, historical events, a prayer prompt, tips for personal and business growth, and more. Spend a few minutes each day on the corresponding date. Pray over the scripture. Consider how you can use the information to deepen your faith as you grow your business or advance your career. Think about how the historical events and businesspeople who were born or died on that day contributed to our current business landscape and the abundance of opportunities we enjoy.

We invite you to share the motivational memes featured throughout the *Almanac*. Visit CreateTeachInspire.com/CBAmemes to download full-color images you are welcome to use on your website, social media, presentations, or anywhere else.

We pray you and your career or business will be as blessed by *Christian Business Almanac* as we were by creating it for you.

Jacquelyn Lynn
Jerry D. Clement

Christian Business Almanac

—•—

January

January is named after the Roman god Janus. He had two faces and could see the future and the past. Janus is a symbol for new beginnings. He was the protector of doorways and gates.

Historical names for January include "Wulfmonath," from the ancient Anglo-Saxons because it was the month hungry wolves came scavenging. King Charlemagne called it "Wintermanoth," which meant "winter/cold month."

January birthstone
Garnet, rose quartz, red zircon

January flower
Carnation

January is ...
- Be Kind to Food Servers Month
- Celebration of Life Month
- Family Fit Lifestyle Month
- Financial Wellness Month
- Get a Balanced Life Month
- Get Organized Month
- International Creativity Month
- National Be On-Purpose Month
- National Clean Up Your Computer Month
- National Eye Care Month
- National Human Resource Month
- National Slavery and Human Trafficking Prevention Month
- National Stalking Awareness Month
- National Thank You Month
- Teen Driving Awareness Month

Mark your calendar for these January holidays and observances

Second Monday in January	National Clean Off Your Desk Day
Second Tuesday in January	National Poetry at Work Day
Second Wednesday in January	National Take the Stairs Day
Second Saturday in January	National Vision Board Day
Third Monday in January	Martin Luther King, Jr. Day
Third Sunday in January	World Religion Day
Fourth Monday in January	Better Business Communication Day
Fourth Tuesday in January	Speak Up and Succeed Day
Fourth Thursday in January	Clashing Clothes Day
Last Thursday in January	NASA's Day of Remembrance
Last Friday in January	National Fun at Work Day
Fourth Sunday in January	National Bible Sunday
Last Tuesday in January	National Plan for Vacation Day
Third Thursday in January	Get to Know Your Customers Day

Fun Facts about January
January originally had 30 days until Julius Caesar added the thirty-first day.
January is considered the coldest month of the year in the Northern Hemisphere.

January 1

Since you have heard about Jesus and have learned the truth that comes from him, throw off your old sinful nature and your former way of life, which is corrupted by lust and deception. Instead, let the Spirit renew your thoughts and attitudes. Put on your new nature, created to be like God—truly righteous and holy. (Ephesians 4:21-24, NLT)

Welcome to a new year!

The first day of a new year brings the delight of a fresh start, the thrill of new challenges, and a task list that may seem overwhelming.

What's the first thing to do?

Stop, take a deep breath, and rejoice and be glad in this day the Lord has made.

Release the negatives of the past—the pain, the regrets, the grudges that weigh us down. Be thankful for the experiences that have brought us to now and keep our focus on the present.

Don't be anxious about tomorrow. Worrying is simply praying for the wrong thing to happen. It's a thief that steals joy.

Should we plan and prepare? Of course. We should set goals and create strategies to reach them. But our top goal should be to live fully in today and leave tomorrow to God.

There is plenty to do. Let the year unfold according to God's plan.

Thought for the day

"It is important to keep a still place in the 'marketplace.' This still place is where God can dwell and speak to us. It is also the place from which we can speak in a healing way to all the people we meet in our busy days. Without that still place we start spinning."

Henri J.M. Nouwen

Read:
Proverbs, Chapter 1

Today we observe

New Year's Day
Copyright Law Day
Ellis Island Day
Public Domain Day
World Day of Peace
Eighth Day of Christmas

On this day in history

Notable events

In 1913, the U.S. Post Office began parcel post deliveries.

In 1919, Edsel Ford succeeded his father, Henry Ford, as president of the Ford Motor Company.

In 1934, Federal Deposit Insurance Corp. (FDIC, U.S. bank guarantor) became effective.

In 1939, Bill Hewlett and Dave Packard founded Hewett-Packard in a garage in Palo Alto, California.

In 1984, AT&T's twenty-two owned Bell system companies divested into eight companies.

In 1985, the internet's domain name system was created.

Births

Mark R. Hughes, American entrepreneur, founder of Herbalife International, Ltd., 1956

Deaths

Leo Steiner, American restaurateur, 1988

Grace Hopper, American computer scientist and U.S. Navy admiral, 1992

I pray that I may focus on what's important to God.

January 2

L et the morning bring me word of your unfailing love, for I have put my trust in you. Show me the way I should go, for to you I entrust my life.
(Psalm 143:8, NIV)

Get holidays on your radar

It's not enough to have holidays on your calendar, you need to get them on your radar so your operation is appropriately prepared. The beginning of a new year is an ideal time to do that.

Think about key holidays with these points in mind:
- Will your business close on the holiday?
- If the holiday falls on a day when you would normally be closed, will you close the day before or after?
- If you will be open on a holiday, will you offer extra holiday pay to your workers?
- How will you manage scheduling workers on the holiday and allowing for time off requests?
- How will you notify your customers and suppliers of your holiday schedule?
- Are there industry standards regarding holidays you should follow?
- What other issues are important for you to consider regarding each holiday?

You probably have a digital calendar that notes important holidays. It's a good idea to add reminders weeks, or even months, in advance so that you can implement an appropriate holiday plan.

Thought for the day

"A man may fail many times but he isn't a failure until he begins to blame somebody else."

John Burroughs

Read:
Proverbs, Chapter 2

Today we observe

World Introvert Day

National Motivation and Inspiration Day

National Run it Up the Flagpole and See if Anybody Salutes it Day

Ninth Day of Christmas

On this day in history

Notable events

In 1906, Willis Carrier received a U.S. patent for the world's first air conditioner.

In 1921, KDKA Pittsburgh became the first radio station to broadcast a religious program.

In 1938, book publisher Simon and Schuster was founded.

In 1942, the U.S. Navy opened a blimp base at Lakehurst, New Jersey.

Births

Charles Thurber, American inventor and firearms maker who made important innovations in the early development of the typewriter, 1803

Florence Lawrence, Canadian-American stage performer, film actress, and inventor; designed the first auto signaling arm, a predecessor of the modern turn signal, and the first mechanical brake signal, 1886

Deaths

Lloyd Hall, American chemist and inventor who contributed to the science of food preservation, 1971

Lillian Moller Gilbreth, American psychologist, industrial engineer, early pioneer in applying psychology to time-and-motion studies, 1972

William P. Carey, American businessman and philanthropist, founder of W.P. Carey & Co., 2012

I pray for new and exciting ways to serve.

January 3

Don't just pretend to love others. Really love them. Hate what is wrong. Hold tightly to what is good. Love each other with genuine affection, and take delight in honoring each other. Never be lazy, but work hard and serve the Lord enthusiastically. *(Romans 12:9-11, NLT)*

Are these holidays on your calendar?

Be sure holidays and observances that don't fall on the same date each year are on your calendar along with reminders. Major religious holidays include:
- Ash Wednesday
- Palm Sunday
- Good Friday
- Easter
- Yom Kippur
- Rosh Hashanah
- Thanksgiving
- Hanukkah

Check the list provided at the beginning of each month for moveable secular holidays and observances that you may want to celebrate.

Thought for the day

"I never perfected an invention that I did not think about in terms of the service it might give others. I find out what the world needs, then I proceed to invent."
Thomas Edison

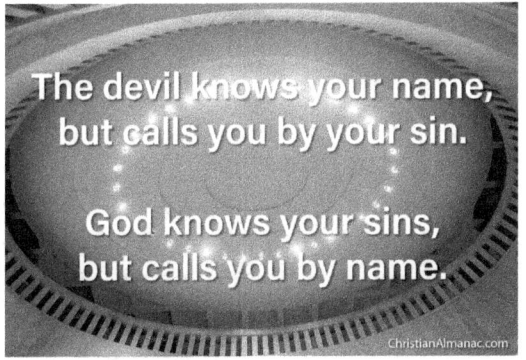

Read:
Proverbs, Chapter 3

Today we observe
National Write to Congress Day
International Mind-Body Wellness Day
Tenth Day of Christmas

On this day in history

Notable events
- In 1521, Martin Luther was excommunicated from the Roman Catholic Church for failing to recant parts of his Ninety-five Theses which started the Protestant Reformation.
- In 1831, the first building and loan association was organized in Frankford, Pennsylvania.
- In 1977, Steve Wozniak and Steve Jobs incorporated Apple Computer, Inc.
- In 2009, the bitcoin network was created when Kakamoto mined the starting block of the chain, known as the genesis block.

Births
- Earl William "Madman" Muntz, American businessman and engineer, television commercial pioneer, creator of the Muntz Stereo-Pak, invented the practice known as Muntzing (simplifying otherwise complicated electronic devices), 1914
- Gordon Moore, American businessman, engineer, cofounder of Intel Corporation, 1929
- Nicole Nordeman, American pop and contemporary Christian singer-songwriter, 1972

Deaths
- James Merritt Ives, American lithographer and businessman (Currier and Ives), 1895
- Conrad Hilton, American hotel mogul, 1979
- Ted Stanley, American entrepreneur and philanthropist, cofounder of the Danbury Mint, 2016

I am grateful for everything that has brought me to where I am.

January 4

Arise, Jerusalem! Let your light shine for all to see. For the glory of the Lord rises to shine on you. *(Isaiah 60:1, NLT)*

Rejection happens—make it work *for* you

Rejection is a part of all aspects of life, not just business. But you'll never get a yes unless you risk hearing a no.

You can respond to rejection with a huge dose of self-pity or you can turn it around and make it work for you.

Accept that rejection hurts and can make you angry. Don't deny your feelings. Treat yourself with compassion. Acknowledge the pain and process your emotions—just don't wallow in them.

Don't let rejection define you. You're not going to close every deal. You're not going to get every job—even the dream job you're perfect for. But you are more than your rejections. Spend some time focusing on your successes.

Learn from rejection. Don't make excuses or dwell on what you did wrong. Instead, consider what you can do differently next time. If you made mistakes or missed some red flags, acknowledge that and use that awareness as a way to improve. Then get out there and try again.

I pray that I may find beauty in the ordinary.

> Grow your faith by reflecting on your spiritual journey. Make a list of the ways your life has been better because you followed Christ.

Today we observe
National Trivia Day

Eleventh Day of Christmas

On this day in history
Notable events

In 1847, Samuel Colt sold his first revolver pistol to the U.S. government.

In 1865, New York Stock Exchange opened its first permanent headquarters at 10-12 Broad St., near Wall St. in New York City.

In 1968, Leo Fender sold Fender Guitars for $13 million to CBS.

In 2000, American businessman and investor Mark Cuban purchased a majority stake in the Dallas Mavericks NBA franchise for $285 million from H. Ross Perot, Jr.

In 2022, Toyota became the first foreign automaker to top U.S. sales, beating GM in 2021, partly due to supply issues.

Births

Isaac Newton, English physicist, mathematician and astronomer, 1643

Don Shula, American professional football player and coach, entrepreneur, 1930

Parker Harris, American business executive, cofounder of Salesforce, 1967

Deaths

Cornelius Vanderbilt, American business magnate who built his wealth in railroads and shipping, 1877

Harry B. Helmsley, American billionaire real estate developer, 1997

Thought for the day

"There are two possible outcomes: if the result confirms the hypothesis, then you've made a measurement. If the result is contrary to the hypothesis, then you've made a discovery."

Enrico Fermi

Read:
Proverbs, Chapter 4

January 5

Dear friends, don't be surprised at the fiery trials you are going through, as if something strange were happening to you. Instead, be very glad—for these trials make you partners with Christ in his suffering, so that you will have the wonderful joy of seeing his glory when it is revealed to all the world. If you are insulted because you bear the name of Christ, you will be blessed, for the glorious Spirit of God rests upon you. *(1 Peter 4:12-14, NLT)*

The 8 rules George Washington Carver lived by:

1. Be clean both inside and out.
2. Neither look up to the rich nor down to the poor.
3. Lose, if need be, without squealing.
4. Win without bragging.
5. Always be considerate of women, children, and older people.
6. Be too brave to lie.
7. Be too generous to cheat.
8. Take your share of the world and let others take theirs.

Failure should always be an option in your organization. Failure is a necessary step toward business success. If you're not failing at least occasionally, you're not innovating enough. Don't punish failure; instead, see it as an investment in education.

Thought for the day

"Dream big, but allow yourself the opportunity to start small, and have your share of struggles in the beginning. The world's greatest composers weren't writing symphonies the day they first sat at a piano."

Kevin O'Rourke

I pray for those who feel trapped.

Today we observe

Carver Day (honoring George Washington Carver)

Twelfth Day of Christmas

On this day in history

Notable events

In 1903, San Francisco-Hawaii telegraph cable opened for public use.

In 1914, Henry Ford, founder of Ford Motor Company, announced his $5 per day minimum wage, doubling most workers' pay from $2.40 for a nine-hour day to $5 for an eight-hour day.

Births

King C. Gillette, American businessman and inventor of inexpensive and disposable safety razor blades, 1855

DeWitt Bristol Brace, inventor of the spectrophotometer, 1859

Byron Bancroft Johnson, American professional baseball executive, founder of the American League, 1864

Sam Phillips, American record producer, founder of Sun Records and Sun Studio, 1923

Hosea Williams, American civil rights leader, ordained minister, businessman, politician, and philanthropist, 1926

Deaths

Calvin Coolidge, 30th U.S. President, 1933

George Washington Carver, African-American agricultural scientist and inventor, 1943

S. Joseph Begun, German-American engineer and inventor known for his contributions to magnetic recording, underwater acoustics, and telecommunications, 1995

Jay Arena, American pediatrician and inventor of the child-proof safety cap, 1996

Read: Proverbs, Chapter 5

January 6

Behold, I will do something new; now it will spring forth; will you not know it? I will even make a roadway in the wilderness, rivers in the wasteland.
(Isaiah 43:19, LSB)

Give others a chance to serve you

Are you quick to do favors but slow to ask for them? Not only are you limiting your own achievements, you're denying others an opportunity to serve.

To build synergy, we need to work together, not just as synchronized parts but as mutually supporting elements. One of a leader's best strengths is the ability to admit they need help and graciously accept it.

If you enjoy serving others, think about how much they likely would enjoy serving you. And when that happens, your relationship will deepen and strengthen as you work together toward a common goal. Your productivity will improve and your knowledge will increase.

People can't help you if they don't know what you need, so tell them. Be clear and specific so they know exactly what they're committing to do. At the same time, be courteous and let them know they can decline if they are unable to meet your needs.

Thought for the day

"Forgiving isn't something you do for someone else. It's something you do for yourself. It's saying, 'You're not important enough to have a stranglehold on me.' It's saying, 'You don't get to trap me in the past. I am worthy of a future.'"
— *Jodi Picoult*

I pray for calm when I am stressed and overwhelmed.

Today we observe
Three Kings Day
Epiphany

On this day in history

Notable events

In 1893, the Washington National Cathedral was chartered by Congress.
In 1914, the stock brokerage firm of Merrill Lynch was founded.
In 1931, Thomas Edison submitted his last patent application.
In 1976, Ted Turner purchased the Atlanta Braves for a reported $12 million.

Births

Abram Nicholas Pritzker, American businessman (Hyatt Hotels, *McCall's* magazine), 1896
Danny Thomas, American actor, comedian, producer, and philanthropist, 1912
John DeLorean, American engineer, inventor, and U.S. automobile industry executive; founder of DeLorean Motor Company, 1925
Fred L. Turner, American businessman, CEO of McDonald's (1977-2004), 1933
Henry R. Kravis, American businessman, investor, and philanthropist, 1944
Eric Trump, American businessman and activist, 1984

Deaths

Philip Danforth Armour, American meatpacking industrialist, founder of Armour & Company, 1901
Theodore Roosevelt, 26th U.S. President, 1919
Tex Rickard, American boxing promoter and entrepreneur, 1929
Albert Rice Leventhal, American publisher (Little Golden Books), 1976
Cy Leslie, American businessman, founder of Voco Records, Pickwick Records, and MGM/UA Home Entertainment Group, 2008
Don Tyson, American businessman and founder of Tyson Foods, 2011

Read:
Proverbs, Chapter 6

January 7

You, my brothers and sisters, were called to be free. But do not use your freedom to indulge the flesh; rather, serve one another humbly in love. For the entire law is fulfilled in keeping this one command: "Love your neighbor as yourself." *(Galatians 5:13-14, NIV)*

Make two lists from last year

Though you may be focused on the new beginnings offered by a new year, take the time to look back.

Michelle Ogden, founder and CEO of Ogden Wealth, LLC (Maitland, Florida), says that every January, she makes two lists from the previous year. One is all the company's successes; the other is what she calls opportunities to learn and grow.

"We review them as a team and talk through what we learned and how we can improve," she says.

When reviewing what didn't work, keep in mind that this isn't the time to cast blame or discipline—that should have been done when the situation occurred. Concentrate on understanding what happened, how to avoid repeating mistakes and what you can do differently in the future. Remember that you can learn as much from reviewing your successes as from your failures, so don't ignore studying what you did right. How can you repeat those wins? Can you be more efficient or do even better?

Incorporate these lessons into your plan for the year and move forward.

Thought for the day

"Sometimes when I'm talking, my words can't keep up with my thoughts. I wonder why we think faster than we speak…Probably so we can think twice!"

Bill Watterson

I pray that I may pass a legacy of faith to the next generation.

Today we observe

I Am a Mentor Day

Orthodox Christmas

On this day in history

Notable events

In 1782, Bank of North America, the first U.S. commercial bank, opened in Philadelphia.

In 1784, the first U.S. seed business was established by David Landreth in Philadelphia.

In 1830, America's first major railroad station opened in Baltimore as the eastern terminus of the recently formed Baltimore and Ohio (B&O) Railroad.

In 1927, commercial transatlantic telephone service between New York and London began.

In 1980, U.S. President Jimmy Carter authorized legislation to bail out the Chrysler Corporation with a $1.5 billion loan.

In 2019, Amazon overtook Microsoft to become the world's most valuable listed company, worth $787 billion.

Births

Millard Fillmore, 13th U.S. President, 1800

Deaths

James Fisk, flamboyant American financier known as "Barnum of Wall Street" for his unscrupulous business practices, 1872

Nikola Tesla, Serbian-American physicist, electrical engineer, and inventor, 1943

Nathaniel Reed, American outlaw who became an evangelist after his release from prison, 1950

Jerome L. Murray, American inventor of the peristaltic heart pump that made open-heart surgery possible, 1998

Fred L. Turner, American businessman, CEO of McDonald's (1977-2004), 2013

Read: Proverbs, Chapter 7

January 8

> Woe to him who builds his house by unrighteousness, and his upper rooms by injustice, who makes his neighbor serve him for nothing and does not give him his wages. *(Jeremiah 22:13, ESV)*

Time for your annual checkup

January is an ideal time to conduct an annual checkup of your business. Take a look at these specific areas:

Mission statement. Is your mission statement still valid? If not, revise it.

Business plan. Compare last year's plan with your actual results, and use that information to create a plan for the current year.

Employee compensation and benefit packages. How do your pay scales, bonus plans, and benefits compare with other employers in the area? How satisfied are your workers? Could your benefit resources be realigned for improved employee relations?

Insurance. Review all your policies with a line-by-line coverage and cost analysis. Let your agent know about any changes in your operation that could require changes in insurance.

Security. Do a check of your physical and virtual security. Change locks, alarm codes, and passwords at least once a year.

Professional relationships. Be sure the people you rely on for advice—your attorney, accountant, financial planner, other consultants, etc.—have the knowledge and skills appropriate for your needs.

Financial relationships. Review the details of your banking agreements, commercial loans, and leases. Renegotiate those contracts if necessary.

Other areas to examine include competitor information, customer satisfaction feedback, supplier terms and relationships, maintenance and service contracts, office furnishings and equipment, computer systems, freight, and telecommunications systems.

Read:
Proverbs, Chapter 8

Today we observe

Show and Tell at Work Day

World Typing Day

On this day in history

Notable events

In 1675, the first American commercial corporation, NY Fishing Co., was chartered.

In 1835, the U.S. national debt was $0 for the first and only time in history.

In 1889, Dr. Herman Hollerith received the first U.S. patent for a mechanical tabulating machine.

In 1945, Youth for Christ organized.

In 1982, AT&T agreed to divest itself of twenty-two Bell System companies.

In 1988, Hewlett-Packard introduced HP-28S Advanced Scientific Calculator.

Births

Joseph Weizenbaum, German-American computer scientist and professor at MIT, created the first chatbot, 1923

Deaths

Galileo Galilei, Italian astronomer, physicist, and engineer, 1642

Eli Whitney, American inventor, 1825

Dave Thomas, American businessman, philanthropist, fast-food tycoon, founder of Wendy's, 2002

Thought for the day

"The illiterate of the 21st century will not be those who cannot read and write, but those who cannot learn, unlearn, and relearn."

Alvin Toffler

I pray for those who are in pain.

January 9

Have I not commanded you? Be strong and courageous. Do not be frightened, and do not be dismayed, for the Lord your God is with you wherever you go. *(Joshua 1:9, ESV)*

Where are you sitting?

Where you sit determines what you see. Is your view a solid wall, the back of someone's head, or a vast panorama?

What you see determines what you do. Are you blocked? Do you need to wiggle around? Or do you have a wide open field?

What you do determines your future.

So, where are you sitting? Be sure you're sitting in a good place—and if you're not, move.

Don't envy what other people have

When you begin to feel envious because of what you see (success, money, things) that other people have, stop and remember that you don't see everything.

You may not be able to see what they had to do to get those things—and it might have been something you're not willing to do.

You may not be able to see behind their façade of material trappings to know if they're truly happy and content or if they're lonely and miserable.

And what do you benefit if you gain the whole world but lose your own soul? (Mark 8:36, NLT)

Admire what successful people have achieved without envying what they have. And focus on what you have to do to get what you really want.

I am grateful for the kind things that strangers have done for me.

Read:
Proverbs, Chapter 9

Today we observe

National Law Enforcement Appreciation Day

National Word Nerd Day

On this day in history

Notable events

In 1847, the first San Francisco newspaper was published.

In 1848, the first commercial bank in San Francisco was established.

In 1894, New England Telephone and Telegraph installed the first battery-operated telephone switchboard in Lexington, Massachusetts.

In 1986, after losing a patent battle with Polaroid, Kodak had to give up its instant camera business.

In 2001, Apple introduced iTunes at the Macworld Expo in San Francisco.

Births

Richard M. Nixon, 37th President of the United States, 1913

Earl Gilbert Graves, Sr., American entrepreneur, publisher (founder of Black Enterprise magazine), and philanthropist, 1935

Mat Hoffman, American BMX rider and entrepreneur, 1972

Deaths

Willis Rodney Whitney, American chemist, founder of the General Electric research laboratory, and pioneer of industrial scientific research, 1958

Thought for the day

"You can do so much in 10 minutes' time. Ten minutes, once gone, are gone for good. Divide your life into 10-minute units and sacrifice as few of them as possible in meaningless activity."

Ingvar Kamprad

January 10

> The generous will prosper; those who refresh others will themselves be refreshed. *(Proverbs 11:25, NLT)*

Holy, Holy, Holy! Lord God Almighty!

Reginald Heber (1783-1826)

Holy, holy, holy! Lord God Almighty!
Early in the morning our song shall rise to Thee;
Holy, holy, holy! merciful and mighty!
God in three Persons, blessed Trinity!

Holy, holy, holy! all the saints adore Thee,
casting down their golden crowns around the glassy sea;
cherubim and seraphim, falling down before Thee,
who wert and art and evermore shalt be.

Holy, holy, holy! though the darkness hide Thee,
though the eye of sinfulness Thy glory may not see;
only Thou art holy, there is none beside Thee,
perfect in pow'r, in love, and purity.

Holy, holy, holy! Lord God Almighty!
All Thy works shall praise Thy name, in earth and sky and sea;
Holy, holy, holy! merciful and mighty!
God in three Persons, blessed Trinity!

Thought for the day

"Entrepreneurs are risk takers, willing to roll the dice with their money or reputation on the line in support of an idea or enterprise. They willingly assume responsibility for the success or failure of a venture and are answerable for all its facets."

Victor Kiam

I pray that I always remember that God has my back, no matter what.

Today we observe

National Shareholders Day

On this day in history

Notable events

In 1776, "Common Sense" by Thomas Paine, advocating American independence, was published.

In 1870, John D. Rockefeller, Henry M. Flagler, and others founded Standard Oil Company of Ohio.

In 1949, RCA introduced the 45 RPM record.

In 1970, the Preview Center (the first building to open) opened at Walt Disney World in Florida.

Births

Jacob Schiff, German-born American banker, businessman, and philanthropist who helped finance the expansion of American railroads, 1847

Roy E. Disney, American businessman, senior executive for The Walt Disney Company, nephew of Walt Disney, son of Roy O. Disney, 1930

George Foreman, American boxer and entrepreneur, 1949

Diane Hendricks, American businesswoman, film producer, and philanthropist, owner of the Hendricks Holding Company and ABC Supply, 1947

Jared Kushner, American real estate developer and son-in-law and advisor to Donald Trump, 1981

Deaths

Samuel Colt, American inventor, industrialist, and businessman who established Colt's Patent Fire-Arms Manufacturing company (now Colt's Manufacturing Company) and made the mass production of revolvers commercially viable, 1862

Ruth Wakefield, American inventor and creator of the Toll House Cookie, the first chocolate chip cookie, 1977

Read:
Proverbs, Chapter 10

January 11

But I trust in you, Lord; I say, "You are my God." My times are in your hands; deliver me from the hands of my enemies, from those who pursue me. Let your face shine on your servant; save me in your unfailing love. *(Psalm 31:14-16, NIV)*

Steps to wise decision-making

1. Define as specifically as possible what the decision is that needs to be made.
2. Brainstorm and write down as many alternatives as you can think of.
3. Think of where you could find more information about possible alternatives, including friends, family, clergy, co-workers, state and federal agencies, professional organizations, online resources, news sources, books, and so on.
4. Check out your alternatives.
5. Evaluate your alternatives to see which ones could work for you.
6. Visualize the outcomes of each realistically workable alternative.
7. Do a reality check. Which of your remaining alternatives are most likely to happen?
8. Review those remaining alternatives and decide which ones feel most comfortable to you.
9. Make a decision and take action.
10. Review your decision at specified points and make changes if necessary.

Thought for the day

"I would rather be what God chose to make me than the most glorious creature that I could think of. For to have been born in God's thought, and then made by God is the dearest, grandest, and most precious thing in all thinking."

George MacDonald

I pray that I see the hand of God everywhere.

Today we observe

International Thank You Day

National Human Trafficking Awareness Day

On this day in history

Notable events

In 1759, Presbyterian Ministers Fund, the first life insurance company in the United States, was incorporated in Philadelphia.

In 1912, the Bread and Roses Strike began in Lawrence, Massachusetts.

In 1964, the first government report by the U.S. Surgeon General warning that smoking may be hazardous was issued.

Births

Ezra Cornell, American businessman and philanthropist, founder of Western Union Telegraph and Cornell University, 1807

Harry Gordon Selfridge, American retail magnate, founder of London-based department store Selfridges, 1858

Roger Lewis, American businessman, CEO of Amtrak, Pan Am, 1912

Carroll Shelby, American automotive designer, racing driver, and entrepreneur, 1923

Deaths

Gail Borden, American manufacturer and inventor of condensed milk, 1874

Nelson Doubleday, American book publisher, president of Doubleday Company (1922-1946), 1949

Ivan Combe, American inventor of personal care products (Clearasil), 2000

Carl Karcher, American entrepreneur and philanthropist, founder of Carl's Jr. hamburger chain, 2008

Sheldon Adelson, American business magnate (CEO of Las Vegas Sands casino company), 2021

Read:
Proverbs, Chapter 11

January 12

And after you have suffered a little while, the God of all grace, who has called you to his eternal glory in Christ, will himself restore, confirm, strengthen, and establish you. *(1 Peter 5:10, ESV)*

Build a problem and solution archive

Are you wasting valuable time reinventing the wheel?

In an ideal world, when we have a problem, we'd solve it and never have to deal with it again. But in the real world, the same (or very similar) problems will occur over and over. When you treat a known problem as a new problem, you're wasting time and money.

That's why you need to create a database of problems and solutions. Make it a simple, searchable, easily accessible system that lists the problems and describes the steps that were taken to solve them. Adding the situation and solution to the database should be the required final step in solving the problem.

When a problem arises, check the problem/solution database to see if the situation or something similar has happened before and how it was handled. If the same solution will work again, you can move quickly to getting the problem resolved. Update the database to reflect that the problem recurred and what you did.

If the problem is not in the database, be sure it gets entered before it's considered a closed matter.

A problem and solution database captures operational knowledge and institutional history even though the employees involved may have moved on.

Today we observe
Stick to your New Year's Resolution Day
Work Harder Day

On this day in history
Notable events
- In 1906, the Dow Jones closed above 100 (100.26) for the first time.
- In 1929, seatrain (railroad cars aboard ships) service began between New Orleans and Havana.
- In 1957, the Southern Christian Leadership Conference (SCLC) was founded at Ebenezer Baptist Church in Atlanta with Martin Luther King, Jr. as its leader.

Births
- William Chapman Ralston, San Francisco businessman and financier, founder of the Bank of California, 1826
- Ruth Benerito, American chemist and inventor in the textile industry, known for the development of wash-and-wear cotton fabrics, 1916
- Rush Limbaugh, American conservative political talk radio personality, 1951
- Jeff Bezos, American entrepreneur and founder of Amazon, 1964

Deaths
- Hiram Walker, American entrepreneur and founder of Hiram Walker and Sons, Ltd. distillery, 1899
- Bill Hewlett, American engineer and businessman, cofounder of Hewlett-Packard, 2001
- Charles H. Price II, American businessman, banker, chairman and CEO of Price Candy Company, U.S. ambassador, 2012

Thought for the day

"Character may be manifested in the great moments, but it is made in the small ones."

Phillips Brooks

I pray for my competitors.

Read:
Proverbs, Chapter 12

January 13

For someone who lives on milk is still an infant and doesn't know how to do what is right. Solid food is for those who are mature, who through training have the skill to recognize the difference between right and wrong. *(Hebrews 5:13-14, NLT)*

Raise prices without losing customers

Price increases are never pleasant, but they are often the only way to maintain profitability when your expenses go up. Review your pricing annually (or even more often) to be sure you're covering your costs and making money.

Ease customers into your new pricing structure to make it as palatable as possible. Let them know that gradual increases are necessary for you to cover your costs, and that those increases will be reflected in future orders.

It's a good idea to avoid across-the-board price hikes if you can. Increasing everything by the same amount at the same time can have a jarring impact on customers. Stagger the increases for a softer reaction.

If possible, don't raise prices to all customers all at once. First increase prices to your least profitable customers. If you lose one of those accounts, you'll probably be better off; take it as an opportunity to find a new, more profitable buyer.

Even if you lose a better account because of higher prices, keep two points in mind: First, chances are your competitors are charging similar rates, so there's an excellent possibility those customers will come back. Second, the only way for your company to grow and thrive is for your business to be profitable.

I pray that I choose my words carefully and say things that will help not hurt.

Read: Proverbs, Chapter 13

Today we observe
Make Your Dream Come True Day

On this day in history

Notable events
- In 1863, the chenille yarn making machine was patented by William Canter in New York City.
- In 1942, Henry Ford patented a method of constructing plastic auto bodies.
- In 1976, American inventor Ray Kurzweil and the National Federation of the Blind unveiled the Kurzweil Reading Machine, the first omni-font optical character recognition system.
- In 2000, Microsoft Chairman Bill Gates stepped aside as chief executive and promoted company president Steve Ballmer to the position.

Births
Horatio Alger, American clergyman and author for whom the Horatio Alger Association of Distinguished Americans was named 1832
Alfred Fuller, Canadian-American businessman, entrepreneur, and philanthropist (Fuller Brush Company), 1885
Kevin McClatchy, American businessman, chairman of McClatchy, former owner of the Pittsburg Pirates baseball team, 1963

Deaths
Bruce Pasternack, American businessman, president and CEO of Special Olympics International (2005-2007), 2021

Thought for the day

"We have to abandon the idea that schooling is something restricted to youth. How can it be, in a world where half the things a man knows at 20 are no longer true at 40—and half the things he knows at 40 hadn't been discovered when he was 20?"

Arthur C. Clarke

January 14

You then, my son, be strong in the grace that is in Christ Jesus. And the things you have heard me say in the presence of many witnesses entrust to reliable people who will also be qualified to teach others. *(2 Timothy 2:1-2, NIV)*

Sync your billing with your customers' payable procedures

A simple but often overlooked technique for improving cash flow is to coordinate your billing system with your customers' payable procedures. Submitting your invoices at the right time with complete information will often speed up payment, particularly with larger companies. Consider these tips:

When setting up a new account, find out what the company's payment procedures are. Ask what you can do to ensure prompt payment.

Be sure your invoice is easy to read and includes all necessary information. Clearly identify your products and services, your terms, payment methods, and indicate any customer reference that will help the accounts payable department determine the validity of your invoice.

If you are billing on a retainer, find out when checks for your type of services are written, and time your invoices to arrive shortly before that date.

Be sure you are sending your invoice to the correct person and location. Some companies may require the purchaser to approve invoices and forward them to accounting; others may pay faster if you send it directly to accounting.

If possible, bill on the delivery of the product or service. That's when the appreciation of your work is highest. When they're thinking about you in a positive way, they're more likely to process your invoice faster.

Read:
Proverbs, Chapter 14

Today we observe
Take a Missionary to Lunch Day

On this day in history

Notable events

In 1799, Eli Whitney (inventor of the cotton gin) received a government contract for 10,000 muskets.

In 1873, "celluloid" was registered as a trademark by its inventor, John Wesley Hyatt.

In 1976, Ted Turner became CEO of the Atlanta Braves.

Births

Thomas J. Watson, Jr., American businessman (president of IBM, 1952-1971) and politician, 1914

Deaths

John Francis Dodge, American automobile pioneer (cofounder of Dodge Brothers Company), 1920

Ray Kroc, American fast-food entrepreneur (McDonald's) and owner of San Diego Padres baseball team, 1984

Thought for the day

"The only thing that stands between a man and what he wants from life is often merely the will to try it and the faith to believe that it is possible."

Richard DeVos

I pray that others will see Christ in me.

Grow your faith through obedience. What will you do to obey the Lord today?

January 15

Endure hardship as discipline; God is treating you as his children. For what children are not disciplined by their father? (Hebrews 11:1, ESV)

Monitor the internet with Google Alerts

Don't get surprised by what's on the internet about you, your company, or your industry. Track it for free with Google Alerts.

Google Alerts is a free content change detection and notification service offered by Google. It allows you to monitor the internet for keywords and phrases of interest, and sends you an email when Google finds a result matching your search query.

With Google Alerts, you can monitor what's being said online about your company and brand, your competitors, your key people, and other relevant topics.

To set an alert, go to Google.com/alerts, type the keyword or phrase into the search bar, choose your options (how often you want the alerts, the sources, the language, the region, how many results, and where to send the results email), and click on the "create alert" button.

Put names and phrases in quotation marks; otherwise, Google will send alerts for the individual words.

If you're tracking companies or people, remember to set alerts for common misspellings and variations. For example, if you're following McDonald's, include an alert for MacDonald's as well. If you're following someone named Richard, include alerts for Dick, Rick, and Rich. If you're following someone named Caroline, include alerts for Carolin, Carolyn, and Karoline.

Experiment with the settings until you find the combination that is most effective for you. Adding, removing, and editing alerts is quick and easy, so you can do it as needed. It's also a good idea to do an annual review of your alerts to be sure you are tracking everything you need to and not what's no longer of interest.

On this day in history

Notable events

In 1782, Superintendent of Finance Robert Morris recommended the establishment of decimal coinage and a national mint to U.S. Congress.

In 1831, the first U.S.-built locomotive to pull a passenger train made its first run.

In 1861, Elisha Otis patented the steam elevator.

In 1907, American inventor Lee De Forest patented the three-element vacuum tube.

In 1943, the world's largest office building, the Pentagon, was completed to house the U.S. military headquarters.

In 2001, Jimmy Wales and Larry Sanger launched Wikipedia, a free Wiki or content encyclopedia.

Births

Pierre S. du Pont, American entrepreneur, businessman (president of DuPont de Nemours, Inc. and president of General Motors), philanthropist, 1870

Martin Luther King, Jr., American clergyman and civil rights leader, 1929

Deaths

Fannie Farmer, American culinary pioneer who revolutionized modern cooking through the introduction of precise measurements, 1915

Thought for the day

"There are two types of people who will tell you that you cannot make a difference in this world: those who are afraid to try and those who are afraid you will succeed."

Ray Goforth

I pray that I worship God in everything I do.

Read:
Proverbs, Chapter 15

January 16

Consider it pure joy, my brothers and sisters, whenever you face trials of many kinds, because you know that the testing of your faith produces perseverance. Let perseverance finish its work so that you may be mature and complete, not lacking anything. *(James 1:2-4, NIV)*

Turn your error page into a marketing message

No matter how well your website is designed, there will be times when some of your site's visitors will land on a "404 error" page. This generally happens when the page they're trying to reach has been moved, deleted, or renamed. The URL might not work anymore but it's still showing up on other sites, blogs, and search engine results pages.

Turn this negative into a positive by customizing your 404 page with a marketing message.

Your 404 page should follow your basic home page design and site navigation so visitors immediately know they're on the right site. Tell them the page they're looking for can't be found and invite them to click around using the search tool or the navigation menu. Also add prominent links to helpful resources on your site, such as your newsletter or an opt-in offer to get them on your email list, but don't make it a hard sell.

It's okay to have fun with your 404 page with a cute image or other entertaining content, but be sure to take the extra step so you don't miss the opportunity to turn a mishap into marketing.

Thought for the day

"It is a waste of time to be angry about my disability. One has to get on with life and I haven't done badly. People won't have time for you if you are always angry or complaining."

Stephen Hawking

Today we observe
Book Publishers Day
National Religious Freedom Day

On this day in history
Notable events
In 1868, William Davis, a fish dealer in Detroit, patented a refrigerator car.

Births
Andre Michelin, French industrialist, tire manufacturer, and publisher of the Michelin Guide, 1853

Frank Zamboni, American entrepreneur, engineer, and inventor of the Zamboni Ice Resurfacer, 1901

Carl Karcher, American entrepreneur and philanthropist, founder of Carl's Jr. hamburger chain, 1917

Cassey Ho, American social media fitness entrepreneur, 1987

Deaths
Marshall Field, American entrepreneur and founder of Marshall Field and Company, 1906

Lydia Moss Bradley, American bank president, philanthropist, and college founder, 1908

Thaddeus S. C. Lowe, American aeronaut and inventor, 1913

John C. Bogle, American investor, business magnate, and philanthropist; founder and chief executive of The Vanguard Group, 2019

I pray for supervisors and managers who must discipline or provide negative feedback to their teams.

Read:
Proverbs, Chapter 16

January 17

Do not steal. Do not lie. Do not deceive one another. Do not swear falsely by my name and so profane the name of your God. I am the Lord. Do not defraud or rob your neighbor. Do not hold back the wages of a hired worker overnight. *(Leviticus 19:11-13, NIV)*

Get a lift from love notes

No matter how positive you are naturally, no matter how many spirit-lifting techniques you know, you're going to have bad days—days when suppliers don't deliver, customers are unreasonable, the computer has a mind of its own, and you can't seem to do anything right.

Set up a "love notes" file—a special file of complimentary messages (cards, notes, emails) you've received from customers and colleagues. When you're having "one of those days," go through your morale-boosting messages to remind yourself of the difference you make for the customers you serve and the people you work with.

If you get a lift from positive written feedback, remember others do as well, so be a source of content for someone else's "love notes" file. When appropriate, let others know in writing that you appreciate them and why.

Thought for the day

"The truth is that many people set rules to keep from making decisions. Not me. I don't want to be a manager or a dictator. I want to be a leader—and leadership is ongoing, adjustable, flexible, and dynamic."

Mike Krzyzewski

I pray for those who need direction.

Read:
Proverbs, Chapter 17

Today we observe

Kid Inventors' Day

Customer Service Day

On this day in history

Notable events

In 1871, Andrew Smith Hallidie patented the first cable car in the U.S.

In 1916, Rodman Wanamaker organized a lunch in New York to discuss forming a golfers association which would become the PGA.

In 1928, the first fully automatic photographic film developing machine was patented.

In 1934, President Franklin Roosevelt created the Electric Home and Farm Authority to increase sales of large electrical appliances to Americans of low and moderate income.

Births

Benjamin Franklin, U.S. Founding Father, inventor, writer, ambassador, 1706

Catherine Booth, co-founder of the Salvation Army, 1829

Carl Laemmle, German-American film producer and cofounder of Universal Pictures, 1867

Glenn Luther Martin, American pioneering aviator, founder of what became Lockheed Martin, 1886

George Sperti, American inventor (Preparation H, Sperti Ultraviolet Lamp, Aspercreme), 1900

Vidal Sassoon, British-American hairstylist, businessman, and philanthropist, 1928

Anne F. Beiler, American businesswoman, author, motivational speaker, founder of Auntie Anne's Pretzels, 1949

Deaths

Rutherford B. Hayes, 19th U.S. President, 1893

Juliette Gordon Low, American activist and founder of the Girl Scouts of America, 1927

Walter O. Briggs Sr., American entrepreneur (Briggs Manufacturing company, automobile body manufacturer), and sports team owner, 1952

January 18

> **B**ut Jesus, aware of this, replied, "Why criticize this woman for doing such a good thing to me? You will always have the poor among you, but you will not always have me. She has poured this perfume on me to prepare my body for burial. I tell you the truth, wherever the Good News is preached throughout the world, this woman's deed will be remembered and discussed."
> *(Matthew 26:10-13, NLT)*

Take a vacation

Vacations are essential to your mental and physical health. If you're someone who finds it hard to take time off, these tips may help:

Plan ahead. Schedule your vacation time far enough in advance that you can organize your workload around your time off.

Build a backup network. Look for people you trust who can handle work that can't wait while you're gone. If you're a solo operator, develop a strong network of similarly situated business owners who can help you and whom you can help. Draw up a written agreement to protect everyone in terms of the client's status, obligations, and compensation.

Notify your regular clients. About a week before you leave, tell the clients with whom you communicate regularly that you'll be unavailable. You may need to tell them sooner if it means rescheduling some of their work.

Take some work with you. Sometimes a change of scenery is worthwhile even if you can't totally escape your business—just don't work the entire time.

Consider several short breaks instead of one long vacation. A Friday-through-Monday break can often be achieved without your clients even knowing you were gone.

Thought for the day

"It's so simple to be wise. Just think of something stupid to say and then don't say it."

Sam Levenson

Today we observe

National Thesaurus Day

Week of Prayer for Christian Unity
(Jan. 18-25)

On this day in history

Notable events

In 1903, the first transatlantic radio transmission to originate in the United States was sent by a transmitter in Massachusetts.

In 1964, plans for the World Trade Center in New York City were announced.

In 1991, Eastern Air Lines, once one of the world's largest airlines, went out of business after 62 years, citing financial problems.

Births

Joseph Glidden, American businessman, farmer, philanthropist, inventor of modern barbed wire, 1813

Thomas A. Watson, American telephone pioneer, shipbuilder, assistant to Alexander Graham Bell, one of the original organizers of the Bell Telephone Company, 1854

Ray Dolby, American engineer, sound expert, and inventor, 1933

Deaths

Alfred Vail, American inventor and early telegraph pioneer, 1859

John Tyler, 10th U.S. President, 1862

Georgia Frontiere, American businesswoman, entertainer, and philanthropist, NFL team owner, 2008

I pray that I will not be afraid of being disliked.

Read:
Proverbs, Chapter 18

January 19

> Good will come to those who are generous and lend freely, who conduct their affairs with justice. *(Psalm 112:5, NIV)*

Get paid what you're worth

Remember the concept of perceived value: If something is priced too low, it must not be worth much. If it's priced high, it must be valuable.

Make it a policy to always get paid what you're worth.

You may be tempted to offer a deep discount to a new client or as a favor to someone who can't afford your regular prices. If you're willing to charge so little for your work, why should the receiver value it any higher than you do? And why should they be willing to pay more later?

Set the tone of your relationship from the start by pricing your products and services at what they're worth. Consider it a red flag when a prospective customer tries to get you to charge less.

The only exception is when you are clearly donating your products or services to a bona fide charity.

Thought for the day

"Be so strong that nothing can disturb your peace of mind. Talk health, happiness, and prosperity to every person you meet. Make all your friends feel there is something special in them. Look at the sunny side of everything. Think only of the best, work only for the best, and expect only the best. Be as enthusiastic about the success of others as you are about your own. Forget the mistakes of the past and press on to the greater achievements of the future. Give everyone a smile. Spend so much time improving yourself that you have no time left to criticize others. Be too big for worry and too noble for anger."

Christian Larsen

Today we observe

Good Memory Day

National Tin Can Day

On this day in history

Notable events

In 1825, Ezra Daggett and nephew Thomas Kensett patented food storage in tin cans.

In 1883, the first electric lighting system employing overhead wires, built by Thomas Edison, began service in Roselle, New Jersey.

In 1915, the neon-lighting tube was patented by Georges Claude.

In 1935, Coopers Inc. sold the world's first men's briefs called the "Jockey" in Chicago.

In 1938, General Motors began mass production of diesel engines.

Births

Anne Hummert, American radio pioneer and producer of daytime radio serials, 1905

John H. Johnson, African-American publisher (*Negro Digest, Ebony, Jet*), 1918

Dolly Parton, country singer-songwriter, actress, entrepreneur, philanthropist, literacy advocate, 1946

J.B. Pritzker, American businessman (cofounder of Pritzker Group Private Capital), philanthropist, and politician, 1965

Deaths

Hedy Lamarr, Austrian-American actress and inventor (radio guidance system for Allied torpedoes), 2000

I pray to find joy in messes.

Grow your faith by attending church regularly.

Read:
Proverbs, Chapter 19

January 20

However, as it is written: "What no eye has seen, what no ear has heard, and what no human mind has conceived"—the things God has prepared for those who love him. *(1 Corinthians 2:9, NIV)*

Thriving in change

Change can be overwhelming and unsettling, but it can also present a wealth of opportunities if you develop these habits:

Accept the certainty of uncertainty. Our world is filled with ambiguity, shifting priorities, differing expectations, unanswered questions, new ways of doing old things, and phenomenal growth, so accept the certainty of uncertainty.

Stop fighting change. It's natural to resist change and want to maintain a familiar environment, but that path is a dead-end street. Success requires you to abandon the status quo, overcome addictions to your comfort zone, and quickly adapt to new situations and ways of doing things.

Keep learning. Spend at least thirty minutes daily seeking out new information and deciding how to apply it to your life.

Discard your prejudices. Prejudices can stifle your creativity and limit your ability to respond to change.

Watch trends and collect ideas. Pay attention to what's going on and create an idea file where you can stash tidbits for later review and use.

Cultivate and maintain a solid resource network. Never pass up an opportunity to interact with another human being. *Be a fixer, not a finger-pointer.* Don't just complain about problems; welcome the opportunity for creative problem-solving.

Lighten up. Negativism and stress cloud judgment and interfere with objectivity. The benefits of optimism and a sense of humor cannot be overestimated in a climate of change and chaos.

Stop waiting. Change doesn't wait, and the opportunities found in change today may not be there tomorrow. Develop a sense of urgency and couple it with action.

Today we observe

Take a Walk Outdoors Day

On this day in history

Notable events

In 1920, the American Civil Liberties Union was founded.

In 1937, the first U.S. Presidential Inauguration Day held on January 20 (previously on March 4).

Births

William R. Pettiford, African-American minister and banker, founder of Alabama Penny Savings Bank, 1847

Julia Morgan, American architect (Hearst Castle and other Hearst properties), 1872

Allan Lockheed (born Allan Loughead), American aviation engineer and businessman, founder of the Alco Hydro-Aeroplane Company, which became Lockheed Corporation, 1889

Deaths

John Coleman, American journalist, cofounder of The Weather Channel, and broadcaster, 2018

Thought for the day

"You are a beautiful creation, perfectly imperfect, a work in progress. You have everything you need to fulfill your purpose. Don't dilute yourself for any person or any reason. You are enough. Be unapologetically you."

Steve Maraboli

I pray on Solomon's prayer for wisdom in 1 Kings 3.

Read:
Proverbs, Chapter 20

January 21

> Then we will no longer be immature like children. We won't be tossed and blown about by every wind of new teaching. We will not be influenced when people try to trick us with lies so clever they sound like the truth. *(Ephesians 4:14, NLT)*

When you should just say no

Sometimes you can't do what your customers want.

There are three reasons to say no to a client: when you're too busy to do the job right and on time; when you don't possess the right skills for the job; and when there's a conflict of ethics. If you handle the situation with tact and diplomacy, you should be able to retain the client for future work if you want.

If you're too busy to meet the client's stated deadline, be honest. Explain your own time constraints and let them know what deadline you can meet. They may be willing to wait, but if they can't, consider referring them to someone else who can handle the project. If you don't have time to do the job right, don't accept it and then either miss the deadline or deliver substandard work.

Take a similar approach when you don't possess the right skills. When possible, make a referral to someone more qualified. You might consider accepting the project and subcontracting to someone else. If you do this, remember that you are ultimately responsible for the quality and delivery of the work.

Ethical issues are more delicate to handle. Never do anything that makes you feel uncomfortable or that you wouldn't want the world to know about. Be professional and diplomatic, but stand your ground and don't let a client bully you into doing something you don't want to.

Turning down clients may well be one of the hardest things you have to do in business, but you have to be true to yourself and have the strength to say no when it's appropriate.

Today we observe

Own Your Own Home Day
Thank Your Mentor Day

On this day in history

Notable events
In 1915, Kiwanis International was founded in Detroit.
In 1970, the first wide-body jet, a Boeing 747, was put into service by Pan Am.

Births
John Fitch, American inventor, clockmaker, entrepreneur, and engineer 1743
William Wrigley III, American chewing gum mogul, 1933
Paul Allen, American businessman, investor, and philanthropist, cofounder of Microsoft, 1953
Keith Hufnagel, American skateboarder, entrepreneur, and fashion designer, founder of the streetwear brand HUF, 1974

Deaths
John Blair Scribner, American magazine and book publisher (Charles Scribner's Sons), 1879
Elisha Gray, American electrical engineer (developed a telephone prototype) and cofounder of Western Electric Manufacturing Company, 1901

Thought for the day

"I don't forgive people because I'm weak, I forgive them because I am strong enough to know people make mistakes."
Marilyn Monroe

I pray that I will hold fast to the anchor that is Christ.

Read:
Proverbs, Chapter 21

January 22

G od is not man, that he should lie, or a son of man, that he should change his mind. Has he said, and will he not do it? Or has he spoken, and will he not fulfill it? *(Numbers 23:19, ESV)*

Business is simple, failure is okay

The late Larry H. Miller presided over a multimillion-dollar financial empire that began with a single automobile dealership. The company still bears his name and includes real estate, senior health, finance and lending, and sports and entertainment.

He said there were three primary reasons he was successful. First, he learned that business is simple. "It is simply a function of having quality goods and/or services consistently delivered at a fair price. Supply and demand works," he said. "I take things one day at a time. It's one phone call, one experience, and one negotiation at a time."

Second, he found a niche for his business interests, particularly the auto dealerships, that suited his style and abilities.

Third, he wasn't afraid to fail. "I lost my fear of failure a long time ago," he said. "I learned that I was going to fail on some things, but that wasn't catastrophic. Failure is not the end of the world." He also learned to capitalize on the positives. "Successes give confidence, and strength leads to strength."

He said there's no substitute for hard work, but it needs to be smart work. "It's easy to confuse motion and progress. Progress always needs motion, but motion isn't always progress."

To work smart, he repeated: Keep things simple. Don't get caught up in sophisticated or complex trappings. Pay attention to the basics. "I don't have to look at many numbers to know what's going on in any given store. Every department has two or three key numbers that tell the story. Focus on the simple things and then let yourself get more sophisticated. You can't lose sight of the core issues; if you do, you'll forget what made you great."

On this day in history

Notable events

In 1895, the National Association of Manufacturers (NAM) was founded in Cincinnati, Ohio. One of NAM's earliest efforts was to call for the creation of the U.S. Department of Commerce.

In 1984, Apple's iconic "1984" commercial aired during Super Bowl XVIII.

Births

Sam Cooke, American singer and entrepreneur, 1931

Deaths

David Edward Hughes, British-American inventor (microphone, teleprinter), 1900

Lyndon B. Johnson, 36th U.S. President, 1973

William M. Batten, American businessman (J. C. Penney Company, New York Stock Exchange), 1999

Harold Stanley Marcus, American business executive (Neiman Marcus), 2002

Stephen Mather, American industrialist and conservationist (organized U.S. National Park Service), 1930

Irving B. Kahn, American media proprietor, inventor (teleprompter), founder of TelePrompTer Corporation, early cable television developer, 1994

Thought for the day

"Our lives improve only when we take chances—and the first and most difficult risk we can take is to be honest with ourselves."

Walter Anderson

I pray that I trust God over myself or anyone else.

Read: Proverbs, Chapter 22

January 23

The counsel of the Lord stands forever, the plans of his heart to all generations. Blessed is the nation whose God is the Lord, the people whom he has chosen as his heritage! *(Psalm 33:11-12, ESV)*

Ten reasons to keep a journal

1. *Create a greater awareness of actions and behaviors.* If you're writing down what's happening, you'll be more aware of what you're doing in response. Use journaling as a tool to reinforce your good habits and avoid slipping into negative patterns.

2. *Keep your thoughts organized.* The exercise of writing down your thoughts and feelings forces you to present them in a reasonably organized manner.

3. *Set and track goals.* A journal is a great place to record your goals and track your plans to achieve them. It's also a place to make adjustments to your plans.

4. *Manage stress.* Writing about your anxieties, frustrations, and fears can be a release that frees you from constant worry.

5. *Create the foundation for a book.* You may be able to use information from your journal to write a book that will help others.

6. *Solve problems and resolve conflicts.* Writing about a problem and possible solutions can help you reach a resolution.

7. *Boost your creativity.* Writing helps you process ideas and communicate them more effectively. The more you write, the more creative you're likely to become.

8. *Build your self-esteem.* Use a journal to give your ego a lift by recording your achievements and the positive input you've received from others.

9. *Get to know yourself better.* Keeping a record of your feelings will increase your self-understanding. You'll also learn what makes you feel good and what situations and people you should avoid.

10. *Capture your perspective for posterity.* A record of your life may not make a bestselling book, but it will be fascinating reading for your grandchildren and great-grandchildren.

Today we observe

National Handwriting Day

On this day in history

Notable events

In 1849, Jesse K. Park and Cornelius S. Watson received a U.S. patent for an envelope-making machine.

In 2020, China locked down the city of Wuhan in response to the COVID-19 pandemic.

Births

John Hancock, American merchant, statesman, and first signer of the Declaration of Independence, 1737

John Browning, American firearm designer, founder of Browning Arms Company, 1855

Gertrude B. Elion, American biochemist and drug researcher who developed groundbreaking leukemia and herpes drug treatments, 1918

Deaths

Jay Pritzker, American entrepreneur (cofounder of Hyatt Hotels), philanthropist, 1999

Jack LaLanne, American fitness and nutrition guru, motivational speaker, known as the godfather of fitness, 2011

Lee "Q" O'Denat, American internet entrepreneur (WorldStarHipHop.com), 2017

Thought for the day

"There are those who work all day. Those who dream all day. And those who spend an hour dreaming before setting to work to fulfill those dreams. Go into the third category because there's virtually no competition."

Steven J. Ross

I pray for our nation.

Read:
Proverbs, Chapter 23

January 24

Likewise, every good tree bears good fruit, but a bad tree bears bad fruit. A good tree cannot bear bad fruit, and a bad tree cannot bear good fruit. Every tree that does not bear good fruit is cut down and thrown into the fire. (Matthew 7:17-19, NIV)

Tips for effective journaling

Journal every day. Make writing in your journal a priority. Schedule time on your calendar and give it the same importance you would a meeting with a key client.

Make it private. Do whatever you need to do to keep your journal private. If you're using a computer, password protect your journal files. If you're using a paper diary, store it in a locked place. Even though you may eventually share parts of your journal, it needs to be private while you're writing in it.

Tell your story, don't just express emotions. Write down what happened along with how you felt about it.

Don't censor or edit as you go. Just write. Don't worry about what someone else might think about what you're writing. Don't worry about grammar and punctuation—you can always fix that later if you decide to publish any parts of your journal.

Read old journal entries. Your journal is your history. Periodically look back to review your personal and professional growth.

Thought for the day

"A friend is one that knows you as you are, understands where you have been, accepts what you have become, and still, gently allows you to grow."

William Shakespeare

I pray to avoid spiritual junk food.

Read:
Proverbs, Chapter 24

Today we observe

International Day of Education

National Compliment Day

On this day in history

Notable events

In 1848, James Marshall found gold in Sutter's Mill in Coloma, California, beginning the California Gold Rush.

In 1908, Robert Baden-Powell published "Scouting for Boys," a manual for self-instruction in outdoor skills and self-improvement, which became the inspiration for the Scout Movement.

In 1935, the first canned beer, Krueger's Cream Ale, was sold by American company Krueger Brewing Co.

In 1975, the first McDonald's drive thru opened in Sierra Vista, Arizona. The restaurant was losing sales because soldiers at nearby Fort Huachuca Army Base had to stay in their vehicles when wearing fatigues when off base; a simple sliding window installed in the wall solved the problem.

In 2017, President Donald Trump withdrew the U.S. from the Trans-Pacific Partnership Agreement (TPPA).

Births

J. Howard Marshall, American billionaire businessman, academic, and government official, involved with and invested in the petroleum industry 1905

Walter Haas, Jr., American businessman (Levi Strauss & Co.) and sports team owner, 1916

Oral Roberts, American televangelist, founder of Oral Roberts College, 1918

Deaths

Alfred Carlton Gilbert, American athlete, businessman, inventor (Erector Set), 1961

Bill W., American co-founder of Alcoholics Anonymous, 1971

Marvin Minsky, American artificial intelligence computer scientist (MIT), 2016

January 25

But grow in the grace and knowledge of our Lord and Savior Jesus Christ. To him be the glory both now and to the day of eternity. Amen. *(2 Peter 3:18, ESV)*

Why we work and rest

We are made in the image of God—the same God who creates, loves, forgives, cares, guides, works, and rests.

God created the heavens and earth. He created all the creatures. Once his initial work of creation was done, he rested and then went back to work.

He takes care of us. He listens to us and answers our prayers. He performs miracles.

He works. And he rests.

Because we are made in his image, we are at our best when we are doing what he does: working and resting. We are at our best when, in the course of our work, we allow ourselves to be God's instruments. We are at our best when, after we have worked, we take the time we need to rest, to relax, to revitalize ourselves so that we can do more work.

We were made to do meaningful, purposeful activities that serve the world God created. We see that early in the Bible when God placed Adam in the garden to "work it and take care of it" *(Genesis 2:15, NIV)*.

God's message to work joyfully and to the best of our ability continues throughout the Bible. "Whatever you do, work at it with all your heart, as working for the Lord, not for human masters" *(Colossians 3:23, NIV)*.

The message to rest is equally clear. God rested. Jesus rested. And we are to rest and trust God to take care of things.

Work and rest are fundamental to who we are. They are what our Creator intended for us. They are how we live out our faith and serve him and one another.

We work and we rest because that's what God does.

Read: Proverbs, Chapter 25

Today we observe

Observe the Weather Day

On this day in history

Notable events

In 1881, Thomas Edison and Alexander Graham Bell formed the Oriental Telephone Company.

In 1955, the tax preparation company H&R Block was founded by brothers Henry W. Bloch and Richard Bloch.

Births

Ernst Alexanderson, Swedish-American electrical engineer, inventor (held 344 patents), and pioneer in radio and television development, 1878

Brian Armstrong, American businessman (CEO and co-founder of Coinbase), 1983

Deaths

Vivien Kellems, American industrialist, inventor, and public speaker, known for her battle with the U.S. government over income tax withholding and other tax issues, 1975

Florence Knoll Bassett, American architect, interior designer, furniture designer, and entrepreneur who revolutionized office design, 2019

Thought for the day

"Refuse to emotionally succumb to the negative events around you and tap your mental toughness to thrive in any environment. The good guy doesn't always win and justice doesn't always prevail, but where you direct your mental energy will always determine your attitude and it will always be controlled by you."

Steve Siebold

I pray that I may always see problems as possibilities.

January 26

Woe to those who call evil good and good evil, who put darkness for light and light for darkness, who put bitter for sweet and sweet for bitter! Woe to those who are wise in their own eyes, and shrewd in their own sight! (Isaiah 5:20-21, ESV)

Five reasons to pray for others

1. It's hard to be angry at someone we're praying for.

There's something about taking a genuine prayer to God that removes anger from our hearts, even if that's not what we're praying about. And when that happens, it leads to reconciliation.

2. It makes us more aware of what we have to be thankful for.

When we pray for someone who is experiencing hard times or health issues, it's natural to think about our own blessings—and it's a good time to thank God for those blessings.

3. It gives us a chance to listen to God so we know how we can help.

Prayer is powerful and sometimes it's the only thing we can do, but it's also a chance to let God tell us how we can be his hands in the world.

4. It helps us actively focus on the needs of others instead of ourselves.

Praying for others forces us to think about what they need. That process can lead to us being more outwardly focused in all of our relationships.

5. When we pray for others, we are doing what Jesus did.

The Bible tells us of the many times Jesus prayed for others and told us to do the same.

Does God *need* us to pray to work in other people's lives? Of course not. But God wants us to pray. Prayer brings us closer to God, it strengthens our relationship with him.

Today we observe

Dental Drill Appreciation Day

Lotus 1-2-3 Day

National Spouses Day

On this day in history

Notable events

In 1875, an electric dental drill was patented by George F. Green.

In 1989, AT&T reported its first loss in 103 years: $1.67 billion in 1988.

Births

Paul Newman, American actor, entrepreneur, and philanthropist, 1925

Deaths

Abner Doubleday, American Union Army major general, inventor (San Francisco cable cars), 1893

Nelson Rockefeller, American businessman and politician, 1979

Kobe Bryant, American professional basketball player, entrepreneur, author, and philanthropist, 2020

Thought for the day

"No man ever got very high by pulling other people down. The intelligent merchant does not knock his competitors. The sensible worker does not knock those who work with him. Don't knock your friends. Don't knock your enemies. Don't knock yourself."

Lord Alfred Tennyson

Read:
Proverbs, Chapter 26

I pray that I remember to pray when I'm under pressure.

January 27

I pray that your love will overflow more and more, and that you will keep on growing in knowledge and understanding. For I want you to understand what really matters, so that you may live pure and blameless lives until the day of Christ's return. *(Philippians 1:9-10, NLT)*

Rules for life:

1. Compliment three people every day.
2. Watch a sunrise at least once a year.
3. Be the first to smile and say, "Hello."
4. Live beneath your means.
5. Treat everyone like you want to be treated.
6. Never give up on anybody. Miracles happen.
7. Forget the Joneses.
8. Never deprive someone of hope. It may be all they have.
9. Pray not for things, but for wisdom and courage.
10. Be tough-minded but tenderhearted.
11. Be kinder than necessary.
12. Remember that a person's greatest emotional need is to feel appreciated.
13. Keep your promises.
14. Learn to show cheerfulness even when you don't feel like it.
15. Remember that overnight success usually takes about fifteen years.
16. Leave everything better than you found it.
17. Remember that winners do what losers don't want to do.
18. When you arrive at your job in the morning, let the first thing you say brighten everyone's day.
19. Don't rain on other people's parades.
20. Never miss an opportunity to tell someone you love them.

Read:
Proverbs, Chapter 27

Today we observe

Holocaust Memorial Day

Punch the Clock Day

Thomas Crapper Day

On this day in history

Notable events

In 1880, Thomas Edison received the patent embodying the principles of his incandescent lamp that paved the way for the universal domestic use of electric light.

In 1967, a fire in the Apollo 1 command module killed astronauts Gus Grissom, Ed White, and Roger B. Chaffee during a launch rehearsal.

Births

Samuel Gompers, American labor union leader (American Federation of Labor), 1850

William Randolph Hearst, Jr., American businessman and newspaper publisher 1908

Bill English, American computer engineer who helped develop the computer mouse and the NLS computer system, 1929

Deaths

Julian W. Hill, American research chemist who developed nylon, 1996

Charles Hard Townes, American physicist, inventor (maser), advisor to U.S. Presidents, Nobel Prize winner, 2015

Ingvar Kamprad, Swedish businessman, founder of IKEA, 2018

Thought for the day

"We are all faced with a series of great opportunities brilliantly disguised as unsolvable problems."

John W. Gardner

I pray that I will be guided by the simplicity and majesty of God's commandments.

January 28

> This is the confidence we have in approaching God: that if we ask anything according to his will, he hears us. *(1 John 5:14, NIV)*

Keep it simple to make it interesting

A key communication challenge we face is that information we need to share may be complex and not always easy to explain. The solution is to keep it simple.

Simple does *not* mean stupid. Presenting your ideas in a way that is simple and easy to understand is not the same as dumbing them down. You can communicate your complex information in a simple way without compromising it.

Lee Iacocca said, "You can have brilliant ideas, but if you cannot get them across, your ideas will not get you anywhere."

The first step is basic: Know your audience. Who are these people? What challenges are they struggling with that you can solve? What do they want to know? What do they need to know? Why do they care about what you have to say?

Once you know who you're talking to, you can figure out what to say and how to best say it. Throughout the process, use examples, stories, and analogies so your audience can engage with you and get excited about your message.

Always avoid using jargon your audience may not understand. It doesn't make you look smart—it makes them lose interest.

It comes down to this: If you can't communicate your ideas, they're worthless. When you can communicate your ideas and your message has value, you're unstoppable.

I pray that I may be a strong representative of my faith.

Read: Proverbs, Chapter 28

Today we observe
Data Privacy Day

Thank a Plugin Developer Day

On this day in history

Notable events

In 1855, the first locomotive ran from the Atlantic Ocean to the Pacific Ocean on the Panama Railway.

In 1902, the Carnegie Institute was founded in Washington, D.C.

In 1932, the first U.S. state unemployment insurance act was enacted in Wisconsin.

In 1958, the Lego Group patented their design of interlocking Lego bricks.

In 1986, Space Shuttle Challenger exploded 73 seconds after liftoff from Cape Canaveral, killing Christa McAuliffe, Ellison S. Onizuka, Francis R. Scobee, Greg Jarvis, Judith Resnik, Michael J. Smith, and Ronald E. McNair.

Births

William Seward Burroughs, American inventor of the first workable adding machine, 1855

Luther George Simjian, Armenian-American inventor and entrepreneur who held more than 200 patents (most significant were a pioneering flight simulator, the first ATM, and improvement to the teleprompter), 1905

Rick Warren, American pastor and author, 1954

Christopher Ruddy, American journalist, CEO and majority owner of Newsmax Media, 1965

Thought for the day

"[T]he devil is a liar. And this is one of his favorite deceptions. He convinces us that our value can somehow be achieved if we do this and don't do that, get this, and lose that. And so we rush, strive, and live discontentedly, but in the end we're still empty. When we pin our worth to any person, goal, achievement, we will never know our true value that is found only in God."

Jackie Greene

January 29

Therefore humble yourselves under the mighty hand of God, that He may exalt you at the proper time, casting all your anxiety on Him, because He cares for you. *(1 Peter 5:6-7, LSB)*

Make your no sound like yes

Don't tell a customer what you can't do. Instead, respond to requests by telling them what you *can* do.

For example, if a customer wants 100 widgets delivered by Friday and you don't have enough of them in stock, say, "We'll have 50 widgets on your dock before noon on Friday and the remaining 50 to you by the following Wednesday, and we'll give you the quantity discount for ordering 100."

You might be tempted to say something like, "I'm sorry we can't do that, but we can do this." Drop the first half of that and go straight to what you can do.

Most customers will be reasonable and work something out with you. Don't plant the negative seed in their minds that you can't meet their needs.

Walking in faith means putting one foot in front of the other with both eyes on God.

Thought for the day

"Seek out that particular mental attribute which makes you feel most deeply and vitally alive, along with which comes the inner voice which says, 'This is the real me,' and when you have found that attitude, follow it."

James Truslow Adams

I am grateful for my business colleagues and how they enrich my professional life.

Read: Proverbs, Chapter 29

Today we observe
Freethinkers Day

On this day in history

Notable events
- In 1892, the Coca-Cola Company was incorporated in Atlanta, Georgia.
- In 1912, martial law was declared in the textile strike in Lawrence, Massachusetts.
- In 1920, Walt Disney started work as an artist with KC Slide Co. for $40 a week.
- In 1924, Carl Taylor patented an ice cream cone rolling machine.

Births
- William McKinley, 25th U.S. President, (third President to be assassinated), 1843
- John D. Rockefeller, Jr., American businessman, financier, and philanthropist, 1874
- Allen B. DuMont, American engineer and inventor (perfected commercial practical cathode ray tube), 1901
- Lewis Urry, Canadian-American chemical engineer and inventor; invented both the alkaline battery and lithium battery while working for Eveready Battery, 1927
- Oprah Winfrey, American talk show host, actress, entrepreneur, 1954

Deaths
- Seth Thomas, American manufacturer and pioneer in the mass production of clocks, 1859
- Bion J. Arnold, American electrical engineer and inventor (railroad electrification), 1942

God is still writing your story. Stop trying to steal the pen! Trust the true author of your life.

ChristianAlmanac.com

January 30

> **B**ut where can wisdom be found? Where does understanding dwell?
> *(Job 28:12, NIV)*

Hiring convicted criminals

If you have employees, sooner or later you're going to have an applicant who has a criminal history. Should you automatically reject that candidate? No. You may find some excellent employees who have criminal backgrounds and deserve a second chance.

To develop a policy on hiring convicted criminals, identify all applicable legal requirements. Many states have laws governing when you can ask about criminal histories and prohibiting employers from rejecting an applicant strictly on the grounds of a past conviction. However, a criminal conviction may make an applicant ineligible for a job that requires bonding or special licensing.

With that in mind, you can assess whether the applicant is the right person for the job. Consider the conviction (what was the crime and how long ago did it happen?) in the overall context of the applicant's background, skills, and abilities, and your staffing needs.

One of the most common convictions employers have to consider is driving while intoxicated (or driving under the influence). If the person will be driving a company vehicle or driving their own car on company business, you'll need to determine if they're insurable.

Thought for the day

"If a man is called to be a street sweeper, he should sweep streets even as Michelangelo painted, or Beethoven composed music or Shakespeare wrote poetry. He should sweep streets so well that all the hosts of heaven and earth will pause to say, 'Here lived a great street sweeper who did his job well.'"
— *Martin Luther King Jr.*

Today we observe
National Escape Day

On this day in history

Notable events

In 1928, the first radio telephone connection between Netherlands and U.S. was established.

In 1963, computer scientist Ivan Sutherland submitted a thesis containing his Sketchpad program, a forerunner to modern-day graphic user interfaces and computer-aided design programs.

In 1975, Erno Rubik applied for a patent for his "magic cube" invention, which would later be known as a Rubik's cube.

In 2015, Shake Shack, founded by Danny Meyer, was first listed on the New York Stock Exchange.

Births

Franklin D. Roosevelt, 32nd U.S. President (longest-serving President), 1882

Francis A. Schaeffer, American evangelical theologian, philosopher, author, and Presbyterian pastor, 1912

Douglas Engelbart, American engineer, computer scientist, and inventor (computer mouse), 1925

Deaths

Frank Nelson Doubleday, American publisher (founder of Doubleday & Co.), 1934

Orville Wright, American aviator (Wright Brothers), 1948

John Bardeen, American physicist, electrical engineer, and co-inventor of the transistor, 1991

I pray for everyone to have the opportunity to be a part of something bigger than themselves.

Read:
Proverbs, Chapter 30

January 31

For the kind of sorrow God wants us to experience leads us away from sin and results in salvation. There's no regret for that kind of sorrow. But worldly sorrow, which lacks repentance, results in spiritual death. Just see what this godly sorrow produced in you! Such earnestness, such concern to clear yourselves, such indignation, such alarm, such longing to see me, such zeal, and such a readiness to punish wrong. You showed that you have done everything necessary to make things right. (2 Corinthians 7:10-11, NLT)

The upside of getting knocked down

Sometimes life knocks us to our knees.

For most of us, it's happened not just once, not just twice, but over and over.

When it does, we can't stay down. We need to get up and keep going.

But first, while we're on our knees, we should pray.

God doesn't care about our posture when we're praying—what he cares about is that we're praying. Even so, there is something meaningful about going down on our knees to pray, about getting into that special position to talk to God and—more important—to listen to him.

So the next time it feels like life has knocked you to your knees, before you get up, take the time to pray. Take the time to surrender yourself and your situation to God. Wait for guidance so you know what to do.

Then get up and get back in the game.

Though it might not feel this way at the time, there's always an upside to getting knocked down, whether we've tripped and stumbled on our own or been knocked down by other people or circumstances. And that upside is that being down is an ideal time to look up and seek consolation and direction from God.

Find joy in knowing that God is with you and will pick you up every time you fall.

Today we observe

Hug an Economist Day

Scotch Tape Day

On this day in history

Notable events

In 1865, by a vote of 121-24, Congress passed the 13th Amendment to the U.S. Constitution, abolishing slavery in the U.S.

Births

Irving Langmuir, American chemist, engineer, inventor of gas-filled-incandescent lamp, 1881

S. Newman Darby, American inventor of the sailboard, 1928

Deaths

Samuel Goldwyn, film producer and movie magnate, 1974

Anne Cox Chambers, American media owner (Cox Enterprises) and U.S. ambassador to Belgium, 2000

Henry Kloss, American audio engineer (acoustic loudspeaker), 2002

Edwin H. Armstrong, U.S. radio inventor (FM), 1954

John Mott, evangelist, long-serving leader of the Young Men's Christian Association (YMCA), Nobel Peace Prize winner, 1955

Thought for the day

"Aim at heaven and you will get earth thrown in. Aim at earth and you get neither."

C.S. Lewis

Read:
Proverbs, Chapter 31

I pray for my spouse.

Christian Business Almanac

February

February was named after the Roman *Februalia*, a month-long festival of purification and atonement. It comes from the Latin word *februa*, which means "to cleanse".

February birthstone
Amethyst

February flower
Violet, primrose

February is ...
- American Heart Month
- Bike to Work Month
- Black History Month
- Celebration of Chocolate Month
- Declutter for a Cause Month
- Free Open Source Software Month
- International Boost Self-Esteem Month
- National Cancer Prevention Month
- National Children's Dental Health Month
- National Enrolled Agents Month
- National Library Lovers Month
- National Self-Check Month
- National Spay/Neuter Month
- National Teen Dating Violence Awareness and Prevention Month
- National Time Management Month
- Responsible Pet Owners Month
- Return Shopping Carts to the Supermarket Month
- Youth Leadership Month

Mark your calendar for these February holidays and observances

First Thursday in February	Optimist Day
Second Monday in February	National Clean Out Your Computer Day
Third Friday in February	National Caregivers Day
Third Monday in February	Presidents' Day
Last Friday in February	International Stand Up to Bullying Day*
Fourth Wednesday in February	Inconvenience Yourself Day
Third week in February	National Entrepreneurship Week

*also observed in November

Fun Facts about February

February is the only month to have fewer than 30 days. Though it's usually 28 days, in leap years February is 29 days long.

Originally February was the last month of the calendar year; around 450 BC, it was moved to its place as the second month.

U.S. Presidential election years are always leap years.

February 1

And in fact, you do love all of God's family throughout Macedonia. Yet we urge you, brothers and sisters, to do so more and more, and to make it your ambition to lead a quiet life: You should mind your own business and work with your hands, just as we told you, so that your daily life may win the respect of outsiders and so that you will not be dependent on anybody. *(1 Thessalonians 4:10-12, NIV)*

Help employees bond with each other

People aren't loyal to companies, they're loyal to other people. Smart leaders encourage team loyalty to build employee commitment. Some ways to do that:

Create teams or groups that interact frequently within the organization, and make sure every employee is an active participant in at least one of them.

If people on a particular team aren't working well together, make changes. Move anyone who isn't happy on their team to a different team. Don't try to force people to get along or like each other; instead, put them where they will be happiest and most productive.

Provide opportunities for team members to relax, have fun, and bond with each other. Don't restrict their interactions to task-specific meetings.

Be sure the work the teams are doing is interesting, challenging, and rewarding so that the team members feel they have a purpose and they share a sense of accomplishment.

Thought for the day

"It is not because things are difficult that we do not dare, it is because we do not dare that they are difficult."

Seneca

Read:
Proverbs, Chapter 1

Today we observe
Car Insurance Day
Change Your Password Day
National Freedom Day

On this day in history

Notable events

In 1843, the oldest continuous writer of insurance in America, The Mutual Life Insurance Company of New York (MONY), opened.

In 1893, Thomas Edison completes the world's first movie studio in West Orange, New Jersey.

In 1926, land at Broadway & Wall Street sold at a record $7 per square inch.

In 2003, Space Shuttle Columbia disintegrated during reentry into the Earth's atmosphere, killing Michael P. Anderson, David Brown, Kalpana Chawla, Laurel Clark, Rick D. Husband, William C. McCool, and Ilan Ramon.

Births

Andrew Breitbart, American conservative blogger and publisher, 1969

Deaths

Edwin Howard Armstrong, American electrical engineer and inventor who developed FM radio and the superheterodyne receiver system, 1954

Donald Wills Douglas, American aircraft industrialist (McDonnell Douglas) and aviation pioneer, 1981

Paul Mellon, American philanthropist and owner/breeder of Thoroughbred racehorses, 1999

I am thankful that I can pray any place, any time and God hears me.

February 2

> One night the Lord spoke to Paul in a vision: "Do not be afraid; keep on speaking, do not be silent. *(Acts 18:9, NIV)*

How to evaluate a business investment

Are you considering a particular type of business? Have you been asked to invest in someone else's operation? Before you make a decision, ask yourself these questions and do the necessary research to have complete and accurate answers to all of them:

- What is my total investment of time and money?
- What can I realistically expect the return on my investment to be, and is the gain sufficient?
- What are all the upsides of this investment?
- What are all the downsides?
- What is the best case scenario?
- What is the worst case scenario?
- Can I handle the worst case scenario?

Thought for the day

"In order to develop ourselves, for our companies to flourish, and for our world to improve, we need to be able to think creatively, not just solve problems. We require the ability to create brilliant new solutions, to invent what has never existed before. In the real world, the most valued skills are the ones for which we have little training and no rulebook."

— Gerald Sindell

> Grow your faith by reflecting on God's promises and how you have seen them manifest in your life.

Today we observe
Candlemas Day
National Women's Heart (Wear Red) Day
Self Renewal Day

On this day in history

Notable events
In 1888, Frank Sprague opened the first successful U.S. electric street railway system (Richmond Union Passenger Railway) in Richmond, Virginia.
In 1892, William Painter patented the bottle cap.

Births
Solomon R. Guggenheim, American businessman, art collector, and philanthropist, 1861
Howard Deering Johnson, American entrepreneur, businessman, and founder of the Howard Johnson's chain of restaurants and motels, 1897
Barry Diller, American businessman, founder of Fox Broadcasting Company and USA Broadcasting, 1942
Christopher Buskirk, publisher and editor of *American Greatness*, cofounder and CIO of 1789 Capital, author, 1969

Deaths
Thomas W. Lamont, American banker and philanthropist, 1948
Willie Mae Ford Smith, American musician and Christian evangelist instrumental in the development and spread of gospel music in the U.S., 1994
Roger L. Stevens, American real estate magnate, theater producer, and fundraiser, 1998

I pray that I will be brave when the need arises.

Read:
Proverbs, Chapter 2

February 3

Therefore, since we are surrounded by so great a cloud of witnesses, let us also lay aside every weight and the sin that clings so closely, and let us run with perseverance the race that is set before us, looking to Jesus, the pioneer and perfecter of faith, who for the sake of the joy that was set before him endured the cross, disregarding its shame, and has taken his seat at the right hand of the throne of God. *(Hebrews 2:1-2 NRSVue)*

Keep an eye on the future

It's easy to get wrapped up in day-to-day operations, but growing a business requires long-term strategic planning. Set aside time every week to think about where your company will be in three to five years and how it's going to get there. Talk with your team and get them thinking the same way. Don't let new technologies or industry changes sneak up on you; research and plan so that you stay ahead of market shifts and customer demands.

Are you going global?

Don't assume that if it works in America, it will work anywhere. Tailor your sales and marketing efforts to each country. The same goes for pricing, shipping, payment terms and packaging.

Don't ignore the cultural differences that shape the various marketplaces you're targeting. Do your homework ahead of time so you won't risk offending prospective international customers with an innocent but inappropriate gesture or remark.

Thought for the day

"No religion has accomplished what Christianity has accomplished. No ideology. No school of thought. No idea, no government, no political system. Nothing else has ever lit the world on fire like the Gospel."
Matt Walsh

Read:
Proverbs, Chapter 3

Today we observe

National Missing Persons Day

On this day in history

Notable events
In 1882, circus owner P.T. Barnum bought his world-famous elephant, Jumbo.
In 1999, Salesforce, Inc., an American cloud-based software company, was founded by Marc Benioff, Parker Harris, Dave Moellenhoff, and Frank Dominguez.

Births
Horacy Greeley, founder and editor of the *New York Tribune*, 1811
George Nissen, American inventor (the trampoline), 1914
Henry Heimlich, surgeon and inventor of the Heimlich maneuver, 1920

Deaths
Woodrow Wilson, 28th U.S. President, 1924
Alexander Goode, Clark Poling, George Fox, John Washington (The Four Chaplains) drowned in the sinking of the *Dorchester*, 1943

I pray for those I have the privilege of mentoring.

Do what you can, and leave the rest to God.

February 4

> "You have heard the law that says, 'Love your neighbor' and hate your enemy. But I say, love your enemies! Pray for those who persecute you! *(Matthew 5:43-44, NLT)*

Five easy ways ...

To prevent crises

1. Stop and carefully think about what failure to prepare for crises could mean on a very personal basis to all the people with whom you work and to those your organization serves. Let your conscience, not just your business instinct, guide your actions.
2. Never implement a major operational decision without asking a PR-savvy person to help you anticipate the response from all stakeholders, internal and external.
3. Ensure that at least two members of your leadership team are extremely internet and social media savvy.
4. When you're being criticized, don't get defensive. Say sincerely, "You could be right," then smile and end the conversation.
5. When you're caught up in a disagreement where you're attempting to change someone's perspective or "fix" things, stop and ask yourself, "How important is this?"

To cause crises

1. Underestimate the power of a single angry consumer with a smartphone.
2. Have critical policies for which employees receive little or no training and/or refresher training.
3. Use lawyers as a default response to detractors.
4. Fail to consider and plan for the impact of losing a key contractor or vendor.
5. Hire senior level executives from other organizations without conducting thorough background checks.

Today we observe

International Day of Human Fraternity
National Thank a Mail Carrier Day
Torture Abolition Day
USO Day

On this day in history

Notable events

In 1824, J.W. Goodrich introduced rubber galoshes to the public.
In 1913, the National Institute of Arts & Letters was founded.
In 1971, the NASDAQ stock exchange was founded in New York City.
In 2004, Mark Zuckerberg launched Facebook from his Harvard dormitory room.

Births

Charles Lindbergh, American aviator, 1902
Rosa Parks, American civil rights activist, 1913
Theodore Henry Stanley, American anesthesiologist and medical entrepreneur, known for creating the fentanyl lollipop, 1940

Deaths

Raiford "Ossie" Davis, American actor, director, author, and civil rights activist, 2005

Thought for the day

"If things are not going well with you, begin your effort at correcting the situation by carefully examining the service you are rendering, and especially the spirit in which you are rendering it."

Roger Babson

I pray to see beyond the immediate and focus on eternity.

Read:
Proverbs, Chapter 4

February 5

Blessed is the one who does not walk in step with the wicked or stand in the way that sinners take or sit in the company of mockers, but whose delight is in the law of the Lord, and who meditates on his law day and night. That person is like a tree planted by streams of water, which yields its fruit in season and whose leaf does not wither—whatever they do prospers. *(Psalm 1:1–3, NIV)*

Market research resource

The other players in your field are a great resource for information on your industry and market. Some may be direct competitors; others may be in your general space but serving different markets. They're all putting out information to the public that you can benefit from having as well.

Visit their websites regularly. Sign up for all their newsletters, white papers, technical papers, industry surveys, and conference reports. Subscribe to their email lists. Monitor their social media. You don't need to copy what they're doing; just let that knowledge factor into your own planning and decision-making.

Thought for the day

"Know how to listen, and you will profit even from those who talk badly."
— Plutarch

I pray on the message of Deuteronomy 7:7-8 and let it lift me up.

Shareable Saturday

An inspirational thought, brief video, and more delivered to your inbox weekly.

Read:
Proverbs, Chapter 5

Today we observe
Disaster Day

On this day in history

Notable events

In 1817, the first U.S. gas company (coal gas for street lights) was incorporated in Baltimore.
In 1870, the first motion picture was shown to a theater audience in Philadelphia.
In 1901, the loop-the-loop centrifugal RR (roller coaster) was patented by Ed Prescot.
In 1901, Pierpont Morgan formed U.S. Steel Corp.
In 1919, the film studio United Artists was founded.
In 2014, Google vice president Susan Wojcicki was named CEO of YouTube.

Births

Hiram Stevens Maxim, American-British inventor (automatic fire sprinkler, curling iron, steam inhaler, more) known as the creator of the first automatic machine gun, 1840
Joan Whitney Payson, American heiress, businesswoman, MLB team owner, and philanthropist, 1903
Norton Simon, American industrialist (Hunt's Foods, Norton Simon Museum), 1907
Nolan Bushnell, American electrical engineer, founder of Atari, creator of Pong, 1943
Jeremy Boreing, American screenwriter, director, producer, entrepreneur, and political commentator; co-CEO of *The Daily Wire*, 1979

Deaths

Leon Leonwood Bean, American inventor, author, founder of L.L. Bean, a retailer specializing in clothing and outdoor recreation equipment, 1967
Conrad "Nicky" Hilton, Jr., American socialite, hotel heir, and businessman, 1969
E. Michael Burke, American businessman and sports executive, 1987

February 6

A*ll who are victorious will inherit all these blessings, and I will be their God, and they will be my children. (Revelation 21:7, NLT)*

Are your suppliers covered?

There are times when it's appropriate for you as a customer to ask about your suppliers' insurance and even insist that they have certain coverages. Generally, you'll be concerned with property insurance (which covers your interest in tangible property) and liability coverage (which protects you in case of a lawsuit).

Consider the other party's insurance as additional protection. Who buys the insurance is a matter of bargaining power, custom, and practicality.

For example, if you buy your product components from a variety of different sources, you may want to insist that your suppliers carry liability coverage to protect you should a claim be made based on a product failure due to a specific component.

Or if your period of exposure to potential liability or property damage is of limited duration—perhaps because your business is seasonal or event-driven—it may be more practical and customary for the supplier to provide coverage than for you to do so.

Once you've determined that it's appropriate to require your supplier to have specific coverage, make sure what you ask for is actually enforced.

One way is to get a certificate of insurance, which is a document that typically describes the type of coverage a company has. A safer approach is to ask your vendors to name you as an additional insured on their policy. You'll not only get the benefits of the policy, but you'll be notified if the policy is canceled for any reason.

Today we observe
Pay a Compliment Day
Time to Talk Day

On this day in history

Notable events

In 1867, American financier and philanthropist George Peabody established the Peabody Education Fund to provide improvements to existing schools in poor areas of the southern United States.

In 1882, the Knights of Columbus (Catholic fraternal organization) was formed in New Haven, Connecticut.

In 1894, William Painter patented the bottle opener.

In 1935, the board game *Monopoly* went on sale for the first time.

Births

Doc Durant, American financier and railroad promoter, 1820

Ronald Reagan, 40th U.S. President, 1911

J. Howard Marshall III, American businessman, owner of MDH Industries, 1936

Robert H. Brooks, American businessman, restaurateur, executive, founder of Naturally Fresh, Inc., creator of Hooters of America, 1937

Deaths

Kenneth H. Olsen, American electrical engineer and cofounder of Digital Equipment Corporation, 2011

Thought for the day

"Look at a day when you are supremely satisfied at the end. It's not a day when you lounge around doing nothing, it's when you've had everything to do and you've done it."

Margaret Thatcher

I am grateful for a fresh outlook.

Read:
Proverbs, Chapter 6

February 7

Look at the birds of the air; they do not sow or reap or store away in barns, and yet your heavenly Father feeds them. Are you not much more valuable than they? Can any one of you by worrying add a single hour to your life? *(Matthew 6:26-27 NIV)*

Entrepreneurial characteristics: blessing or curse?

The very characteristics that are the mark of an entrepreneur are also characteristics that can cause trouble in companies and personal lives. Recognizing and understanding this reality can go a long way toward preventing problems with which many entrepreneurs struggle.

For example, entrepreneurs are notorious for being good at starting but bad at running a business. The difference between the entrepreneur and the manager is that the entrepreneur has a talent and gift in the creation process, while the manager has the ability to organize the details. Entrepreneurs need to either develop their management skills or hire a manager to run their company.

Entrepreneurs are often too optimistic, which can set them up for failure. Their line of reality gets swayed by their passion for their idea. Step back and set reasonable goals, and then create a practical plan to reach those goals.

Along with realistic goals, entrepreneurs need to be realistic about the quality of their ideas. Entrepreneurs have a desire to create something, and often think it's new and different when it's actually not. Pay attention to what market research and your advisors tell you.

Finally, entrepreneurs can get so wrapped up in their business that their personal relationships suffer. They don't even realize how their business is affecting their families. Schedule time every week to look at other issues in your life, to be with your family, and to take care of your personal needs.

Today we observe
National Send a Card to a Friend Day

On this day in history

Notable events
In 1904, a fire in Baltimore destroyed 1500 buildings in 80 blocks.
In 1915, the first wireless message sent from a moving train to a station was received.

Births
John Deere, American blacksmith and manufacturer, founded Deere & Company, 1804
An Wang, Chinese-American computer engineer and inventor, cofounder of Wang Laboratories, 1920

Deaths
Henry Steinway, German-American piano manufacturer, 1871
Robert Wood Johnson I, American industrialist and cofounder of Johnson & Johnson, 1910
Harvey S. Firestone, American manufacturer and founder of Firestone Tire and Rubber Company, 1938
Jack Cover, American aerospace scientist and inventor of the Taser stun gun, 2009

Thought for the day
"Good can exist without evil, whereas evil cannot exist without good."
Thomas Aquinas

I pray for all those who are trying to do what they believe is right.

Read:
Proverbs, Chapter 7

February 8

For to this you have been called, because Christ also suffered for you, leaving you an example, so that you might follow in his steps. He committed no sin, neither was deceit found in his mouth. When he was reviled, he did not revile in return; when he suffered, he did not threaten, but continued entrusting himself to him who judges justly. *(1 Peter 2:21-23, ESV)*

Praise Ye the Lord, the Almighty

Joachim Neander, 1680
Trans. Catherine Winkworth

Praise ye the Lord, the Almighty, the King of creation!
O my soul, praise him, for he is thy health and salvation!
All ye who hear; now to his temple draw near,
join me in glad adoration.

Praise to the Lord, who o'er all things so wondrously reigneth;
shelters thee under his wings, yea so gently sustaineth!
Hast thou not seen how thy desires e'er have been
Granted in what He ordaineth?

Praise to the Lord, who will prosper your work and defend you;
surely his goodness and mercy shall daily attend you.
Ponder anew what the Almighty can do,
if with his love he befriends you.

Praise ye the Lord! O let all that is in me adore him!
All that hath life and breath, come now with praises before him.
Let the Amen sound from his people again;
Gladly for aye we adore him.

I pray for all the churches across our country and around the world.

Read:
Proverbs, Chapter 8

Today we observe

Laugh and Get Rich Day

On this day in history

Notable events

In 1802, Simon Willard patented his eight-day "Improved Timepiece," a wall clock that came to be known as the banjo clock.

In 1898, John Ames Sherman patented the first envelope folding & gumming machine.

In 1910, the Boy Scouts of America was incorporated by William D. Boyce.

Births

Chester Carlson, American physicist, inventor, and patent attorney known for inventing electrophotography (xerography, the dry photocopying process), 1906

Deaths

Connie Mack, American Baseball Hall of Fame catcher, manager, and team owner, 1956

John von Neumann, Hungarian-American mathematician, physicist, computer scientist, engineer, and polymath, known for mathematical formulation of quantum mechanics, game theory, spectral theory, ergodic theory, and more, 1957

Thought for the day

"Success comes in a lot of ways, but it doesn't come with money and it doesn't come with fame. It comes from having a meaning in your life, doing what you love and being passionate about what you do. That's having a life of success. When you have the ability to do what you love, love what you do and have the ability to impact people. That's having a life of success. That's what having a life of meaning is."

Tim Tebow

February 9

"I have swept away your sins like a cloud. I have scattered your offenses like the morning mist. Oh, return to me, for I have paid the price to set you free." Sing, O heavens, for the Lord has done this wondrous thing. Shout for joy, O depths of the earth! Break into song, O mountains and forests and every tree! For the Lord has redeemed Jacob and is glorified in Israel. *(Isaiah 44:22–23 NLT)*

You can fire your attorney

Remember that in the attorney-client relationship, the client is the boss. You can fire your attorney at any time. If you are not satisfied with the work your attorney is doing for you, you are entitled to terminate their services; however, you must pay for services rendered up to the date of termination.

It's common for problems between attorneys and clients to be due to poor communication. Let your attorney know if you are not pleased and try to reach a solution before taking further action. If your attorney has appeared in court on your behalf and the case is pending, a judge may have to approve the decision to remove the attorney from the case.

Stay productive

In today's complex business world, you need to make every minute count. Try these strategies:

Be effective, not just efficient. It's not enough to get things done more quickly, make sure those things need to be done and are producing the results you want.

Measure and respond. Evaluate your business metrics to identify what you're doing well and where improvements are needed.

Review progress against goals. This is not a once-a-year exercise. Conduct weekly or monthly check-ins and take appropriate action to stay on track or adjust the plan or goals as needed.

Today we observe

Chocolate Day

On this day in history

Notable events

In 1870, the U.S. Army established the U.S. National Weather Service.

Births

William Henry Harrison, 9th President of the United States, 1773

John Garnet Carter, American entrepreneur and inventor, the first to patent a version of miniature golf, 1883

Garner Ted Armstrong, American evangelist, minister, author, educator, radio and television commentator, 1930

Deaths

William E. Dodge, American businessman, politician, and activist, cofounder of Phelps Dodge Corporation (one of America's largest mining companies), founding member of YMCA of the U.S., 1883

Walter Frederick Morrison, American entrepreneur and inventor (Frisbee), 2010

Thought for the day

"True heroism is remarkably sober, very undramatic. It is not the urge to surpass all others at whatever cost, but the urge to serve others at whatever cost."

Arthur Ashe

I pray for a pure heart.

Read:
Proverbs, Chapter 9

February 10

My dear brothers and sisters, take note of this: Everyone should be quick to listen, slow to speak and slow to become angry, because human anger does not produce the righteousness that God desires. Therefore, get rid of all moral filth and the evil that is so prevalent and humbly accept the word planted in you, which can save you. *(James 1:19-21, NIV)*

Test your marketing strategies

Even with the greatest idea and thorough planning, concept and reality can be two different things. Before you roll out any marketing campaign, test it to be sure it will produce the results you want.

The easiest way to test a marketing strategy is to implement it on a small scale before committing to a larger-scale effort. It's also a good idea to do some comparison testing. Run two different ads and see which one pulls better. Mail two different pieces and see which one draws the higher response. Compare the cost and results generated by various strategies and go with the ones that deliver the best results for you.

Be careful not to extend the conclusion of your test beyond the test itself. Don't assume that a different set of circumstances will produce the same results; instead, test every possible angle. For example, if you tested a free printed newsletter and the test indicated you wouldn't get enough of a response to justify the cost, don't assume an online newsletter will produce the same poor results. Test that as well.

If the test tells you something won't work, the test itself was not a failure, it was a tremendous success—and it saved you a lot of time, money, and energy pursuing a strategy that would have failed.

Thought for the day

"The past is a place of reference, not a place of residence; the past is a place of learning, not a place of living."
— *Roy T. Bennett*

Today we observe
Umbrella Day

On this day in history

Notable events
In 1863, Alanson Crane patented the first U.S. fire extinguisher.
In 1870, the Young Women's Christian Association (YWCA) was formed in New York City.
In 1942, American chemist James Franklin Hyde patented fused silica.

Births
Jesse G. Vincent, American aircraft, marine, and automobile engine designer, chief engineer for Packard automobiles, 1880
John Franklin Enders, American microbiologist, developed measles vaccine, 1897
Walter Houser Brattain, American physicist and Nobel laureate for his work on transistors, 1902
Walter A. Brown, American sports executive, founder and original owner of the Boston Celtics, which he funded with a mortgage on his home, 1905

Deaths
Jerome Namias, American meteorologist who helped develop the system of passenger flight weather forecasting and researched the interaction between the oceans and atmosphere, 1997
Charles Rudolph Walgreen, Jr., American businessman, son of Walgreens founder, increased profit and size of the drug store during his tenure as president, 2007
Mike Ilitch, American businessman (founded Little Caesars Pizza), 2017

I am grateful that God will never abandon me.

Read:
Proverbs, Chapter 10

February 11

> "What do you want me to do for you?" Jesus asked him. The blind man said, "Rabbi, I want to see." "Go," said Jesus, "your faith has healed you." Immediately he received his sight and followed Jesus along the road. *(Mark 10:51-52, NIV)*

When things aren't right

Sometimes you feel dissatisfied. Things aren't right, but they're not totally wrong. You're irritated and agitated, and you know something needs to change. Do you stick with it? Or toss it and either start over or do something else?

To make the right decision, take a step back and ask yourself these questions:
- What's working well?
- What's not working?
- Can you fix what's not working and, if so, what will it take?
- Will you be satisfied with the fixes?

Your answers will tell you what you should do.

This technique can work with businesses, jobs, relationships (business and personal), living situations, and any other part of your life.

Thought for the day

"Before the Resurrection of Christ, the Holy Spirit came upon individuals only on certain occasions for special tasks. But now, after the Resurrection, Christ through the Holy Spirit dwells in the heart of every believer to give us supernatural power in living our daily lives."

Billy Graham

I pray for the wisdom to deal with whatever unexpected circumstances I encounter.

Read: Proverbs, Chapter 11

Today we observe

Don't Cry Over Spilled Milk Day
National Make a Friend Day
National Inventors' Day

On this day in history

Notable events

In 1752, the Pennsylvania Hospital (the first in America, founded through the efforts of Benjamin Franklin) received its first patient.

In 1809, Robert Fulton patented the steamboat.

Births

Thomas Edison, American inventor and businessman, 1847

Arthur Davidson, American businessman, cofounder of the Harley-Davidson Motor Company, 1881

Deaths

William Kelly, American inventor (pneumatic process of steelmaking), 1888

Charles Scribner, III, American book publisher, 1952

Ben Abruzzo, American balloonist and businessman, 1985

George A. Stephen, inventor (Weber Kettle Grill), 1993

Samuel W. Alderson, American inventor best known for developing the crash test dummy, 2005

Frank Piasecki, American engineer and helicopter aviation pioneer, 2008

Grow your faith by keeping a daily gratitude journal. Being intentional by recording what you are grateful for will increase your awareness of your abundant blessings.

February 12

T he Lord is good, a refuge in times of trouble. He cares for those who trust in him, *(Nahum 1:7, NIV)*

Team devotions for growth

Lois Rosenberry, president and CEO of Children's Discovery Center (Toledo, Ohio), has always opened administrative meetings with prayer and a devotion. She realized that even though they were providing Christian early childcare and education, some members of her leadership team had limited knowledge of the Bible.

She came up with the idea to let them research and lead the devotions for the monthly meetings—an idea that was enthusiastically embraced by the executives and administrators. She began by letting them choose what they wanted to study, which ranged from topics such as what the Bible says about leadership to what they could learn from specific characters.

The next step was to give them the tools they needed. To help them with their research, she bought each of them a basic Bible storybook written for eight- to twelve-year-olds. Even though her team consists of highly credentialed educators, Rosenberry wanted something that would be accurate but easy to read, not a complex scholarly commentary.

"How they responded was fascinating," Rosenberry says. Working solo and in pairs, the team members developed creative devotion presentations on their topic or character. They've done PowerPoints and even videos.

After each devotion presentation, Rosenberry leads a discussion. "What did we learn about Esther's leadership skills? What did we learn about Ruth? What can we learn and how can we apply that to our own leadership here in a Christian center?"

As the leadership team grows professionally, they are also growing personally and spiritually. Rosenberry says, "It has worked out beautifully."

On this day in history

Notable events

In 1978, Harvard player Frederick Thayer patented a baseball catcher's mask.

In 1998, Intel unveiled its first graphics chip, the i740.

Births

Peter Cooper, American industrialist, inventor, philanthropist, and politician, designed and built the first American steam locomotive, designed the first steel chair (a rocking chair) in America, founded Cooper Union for the Advancement of Science and Art, 1791

Abraham Lincoln, 16th U.S. President (first U.S. President to be assassinated), 1809

Deaths

Thomas L. Jennings, American tailor and inventor (dry-cleaning), abolitionist, and desegregationist, 1856

George Antheil, American composer, pianist, and inventor (developed radio guidance system for Allied torpedoes with Hedy Lamarr), 1959

James Cash Penney, American department store founder (JCPenney), 1971

Thought for the day

"The willingness to forgive is a sign of spiritual and emotional maturity. It is one of the great virtues to which we all should aspire. Imagine a world filled with individuals willing both to apologize and to accept an apology. Is there any problem that could not be solved among people who possessed the humility and largeness of spirit and soul to do either—or both—when needed?"

Gordon B. Hinckley

I pray for those who are traveling.

Read:
Proverbs, Chapter 12

February 13

If I speak in the tongues of men or of angels, but do not have love, I am only a resounding gong or a clanging cymbal. If I have the gift of prophecy and can fathom all mysteries and all knowledge, and if I have a faith that can move mountains, but do not have love, I am nothing. If I give all I possess to the poor and give over my body to hardship that I may boast, but do not have love, I gain nothing. *(1 Corinthians 13:1-3, NIV)*

Five mistakes that make networking events a waste of time

When you go to a networking event, go prepared to get the maximum benefit of your investment of time and money. Don't make these mistakes:

1. Forgetting your business cards or not bringing enough.
2. Giving out business cards with out-of-date or incomplete information.
3. Being unprepared to receive business cards from others.
4. Sitting and talking only with people you already know.
5. Describing your business in an unclear, incomplete or rambling way.

Bring plenty of cards that are well-designed and include current information. Have a place to put cards you collect. Meet new people. And be prepared with an effective introduction. No matter how popular social media and online networking becomes, nothing will ever match the power of a face-to-face contact—don't waste the opportunity.

Consider the source

It's natural for criticism to affect us, especially when someone tells us we aren't performing as well as we thought we were.

Before you take negative feedback to heart, filter it by the source. Is it coming from someone who is knowledgeable and worthy of respect? If so, process it and figure out how to benefit from it. If not, take it with a grain of salt—or even ignore it completely.

Today we observe
National Internet Friends Day

World Radio Day

On this day in history

Notable events

In 1799, the first U.S. law regulating insurance was passed by the Massachusetts legislature.

In 1914, the American Society of Composers, Authors & Publishers (ASCAP) was founded in New York City.

In 1957, the Southern Christian Leadership Conference organized in New Orleans with Martin Luther King, Jr. as president.

In 1985, the Dow Jones closed at a record high of 1297.92 after topping 1300 earlier.

Births

William Shockley, American inventor, physicist, and eugenicist, Nobel prize winner, known (with Frederick Terman) for being the father of Silicon Valley, 1910

Dr. Don Panoz, American entrepreneur and motorsports impresario (ALMS), 1935

Thought for the day

"When we walk to the edge of all the light we have and take the step into the darkness of the unknown, we must believe that one of two things will happen. There will be something solid for us to stand on or we will be taught to fly."

Patrick Overton

I pray to recognize grace when I see it.

Read:
Proverbs, Chapter 13

February 14

Love is patient, love is kind. It does not envy, it does not boast, it is not proud. It does not dishonor others, it is not self-seeking, it is not easily angered, it keeps no record of wrongs. Love does not delight in evil but rejoices with the truth. It always protects, always trusts, always hopes, always perseveres. *(1 Corinthians 13:4-7, NIV)*

On education ...

At the entrance gate of a university in South Africa, the following message was posted for contemplation:

"Destroying any nation does not require the use of atomic bombs or the use of long range missiles. It only requires lowering the quality of education and allowing cheating in the examinations by the students."

Patients die at the hands of such doctors.

Buildings collapse at the hands of such engineers.

Money is lost at the hands of such economists and accountants.

Humanity dies at the hands of such religious scholars.

Justice is lost at the hands of such judges.

The collapse of education is the collapse of the nation.

Thought for the day

"Listen to the mustn'ts, child. Listen to the don'ts. Listen to the shouldn'ts, the impossibles, the won'ts. Listen to the never haves, then listen close to me... Anything can happen, child. Anything can be."

Shel Silverstein

I am thankful for the acts of kindness that have been done for me.

Read:
Proverbs, Chapter 14

Today we observe

Organ Donor Day

Valentine's Day

On this day in history

Notable events

In 1876, Alexander Graham Bell and Elisha Gray applied separately for telephone patents. The Supreme Court eventually ruled Bell the rightful inventor.

In 1903, President Theodore Roosevelt signed a bill into law establishing the U.S. Department of Commerce & Labor.

In 1919, Merchants Parcel Delivery changed its name to United Parcel Service.

In 1924. Thomas J. Watson renamed the Computing-Tabulating-Recording Company (CTR) as International Business Machines (IBM).

In 2019, JP Morgan became the first bank to create its own crypto-currency, JPM Coin.

Births

Otis Tufts, American machinist and inventor, who built printing machines, steam engines, firefighting equipment, and invented the steam pile driver, 1804

Christopher Latham Sholes, American newspaperman, politician, and inventor of the typewriter, 1819

Margaret E. Knight, American businesswoman and inventor, notably of a machine to produce flat-bottomed paper bags, called the most famous 19th-century woman inventor, founder of Eastern Paper Bag Company, 1838

George Washington Gale Ferris, Jr., American engineer and inventor (Ferris Wheel), 1859

Michael Bloomberg, American businessman, mayor of New York City (2002-13), and philanthropist, 1942

Deaths

Walter Zinn, Canadian-American nuclear physicist (invented the breeder reactor), 2000

February 15

A cheerful heart is good medicine, but a broken spirit saps a person's strength. *(Proverbs 17:22, NLT)*

Make it difficult for your customers to leave

Some customers are loyal; others will leave you on a whim. What can you do to keep those customers who are buying from you because it's convenient but would switch to a competitor for a slightly lower price or because you have service failure?

Consider making it so hard for them to leave that they won't because it's not worth the effort. It's what banks do—their strategy to is get customers to have at least four different accounts (checking, savings, investment, consumer loan, mortgage loan, vehicle loan, safe deposit box, etc.). You might get mad at the bank or even find a better deal somewhere else, but when you think about moving your accounts, it's just too much trouble—so you stay. Communication companies (phone companies, cable companies, etc.) are doing the same thing when they offer discounts if you bundle your service. If you have your phone, television, and internet access all with the same company, you're going to think long and hard about switching providers for any reason because it will be a huge hassle.

What can you do to make it difficult for customers to leave? Can you put together product and service packages? Offer loyalty programs that reward long-time customers? Discounts for repeat business?

Ideally, of course, your customers should be staying with you because they want to. But in the real world of business, that's not how it always is. In addition to offering superior service and excellent products, it makes sense to set up barriers to leaving you so that customers have to think twice before they do. Do what you can do to make your customers want to stay and, at the same time, do what you can do to make it hard for them to leave.

Today we observe

Susan B. Anthony Day

On this day in history

Notable events

In 1903, the first teddy bear went on sale when toy store owner and inventor Morris Michtom placed two stuffed bears in his shop window.

Births

Cyrus McCormick, American businessman and inventor (mechanical reaper), founder of McCormick Harvesting Machine Company, which later became part of International Harvester Company, 1809

Charles Lewis Tiffany, American jeweler and founder of Tiffany & Co., 1812

Alfred Carlton Gilbert, American athlete, businessman, inventor (Erector Set), 1884

Deaths

Melville Elijah Stone, American newspaper publisher, founder of the *Chicago Daily News*, 1929

Robert Lee Thornton, Sr., American banker, civic leader, and four-term mayor of Dallas, Texas, 1964

Robert Adler, Austrian-American inventor (television remote control), 2007

Thought for the day

"Forget conventionalisms; forget what the world thinks of you stepping out of your place; think your best thoughts, speak your best words, work your best works, looking to your own conscience for approval."

Susan B. Anthony

I pray to be shielded from negativity.

Read:
Proverbs, Chapter 15

February 16

> We can rejoice, too, when we run into problems and trials, for we know that they help us develop endurance. And endurance develops strength of character, and character strengthens our confident hope of salvation. And this hope will not lead to disappointment. For we know how dearly God loves us, because he has given us the Holy Spirit to fill our hearts with his love. *(Romans 5:3-5, NLT)*

Take your parents to work

Remember when your parents came to school to see what you did all day? Maybe it's time to invite them to your office so they can once again see what you do all day. Consider a Parents' Day to let mothers and fathers see their adult children in their working environment.

Many workers, especially those in high-tech and creative jobs, have a hard time explaining their jobs to their parents. Also, today's younger workers are often accustomed to parents who have been very involved in their lives.

Depending on your particular operation, you can either make your Parents' Day a special company-wide event, schedule it by department, or just let workers know they are welcome to bring their parents in for a visit. The invitation should include not only biological and adoptive parents, but the people in your employees' lives who have played a parental role.

Consider hosting a casual lunch, a tour of the facility, and a presentation that demonstrates what the company does. Allow time for parents to see your staff in action. The overall cost will be minimal; the rewards are tremendous.

Thought for the day

"Your challenge is not your challenge. Your challenge is the way you think about your challenge. Your problem is not your problem; it is the way you look at it. Satan knows this. The devil is always messing with our minds."

Max Lucado

Today we observe

Do a Grouch a Favor Day

On this day in history

Notable events

In 600, Pope Gregory the Great decreed that saying "God bless you" is the correct response to a sneeze.

In 1880, the American Society of Mechanical Engineers formed in New York City.

In 1883, *Ladies' Home Journal* began publishing and in 1903 became the first American magazine to reach one million subscribers.

In 1937, the DuPont Corp. patented nylon (developed by employee Wallace Carothers).

Births

Richard McDonald, American entrepreneur, cofounder (with his brother Maurice McDonald) of McDonald's fast food restaurants, 1909

Carl Icahn, American businessman, investor, and philanthropist, founder of Icahn Enterprises, 1936

Deaths

Jay Cooke, American financier, first major investment banker in the U.S., and creator of the first wire house firm, 1905

James L. Kraft, Canadian-American entrepreneur and inventor (pasteurization process for cheese), founder of Kraft Foods, Inc., 1953

Larry Tesler, American computer scientist (invented copy, cut, paste), 2020

I pray for the ability to train those for whom I am responsible so that they may perform beyond expectations.

Read:
Proverbs, Chapter 16

February 17

But the Lord is faithful; he will strengthen you and guard you from the evil one. *(2 Thessalonians 3:3 NLT)*

How to build self-discipline

Self-discipline is the ability to keep going, stay motivated, and do what needs to be done regardless of how you feel. It takes self-discipline to achieve goals, improve performance, and have healthier, more fulfilling relationships. Some ways to strengthen your self-discipline:

Start small. Set small, achievable goals that will give you a sense of accomplishment and motivate you to move on to bigger and better things.

Change your habits. Identify and systematically eliminate your bad habits. Create and maintain good habits.

Practice self-control. Resist giving in to impulsive behavior and emotions. "Do not be quickly provoked in your spirit, for anger resides in the lap of fools." *(Ecclesiastes 7:9, NIV)*

Exercise. Regular physical exercise helps keep you healthy, improves your mood, and helps build self-discipline.

Reduce your consumption of physical and mental junk food. What you put into your mind and body should be healthful and nutritious.

Create a process of setting and tracking short- and long-term goals. Use the short-term goals to help build a sense of achievement and momentum.

Be self-aware. Understand your strengths, weaknesses, and triggers, and use that awareness to build self-discipline.

Find and use tools. Identify resources that will help and support your self-discipline journey.

I am thankful that even when I don't know where I'm going, I know that God does and he will lead me on the right road.

Today we observe

Random Acts of Kindness Day

On this day in history

Notable events

In 1943, Dow Chemical and Corning Glass Works formed a joint venture to explore and produce silicon materials based on the work of James Franklin Hyde.

In 1972, sales of the Volkswagen Beetle model exceeded those of the Ford Model T.

In 1981, Chrysler Corporation reported the largest corporate losses in U.S. history.

Births

Aaron Montgomery Ward, American retailer, founder of Montgomery Ward, 1844

Thomas J. Watson, American businessman, chairman and CEO of IBM (1914-56), 1874

Jensen Huang, Taiwanese-American businessman, founder of Nvidia Corp., 1963

Michael Jordan, former professional basketball player and businessman, 1963

Deaths

Christopher Latham Sholes, American newspaperman, politician, and inventor of the typewriter, 1890

Rush Limbaugh, American conservative political talk radio personality, 2021

Thought for the day

"Now if you are going to win any battle you have to do one thing. You have to make the mind run the body. Never let the body tell the mind what to do. The body will always give up. It is always tired morning, noon, and night. But the body is never tired if the mind is not tired. When you were younger the mind could make you dance all night, and the body was never tired… You've always got to make the mind take over and keep going."

George S. Patton

Read:
Proverbs, Chapter 17

February 18

As the mountains surround Jerusalem, so the Lord surrounds his people from this time on and forevermore. (Psalm 125:2, NRSVue)

You need written, detailed contracts—even with people you trust

Insisting on a detailed contract does not indicate a lack of trust. Rather, it provides a vehicle for you to confirm your mutual understanding of your agreement.

Contracts don't have to be formal, complex documents (depending, of course, on what they cover); they just have to clearly outline the deal you're making. This is the chance for you to say, "Wait, that's not what I meant," or "That's exactly what I expect."

Some tips on contracts:

Make standard provisions apply to both parties. If, for example, the contract exempts the supplier from specific liabilities, the language should be revised to exempt the customer as well.

Use precise language. It's difficult to enforce vague language, so be specific. A clause that states a supplier isn't responsible for failures due to causes "beyond the vendor's control" leaves a lot of room for interpretation. More precise language forces a greater level of accountability.

Include a default provision and an escape clause. Describe the circumstances under which either party would be considered in default and what will happen. Also define what's necessary to terminate the contract if either party wants out.

Don't assume anything not in writing. If it's in the contract, it's enforceable; if it's not in the contract, it's not enforceable. Period.

Consider a legal review. Depending on the amount of money and the degree of risk and liability involved, you may want to have an attorney take a look at your contracts.

Today we observe
National Battery Day
Thumb Appreciation Day

On this day in history
Notable events
In 1986, anti-smoking ads aired for the first time on TV.

Births
George Peabody, American financier and philanthropist, considered the father of modern philanthropy, 1795

Deaths
Charles Lewis Tiffany, American jeweler and founder of Tiffany & Co., 1902
John Batterson Stetson, American hat manufacturer, philanthropist, inventor of the cowboy hat, founder of John B. Stetson Company, 1906
George Dayton, American businessman, philanthropist, founder of Dayton's department store which became Target Corp., 1938
Charles Bedaux, French-American efficiency engineer who developed the Bedaux plan for measuring and compensating industrial labor, 1944
Jack Northrup, American aircraft industrialist and designer, founder of the Northrop Corporation, 1981

Thought for the day

"Consult not your fears but your hopes and your dreams. Think not about your frustrations, but about your unfulfilled potential. Concern yourself not with what you tried and failed in, but with what it is still possible for you to do."

— *Pope John XXIII*

I pray for my family.

Read: Proverbs, Chapter 18

February 19

Consequently, faith comes from hearing the message, and the message is heard through the word about Christ. But I ask: Did they not hear? Of course they did: "Their voice has gone out into all the earth, their words to the ends of the world." *(Romans 10:17-18 NIV)*

Give your weaknesses to God

Should you fake it until you make it?

A popular school of thought is that if we pretend to be what we want to be, we will ultimately manifest the role we're playing.

That might work with people, but it won't work with God. God knows our weaknesses even better than we do. When we have doubts as to our abilities, when we are afraid, God is there, waiting for us to ask for his help. He wants us to be willing to accept it.

The Bible is full of stories of people who didn't think they could do what God was calling them to do—and yet, they did. God doesn't depend on our abilities, he wants our obedience and then he will equip us.

Don't pretend you're something you're not. Don't operate with a false sense of self-confidence. Don't hide from your weaknesses. Give them to God and let God transform and empower you to be the authentic person he created you to be.

Remember what Paul wrote: *Each time he said, "My grace is all you need. My power works best in weakness." So now I am glad to boast about my weaknesses, so that the power of Christ can work through me. … For when I am weak, then I am strong.* (2 Corinthians 12:9-10, NLT)

So should you fake it until you make it? No. Embrace the power of your weaknesses by turning them over to God and letting him work through them.

I pray for my suppliers who provide my company with the goods and services it needs to operate.

Today we observe

Prevent Plagiarism Day

On this day in history

Notable events

In 1856, the tin-type camera was patented by Hamilton Smith.

In 1878, Thomas Edison was granted a patent for his cylinder phonograph.

In 1906, Will Keith Kellogg joined Charles D. Bolin in founding the Battle Creek Toasted Corn Flake Company, now the multinational food manufacturer Kellogg's.

In 1913, the first prize was inserted into a Cracker Jack box.

Births

Mary Elizabeth Anderson, American real estate developer, rancher, viticulturist, and inventor of the windshield wiper, 1866

Bill Bowerman, American track and field coach, co-founder of Nike, 1911

Karen Silkwood, American nuclear lab technician and labor union activist, 1946

Jeffrey Robert Immelt, American businessman, chairman of General Electric, 1956

Deaths

Charles "Charlie O" Finley, American businessman and sports entrepreneur, 1996

Thought for the day

"Everyone has got it in him, if he will only make up his mind and stick at it. None of us is born with a stop-valve on his powers or with a set limit to his capacities. There is no limit possible to the expansion of each one of us."

Charles Schwab

Read:
Proverbs, Chapter 19

February 20

Fools vent their anger, but the wise quietly hold it back. *(Proverbs 29:11, NLT)*

Keep negative emotions from escalating into anger

Recognize the warning signs that you're about to get angry. Anger typically begins with feelings of annoyance and irritation. When you're getting annoyed, look for ways to either change the situation or remove yourself from it. Take control over your precursors to anger.

Change your perspective. Angry people often think things are worse than they actually are. Before you get to that point, step back and be logical. Try replacing your negative view with a positive—or at least a more reasonable—one.

Manage your expectations. Be realistic in what you expect from yourself and others. Don't make impossible demands that will only leave you frustrated and angry when they're not met.

Use relaxation techniques that work for you. Try taking slow, controlled, deep breaths or visualizing yourself in a relaxed place or situation.

Move. Go for a walk or a run. Do a yoga practice. Dance. Getting yourself in motion can help you decompress and burn off feelings that can grow into anger.

Communicate. Have a calm, rational conversation with the other person or people involved. Let them talk and listen to what they have to say. Consider your response carefully.

Turn it over to God. Pray and ask God to handle it, then let it go.

from *Seven Day Anger-Free Challenge* by Jacquelyn Lynn

Today we observe
Clean Out Your Bookcase Day
National Leadership Day
National Student Volunteer Day

On this day in history

Notable events

In 1768, the first American chartered fire insurance company opened in Pennsylvania.

In 1872, Cyrus Baldwin patented the hydraulic electric elevator.

In 1909, the Hudson Motor Car Company was founded in Detroit, Michigan by retail titan Joseph L. Hudson and other investors.

Births

Robert Wood Johnson I, American industrialist and cofounder of Johnson & Johnson, 1845

E. H. Harriman, American financier and railroad executive, 1848

Cornelius Vanderbilt Whitney, American businessman, film producer, government official, writer, and philanthropist, 1899

Gloria Vanderbilt, American fashion designer, artist, heiress, and socialite, 1924

Kenneth H. Olsen, American electrical engineer and cofounder of Digital Equipment Corporation, 1926

Cindy Crawford, American supermodel and businesswoman, 1966

Deaths

Larry H. Miller, American entrepreneur (owner of more than 60 automotive dealerships and a variety of other ventures), philanthropist, and owner of NBA's Utah Jazz, 2009

Thought for the day

"Three Rules of Work: Out of clutter find simplicity; from discord find harmony; in the middle of difficulty lies opportunity."

Albert Einstein

I pray for the wisdom and strength to set appropriate boundaries in all areas of my life.

Read:
Proverbs, Chapter 20

February 21

Don't worry about anything; instead, pray about everything. Tell God what you need, and thank him for all he has done. *(Philippians 4:6, NLT)*

Schedule vacations

Now is the time to get vacations on your company's schedule. Determine how many people can be out at the same time and set up a vacation calendar so they can reserve their time off. This is an ideal time to remind your employees of the benefits of vacations, which include improving physical and mental health, motivation, relationships, job performance, and perspective.

Create a system (such as first come, first served or seniority) that works with your organization for how employees can schedule their vacations. Set a deadline for making requests so that other employees aren't left in limbo.

Be as flexible as possible, because life happens and plans will change. But let employees know that it's important for you to have sufficient time to prepare for their absences.

It's not what you do that counts, it's what problems you solve

You can spend your days working, but if you're not solving problems, you're not likely to feel satisfied. And if you're not finding solutions that will make a difference in the world, you won't feel fulfilled.

What problems are you solving?

I am grateful for my friends.

> Grow your faith by reading a book about Christian life or doctrine.

On this day in history

Notable events

In 1842, the first known sewing machine was patented in the U.S. by John Greenough.

In 1878, the world's first telephone directory was issued in New Harbor, Connecticut; it had 50 subscribers.

In 1931, Alka Seltzer was introduced.

In 1947, the first instant developing camera, the Polaroid Land Camera Model 95, was demonstrated by Edwin Land at the Optical Society of America.

In 1948, NASCAR was incorporated.

Births

Kelsey Grammer, American actor, comedian, director, producer, and activist, 1955

Kevin Rose, American television host and internet entrepreneur, 1977

Deaths

Frederick McKinley Jones, American inventor, entrepreneur, and engineer best known for his work in refrigeration technology, 1961

Tim Horton, Canadian ice hockey player and cofounder of the Tim Hortons restaurant chain, 1974

Gertrude B. Elion, American biochemist, drug researcher, Nobel Prize winner, 1999

Barney Rosset, pioneering American book and magazine publisher, founder of Grove Press and *Evergreen Review*, 2012

Billy Graham, American Baptist evangelist, 2018

Thought for the day

"All of the great leaders have had one characteristic in common: it was the willingness to confront unequivocally the major anxiety of their people in their time. This, and not much else, is the essence of leadership."

John Kenneth Galbraith

Read:
Proverbs, Chapter 21

February 22

As obedient children, do not be conformed to the passions of your former ignorance, but as he who called you is holy, be holy yourselves in all your conduct; *(1 Peter 1:14–15 RSV)*

To get what you want, say thank you in advance

The next time you're in a situation where you're not getting the performance out of a person that you need, try thanking them for doing what you want them to do—even if they haven't done it yet.

Most people will respond by trying to earn the appreciation you expressed.

For example: You have an IT person on your staff who tends to be abrupt and doesn't explain things clearly, which is affecting morale and productivity.

Instead of telling her she needs to be more pleasant, avoid techno-speak, and be sure others understand her, thank her for being that way. Say, "Jessica, I really appreciate you taking the time to make sure the customer service reps understand how to use all the features of the new tracking system. You talk to them in plain English, using terms they understand, and you treat them with respect. Thanks."

You know that's not what Jessica is really doing. She may or may not realize that's not what she's doing. But you've paid her a compliment, and it's human nature to respond to something nice that's said about us by trying to be more of whatever that is. Jessica is very likely to start demonstrating the behavior you just praised her for.

It's part of the law of reciprocity. You create a sense of obligation on the part of the person you thank or compliment to fulfill the expectation you've set.

Thought for the day

"Creativity is allowing yourself to make mistakes. Art is knowing which ones to keep."

Scott Adams

Today we observe

Be Humble Day

World Thinking Day

On this day in history

Notable events

In 1879, the first Woolworth's Great Five Cent Store opened by Frank Winfield Woolworth in Utica, New York; it failed almost immediately.

Births

George Washington, American Founding Father, Commander-in-Chief of the Continental Army during the War for Independence, and first President of the United States, 1732

Isaac Rice, German-American businessman, investor, author (founder of General Dynamics Electric Boat, Electric Vehicle Company), 1850

Robert Baden-Powell, founder of the modern scouting movement, 1857

Ralph C. Smedley, founder of Toastmasters International, 1878

Al Gross, American inventor (walkie-talkie), 1918

Charles "Charlie O" Finley, American businessman and sports entrepreneur, 1918

Joseph Lechleider, American electrical engineer, inventor (DSL/high speed internet technology), 1933

Deaths

John Jacob Astor III, American businessman, financier, philanthropist, and soldier during the Civil War, 1890

Wesley A. Clark, American physicist credited with designing the first modern personal computer, 2016

I pray to be a constant reflection of God's goodness, generosity, and infinite mercy.

Read:
Proverbs, Chapter 22

February 23

Then they gathered around him and asked him, "Lord, are you at this time going to restore the kingdom to Israel?" He said to them: "It is not for you to know the times or dates the Father has set by his own authority. But you will receive power when the Holy Spirit comes on you; and you will be my witnesses in Jerusalem, and in all Judea and Samaria, and to the ends of the earth." *(Acts 1:6-8, NIV)*

Political campaigns: big market, big risk

Political campaigns spend billions of dollars buying the goods and services necessary (and maybe not necessary but stuff they buy anyway) to get their candidates elected.

It's not just advertising. Campaigns buy other promotional items, food, transportation, computers, communication equipment, office equipment and supplies, audio-visual equipment and services, consulting services and more.

If you can get your share of that money, great!

Just remember: Not every company that has political campaigns for customers gets paid.

When a political campaign leaves a business owner holding a bad debt, even when the amount is a relatively small portion of the campaign's total budget, the damage to the supplier can be significant. And the money is virtually impossible to collect.

What's the answer?

The safest strategy is to insist that political campaigns pay in advance. Only extend credit to a campaign if you support the candidate or the issue enough to be willing to risk the amount of the sale as an involuntary donation.

Could this approach cost you business? Sure. But it could also prevent losses—and only you can decide how much your company can afford to risk.

I pray for talented people and that they will seek to use their gifts for God's glory.

Today we observe
Diesel Engine Day
World Understanding and Peace Day

On this day in history

Notable events
In 1455, Johannes Gutenberg printed his first Bible (estimated date).
In 1883, the American Anti-Vivisection Society was organized in Philadelphia; it's original goal was to regulate the use of animals in science and society; today, its mission is to end the use of animals in science.
In 1905, the first Rotary Club was formed by four men in the Unity Building, Chicago.
In 1927, President Calvin Coolidge created the Federal Radio Commission.

Births
James G. Batterson, American designer, builder, and a founder of Travelers Insurance Company, 1823
W.E.B. Du Bois, American civil rights activist, cofounder of the NAACP, 1868
Michael Dell, American businessman, investor, and philanthropist, founder of Dell Technologies, 1965

Deaths
John Quincy Adams, 6th U.S. President, 1829
John Robert Gregg, Irish-American inventor of Gregg Shorthand system, 1948

Thought for the day

"The trouble with most of us is that we would rather be ruined by praise than saved by criticism."

Norman Vincent Peale

Read:
Proverbs, Chapter 23

February 24

> I praise you because I am fearfully and wonderfully made; your works are wonderful, I know that full well. *(Psalm 139:14, NIV)*

Selecting a trainer

Training has a direct impact on your organization's productivity and performance. Investing in training can generate tremendous returns, but if you're bringing in an outside trainer, it's important to choose one who can deliver the results you need. Before you choose a trainer, consider this advice:

Determine exactly what you need before you begin interviewing trainers. Protect yourself and the outside trainer from possible misunderstandings by outlining clearly what you expect. This spares both of you from potential unpleasantness or ineffectiveness after the project is underway.

Ask for written proposals. By getting it in writing, you'll be able to determine if the trainer truly understands the scope of the project and has the resources to meet your needs.

Check references. If the proposal looks good, contact some of the trainer's current and/or former clients.

Ask for work samples. If you want the trainer to create manuals or other types of training aids, take a look at the items they've produced in the past. If it's not what you have in mind, ask if they have the capability to handle something different. And be sure your contract stipulates who owns any training tools they create.

Develop a project timeline. The only way to be sure a trainer will meet your deadlines is to put them in writing and make them part of the contract.

I am thankful for my home.

Read:
Proverbs, Chapter 24

On this day in history

Notable events

In 1582, Pope Gregory XIII announced a new style of calendar, commonly known as the Gregorian calendar.

In 1938, DuPont began manufacturing synthetic bristle toothbrushes with molded plastic handles advertised as Dr. West's Miracle Tuft Toothbrush.

Births

Steve Jobs, American computer entrepreneur and cofounder of Apple, 1955

Terry Semel, American executive (chairman and CEO of Yahoo! Inc., chairman and co-CEO of Warner Bros.), 1943

Deaths

Robert Fulton, American inventor and engineer (first commercial steamboat), 1815

Malcom Forbes, American entrepreneur and politician, publisher of Forbes magazine, 1990

Larry David Norman, American musician, a pioneer of Christian rock music, 2008

Thought for the day

"If you envy successful people, you create a negative force field of attraction that repels you from ever doing the things that you need to do to be successful. If you admire successful people, you create a positive force field of attraction that draws you toward becoming more and more like the kinds of people that you want to be like."

Brian Tracy

Answer to God, answer to your spouse, answer to people who are in authority in your own life, but don't bow to public opinion.

February 25

Yes, they knew God, but they wouldn't worship him as God or even give him thanks. And they began to think up foolish ideas of what God was like. As a result, their minds became dark and confused. Claiming to be wise, they instead became utter fools. *(Romans 1:21-22 NLT)*

Conduct credit reviews on your long-time customers

If you extend credit to your customers, how long has it been since you've done a credit check on your accounts?

If it's been more than a year, it's been too long.

Just because a company has paid its bills on time in the past doesn't mean it will do so in the future. It's good business practice to do a full credit review of every customer at least annually and always be on the alert for signs that a customer is in trouble.

Some red flags include:
- Slowdown in payments
- Increased returns of merchandise
- Difficulty getting answers to your payment inquiries

Even a sharp increase in ordering could signal trouble. Companies concerned that they may lose their credit privileges may try to stock up while they can.

Something else to monitor is a major change in your customers' product line(s) or customer base. These are issues that could affect their cash flow and ability to pay.

Most customers understand routine credit reviews and accept them as sound business practice. A customer who objects may well have something to hide—and that's something you need to know.

I pray for my friends and colleagues to get through the challenges they don't talk about.

Read:
Proverbs, Chapter 25

Today we observe
National Chocolate Covered Nut Day

Quiet Day

On this day in history

Notable events

In 1836, Samuel Colt patented the first multi-shot revolving-cylinder revolver, enabling the firearm to be fired multiple times without reloading.

In 1913, the Sixteenth Amendment to the U.S. Constitution became law, providing the legal basis for the institution of a graduated income tax.

Births

Charles Lang Freer, American industrialist (founder of Peninsular Car Company), art collector, and patron, 1854

Deaths

James D. Norris, American businessman, investor, commodities dealer, sports team owner, racehorse owner/breeder, 1966

Thought for the day

"When we think life is dark, Christ knows better. Look up. The light is coming."

Bear Grylls

Celebrate your children

Let your children know how important they are to you by making their birthday the special occasion it is. If your child's birthday falls on a workday, take vacation time (or whatever paid time off you have available) so you can spend the entire day celebrating with them. Schedule it well in advance so you can commit to being with your family on that day.

February 26

"Therefore go and make disciples of all nations, baptizing them in the name of the Father and of the Son and of the Holy Spirit, and teaching them to obey everything I have commanded you. And surely I am with you always, to the very end of the age." *(Matthew 28:19-20 NIV)*

Turn old employers into new customers

If you started your own business after a stint in the corporate world, you may find your former employer is a prime prospective customer.

Assuming you left on good terms, you have significant advantages selling to your former employer. You know the system, the company way, but that knowledge will only get you in the door.

It's critical to recognize that your relationship with the company has changed. As a supplier, you may be dealing with different people, perhaps higher up on the corporate ladder, than you did before. Some of your former co-workers may see you as a threat to their own job security. Also, their bosses may not be entirely comfortable if you have overt personal relationships with company employees, so you may need to stop socializing with former co-workers.

If, on the other hand, those former co-workers see you as an ally, they can be very helpful—but it's help you shouldn't count on. Don't expect to be told company secrets, or to be able to neglect the account and continue to retain it. You go into the relationship with an edge, but that just gets you your first assignment. The future depends on the quality of product or service you provide, and you're going to be expected to perform as well or better than anyone else out there.

I pray to stay focused on my purpose and not wander aimlessly.

Read:
Proverbs, Chapter 26

Today we observe
Carpe Diem Day
National Letter to an Elder Day

On this day in history

Notable events
- In 1935, RADAR (radio detection and ranging) was first demonstrated by Robert Watson-Watt.
- In 2013, a flexible battery capable of being charged wirelessly and folded and stretched was developed.

Births
- Levi Strauss, German-born American clothing designer who founded the first company to manufacture blue jeans (Levi Strauss & Co.), 1829
- John Harvey Kellogg, American businessman, inventor, and physician, director of the Battle Creek Sanitarium, developer of a variety of bland vegetarian foods including granola and flaked breakfast cereal, 1852
- Herbert Henry Dow, American industrialist (Dow Chemical) and inventor, 1866

Deaths
- Richard Jordan Gatling, American inventor (Gatling gun, first hand-cranked machine gun), 1903

Thought for the day

"People love to talk but hate to listen. Listening is not merely not talking, though even that is beyond most of our powers; it means taking a vigorous, human interest in what is being told us. You can listen like a blank wall or like a splendid auditorium where every sound comes back fuller and richer."

Alice Duer Miller

February 27

We think you ought to know, dear brothers and sisters, about the trouble we went through in the province of Asia. We were crushed and overwhelmed beyond our ability to endure, and we thought we would never live through it. In fact, we expected to die. But as a result, we stopped relying on ourselves and learned to rely only on God, who raises the dead. *(2 Corinthians 1:8-9, NLT)*

Do your suppliers understand how you operate?

Your suppliers will be able to serve you better if they know as much as possible about how you operate. A savvy salesperson will seek this information, but if that doesn't happen, take the initiative to make sure your suppliers know:

Your purchasing process. Tell them who the decision-makers are and explain the internal steps required to make a buying decision.

Your internal policies governing relationships with suppliers. For example, are your employees allowed to accept gifts or entertainment from vendors?

Your payment process. Tell them how long it takes you to process invoices and what information (purchase order, proof of delivery, etc.) you need from suppliers to get them paid quickly, efficiently, and accurately.

If suppliers are irritating you by not doing things the way you'd prefer, it might be that they just aren't aware of how they can best work with you. Tell them and you'll both reap the benefits.

Thought for the day

"Surround yourself with the best people you can find, delegate authority, and don't interfere as long as the policy you've decided upon is being carried out."

Ronald Reagan

Read:
Proverbs, Chapter 27

Today we observe
World NGO Day

On this day in history

Notable events
- In 1879, saccharin, the first widely commercialized non-nutritive sweetener, was accidentally discovered by Constantin Fahlberg at Johns Hopkins University.
- In 1998, Apple discontinued the development of the Newton computer.

Births
- Henry E. Huntington, American railroad magnate, real estate investor, and major booster for Los Angeles, 1850
- Walter O. Briggs Sr., American entrepreneur (Briggs Manufacturing company, automobile body manufacturer), and sports team owner, 1877
- Charles Strite, American inventor (automatic pop-up toaster), 1878
- David Sarnoff, Russian-American businessman who headed a conglomerate of telecommunications and media companies (including RCA and NBC), credited with Sarnoff's Law, which states that the value of a broadcast network is proportional to the number of viewers, 1891
- Elizabeth Taylor, English-American actress, businesswoman, and humanitarian, 1932
- Ralph Nader, American consumer advocate, 1934

Deaths
- Kingsley Davis, American sociologist and demographer, coined the terms "population explosion" and "zero population growth," 1997
- Fred Rogers, American children's TV host, Presbyterian minister, 2003

I am thankful for the privilege of prayer.

February 28

> Honor the Lord with your wealth and with the best part of everything you produce. Then he will fill your barns with grain, and your vats will overflow with good wine. *(Proverbs 3:9–10 NLT)*

Important internal controls

Protect your business financially with these internal controls:

- Create a system of internal checks and balances so that financial duties are handled by two or more unrelated employees.
- To avoid the possibility of a single employee embezzling funds undetected, the same employee should not authorize, process, and record financial transactions.
- Review credit card statements carefully.
- Require two signatures on checks; check with your bank on creating a comparable requirement for electronic payments.
- Conduct periodic internal audits, both scheduled and unscheduled. Have an external source audit your finances at least once a year.
- Make vacations mandatory. Employees who never take time off may be afraid that irregularities will be discovered in their absence.
- Set up a system so employees can report fraud anonymously, without fear of retaliation.

Thought for the day

"Be strong enough to stand alone, be yourself enough to stand apart, but be wise enough to stand together when the time comes."

— *Mark Amend*

I pray that when I get frustrated, Lord, you will calm me and guide me in the right direction.

Today we observe

International Repetitive Strain Injury Awareness Day (Feb. 29 in leap years)

National Essay Day

On this day in history

Notable events

In 1646, Roger Scott, of Lynn, Massachusetts, was tried and found guilty of sleeping in church.

In 1759, Pope Clement XIII allowed the Bible to be translated into various languages.

In 1827, the first commercial railroad in the U.S., Baltimore & Ohio (B&O), was chartered.

In 1953, Francis Crick and James Watson discovered the chemical structure of DNA-molecule using studies of x-ray diffraction developed by Rosalind Franklin and Maurice Wilkins.

In 1956, American engineer Wright Forrester was issued a patent for computer core memory.

Births

Linus Pauling, American chemist, chemical engineer, author, educator, and peace activist, winner of the Nobel Prize in Chemistry and the Nobel Peace Prize, 1901

Deaths

George Hearst, American businessman and politician, 1891

Henry Luce, American magazine publisher (Time, Fortune, Life), 1967

Owen Chamberlain, American physicist known for particle physics, Nobel Prize winner, 2006

Joseph M. Juran, Romanian-born American engineer, management consultant, and author, advocate for quality and quality management, 2008

Paul Harvey, American news commentator and radio broadcaster, 2009

Read:
Proverbs, Chapter 28

February 29

> I thank him who has given me strength, Christ Jesus our Lord, because he judged me faithful, appointing me to his service, though formerly I was a blasphemer, persecutor, and insolent opponent. But I received mercy because I had acted ignorantly in unbelief, and the grace of our Lord overflowed for me with the faith and love that are in Christ Jesus. *(1 Timothy 1:12-14, ESV)*

O God Our Help in Ages Past

Isaac Watts, 1719

O God, our Help in ages past,
our Hope for years to come,
our Shelter from the stormy blast,
and our eternal Home.

Under the shadow of Thy throne
Thy saints have dwelt secure;
sufficient is Thine arm alone,
and our defense is sure.

Before the hills in order stood,
or earth received its frame,
from everlasting Thou art God,
to endless years the same.

A thousand ages in Thy sight
are like an evening gone,
short as the watch that ends the night
before the rising sun.

Time, like an ever-rolling stream
Soon bears us all away;
we fly forgotten, as a dream
dies at the op'ning day.

O God, our Help in ages past,
our Hope for years to come,
be Thou our Guard while life shall last,
and our eternal Home!

Today we observe

International Repetitive Strain Injury Awareness Day

Leap Day

On this day in history

Notable events
In 1960, the first Playboy Club opened in Chicago.

Births
Ann Lee, American founder of the Shakers, 1736.
Herman Hollerith, American businessman and inventor (first electric tabulating machine), founder of a company that was combined with several other companies in 1911 to form what would eventually become IBM, 1860.
Tony Robbins, American motivational speaker, 1960.

Deaths
Bill Roe, American sports executive, 2020.

Thought for the day

"The truth of the resurrection gives life to every other area of gospel truth. The resurrection is the pivot on which all of Christianity turns and without which none of the other truths would much matter. Without the resurrection, Christianity would be so much wishful thinking, taking its place alongside all other human philosophy and religious speculation."

John MacArthur

Shareable Saturday

An inspirational thought, brief video, and more delivered to your inbox weekly.

I pray for Jesus to be my peace.

Read:
Proverbs, Chapter 29

Christian Business Almanac

March

The name of March comes from *Martius*, the first month of the earliest Roman calendar and the beginning of the season for warfare. It was named after Mars, the Roman god of war.

March birthstone
Aquamarine, bloodstone

March flower
Daffodil, jonquil

March is ...
- American Red Cross Month
- Bleeding Disorders Awareness Month
- Brain Injury Awareness Month
- Colorectal Cancer Education and Awareness Month
- Employee Spirit Month
- International Ideas Month
- Kidney Cancer Awareness Month
- Listening Awareness Month
- National Cerebral Palsy Awareness Month
- National Clean Up Your IRS Act Month
- National Ethics Awareness Month
- National Kidney Month
- National March into Literacy Month
- National Sleep Awareness Month
- Poison Prevention Awareness Month
- Supply Management Month
- Women's History Month

Mark your calendar for these March holidays and observances

First Friday in March	National Dress in Blue Day
First Friday in March	National Speech and Debate Education Day
First Friday in March	World Day of Prayer
First full week in March	Women in Construction Week
First Tuesday in March	National Sportsmanship Day
First Wednesday in March	Stop Bad Service Day
Second Sunday in March	Check Your Batteries Day
Second Sunday in March	Daylight Saving Time begins (most of U.S.)
Second Friday in March	National Freelancers Day
Second Tuesday in March	National Organize Your Home Office Day
Second Wednesday in March	No Smoking Day
Second full week in March	National Older Workers Employment Week
Third Saturday in March	International Sports Car Racing Day
Third Wednesday in March	Small Business Development Centers Day
Fourth Wednesday in March	American Red Cross Giving Day

Fun Facts about March

March is the second of seven months to have 31 days.
Martius remained the first month of the Roman calendar year until as late as 153 BC.
March is the only month with three consecutive consonants in the English language.

March 1

I solemnly urge you in the presence of God and Christ Jesus, who will someday judge the living and the dead when he comes to set up his Kingdom: Preach the word of God. Be prepared, whether the time is favorable or not. Patiently correct, rebuke, and encourage your people with good teaching. *(2 Timothy 4:1-2, NLT)*

Important website detail

There's a lot to think about when you're building a website—design, functionality, content, marketing and more. Be sure to include these four documents:

Privacy policy. If you collect information from your site's visitors—even if it's just names and email addresses—you should have a policy in place to safeguard that data and let your users know what that policy is.

Terms of use. Tell users what they can and can't do on your site and how you will resolve disputes.

Disclaimers. You can't disclaim all liability, but if you're selling a product or service that has a warranty associated with it, or if you offer advice or even links to other sites, include appropriate and clearly-stated disclaimers on your website.

Copyright policy. If you allow others to post information on your site (comments on your blog, information on discussion boards, etc.), have a copyright policy that explains what may and may not be shared and how you will address copyright infringement.

Thought for the day

"Good management consists of showing average people how to do the work of superior people."

John D. Rockefeller

I pray that I will find a way to ease the burden of someone I work with.

Read:
Proverbs, Chapter 1

Today we observe

Global Day of Unplugging

National Employee Appreciation Day

On this day in history

Notable events

In 1790, the first U.S. census was authorized.

In 1933, to prevent a run on banks, bank holidays were declared in six states.

In 1937, U.S. Steel raised workers' wages to $5 a day.

In 1962, Kresge Corporation opened the first Kmart store in Garden City, Michigan.

Births

Michael Lampton, American astronaut and founder of the optical ray tracing company Stellar Software, 1941

Deaths

Halsey William Wilson, American publisher of reference books *(Readers' Guide, Cumulative Book Index, Book Review Digest)*, founder of H. W. Wilson Company, 1954

Wilhelmina Cooper, Dutch-American model and founder of Wilhelmina Models, 1980

Edwin Land, American inventor of instant photography and cofounder of the Polaroid Corporation, 1991

Orrin Keepnews, American jazz producer and founder of Riverside Records and Milestone Records, 2015

Jim Kimsey, American businessman and philanthropist, cofounder of America Online (AOL), 2016

Orin C. Smith, American businessman & CEO of Starbucks (2000-2005), 2018

Jack Welch, American businessman and CEO of General Electric, 2020

Vernon Jordan, American businessman and civil rights activist, 2021

Jerry Richardson, American businessman, football player, founder of the Carolina Panthers, philanthropist, 2023

March 2

"I have set my rainbow in the clouds, and it will be the sign of the covenant between me and the earth. Whenever I bring clouds over the earth and the rainbow appears in the clouds, I will remember my covenant between me and you and all living creatures of every kind. Never again will the waters become a flood to destroy all life. Whenever the rainbow appears in the clouds, I will see it and remember the everlasting covenant between God and all living creatures of every kind on the earth." *(Genesis 9:13-16, NIV)*

Don't set and forget

One of the wonderful things about the abundance of content marketing and social media tools is that they allow us to manage our messages without having to do it in real time.

But when a crisis occurs or a major news story (such as a natural disaster, mass shooting, or other traumatic incidents) breaks, immediately check your pre-scheduled social media and blog articles to be sure you aren't posting anything that might be interpreted as insensitive—or worse.

Your content marketing strategy and crisis management plan should include checking the content of any pre-scheduled material to make sure that you don't cause or become collateral damage in the event of a tragedy.

Responsible team members should have access to your various content and social media tools at all times. Authorize and train them to suspend any posts that might be questionable in light of unexpected events.

When breaking news alerts start flooding your newsfeed, check your scheduled emails, blog articles and social media posts and make adjustments as needed.

Thought for the day

"And this I believe: that the free, exploring mind of the individual human is the most valuable thing in the world."
John Steinbeck

Read:
Proverbs, Chapter 2

Today we observe

National Read Across America Day
World Teen Mental Wellness Day

On this day in history

Notable events
- In 1799, Congress standardized U.S. weights and measures.
- In 1807, Congress banned the slave trade within the U.S., effective January 1, 1808.
- In 1866, the first U.S. company to make sewing needles by machine incorporated.
- In 1983, compact disc recordings developed by Phillips & Sony were introduced.

Births
- Jheri [Robert] Redding, American hairdresser and businessman, 1907
- Orrin Keepnews, American jazz producer and founder of Riverside Records and Milestone Records, 1923

Deaths
- Harry Soref, American locksmith, inventor (held 80 patents), and businessman, founder of the Master Lock company, 1957

I am thankful for the countless times I have been forgiven.

Along with the privilege of being a child of God comes responsibility.

March 3

The Lord will keep you from all evil; he will keep your life. The Lord will keep your going out and your coming in from this time on and forevermore. *(Psalm 121:7-8, NRSVue)*

Jesus was a businessman

The Bible doesn't tell us much about Jesus' youth and early adulthood, but we know he was a craftsman with a business. We know he learned his trade from Joseph.

And Jesus grew in wisdom and stature, and in favor with God and man. (Luke 2:52, NIV)

"Skill doesn't just develop on its own," says Bristan Heaven, Kingdom-driven Leadership Strategist with Kingdom Reach Leadership (Eustis, Florida) and co-president of the Central Florida Christian Chamber of Commerce. "Jesus had to increase in wisdom, in the skill of his craft. He had to grow in understanding and maturity."

Part of maturity, Heaven says, is the ability to get things done by leveraging the help of others.

"Maturity brings an understanding of what is it that I need to do that only I can do and what is it that others can do even better than I in order to get the work done quicker," Heaven says. "Immaturity says I have to do it all. Maturity says I only need to do what I need to do and let others do the rest."

Running his business gave Jesus a solid foundation for running his ministry. We see it in how he recruited and managed the disciples. We see it in how he interacted with his followers and taught them what they needed to know. We see it in how he managed his time, how he balanced work and rest. And we see it in ourselves when we operate our businesses on clear Christian principles.

Read:
Proverbs, Chapter 3

Today we observe

Caregiver Appreciation Day

Simplify Your Life Day

On this day in history

Notable events

In 1821, American tailor and inventor Thomas L. Jennings received a patent for his dry-scouring process, the forerunner of today's modern dry-cleaning.

In 1910, John D. Rockefeller retired from managing his businesses so he could devote full time to being a philanthropist.

Births

George Pullman, American industrialist and inventor (railway sleeping car), 1831

Alexander Graham Bell, Scottish-born British-American inventor, scientist, and engineer; cofounder of the American Telephone and Telegraph Company, 1847

Elmer McCollum, American biochemist known for his work on the influence of diet on health, discovered vitamins A, B, and D, devised the vitamin naming system, 1879

Jay Arena, American pediatrician, inventor of the child-proof safety cap, 1909

Deaths

Arthur Murray, American ballroom dancer and businessman, 1991

Albert Sabin, Polish-American physician, inventor of the oral polio vaccine, 1993

Thought for the day

"I'm not going to limit myself just because people won't accept the fact that I can do something else."

Dolly Parton

I pray that knowing my prayers are heard is enough, regardless of how they may be answered.

March 4

> "Look! I stand at the door and knock. If you hear my voice and open the door, I will come in, and we will share a meal together as friends. Those who are victorious will sit with me on my throne, just as I was victorious and sat with my Father on his throne. *(Revelation 3:20-21, NLT)*

Turn thoughts into prayers

Our minds are complex and powerful. What we think about today will have a significant impact on our tomorrow.

So turn your thoughts into prayers. It's the easiest way to let God run your show.

Maybe you're preparing for a major presentation. "God, be with me, speak through me, and let this go according to your plan."

Or you're waiting for the client to make a decision. "God, this is important to our company and to me. I've done the best I could and now I'm turning it over to you."

Or you have a disciplinary meeting with an employee who has committed a serious violation of company policy. "God, this is going to be a difficult conversation. Please give me the right words."

Or you're facing a difficult challenge. "God, I don't know how I'm going to do this, but you do. Give me the strength and perseverance I need to achieve the results you want."

Whatever you're thinking, turn it into a prayer and let God handle it.

Today we observe

Courageous Follower Day
Holy Experiment Day
National Grammar Day
National Safety Day

On this day in history

Notable events

In 1809, James Madison became the first U.S. President to be inaugurated in American-made clothes.

In 1902, the American Automobile Association (AAA) was founded in Chicago.

In 1957, the S&P 500 stock market index was introduced, replacing the S&P 90.

Births

Benjamin Waterhouse, American physician, cofounder of Harvard Medical School, and smallpox vaccine pioneer, 1754

Garrett Morgan, American inventor (gas mask, traffic signal), 1877

Charles Rudolph Walgreen, Jr., American businessman, son of Walgreens founder, increased profit and size of the drug store chain during his tenure as president, 1906

T.R.M. Howard, American civil rights leaders, entrepreneur (founded an insurance company, restaurant, hospital, construction firm, and farm), and surgeon, 1908

Richard DeVos, American businessman, cofounder of Amway, 1926

Frank Wells, American entertainment executive, president of the Walt Disney Company, 1932

Mike Krieger, Brazilian-American entrepreneur, software engineer, cofounder of Instagram, 1986

Deaths

Christian K. Nelson, American inventor of Eskimo Pie, 1992

Thought for the day

"I, not events, have the power to make me happy or unhappy today. I can choose which it shall be. Yesterday is dead, tomorrow hasn't arrived yet. I have just one day, today, and I'm going to be happy in it."

Groucho Marx

I pray to hear God's voice in my everyday activities and interactions.

Read:
Proverbs, Chapter 4

March 5

An overseer, then, must be above reproach, the husband of one wife, temperate, sensible, respectable, hospitable, able to teach, not addicted to wine or pugnacious, but considerate, peaceable, free from the love of money; leading his own household well, having his children in submission with all dignity [but if a man does not know how to lead his own household, how will he take care of the church of God?], and not a new convert, so that he will not become conceited and fall into the condemnation of the devil. And he must have a good reputation with those outside the church, so that he will not fall into reproach and the snare of the devil. *(1 Timothy 3:2–7 LSB)*

When clients ask for a discount

What do you say when clients ask for a discount?

A great way to deal with customers who want you to lower your price is to ask why.

Whether you sell a product or service, when you quote a price and the customer asks you to reduce it, ask them why they feel they're entitled to a discount.

Be polite but toss the request back to the customer. Gently force them to consider and explain what they're asking.

Don't justify your price. Ask them to justify why they should pay less.

Sometimes their request is valid, sometimes it isn't. And sometimes the simple act of asking the question will prompt the customer to withdraw the request.

When you know *why* they're asking to pay less, you can make a good decision on whether to negotiate or walk away.

If someone is on your mind, don't just think about them, pray for them. And then reach out to them. God may have put them on your mind for a reason— perhaps because God wants you to be his hands and feet in in their world.

I pray that I recognize the lies the enemy wants me to believe for what they are.

Read:
Proverbs, Chapter 5

Today we observe
International Open Data Day

On this day in history

Notable events
In 1853, piano company Steinway & Sons was founded.
In 1872, George Westinghouse patented the triple air brake for trains.
In 2019, Kylie Jenner became the world's youngest-ever billionaire at 21.

Births
James Merritt Ives, American lithographer and businessman (Currier and Ives), 1824
Emmett J. Culligan, American entrepreneur (found of Culligan, Inc.), 1893
Carroll Rosenbloom, American businessman and owner of two NFL franchises, 1907
Lawrence Tisch, American businessman, cofounder of Loews Corp., 1923

Deaths
Hiram Bond Everest, American businessman, investor, inventor, and farmer, cofounder of the Vacuum Oil Company, 1913
Ray Tomlinson, American computer programmer (invented email and the @ sign), 2016
Joseph Weizenbaum, German-American computer scientist, MIT professor, creator of computer program ELIZA (a forerunner to today's chatbots), 2008

Thought for the day

"It's understandable when children are afraid of the dark. It's sad when adults are afraid of the light."

Jacquelyn Lynn

March 6

The godly eat to their hearts' content, but the belly of the wicked goes hungry. *(Proverbs 13:25 NLT)*

Generate revenue and leads with ebooks

Generating quality leads is often one of the biggest challenges in marketing. But what if your prospective customers were willing to pay you to receive your basic message and then contact you to tell you they want to know more?

That's what happens when ebooks are part of your marketing strategy.

Here's how it works:

- Write a book addressing a key issue related to your product or service.
- Publish that book on one or more of the popular online platforms, such as Amazon, Apple, Barnes & Noble, Kobo, and others.
- Include links in the book to more information and to a page where readers can either purchase or request a salesperson to call (depending on what's appropriate for your product or service).

The result: Your readers have paid to receive your initial marketing message and when they ask for more information, they're coming to you as a warm lead.

Of course, your ebook must have genuine value. It can't just be a brochure or a written sales pitch—it must stand alone as a complete information product.

If you're going to market with ebooks, you should invest in creating a quality product. Your book should deliver significantly more value than it costs. It should also be written and produced professionally—after all, this represents you and your company, so make it something you're proud of.

I am thankful that nothing can separate me from God.

Today we observe
National Oreo Cookie Day

On this day in history

Notable events

In 1933, President Franklin D. Roosevelt declared a nationwide bank holiday to shut down the banking system, pass the Emergency Banking Act, and restore public confidence.

In 1945, George Nissen received a patent for the first modern trampoline.

In 1950, Silly Putty went on sale in the U.S.

In 2018, Forbes named Amazon founder Jeff Bezos the world's richest person for the first time at $112 billion.

Births

George Dayton, American businessman, philanthropist, founder of Dayton's department store which became Target Corp., 1857

Richard L. Simon, American book publisher, cofounder of Simon & Schuster, 1899

Harold Alfond, American businessman who founded the Dexter Shoe Company and established the first factory outlet store, 1914

Bob Akin, American business executive, journalist, and champion sports car racing driver, 1936

Deaths

Davy Crockett, American frontiersman, adventurer, and politician, 1836

Thought for the day

"Excellence is often insubordinate. It's why it is usually on the move professionally. Organizations of all sorts cheer excellence until it gets too much that way. Then they tear it down, like a band that fires its lead singer."

Jeffrey A. Tucker

Read:
Proverbs, Chapter 6

March 7

And Nehemiah continued, "Go and celebrate with a feast of rich foods and sweet drinks, and share gifts of food with people who have nothing prepared. This is a sacred day before our Lord. Don't be dejected and sad, for the joy of the Lord is your strength!" *(Nehemiah 8:10, NLT)*

Use social media to breathe new life into old blog posts

Is your blog rich with content you've written over the last several years that's still relevant and valuable?

Use social media to drive fresh eyes to those articles.

Set up a series of social media posts (Facebook, X, LinkedIn, and whatever other platforms your target market uses) with brief snippets of information and a link to those older blogs. Encourage readers to follow the link to read the old blog posts and join in the conversation.

Consider making this a regular type of social media message, maybe with a tag such as *Worth Repeating* or *Flashback*. Just be sure the article is not outdated and the information is still useful.

Thought for the day

"If we as a nation are serious about addressing/confronting loneliness, and if we want to reduce youth suicide, the best manner to do this is through the strengthening of families, marriage, parenting, and the deepening of our faith, not ignoring these critical factors for our overall mental and spiritual health."

Timothy S. Goeglein

I pray to speak with wisdom and clarity, and to be silent in the same way.

Grow your faith by practicing contentment.

Today we observe
Alexander Graham Bell Day
National Be Heard Day

On this day in history

Notable events
In 1854, Charles Miller patented the first U.S. sewing machine to stitch buttonholes.
In 1876, Alexander Graham Bell received a U.S. patent for the telephone.
In 1911, Willis Farnworth patented the coin-operated locker.
In 1932, a demonstration by unemployed auto workers (known as the Ford Hunger March or the Ford Massacre) in Detroit, Michigan, ended in a confrontation in which four workers were shot to death (a fifth died later) and more than 60 workers were injured by Dearborn police and security guards employed by the Ford Motor Company.
In 1990, Wayne Huizenga purchased half of Joe Robbie Stadium and 15 percent of the Miami Dolphins for $30 million.
In 1994, the U.S. Supreme Court ruled that parodies of an original work are generally covered by the fair use doctrine (Campbell v. Acuff-Rose Music, Inc.).

Births
Whitcomb Judson, American inventor (zipper), 1846
Luther Burbank, American horticulturist who developed more than 800 strains and varieties of plants, 1849
Michael Eisner, American businessman, former chairman and CEO of The Walt Disney Company, 1942

Deaths
Hinsdale Smith, developer of roll-down auto windows, 1959

Read:
Proverbs, Chapter 7

March 8

> And we know that in all things God works for the good of those who love him, who have been called according to his purpose. *(Romans 8:28, NIV)*

Protect your company from employee dishonesty

One of the most damaging things that can happen to a company is for an employee to commit a dishonest act, whether it's stealing from the company or a customer, deliberately lying, or doing something else that isn't honest.

Here's how to protect your company from dishonest conduct by employees:

Admit that it could happen. Admitting that employee dishonesty could happen is not saying that you don't trust your employees; it's simply recognizing that these things happen and your organization is not immune.

Screen your employees thoroughly. Conduct comprehensive background checks even when you're hiring people you know.

Know your legal responsibilities. Consult with an attorney to be sure you understand exactly what you are and are not liable for when it comes to employee conduct. Find out those answers before you need to know them.

Have the right insurance in place. Talk to your insurance agent about the different types of insurance that can cover you for crimes committed by employees. Be adequately covered but not over-insured.

Put procedures and controls in place to make it difficult for dishonesty to occur. These will vary tremendously depending on your type of business, but they can often be implemented easily and affordably. Make it clear to your employees that you don't suspect them of any wrongdoing, but you are simply establishing systems that protect them as well as the company.

Read: Proverbs, Chapter 8

Today we observe
National Proofreading Day

On this day in history

Notable events
In 1817, the New York Stock Exchange was founded.
In 1855, the first train crossed the first U.S. railway suspension bridge at Niagara Falls.

Births
LaMarcus Thompson, American inventor known as the father of the American roller coaster, 1848
Howard H. Aiken, American physicist and pioneer in computing (IBM's Harvard Mark I), 1900

Deaths
Millard Fillmore, 13th U.S. President, 1874
James Buchanan Eads, American engineer and inventor, 1887
John Ericsson, Swedish-American inventor (screw propeller, rotating turret), 1889
William H. Taft, 27th U.S. President and 10th Chief Justice of the U.S., the only person to have served in both offices, 1930
Emily Bissell, American welfare worker and founder of Christmas Seals, 1948

Thought for the day

"Don't just learn, experience. Don't just read, absorb. Don't just change, transform. Don't just relate, advocate. Don't just promise, prove. Don't just criticize, encourage. Don't just think, ponder. Don't just take, give. Don't just see, feel. Don't just dream, do. Don't just hear, listen. Don't just talk, act. Don't just tell, show. Don't just exist, live."

Roy T. Bennett

I pray that broken relationships will be restored.

March 9

This God—his way is perfect; the promise of the LORD proves true; he is a shield for all who take refuge in him. *(Psalm 18:30, NRSVue)*

Quitting can make you a winner

Here are seven things you could quit right now that will make your life happier, richer and far more fulfilling:

1. Quit doing things that aren't moving you closer to your goals. If you're going to quit this, you need to first articulate your goals—professional and personal—and know what you have to do to reach them.

2. Quit making excuses. Excuses just shift the blame to someone or something else outside yourself. Take responsibility for yourself.

3. Quit doing things that don't bring you joy. If it's not making you happy, stop doing it.

4. Quit doing things that aren't good for you emotionally or physically. You know the main ones: smoking, overeating, eating junk food and excessive alcohol consumption. What else are you doing that isn't good for you? Figure it out and quit.

5. Quit saying yes when you really want to say no. It's okay to say no, regardless of your reason.

6. Quit refusing to take care of yourself because you've somehow come to believe that doing so is selfish. If you aren't taking care of yourself, you can't take care of anyone else for long.

7. Quit holding onto things that are poisoning your life. Let go of anger, grudges and hurt feelings. The only person these emotions are hurting is you.

I pray for unexpected ways to serve.

Read:
Proverbs, Chapter 9

Today we observe
National Dish Washer Appreciation Day
National Get Over It Day

On this day in history

Notable events

In 1522, Martin Luther began preaching his "Invocavit Sermons" in Wittenberg, Germany, helping to bring the revolutionary stage of the Reformation to a close by reminding citizens to trust God's Word rather than violence.

In 1984, the Competitive Enterprise Institute was founded.

Births

Leland Stanford, American business tycoon (Southern Pacific Railroad) and founder of Stanford University, 1824

Frederick A. Schroeder, American industrialist and mayor of Brooklyn, 1833

Andrew Viterbi, American telecommunications scientist and businessman (Qualcomm, Inc.), 1935

Rob Cheng, American businessman and entrepreneur, founder of PC Matic, 1959

Deaths

John Alexander Dowie, Scottish-American evangelist, founder of Zion, Illinois, 1907

Edward Bernays, a pioneer in the field of public relations and propaganda, known as "the father of public relations," 1995

Ian Ballantine, American publisher (Ballantine Books), 1995

John Gutfreund, American banker, business, investor, CEO of Salomon Brothers, Inc., 2016

Thought for the day

"The simple step of a courageous individual is not to take part in the lie. One word of truth outweighs the world."

Aleksandr I. Solzhenitsyn

March 10

But Jesus told him, "No! The Scriptures say, 'People do not live by bread alone, but by every word that comes from the mouth of God.'" (Matthew 4:4, NLT)

Staying hopeful

Sometimes it seems like we live in a world that wants to drain hope out of us. Chet Gladkowski, author of *PHD in Hope*, says that staying hopeful takes consistent effort and practice. He writes, "Hope isn't about yesterday or even today—it's always, always, always about tomorrow. It's about the future. Hope says that we want to walk with God towards his future."

Gladkowski says we all need more hope, that we can never have enough hope. He writes, "Make it a point to be searching for hope with every breath and person you meet."

Two ways to do that are to avoid unhopeful people and seek out hopeful people. Gladkowski writes, "You need to be on the lookout for unhopeful people. Avoid them, even run away from things and people whose purpose is to drain hope out of you. It doesn't take some master class or advanced education to spot someone who's hopeful. Be on the lookout for them. And when you find them, get to know them. You may even want to ask them to teach you to be a more hopeful person."

Thought for the day

"The brave die never, though they sleep in dust, their courage nerves a thousand living men."

Minot J. Savage

I am thankful for the guiding hand of a loving God as I go through my day.

Read:
Proverbs, Chapter 10

Today we observe

International Day of Awesomeness
National Landline Telephone Day
National Pack Your Lunch Day

On this day in history

Notable events

In 1849, Abraham Lincoln applied for a patent for a device to lift a boat over shoals and obstructions; he was the only U.S. President to apply for a patent.

In 1876, Alexander Graham Bell made the first telephone call to his assistant.

In 1891, American inventor Almon Strowger patented the Strowger switch, a device that led to the automation of telephone circuit switching.

In 1903, Harry Gammeter (inventor, cofounder of American Multigraph Co.) patented a multigraph duplicating machine.

In 1997, the PalmPilot, developed by Jeffrey Hawkins, was released.

In 2000, the NASDAQ Composite stock market index peaked at 5132.52, signaling the end of the dot-com boom.

In 2023, Silicon Valley Bank, the main bank for tech start-ups, collapsed.

Births

Alfred H. Peet, entrepreneur and founder of Peet's Coffee & Tea in Berkeley, California; Peet is credited with starting the specialty coffee revolution in the U.S., 1920

Tom Scholz, American musician (original member of the rock band Boston), inventor (music technology products), philanthropist, and founder of Scholz Research & Development, Inc., 1947

Biz Stone, American entrepreneur, cofounder of Twitter (now X) and other technology companies, 1974

Deaths

Charles Gordon Curtis, American inventor (Curtis steam turbine), 1953

March 11

A sk me and I will tell you remarkable secrets you do not know about things to come. *(Jeremiah 33:3, NLT)*

The "I don't know" prayer

When the challenges and decisions— whether related to business or personal issues— seem overwhelming and you need help, go to a quiet, private place and tell God.

"Dear God, I don't know. I don't know the answer. I don't know what the right choice is. I don't know how to deal with my feelings. I don't know how to handle this situation. I don't know what to do about this relationship. I don't know what I'm supposed to do. But you know."

Then leave it in God's hands.

Is your Linkedn profile current?

LinkedIn is a powerful business networking platform and a great way to market yourself and your business. It works best if your profile's content is complete and current.

At least once a year, check all your social media profiles to make sure they accurately reflect you and your company. Be sure they include relevant keywords, a strong call to action, up-to-date photographs, and other elements that will allow them to work *for* you and not *against* you.

Thought for the day

"Winning is great, sure, but if you are really going to do something in life, the secret is learning how to lose. Nobody goes undefeated all the time. If you can pick up after a crushing defeat, and go on to win again, you are going to be a champion someday."
Wilma Rudolph

Today we observe
Johnny Appleseed Day (also on September 26)

On this day in history
Notable events
In 2009, Toyota Motor Company announced it had sold over one million gas-electric hybrid vehicles in the U.S. under its six Toyota and Lexus brands.

Births
Vannevar Bush, American engineer, inventor, and science administrator who headed the U.S. Office of Scientific Research and Development during World War II; founder of the company that became Raytheon Company; known for his work on analog computers, 1890

James Franklin Hyde, American inventor who created silica, 1903

Dorothy Schiff, American businesswoman, owner and publisher of the New York Post, 1903

J.C.R. Licklider, American computer scientist who helped lay the groundwork for computer networking and ARPANET, the predecessor of the internet, 1915

Rupert Murdock, Australian-born American media mogul, 1931

Deaths
John Jay McCloy, American lawyer and banker, 1989

Joseph S. Cullinan, American oil industrialist, founder of The Texas Company, which would eventually be known as Texaco, Inc., 1937

Charles Lewis, Jr., American businessman, promoter, entertainer, and founder of the Tapout clothing line, 2009

I pray for a warrior mindset as I fight the spiritual battles in the world.

Read:
Proverbs, Chapter 11

March 12

But the Pharisees went out and plotted how they might kill Jesus. Aware of this, Jesus withdrew from that place. A large crowd followed him, and he healed all who were ill. *(Matthew 12:14-15, NIV)*

What makes quality content?

While there are a lot of ingredients that must be combined to create an effective, successful blog or content marketing campaign, the most important is quality content.

Quality content is:

Well-written. Use correct grammar, spelling, punctuation, syntax, and sentence structure. Avoid jargon and abbreviations your reader may not understand. Clarity is essential.

Accurate. Double-check all facts, dates, figures and formulas. Be sure everything you post is true. If you're not sure about something but you want to speculate, make it clear that you are offering an opinion not a proven fact.

Interesting. Write on subjects your readers care about. Give them information they'll want to know, will find useful and will share.

Appropriate. Make your content suitable for your target audience. If your blog is part of your company's website, your posts should be consistent with your site's overall message and tone.

I pray on the promise of Psalm 23.

Thought for the day

"Dreams are the seeds of change. Nothing ever grows without a seed, and nothing ever changes without a dream."

Debby Boone

Read:
Proverbs, Chapter 12

Today we observe
Working Moms Day

On this day in history

Notable events

In 1894, Coca-Cola was sold in bottles for the first time in a candy store in Vicksburg, Mississippi.

In 1904, Andrew Carnegie established the Carnegie Hero Fund.

In 1912, Juliette Gordon Low founded the Girl Guides (Girl Scouts) in Savannah, Georgia.

In 2008, the streaming service Hulu launched for public access.

Births

Clement Studebaker, American wagon and carriage manufacturer, cofounder of the H&C Studebaker company, precursor of the Studebaker Corporation, 1831

George W. Mason, American industrialist, served as chairman and CEO of the Kelvinator Corporation, the Nash-Kelvinator Corporation, and American Motors Corporation, known for introducing several compact car lines, 1891

Herbert Kelleher, Southwest Airlines cofounder, 1931

Deaths

Henry Bergh, American activist, founder of the American Society for the Prevention of Cruelty to Animals (ASPCA) and assisted in founding the New York and Massachusetts Society for the Prevention of Cruelty to Children, 1888

George Westinghouse, American entrepreneur and engineer, founder of the original Westinghouse Electric Corp., 1914

Edward Willis Scripps, American newspaper published and cofounder of the E. W. Scripps Company and United Press Associations (later United Press International), 1926

Asa Griggs Candler, Sr., American business tycoon and politician who developed Coca-Cola into a major company after buying the recipe for $238.98, 1929

March 13

> The Lord is my strength and shield. I trust him with all my heart. He helps me, and my heart is filled with joy. I burst out in songs of thanksgiving. *(Psalm 28:7, NLT)*

Exposure through newsjacking

Newsjacking is one of the most effective ways to position yourself as an expert, generate media coverage, and increase your social media engagement. It's a process by which you inject yourself into breaking news in real-time.

Have you ever wondered where media outlets find the sources they quote? In most cases, those expert sources have mastered the art and science of newsjacking. They identified the story early, got out in front of it with a combination of facts and opinion, provided a unique perspective, and made sure their audience saw it.

Of course, it's not enough to simply have an opinion, your thoughts must add value to the discussion. An article or blog post using the newsjacking strategy would follow a structure similar to this:

- Headline naming the issue/event and promising more information
- A more detailed description of the event and why it matters to your audience
- Analysis that includes your opinion
- Advice or predictions, such as what steps your readers can take to avoid problems or take advantage of opportunities, or the impact the situation will have on your audience or another defined group
- A brief bio with your photo and credentials

Apply a sound keyword strategy so that journalists and others looking for information on the story can find you. Use your social media network to further increase your exposure.

Establishing yourself as an authority is just one way to use the newsjacking strategy. You can also use it for general exposure, promoting brand awareness, increasing fan loyalty and more.

Today we observe
K-9 Veterans Day

On this day in history

Notable events

In 1877, American engineer Chester Greenwood patented earmuffs after inventing them at age 15.

In 1933, U.S. banks were allowed to reopen after a government-imposed bank holiday.

In 2020, Microsoft cofounder Bill Gates stepped down from the company's board to focus on philanthropic activities.

Births

Walter Annenberg, American businessman, investor, philanthropist, and diplomat who owned and operated Triangle Publications, 1908

Ralph J. Roberts, American businessman and founder of Comcast, 1920

Dave Cutler, American software engineer, developer of Microsoft's Windows NT and Digital Equipment Corp.'s RSX-11M, VAXELN, and VMS, 1942

Jamie Dimon, American business executive and CEO of JPMorgan Chase, 1956

Deaths

Benjamin Harrison, 23rd U.S. President, 1901

Robert C. Baker, American inventor of the chicken nugget and other poultry-related inventions, 2006

Thought for the day

"The recipe for perpetual ignorance is: be satisfied with your opinions and content with your knowledge."

Elbert Hubbard

I am thankful for new beginnings.

Read:
Proverbs, Chapter 13

March 14

No temptation has overtaken you that is not common to man. God is faithful, and he will not let you be tempted beyond your ability, but with the temptation he will also provide the way of escape, that you may be able to endure it. *(1 Corinthians 10:13 ESV)*

Give to gain: five reasons it pays to be generous with your services and expertise

Being generous with information on your website and through social channels is a great way to grow your business.

It's a case of the more you give, the more you'll get. Here's why:

1. People are accustomed to easy access to information through the internet and search engines, and you need to meet that expectation if you want to be taken seriously as service providers.
2. Quality content on your website enhances your credibility and automatically positions you as an authority and expert in your field.
3. Providing information, especially in your own voice through blogs, video, audio and images, lets prospective clients get to know you.
4. Accurate, clearly presented information builds trust.
5. Demonstrating what you know through your website and social channels increases your value when that prospect becomes a client; you can charge higher fees and your clients will be confident you're worth it.

Thought for the day

"Apply yourself. Get all the education you can, but then do something. Don't just stand there, make it happen."

Lee Iacocca

Read:
Proverbs, Chapter 14

Today we observe
Crowdfunding Day
International Ask a Question Day
National Write Your Story Day

On this day in history

Notable events
In 1794, Eli Whitney patented the cotton gin.
In 1899, Ferdinand von Zeppelin received a U.S. patent for a navigable balloon.
In 2002, Elon Musk founded SpaceX.

Births
William Marsh Rice, American businessman and investor who bequeathed his fortune to found Rice University in Houston, Texas, 1816
Albert Einstein, German-born theoretical physicist, 1879
S. Truett Cathy, American businessman, investor, author, and philanthropist, founder of Chick-fil-A, 1921
Frank Borman, American astronaut and CEO of Eastern Air Lines, 1928
Jerry Greenfield, American businessman and cofounder of Ben & Jerry's ice cream, 1951

Deaths
John M. Mack, American inventor (Mack "Bulldog" truck engine) and manufacturer, cofounder of the Mack Brothers Company which became Mack Trucks Inc., 1924
George Eastman, American entrepreneur, inventor and founder of Eastman Kodak Company, 1932
Howard H. Aiken, American physicist and pioneer in computing (IBM's Harvard Mark I), 1973

I pray that those who are at the beginning of their faith journey will be inspired by my example.

March 15

Stay alert! Watch out for your great enemy, the devil. He prowls around like a roaring lion, looking for someone to devour. Stand firm against him, and be strong in your faith. Remember that your family of believers all over the world is going through the same kind of suffering you are. *(1 Peter 5:8-9 NLT)*

Who won your contest?

Contests are a great way to generate sales leads, get customers to engage on social media, build loyalty and more.

But how often have you entered a contest and then never heard another thing about it?

The final step of your contest is to tell your audience who won. If possible, include photos of the winners. Issue a news release, post it on your website, and send an email to everyone who entered. Here's why:

- It's one more way to connect—a legitimate reason for you to communicate with your audience, to put your name in front of them in a positive way.
- It reminds your audience of your contest, giving you a way to maximize the investment of that particular contest.
- It gives you a chance to remind people of future contests. In your email to all entrants, say something like, "If you didn't win this time, try again. We'll be launching our next contest [provide date and a few details]."
- It proves that the prizes were actually awarded to legitimate winners.
- It gives the winners a few minutes in the spotlight.
- It satisfies the curiosity of everyone who took the time to enter.

Your contest terms and conditions should include consent for use of their name and likeness (photo). You may, of course, decide to protect their privacy by using just first name, last initial, and city, state.

Today we observe

International Redefining Wealth Day

World Consumer Rights Day

World Essential Workers Day

On this day in history

Notable events

In 1892, Jesse W. Reno patented the first escalator.

Births

Andrew Jackson, 7th U.S. President, 1767

Arthur Hawley Scribner, American magazine and book publisher, president of Charles Scribner's Sons, 1859

Marjorie Merriweather Post, American socialite, businesswoman, and philanthropist, 1887

Jimmy Lee Swaggart, Pentecostal preacher, televangelist, recording artist, author, 1935

Deaths

Melville Reuben Bissell, American entrepreneur and inventor of the carpet sweeper, 1889

Jheri [Robert] Redding, American hairdresser and businessman, 1998

Edwin J. Shoemaker, American businessman, inventor (original reclining chair), and philanthropist, cofounder of La-Z-Boy, known as the father of motion furniture, 1998

Thought for the day

Work to recall what *really* matters in life. *What* you do is far less important than *who* you're with and, sometimes, *when* you're together. *Always* make time for your loved ones. The other demands will still be around—trust me.

Paul M. Neuberger

Read:
Proverbs, Chapter 15

I pray for clear vision.

March 16

Don't pick a fight without reason, when no one has done you harm.
(Proverbs 3:30, NLT)

To get results, maximize your time

Consider these suggestions to maximize your time and get the highest and best results from everything you do.

Put top priorities in the right place. Although it makes sense to put your top priority first on your agenda, that's not always the most effective approach. Put your top priorities in the place where you know they will receive the right amount of attention and effort, and that may not always be first.

Close your door. Managers who adopt an open-door policy to demonstrate their accessibility are inviting constant interruptions that will prevent them from accomplishing their goals. Certainly you want to be accessible, but you also need to control your schedule rather than letting everyone else do it for you.

Respect the value of time—yours and others'. Just as you work to maximize your own time, you must also respect the value of other people's time. Being late is not only rude, it also tells the person with whom you are dealing that you believe his time is worthless.

Take naps. Schedule rest into your day and don't let anything interrupt that time.

Thought for the day

"If it really was a no-brainer to make it on your own in business there'd be millions of no-brained, harebrained, and otherwise dubiously brained individuals quitting their day jobs and hanging out their own shingles. Nobody would be left to round out the workforce and execute the business plan."

Bill Rancic

Today we observe
Freedom of Information Day

No Selfies Day

On this day in history

Notable events

In 1968, General Motors produced its 100 millionth automobile, the Oldsmobile Toronado.

In 1926, American engineer Robert H. Goddard successfully launched the world's first liquid-fueled rocket.

In 2008, the 85-year-old investment bank Bear Stearns avoided bankruptcy by its sale to JP Morgan Chase at $2 per share.

Births

James Madison, 4th U.S. President, 1751

Phillippe Kahn, American-French engineer, entrepreneur, and philanthropist, founder of four technology companies: Borland, Starfish Software, LightSurf Technologies, and Fullpower Technologies, 1952

Deaths

Daniel Frank Gerber, American baby food manufacturer, 1974

I pray to remember that often people who look perfect on the outside are a mess on the inside, and they need prayers.

Read:
Proverbs, Chapter 16

March 17

We should help others do what is right and build them up in the Lord. For even Christ didn't live to please himself. As the Scriptures say, "The insults of those who insult you, O God, have fallen on me." (Romans 15:2-3 NLT)

More ways to maximize your time

Know your limitations. To effectively maximize your time, you must know what you realistically can and can't accomplish with the resources you have. Over-booking your time and over-committing yourself only sets you up for failure. And if there's something you don't do well, delegate it to someone who can do it better.

Ask the right questions. When you're seeking information, ask questions that are clear, targeted and designed to generate only the information you actually need, rather than a plethora of data you must then sort through.

Understand the difference between a schedule and a to-do list. Your to-do list may be the first step in creating a schedule, but a schedule is more than just tasks, it also includes an established time frame for the completion of each item.

Accept the fact that not everything must be done perfectly. Certainly some tasks allow little room for error, but you can save a lot of time by letting go of the need for perfection when it isn't absolutely necessary.

Distinguish tools from toys. Some technological advances are truly valuable tools; others are nothing more than toys, and the difference is not the item but the user. Before you invest in a new item, be sure it will be a tool that will help you be more effective, not just a toy, or worse, something that will actually reduce your effectiveness.

Today we observe
St. Patrick's Day

On this day in history

Notable events
In 1929, General Motors acquired German auto manufacturer Adam Opel.

Births
Norbert Rillieux, American chemical engineer and inventor (sugar refiner), 1806
Charles Francis Brush, American engineer, inventor (arc lamp), entrepreneur, and philanthropist, 1849

Deaths
Roland E. Arnall, American businessman (owner of ACC Capital Holdings) and diplomat, cofounder of the Simon Wiesenthal Center, 2008

Thought for the day

"Humour is, in fact, a prelude to faith; and laughter is the beginning of prayer. Laughter must be heard in the outer courts of religion, and the echoes of it should resound in the sanctuary; but there is no laughter in the holy of holies. There laughter is swallowed up in prayer and humour is fulfilled by faith. The intimate relation between humour and faith is derived from the fact that both deal with the incongruities of our existence. ... Laughter is our reaction to immediate incongruities and those which do not affect us essentially. Faith is the only possible response to the ultimate incongruities of existence, which threaten the very meaning of our life."

Reinhold Niebuhr

Read: Proverbs, Chapter 17

I am grateful for good health.

March 18

But the wisdom that comes from heaven is first of all pure; then peace-loving, considerate, submissive, full of mercy and good fruit, impartial and sincere. Peacemakers who sow in peace reap a harvest of righteousness. *(James 3:17-18, NIV)*

Pricing your services

Are you charging enough? Many small and home-based business owners don't, often because they aren't sure what a fair rate is, or don't have enough confidence in the value of what they have to offer. To help with the challenge of pricing your services, keep these points in mind.

The going rate. Find out what the acceptable rate—both high and low—in your industry is. Ask around among your colleagues, contact professional or trade organizations that track such information, and do online searches. Then mediate that rate with your own level of experience and expertise.

Exclusivity. If you are considered an expert or are just one or one of a few who do what you do, you can likely charge more than if your field is crowded with competition.

Capacity. Think about how busy you are and how much work you can actually handle. Raise your rates when you're busy; you may end up pricing yourself out of some business, but the business you keep will be more profitable.

Target market. Examine your target market to determine if it has any pricing limitations.

Value. Analyze the real value of what you do. If you're providing something your clients can't do without, you can charge more for it.

Thought for the day

"I have learned over the years that when one's mind is made up, this diminishes fear."
Rosa Parks

Today we observe

Global Recycling Day

National Supreme Sacrifice Day

On this day in history

Notable events

In 1850, Henry Wells and William Fargo formed American Express.

In 1933, American automaker Studebaker was forced into bankruptcy, however new management got the company back on track and the new Studebaker Corporation was incorporated in 1935.

In 1965, the Poppin' Fresh Pillsbury Dough Boy was introduced.

Births

Grover Cleveland, 22nd and 24th U.S. President, 1837

Andy Granatelli, American motorsports entrepreneur, author, CEO of STP, 1923

Lillian Menasche, founder and CEO of the Lillian Vernon Corporation (first company traded on the American Stock Exchange founded by a woman), 1927

Ben Cohen, American cofounder of Ben & Jerry's ice cream, 1951

Deaths

Johnny Appleseed (John Chapman), American pioneer nurseryman and missionary, 1845

William C. Durant, American automobile industry pioneer, cofounder of General Motors and Chevrolet, founder of Frigidaire, 1947

Albert Einstein, German-born theoretical physicist, 1955

I pray to always remember how much people are counting on me to do my job to the absolute best of my ability.

Read:
Proverbs, Chapter 18

March 19

You go before me and follow me. You place your hand of blessing on my head. *(Psalm 139:5, NLT)*

Cause marketing

Cause marketing is a method of doing good works while promoting your company's products and services. It essentially involves choosing a nonprofit organization and supporting it with direct financial assistance, in-kind donations, and/or volunteer time. Done correctly, cause marketing builds community goodwill, customer loyalty, and a stronger bond among your employees. But there are pitfalls. Keep the following points in mind.

Choose the cause carefully. Avoid controversial issues that might offend some of your customers; support those on your own time. The cause should have some relevance to and be compatible with your business.

Check out the organization. Be sure it's legitimate, well-run, and demonstrates a strong degree of accountability.

Be totally committed. Embrace the cause completely, and follow through on your promises. If you're not sincere, it will show.

Get your employees on board. Enthusiasm is contagious, so lead by example.

Promote and publicize your efforts. Make customers and the public aware of what you're doing with discreet but visible mentions in your promotional materials.

Keep good records. In addition to being important from a tax and general business perspective, you should be ready if someone wants to see evidence that you're keeping your word.

I pray to be a source of strength, encouragement, and hope to everyone I encounter.

On this day in history

Notable events

In 1831, the first U.S. bank robbery occurred; the City Bank in New York was robbed of $245,000.

In 1987, Fred Currey acquired Greyhound Bus Company.

In 1991, the five millionth U.S. patent was granted to a team of inventors from the University of Florida for an innovative way to produce fuel ethanol.

Births

Moorfield Storey, American lawyer, activist, and civil rights leader; first president of the NAACP, 1845

Jerome Namias, American meteorologist who helped develop the system of passenger flight weather forecasting and researched the interaction between the oceans and atmosphere, 1910

Deaths

Samuel Cate Prescott, American food scientist and microbiologist involved in the development of food safety, food science, public health, and industrial microbiology, 1962

John DeLorean, American engineer, inventor, and U.S. automobile industry executive; founder of DeLorean Motor Company, 2005

Thought for the day

"When you reach an obstacle, turn it into an opportunity. You have the choice. You can overcome and be a winner, or you can allow it to overcome you and be a loser. The choice is yours and yours alone. Refuse to throw in the towel. Go that extra mile that failures refuse to travel. It is far better to be exhausted from success than to be rested from failure."

Mary Kay Ash

Read:
Proverbs, Chapter 19

March 20

Know therefore that the Lord your God is God; he is the faithful God, keeping his covenant of love to a thousand generations of those who love him and keep his commandments. *(Deuteronomy 7:9, NIV)*

His Eye is on the Sparrow

Civilla D. Martin, 1905

Why should I feel discouraged,
Why should the shadows come,
Why should my heart be lonely,
And long for heav'n and home;
When Jesus is my portion?
My constant Friend is he;
His eye is on the sparrow,
And I know he watches me;
His eye is on the sparrow,
And I know he watches me.

Refrain:
I sing because I'm happy,
I sing because I'm free;
For his eye is on the sparrow,
And I know he watches me.

"Let not your heart be troubled,"
His tender word I hear,
And resting on his goodness,
I lose my doubts and fears;
Though by the path he leadeth,
But one step I may see;
His eye is on the sparrow,
And I know he watches me;
His eye is on the sparrow,
And I know he watches me. *[Refrain]*

Whenever I am tempted,
Whenever clouds arise;
When songs give place to sighing,
When hope within me dies,
I draw the closer to him,
From care he sets me free;
His eye is on the sparrow,
And I know he watches me;
His eye is on the sparrow,
And I know he watches me. *[Refrain]*

Today we observe
Won't You Be My Neighbor Day

On this day in history

Notable events
In 1883, Jan Matzeliger received a patent for a shoe lasting machine which mechanized shoe production.
In 1930, American fast food restaurant chain KFC was founded as Sanders Court & Café by Colonel Harland Sanders.
In 2019, the Walt Disney Company acquired Rupert Murdock's 21st Century Fox entertainment business for $71 billion.

Births
Frederick Winslow Taylor, American mechanical engineer and management consultant, known for his methods to improve industrial efficiency, 1856
Payne Whitney, American businessman, investor, and philanthropist, 1876
Fred Rogers, American children's TV host, Presbyterian minister, 1928

Deaths
David Rockefeller, American investment banker, chairman and chief executive of Chase Manhattan Bank, 2017
Kenny Rogers, American singer and entrepreneur, 2020

Thought for the day

"A clever man reaps some benefit from the worst catastrophe, and a fool can turn even good luck to his disadvantage."
Francois de La Rochefoucauld

I pray for the families of the people who protect us, care for us, and serve us.

Read:
Proverbs, Chapter 20

March 21

> Look, I am sending you out as sheep among wolves. So be as shrewd as snakes and harmless as doves. *(Matthew 10:16, NLT)*

How often should you blog?

How frequently should you post new content on your blog? The short answer is: As often as you need to.

How often you post will depend on your goals and resources. When it comes to content, you should always choose quality over quantity. What sort of posting schedule can you meet with the financial and time resources you have?

If you're using your blog as part of a search engine optimization campaign, frequency is important because the search engines like to see activity on a site. But you must be realistic about what you can produce. It's better to start with a less-ambitious schedule and either supplement it with occasional extra posts or increase it as you go along than to set yourself up for failure by launching with a schedule you can't meet long-term.

If you are using your blog to establish yourself as a thought leader in a relatively narrow niche, you may decide to publish more comprehensive content less frequently.

There's no hard rule. Consider starting with a plan for three or four posts a month. Evaluate the results after the first quarter and decide what adjustments need to be made.

Today we observe
National Common Courtesy Day
National Rosie the Riveter Day

On this day in history

Notable events
- In 2006, the first ever tweet was sent out by Twitter founder Jack Dorsey.
- In 2018, Facebook's Mark Zuckerberg admitted the company "made mistakes" after data on 50 million users was harvested by Cambridge Analytica.

Births
- Jim Thompson, American businessman who helped revitalize the Thai silk industry in the 1950s and 1960s; he disappeared in Malaysia in 1967 and was never found, 1906
- John D. Rockefeller III, American billionaire and philanthropist, 1906

Deaths
- Frederick Winslow Taylor, American mechanical engineer and management consultant, known for his methods to improve industrial efficiency, 1915
- Leo Fender, American inventor and entrepreneur, founder of Fender Musical Instruments Corporation, 1991
- Andrew Grove, Hungarian-American businessman and engineer, pioneer in the semiconductor industry, served as the third CEO of Intel Corporation, 2016

Thought for the day

"Just one mental shift—focusing on the abundance of your environment —switches your psychological settings so that your life automatically improves in many areas you may think are unrelated. This is essentially a leap from fear to faith."

Martha Beck

Read:
Proverbs, Chapter 21

I pray that those who need help will find it.

> Grow your faith by revisiting the pain and trauma in your past and coming to terms with it in a positive way.

March 22

One day Jesus said to his disciples, "There will always be temptations to sin, but what sorrow awaits the person who does the tempting! It would be better to be thrown into the sea with a millstone hung around your neck than to cause one of these little ones to fall into sin. So watch yourselves! (Luke 17:1-3 NLT)

Before you join a coaching or mentoring program

If you're considering joining a coaching or mentoring program, get answers to these questions before signing the contract and paying the fee.

- Are you coaching with the named expert, or is the program farmed out to assistants or even another company?
- Is the program customized to the student?
- How will you communicate with your coach—email, text, phone, online?
- Do you have to make an appointment to speak with your coach or can you call when you need to?
- How long will it take for your coach to respond?
- How long do you have to complete the program?
- What is the total cost and will there be any add-ons?
- Can you speak with people who are currently in the program or have graduated?
- Does the company have a good rating with the Better Business Bureau?
- What industry/professional associations does the company belong to?
- Do you have to pay all fees up front or is there a payment plan available?

Read the contract carefully and make sure what's in the contract matches what you've been told.

> Grow your faith by letting go of guilt and fear.

On this day in history

Notable events

In 1960, Arthur Schawlow and Charles Townes were granted the first patent for lasers.

In 1993, Intel introduced the first Pentium processor.

Births

Pat Robertson, American media mogul, religious broadcaster, political commentator, Southern Baptist minister, 1930

Al Neuharth, American businessman, author, and founder of USA Today, 1924

Deaths

Jonathan Edwards, American revivalist preacher, philosopher, and Congregationalist theologian, 1758

Wayne Huizenga, American businessman and sports team owner, 2018

William Hanna, American animator and cofounder of Hanna-Barbera, 2001

Thought for the day

"Whoever reads the New Testament seriously, or gives thought to the impact which the apostles made upon their generation, must acknowledge that one outstanding historic event alone spurred that small band of 11 ordinary men to an amazing task of evangelization in their generation. Defying every obstacle, loss of home, persecution, even death itself, they evidenced the supreme relevance in their ministry of the resurrection of Jesus Christ."

Erling C. Olsen

I am grateful for my family.

Read:
Proverbs, Chapter 22

March 23

> "Look, I am sending you the prophet Elijah before the great and dreadful day of the Lord arrives. His preaching will turn the hearts of fathers to their children, and the hearts of children to their fathers. Otherwise I will come and strike the land with a curse." *(Malachi 4:5-6 NLT)*

Purchasing tip: talk terms

When you're buying for your business, terms are as important as product price. Beyond the cost of the item itself, look at quantity discounts, add-ons (such as freight and insurance), and payment terms. Every element of the sale is open to negotiation.

Quantity discounts. To determine the true value of a quantity discount, calculate how long you can expect to store the material and what your cost will be for carrying the inventory, then add that to the cost of the goods. Remember to factor in a certain amount of spoilage for items that might get damaged or otherwise become unusable or unsellable while you are storing them. Compare that total with your cost for buying a smaller quantity that you'll move quickly before making your decision on quantity.

Transportation. Freight is an excellent—and often overlooked—negotiating point. If you're paying the freight, you should be selecting the carrier and negotiating the rates. If the vendor insists on choosing the carrier, do some research to make sure you aren't being overcharged on freight. If your suppliers are delivering on their own trucks, negotiate the delivery fee as part of the overall price. Also look at any handling and insurance fees.

Payment terms. Some companies offer substantial discounts for early payment; others will extend what amounts to an interest-free, short-term loan by offering lengthier terms. Find out what your vendor is willing to do and agree on the terms that are best for you.

The bottom line in purchasing is the bottom line: know and negotiate the total amount you're going to pay before you buy.

On this day in history

Notable events

In 1775, Patrick Henry proclaimed, "Give me liberty, or give me death!" in a speech to the Second Virginia Convention.

In 1857, Elisha Otis installed his first elevator at 488 Broadway in New York City.

In 1903, the Wright brothers filed for a patent for a flying machine; the patent was granted three years later.

Births

Fannie Farmer, American culinary pioneer who revolutionized modern cooking through the introduction of precise measurements, 1857

Nathaniel Reed, American outlaw who became an evangelist after his release from prison, 1862

Bette Nesmith Graham, American typist, commercial artist, and inventor (Liquid Paper), 1924

Rex Tillerson, American energy executive (Chair and CEO of ExxonMobil) and the 69th U.S. Secretary of State, 1952

Deaths

Elizabeth Taylor, English-American actress, businesswoman, and humanitarian, 2011

Thought for the day

"Trust yourself. Create the kind of self that you will be happy to live with all your life. Make the most of yourself by fanning the tiny, inner sparks of possibility into flames of achievement."

Golda Meir

I pray for creativity and insight.

Read:
Proverbs, Chapter 23

March 24

But you are a chosen people, a royal priesthood, a holy nation, God's own people, in order that you may proclaim the excellence of him who called you out of darkness into his marvelous light. Once you were not a people, but now you are God's people; once you had not received mercy, but now you have received mercy. *(1 Peter 2:9-10 NRSVue)*

Selling: account penetration

In most organizations, more than one and often several people either influence or actually make buying decisions. A savvy salesperson talks with everyone who is involved in a purchase. Coordinating these efforts among a maze of departments and divisions can be a challenge.

The key to successfully managing sales under these conditions begins by starting off immediately on the right foot. When approaching a new account, use a "top down" selling approach. Start with the highest decision-maker in the company and work your way vertically and horizontally through the organization. The vice president isn't going to say he doesn't have time to see you if the president has suggested the meeting.

At all stages of the process, take care to avoid any action that might alienate anyone. Respect the customer's processes and be prepared to coordinate your sales efforts with several different departments. For example, the marketing director or chief information officer might make the buying decision, but then hand it off to the purchasing department for the details to be negotiated—and the purchasing agent will likely focus on details that weren't an issue before. Find out what the procedures are—all you have to do is ask—and follow them.

Once you close a sale, continue to penetrate the account. Ask the satisfied customer who else in the organization might have need of your products or services. In most cases, they'll be happy to refer you to someone else you should be calling on—and you might even get a referral to a brand new client.

On this day in history

Notable events

In 1868, Metropolitan Life Insurance company was founded.

In 1880, Tobacco Growers' Mutual Insurance company was incorporated.

Births

Andrew W. Mellon, American banker, businessman, industrialist, philanthropist, and politician, 1855

Joseph Barbera, American animator and cofounder of Hanna-Barbera, 1911

Deaths

Stanley Robison, streetcar magnate, MLB team owner, 1911

An Wang, Chinese-American computer engineer and inventor, co-founder of Wang Laboratories, 1990

Gordon Moore, American businessman, engineer, and cofounder of Intel Corporation, 2023

Thought for the day

"You have it easily in your power to increase the sum total of this world's happiness now. How? By giving a few words of sincere appreciation to someone who is lonely or discouraged. Perhaps you will forget tomorrow the kind words you say today, but the recipient may cherish them over a lifetime."

Dale Carnegie

I pray for the wisdom and strength to move on from people and situations that are causing chaos and conflict in my life.

Read:
Proverbs, Chapter 24

March 25

And I know that whatever God does is final. Nothing can be added to it or taken from it. God's purpose is that people should fear him. *(Ecclesiastes 3:14, NLT)*

Don't ignore the competition

Certainly your primary focus should be on your own business, but you must always keep track of your competitors. Pay attention to where they are, what they're offering, and how they're marketing.

- Study their ads.
- Periodically visit their websites.
- Read what's written about them in trade publications and other media.
- "Secret shop" them to find out how they sell.

When it comes to your competitors, you must figuratively sleep with one eye open. Do your best to stay ahead of them, to change your strategy and prevent them from copying you, to stretch and reach so they can't catch you.

Do your best to win every round, but know that you won't always. Sometimes you'll just have to take a hit, clean up the mess after the fact, and move on.

Just like you can take market share away from someone else, someone can do it to you as well. Be vigilant. Know who your competitors are—both old and new players in your market.

Remember that the closer you are to the top, the further you have to fall—and the bigger the crash you'll make if you hit the bottom.

If you're successful, you're going to have competition. If you're making money, somebody else is going to want a piece of your action. So be prepared for it.

Let your competitors push you to be the best you can be.

Read:
Proverbs, Chapter 25

Today we observe

International Day of the Unborn Child

National Medal of Honor Day

On this day in history

Notable events

In 1954, RCA manufactured the first color TV set; it had a 12½" screen, priced at $1,000.

In 1902, Irving W. Colburn patented the sheet glass drawing machine, making the mass production of glass for windows possible.

In 1911, a fire in the Triangle Shirtwaist Company factory in New York City killed 146 workers; the tragedy led to a series of safety laws and regulations that better protected factory workers.

Births

Eileen Ford, American model agency executive and cofounder of Ford Models, 1922

Bill Marriott, American billionaire businessman, executive chairman of Marriott International, 1932

Gloria Steinem, American feminist and publisher, 1934

Tom Monaghan, American entrepreneur, founder of Domino's Pizza, Catholic philanthropist, 1937

Deaths

William C. Bartholomay, American business executive and MLB team owner, 2020

Thought for the day

"When you find a man who knows his job and is willing to take responsibility, keep out of his way and don't bother him with unnecessary supervision. What you may think is cooperation is nothing but interference."

Thomas Dreier

I pray for God's will to be done through me.

March 26

Daniel said: "Blessed be the name of God for ever and ever, to whom belong wisdom and might. He changes times and seasons; he removes kings and sets up kings; he gives wisdom to the wise and knowledge to those who have understanding; he reveals deep and mysterious things; he knows what is in the darkness, and the light dwells with him. *(Daniel 2:20-22, RSV)*

Networking tip: make an introduction

Sometimes we're in networking situations and need help finding something to talk about with someone we've just met. Or we want to learn more about the other person but would like a more effective way to do it than a Q&A (or inquisition).

Try bringing someone else into the conversation. Introduce your new contact to someone else who may also be of interest to you—then let them do the talking.

Introduce each person with a sentence or two explaining what they do in a way that hints at why they would want to know each other.

Example:

"Mary, let me introduce John. John owns an insurance agency that specializes in small businesses. John, Mary is a veterinarian who is in the process of opening her own practice."

Don't let the conversation turn to you—keep the two of them focused on each other. You'll probably learn things you didn't know about them that you'll be able to use to your mutual benefit later.

In addition to gaining additional insight, you've positioned yourself as a master networker and you'll be fresh in their minds after the event.

Of course, you'll want to follow up to maintain that positive impression. Send a note, connect on LinkedIn, make a phone call—however you do it, be sure to reinforce the meeting.

Read:
Proverbs, Chapter 26

On this day in history

Notable events

In 1885, Eastman Film Co. manufactured the first commercial motion picture film.

In 1977, Focus on the Family was founded by Dr. James Dobson.

In 1956, the MedicAlert Foundation was founded.

Births

Condé Nast, American publisher, entrepreneur, and business magnate, founder of the mass media company Condé Nast, 1873

Othmar Ammann, Swiss-American civil engineer whose bridge designs include the George Washington Bridge, Verrazzano-Narrows Bridge, Bayonne Bridge and others; he also directed the planning and construction of the Lincoln Tunnel, 1879

Larry Page, American computer scientist and businessman, cofounder of Google, 1973

Deaths

Frederick Louis Maytag I, American businessman, founder of the Maytag Company, 1937

David Packard, American electrical engineer and cofounder of Hewlett-Packard, 1996

Thought for the day

"Consult not your fears but your hopes and your dreams. Think not about your frustrations, but about your unfulfilled potential. Concern yourself not with what you tried and failed in, but with what it is still possible for you to do."

Pope John XXIII

I pray for the Lord to guide my heart so that I may not only do the right thing but I do it for the right reasons.

March 27

Stand firm then, with the belt of truth buckled around your waist, with the breastplate of righteousness in place, and with your feet fitted with the readiness that comes from the gospel of peace. In addition to all this, take up the shield of faith, with which you can extinguish all the flaming arrows of the evil one. Take the helmet of salvation and the sword of the Spirit, which is the word of God. *(Ephesians 6:14-17, NIV)*

Spelling matters

In these days of email, social media and texting, we probably communicate more in writing than we did decades ago when we had to actually speak with each other because there was no immediate alternative. Everything you put out there should be as close to perfect as you can make it.

Why? The most important reason is: If you can't get basic spelling and grammar right, what else can't you do right?

Of course, your friends and family are likely to forgive a typo or misspelling in a personal text. But when you do it in a public or business arena, you open yourself up to ridicule, could possibly offend someone (especially if the spelling error is that person's name) and risk damaging your credibility.

The solution is to use spellcheck and then proofread, because spellcheck isn't enough—words can be spelled correctly and still be wrong. Look it up if you're not sure.

For really important things, have someone else check what you've written before you send it out. Yes, we're all in a hurry and these things take time. Just remember the adage, "If you don't have time to do it right, how will you find time to do it over?"

Even more important, how will you find time to repair the damage?

I am thankful for all of the casual relationships with people who enrich my life.

Read:
Proverbs, Chapter 27

On this day in history

Notable events

In 1911, the National Exchange Club was founded by a group of businessmen in Detroit, Michigan.

In 1933, the Farm Credit Administration, an independent agency of the federal government, was founded.

Births

John R. Pierce, American engineer (known as one of the two fathers of the communication satellite) and science fiction author, 1910

Mo Ostin, American record executive, 1927

Deaths

Jack Dreyfus, American financial expert and founder of the Dreyfus Funds, 2009

Anita Colby, American model, actress, inventor (chair that converts to inclined bed), author, and business consultant, 1992

Don't offer generic praise

Express your appreciation to your coworkers, employees, suppliers, and anyone else who supports you in the workplace by giving them specific compliments instead of general praise.

Instead of, "You do a great job," say, "Your work on the Smith presentation was excellent. The background research you did was especially valuable." It's a small difference that makes a big impact.

Thought for the day

"I think of life as a good book. The further you get into it, the more it begins to make sense."

Harold S. Kushner

March 28

Don't be selfish; don't try to impress others. Be humble, thinking of others as better than yourselves. *(Philippians 2:3, NLT)*

Guard against cyber threats

Small businesses are easier targets for cybercriminals because they often don't have the internal resources to secure their systems that larger companies do. The Federal Communications Commission offers a free online resource to help small businesses create a customized cybersecurity plan. Visit fcc.gov/cyberplanner for more information about cybersecurity and to get your customized planning guide.

The most common types of cyber attacks

Businesses can be attacked by cybercriminals in a variety of different ways. The most common are:

Phishing. Sending emails and other messages disguised as a communication from a reputable company designed to trick the recipient into revealing confidential information. Some phishing attempts are obvious; some are well-done and hard to detect.

Malware. Malicious software (such as viruses, worms, Trojan viruses, spyware, and adware) used to steal data and destroy computer systems.

Ransomware. A form of malware that prevents users from accessing their systems or files by encrypting the system. The cybercriminals demand a ransom to provide the encryption key that will allow the user to access their data again.

Distributed Denial of Service Attack (DDoS). Cybercriminals flood a company's computing resources and networks with so much traffic that legitimate users (employees, customers, and other intended users) are unable to use websites and networks.

On this day in history

Notable events

In 1881, the Greatest Show on Earth was formed by P.T. Barnum and James Anthony Bailey.

In 1885, the U.S. Salvation Army was officially organized.

Births

Victor Mills, American chemical engineer for Procter & Gamble credited for the creation of modern disposable diapers and the Pampers brand and the production concept for Pringles, 1897

August Anheuser "Gussie" Busch, Jr., American brewing magnate, 1899

Michael W. Young, American biologist and geneticist known for studying genetically controlled patterns of sleep and wakefulness, 1949

Deaths

Byron Bancroft Johnson, American professional baseball executive, founder of the American League, 1931

Dwight D. Eisenhower, 34th U.S. President, 1969

Thought for the day

"Strive to increase order and discipline in your life. Discipline usually means doing the opposite of what you feel like doing. The easy roads to discipline are setting deadlines; discovering and doing what you do best and what's important and enjoyable to you; focusing on habits by replacing your bad habits and thought patterns, one-by-one, over time, with good habits and thought patterns."

Dave Kekich

I pray that the walls that are blocking the message of the Gospel will come down.

Read:
Proverbs, Chapter 28

March 29

Wait patiently for the Lord. Be brave and courageous. Yes, wait patiently for the Lord. *(Psalm 27:14, NLT)*

Create meaningful taglines and slogans

A company's tagline or slogan can be a great marketing tool—or totally useless.

Taglines tend to be more public relations focused, calling the brand's image to mind. Slogans reflect the company's mission and are more advertising focused. To be effective, they have to differentiate the company or product while being catchy and clear.

Consider this actual example:

We focus on customer satisfaction.

Really? How many companies focus on customer dissatisfaction?

Another example:

We live by the creed that the customer is number one.

If you think about that one, you can figure out what they're trying to say, but it still misses the mark. It's not an effective message.

Taglines and slogans are important branding tools—but only when you invest in creating ones that actually work.

Thought for the day

"We should be careful to get out of an experience only the wisdom that is in it—and stop there; lest we be like the cat that sits down on a hot stove lid. She will never sit down on a hot stove lid again—and that is well; but also she will never sit down on a cold one anymore."

Mark Twain

I pray for forgiveness for the times I have desired a seat at a table that Jesus would have flipped.

Today we observe

National Mom and Pop Business Owners Day

On this day in history

Notable events

In 1989, the first U.S. private (Space Services Inc. of America) commercial rocket made a suborbital test flight at White Sands Missile Range in New Mexico.

In 1999, the Dow Jones Industrial Average closed at 10006.78, above the 10,000 mark for the first time.

Births

Edwin Drake, American businessman and first American to successfully drill for oil, 1819

John Tyler, 10th U.S. President, 1790

James E. Casey, American businessman and founder of the American Messenger Company (today known as UPS), 1888

Sam Walton, American business magnate best known for founding Walmart and Sam's Club, 1918

John M. Belk, American head of Belk, Inc., 1920

Julia Montgomery Walsh, American businesswoman and stockbroker, 1923

Roland E. Arnall, American businessman (owner of ACC Capital Holdings) and diplomat, cofounder of the Simon Wiesenthal Center, 1939

Deaths

John Jacob Astor, German-American businessman, merchant, real estate mogul, and investor, 1848

Mark Hopkins, Jr., American business tycoon and railroad executive, 1878

Gustavus Franklin Swift, American founder of the meatpacking firm Swift & Company, 1903

Hobart "Hobie" Alter, American surf and sailing entrepreneur and pioneer, creator of the Hobie Cat catamarans, 2014

Read:
Proverbs, Chapter 29

March 30

Do not let sin control the way you live; do not give in to sinful desires. Do not let any part of your body become an instrument of evil to serve sin. Instead, give yourselves completely to God, for you were dead, but now you have new life. So use your whole body as an instrument to do what is right for the glory of God. *(Romans 6:12-13, NLT)*

Are you subscribed to your own list?

Do you receive the marketing emails your company sends out? Do you open them, look at the design through the eyes of your customers, check the offers and the links, even place the occasional order or put in a help request?

If you don't, you should.

If you're the boss, you may be thinking that you pay other people to do that—and you probably do. But that doesn't relieve you (the company owner and/or senior management team) of the responsibility for making sure your system is working as it should. Here's what to do:

- Set up several email accounts on different systems using fictitious names your team won't recognize. Subscribe to every email list your company maintains.
- Open every email and at least skim it. Is the design user-friendly? Is the style and tone appropriate? Is the information accurate? Is it fresh and creative or has your team resorted to tired, overused tricks and gimmicks?
- Regularly click through all of the links to make sure they work and, if your messages include sales offers, periodically place an order. If you don't do this with every email, at least do it with enough that you can be sure of the overall quality of your campaigns.
- Provide appropriate feedback to the folks doing the work.

Read:
Proverbs, Chapter 30

Today we observe
Grass is Always Browner on the Other Side of the Fence Day

On this day in history
Notable events
In 1858, Hyman L. Lipman patented a pencil with an attached eraser.
In 1950, Bell Telephone Laboratories announced the invention of the phototransistor.
In 2023, key figures in artificial intelligence (AI) including Elon Musk and Steve Wozniak sign an open letter warning the race to develop AI systems is out of control, asking for a suspension of at least six months.

Births
Stanley Robison, streetcar magnate, MLB team owner, 1854
Brooke Astor, American philanthropist, socialite, and writer, 1902
Ingvar Kamprad, Swedish businessman, founder of IKEA, 1926
Paul Crouch, American television evangelist and cofounder with his wife Jan of the Trinity Broadcasting Network, 1934

Deaths
DeWitt Wallace, American magazine publisher, co-founder of *Reader's Digest*, 1981

Thought for the day
"Associate yourself with men of good quality if you esteem your own reputation; for 'tis better to be alone than in bad company."

George Washington

I pray for the strength to forgive when I don't want to forgive.

March 31

In a desert land he found him, in a barren and howling waste. He shielded him and cared for him; he guarded him as the apple of his eye, like an eagle that stirs up its nest and hovers over its young, that spreads its wings to catch them and carries them aloft. The Lord alone led him; no foreign god was with him. *(Deuteronomy 32:10-12, NIV)*

"No" is a complete sentence

You don't need to apologize or offer excuses when you say no. Just say no to anything you can't, don't want to, or just shouldn't do. You'll be more productive and less stressed.

If you feel like a simple "no" is too abrupt, you can soften it; just be sure your message is clear and not open to debate:
"*No, thank you.*"
"*No, but it's sweet of you to offer.*"
"*No, but I appreciate the opportunity.*"

It's not necessary to give a reason when you say no. You can if you want to, but it's likely to open up a dialog that will create pressure on you to change your answer. Of course, if you really want to say yes but circumstances just aren't right at the moment, you should say so.

Never say:
"*I wish I could, but …*" unless you really wish you could.
"*I'd like to, but …*" unless you'd really like to and you're looking for assistance in figuring out a way to do it.
"*I'm not qualified*" or "*I couldn't do the job justice*" unless you can suggest another resource or you want to be told why you *are* qualified or *can* do the job.

Finally, never say yes when what you should and really want to say is no. It's far better to say no in the first place than to say yes and be resentful, do the job poorly, or don't do it at all.

Saying no is one of the most empowering things you can do for yourself.

Today we observe

National Crayon Day
National Farm Workers Day
World Backup Day

On this day in history

Notable events
In 1736, Bellevue Hospital, the first public hospital in the U.S., was founded.

Births
Alfred E. Hunt, American metallurgist and industrialist, founder of the company that would eventually become Alcoa, 1855
Cesar Chavez, American labor leader, civil rights activist, cofounder of the National Farm Workers Association (which became the United Farm Workers labor union), 1927
Liz Claiborne, American fashion designer and entrepreneur, 1929
Stockton Rush, American businessman, engineer, co-founder and CEO of OceanGate, 1962
Evan Williams, American technology entrepreneur, cofounder of Twitter (now X), founder of Blogger and Medium, 1972

Deaths
John Pierpont Morgan, Sr., American financier, investment banker and founder of J.P. Morgan & Co., 1913

Thought for the day

"Don't let the worst people get the best of you. Save it for the best people instead."
Doe Zantamata

Read:
Proverbs, Chapter 31

I am grateful for criticism that helps me improve personally and professionally.

Christian Business Almanac

April

April comes from the Latin word *aperire*, meaning "to open" as flowers do in the spring. April is named for the Greek goddess of love, Aphrodite.

April birthstone
Diamond

April flower
Daisy, sweet pea

April is ...
- Black Women's History Month
- Celebrate Diversity Month
- Confederate History Month
- Distracted Driving Awareness Month
- Faith Month
- Financial Literacy Month
- Humor Month
- Keep America Beautiful Month
- Mathematics and Statistics Awareness Month
- Move More Month
- National Cannabis Awareness Month
- National Card and Letter Writing Month
- National Child Abuse Awareness Month
- National County Government Month
- National Humor Month
- National Internship Awareness Month
- National Safe Digging Month
- National Volunteer Month
- Records and Information Management Month
- Second Chance Month
- Stress Awareness Month
- Workplace Conflict Awareness Month

Mark your calendar for these April holidays and observances

Third Thursday in April	Get to Know Your Customers Day
Fourth Thursday in April	Take Your Daughter and Son to Work Day
Wednesday of the last full week in April	Administrative Professionals Day
Last Wednesday in April	World Stationery Day
Last Friday in April	Arbor Day
Last Saturday in April	Independent Bookstore Day

Fun Facts about April

April is the first of four months to have 30 days and the second of five months to have less than 31 days.

The Lyrids and Eta Aquariids meteor showers appear in April.

April 1

The way of a fool is right in his own eyes, but a wise man listens to advice.
(Proverbs 12:15, ESV)

How to sharpen your mental focus

We all get foggy from time to time. When you're having trouble focusing, try these tips:

Exercise your brain. Search your app store for brain games, memory games, or brain fitness and play the games on your smartphone. Do word puzzles and other brain-training activities.

Exercise your body. Stay active. Even a short, brisk walk can clear the fog.

Listen to positive music. The genre doesn't matter as long as it's upbeat and the lyrics are positive.

Take breaks. A ten-minute break can improve efficiency and focus, even if the break is simply switching tasks for a few minutes.

Do one thing at a time. Don't try to multitask—it drains your ability to concentrate and makes you less accurate and efficient.

Practice mindfulness. Observing your thoughts, feelings, and environment without judgment is a great way to stay focused on the present.

Get enough sleep. Your brain and body need sleep to recharge and function at full capacity.

Thought for the day

"Remember there's no such thing as a small act of kindness. Every act creates a ripple with no logical end."

Scott Adams

I pray for those whose work takes them away from their homes and families.

Today we observe

April Fools' Day
Boomer Bonus Day
International Fun at Work Day

On this day in history

Notable events

In 1778, New Orleans businessman and financier Oliver Pollock created the $ symbol.

In 1826, Samuel Morey received the first U.S. patent for an internal combustion engine, which he called a "gas or vapour engine."

In 1891, the Wrigley Company, an American multinational chewing gum company, was founded.

In 1976, Steve Wozniak and Steve Jobs founded Apple Computer in the garage of Jobs' parents' house.

Births

James Fisk, flamboyant American financier known as "Barnum of Wall Street" for his unscrupulous business practices, 1835

Abraham Maslow, American psychologist and creator of Maslow's hierarchy of needs, 1908

Charles H. Price II, American businessman, banker, chairman and CEO of Price Candy Company, U.S. ambassador, 1931

Norman Abramson, American engineer and computer scientist known for developing the ALOHAnet system, which formed the basis of the protocols essential in the ethernet now in wide use, 1932

Deaths

Charles R. Drew, American surgeon and medical researcher who developed large-scale blood banks early in World War II, 1950

Ed Roberts, American engineer, entrepreneur, and medical doctor who invented the first commercially successful personal computer, known as the father of the personal computer, 2010

Read:
Proverbs, Chapter 1

April 2

Remember this: Whoever sows sparingly will also reap sparingly, and whoever sows generously will also reap generously. Each of you should give what you have decided in your heart to give, not reluctantly or under compulsion, for God loves a cheerful giver. And God is able to bless you abundantly, so that in all things at all times, having all that you need, you will abound in every good work. As it is written: "They have freely scattered their gifts to the poor; their righteousness endures forever." (2 Corinthians 9:6-9, NIV)

Networking tips

Find out what events your ideal customers attend. Those are the places you should be networking.

Have a plan for the event. Don't just show up. Do some advance research and make a plan for how you'll get the most out of the event.

Develop a brief introduction that clearly tells people who you are and what you do. Memorize and practice it so it sounds natural.

Spend most of your time with people you don't know. The reason for attending networking events is to meet new people.

Speak first. Everyone else is there for the same reason you are. Be the one to speak first and you'll find yourself being remembered in a positive way.

Ask questions. Be genuinely interested in the people you're meeting. Ask questions so you can connect on a professional and personal level.

Thought for the day

"If you have something to do that is worthwhile doing, don't talk about it, but do it. After you have done it, your friends and enemies will talk about it."

George W. Blount

I pray for those whose businesses are struggling.

Read:
Proverbs, Chapter 2

Today we observe

International Fact-Checking Day

National Reconciliation Day

On this day in history

Notable events

In 1827, U.S. inventor Joseph Dixon began manufacturing lead pencils.

In 1872, U.S. engineer George Brayton patented a constant pressure internal combustion engine.

In 1978, George de Mestral's patent for "velvet type fabric" expired, putting Velcro in the open market.

Births

Walter Chrysler, American industrial pioneer in the automotive industry, founder of American Chrysler Corporation, 1875

Deaths

Samuel Morse, American inventor and painter, inventor of a single-wire telegraph system and co-inventor of Morse code, 1872

Carroll Rosenbloom, American businessman and owner of two NFL franchises, 1979

John R. Pierce, American engineer (known as one of the two fathers of the communication satellite) and science fiction author, 2002

Robert Schuller, American televangelist, pastor, and author best known for his weekly Hour of Power television program, 2015

April 3

> But let justice roll down like water and righteousness like an ever-flowing stream. *(Amos 5:24, NRSVue)*

Send error-free emails

Have you ever been embarrassed by a mistake in an email you sent?

Whether you're creating marketing emails that go out to thousands of people, writing business emails that go individually or in small groups to colleagues and clients, or just emailing to your family and friends, accuracy and clarity are essential for effective communication.

Here's a list of issues to check when you're proofing your email messages:

Subject line. Be sure it makes sense, reflects the actual content of your message, has no errors, and that placeholder text has been replaced with the actual information.

Sender. It should be a name the recipients will recognize.

Body. Check all the text for spelling, grammar, and clarity. Be sure all the links work and that images display properly. Look for and remove any placeholder text. Check for accuracy—confirm statistics, quotes, the spelling of names, and so on. If you promised to cover five points or provide a list of seven items, be sure your content matches.

Closing. The closing should be appropriate for the message.

Footer. If you're using an email service, check the footer to be sure the content is accurate, up-to-date, and compliant with both best practices and legal requirements.

There is no way to eliminate the risk of mistakes, but taking a little extra time for proofreading and fact-checking will drastically reduce the chances an embarrassing mistake will land in your audience's inboxes.

Today we observe

World Cloud Security Day

National Inspiring Joy Day

On this day in history

Notable events

In 1860, the Pony Express mail service between Missouri and California using relays of horse-mounted riders began.

In 1948, President Truman signed the Economic Recovery Act of 1948, which became known as the Marshall Plan.

In 1953, *TV Guide* published its first issue with a photo of Lucille Ball's newborn baby boy (Desi Arnaz, Jr.) on the cover.

Births

Mellody Hobson, American businesswoman (president and co-CEO of Ariel Investments; chairwoman of Starbucks Corporation; former chairwoman of DreamWorks Animation), 1969

Deaths

Juan Terry Trippe, American commercial aviation pioneer, entrepreneur, and founder of Pan American World Airways, 1981

Frank Wells, American entertainment executive, president of The Walt Disney Company, 1994

David Edgerton, American entrepreneur and cofounder of Burger King, 2018

Thought for the day

"If Jesus rose from the dead, then you have to accept all that he said; if he didn't rise from the dead, then why worry about any of what he said? The issue on which everything hangs is not whether or not you like his teaching but whether or not he rose from the dead."

Timothy Keller

Read: Proverbs, Chapter 3

I am thankful that God is my shield.

April 4

> I have concluded that there is nothing better for people than to be happy and to enjoy themselves as long as they live, and also that everyone should eat and drink, and find enjoyment in all his toil, for these things are a gift from God. *(Ecclesiastes 3:12-13, NET)*

Characteristics of authentic people

We all want to be authentic, but it isn't always easy to consistently make our actions align with our beliefs and needs. Some characteristics truly authentic people share include:

They help others to be authentic. They don't expect others to try to be something they're not. Authentic people accept others as they really are.

They let go of people who treat them badly. They're not interested in changing those people, they just want them out of their lives.

They're confident. Authentic people have nothing to hide, which gives them a degree of confidence many others lack.

They honestly express their feelings and opinions. They don't lie and they don't go-along-to-get-along. They say what they believe, even when it's not popular.

They're internally motivated. They don't depend on external factors to keep them going.

They don't complain. They know there's no point in complaining, so they don't do it. They simply make the best out of any situation.

Thought for the day

"I bet there are things you are holding onto that simply are no longer worthy of your time. It's not that they're not worthy goals for someone... they're just not goals worthy of your life. But it's just not a good use of your life to hang on. Think big, act big. Don't be afraid to move on."

Jason Leister

On this day in history

Notable events

In 1975, Bill Gates and Paul Allen founded Microsoft.

In 1994, Netscape Communications Corporation (originally Mosaic Communications Corporation) was founded.

Births

Linus Yale, Jr., American mechanical engineer, manufacturer, and inventor (cofounder of Yale Lock Company), 1821

Arthur Murray, American ballroom dancer and businessman, 1895

Bill France, Jr., American motorsports executive, CEO of NASCAR, 1933

Deaths

William Henry Harrison, 9th President of the United States, 1841

Peter Cooper, American industrialist, inventor, philanthropist, and politician, designed and built the first American steam locomotive, designed the first steel chair (a rocking chair) in America, founded Cooper Union for the Advancement of Science and Art, 1883

Martin Luther King, Jr., American clergyman and civil rights leader, 1968

Isaac K. Funk, American Lutheran minister, editor, publisher, cofounder of Funk & Wagnalls Company, 1912

Pierre S. du Pont, American entrepreneur, businessman (president of DuPont de Nemours, Inc. and president of General Motors), philanthropist, 1954

Henry John Heinz III, American businessman and politician, 1991

Alfred Mosher Butts, American architect and inventor of the board game *Scrabble*, 1993

I pray that the world finds God.

Read:
Proverbs, Chapter 4

April 5

This is the day that the Lord has made; let us rejoice and be glad in it.
(Psalm 118:24, NRSVue)

Your contracts should include a venue clause

When there's a dispute over a contract, it's not uncommon for the parties to land in court—the question is, which court? If you're doing business with customers and suppliers outside your local area, you could find yourself involved in a courtroom battle being waged hundreds or even thousands of miles away.

Most states have basic venue statutes, but these statutes may not always work to your advantage. And though you may be able to change the venue after a legal proceeding has begun, that process will only delay getting the real dispute settled. Address the issue of venue in your contract so it's settled long before a problem arises.

Your venue clause does not have to be lengthy or complex. It should simply state the location (county), jurisdiction (court), and state law that will apply in the event of a dispute or breach of contract.

If the other party objects to your venue clause, or if you are asked to sign a contract and you object to the venue clause, work toward a resolution in your negotiation process, get legal counsel, and make your final decision based on what is best for your company.

Thought for the day

"If you look to others for fulfillment, you will never truly be fulfilled. If your happiness depends on money, you will never be happy with yourself. Be content with what you have; rejoice in the way things are. When you realize there is nothing lacking, the whole world belongs to you."

Lao Tzu

Today we observe
Go for Broke Day
National Flash Drive Day
Read a Road Map Day

On this day in history

Notable events
- In 1768, the New York Chamber of Commerce, the oldest Chamber of Commerce in America, was formed; it was chartered by King George III in 1770.
- In 1923, Firestone Tire and Rubber Company began producing inflatable tires.

Births
- Booker T. Washington, American educator, author, orator, and adviser to several U.S. Presidents, was born into slavery in Hale's Ford, Westlake Corner, Virginia, 1856
- Washington Atlee Burpee, American horticulturist and founder of Burpee Seeds, 1858
- Samuel Cate Prescott, American food scientist and microbiologist involved in the development of food safety, food science, public health, and industrial microbiology, 1872
- Lawrence Dale Bell, American industrialist and founder of Bell Aircraft Corporation, 1894
- Allan R. Thieme, American plumber credited with designing the first power operated vehicle/scooter, 1937
- Dean Kamen, American engineer, inventor (holder of more than 1,000 patents; invented Segway and iBOT), and businessman, 1951

Deaths
- Howard Hughes, American business magnate, record-setting pilot, engineer, film producer, and philanthropist, 1976
- Sam Walton, American business magnate best known for founding Walmart and Sam's Club, 1992

I pray for empathy.

Read:
Proverbs, Chapter 5

April 6

> Therefore, I urge you, brothers and sisters, in view of God's mercy, to offer your bodies as a living sacrifice, holy and pleasing to God—this is your true and proper worship. Do not conform to the pattern of this world, but be transformed by the renewing of your mind. Then you will be able to test and approve what God's will is—his good, pleasing and perfect will. *(Romans 12:1-2, NIV)*

How Netflix got its name

In his memoir *That Will Never Work*, Netflix cofounder Mark Randolph explained how the company got its name. He writes:

"Soon after we'd moved in the building, Christina and I had written two columns on the whiteboard. One was filled with words related to the internet. The other was filled with words related to movies. We'd decided that the best name for our company would combine two words: one related to movies, one related to the internet. The best name would combine both terms seamlessly, with a minimum of syllables and letters.

"Picking a name is incredibly difficult. For one thing, you need something catchy, something that rolls off the tongue and is easy to remember. One- or two-syllable words are best...

"...Too many syllables, too many letters, and you run the risk of people misspelling your website. Too few letters, and you risk them forgetting the name."

Appearances can be deceiving

Some of the nicest people you'll ever meet will look like thugs and villains. Some of the meanest people you'll ever meet will look like they stepped off the pages of a fashion magazine. Don't judge people on appearances; take the time to find out who they really are.

I am thankful for everyone who didn't give up on me.

Today we observe

Drowsy Drive Awareness Day
National Employee Benefits Day

On this day in history

Notable events

In 1808, John Jacob Astor incorporated the American Fur Company.
In 1889, George Eastman began selling Kodak flexible rolled film.
In 1938, Roy J. Plunkett invented Teflon.
In 1980, Post-it Notes debuted in U.S. stores.

Births

Donald Wills Douglas, American aircraft industrialist (McDonnell Douglas) and aviation pioneer, 1892
Jack Cover, American aerospace scientist and inventor of the Taser stun gun, 1920
James Dewey Watson, American molecular biologist, geneticist, and zoologist, who co-discovered the structure of DNA, 1928

Deaths

Bradley A. Fiske, American naval officer, author, and inventor of more than 130 electrical and mechanical devices including the rangefinder, 1942

Thought for the day

"Two thousand years ago, in the Middle East, an event occurred that permanently changed the world. Because of that event, history was split. Every time you write a date, you're using the Resurrection of Jesus Christ as the focal point."

Rick Warren

Read:
Proverbs, Chapter 6

April 7

> Jesus died for us so that we can live together with him, whether we are alive or dead when he comes. So encourage each other and give each other strength, just as you are doing now. *(1 Thessalonians 5:10-11, NCV)*

Speak the same language your customers do

Do the people in your audience (prospective customers, colleagues, etc.) understand you?

It makes sense that people working together in small groups develop their own verbal shorthand. However, if you use that verbal shorthand when speaking to anyone outside the group (or even someone new to the group), misunderstandings ranging from minor inconveniences to major problems can result.

Of course, even as you make the effort to be sure your audience understands you, you need to take care not to come across as condescending. That's just as bad—if not worse—than using jargon your audience might not know.

When people don't understand you, their first reaction is *not* to be impressed with how smart you are. They're more likely to be frustrated or annoyed. If you make it difficult for them to grasp your message—whether you're selling, servicing or just entertaining—they're going to thinking about where they can go to find someone who will be easier to understand.

If your goal is to educate, fine—but the student has to start with a basic understanding before being able to grasp more advanced concepts.

It all comes down to knowing your audience and making the effort to communicate effectively. The number one way to do that is to speak the same language your audience speaks.

I pray that I will be the hands and feet of the Lord in the world.

Today we observe
Walk to Work Day

On this day in history

Notable events

In 1969, the Advanced Research Projects Agency awarded a contract to build a precursor of today's world wide web to BBN Technologies.

Births

William Keith Kellogg, American industrialist in food manufacturing, founder of the Kellogg Company, 1860

Francis Cabot Lowell, American businessman instrumental in bringing the Industrial Revolution to the U.S. for whom the city of Lowell, Massachusetts is named, 1775

MacKenzie Scott, American novelist and philanthropist, 1970

Deaths

P. T. Barnum, American showman, businessman, politician, and founder of the Barnum & Bailey Circus, 1891

Henry Ford, American industrialist and business magnate, founder of Ford Motor Company and chief developer of the assembly line technique of mass production, died in Dearborn, Michigan, 1947

George Nissen, American inventor (the trampoline), 2010

Thought for the day

"That you may retain your self-respect, it is better to displease the people by doing what you know is right, than to temporarily please them by doing what you know is wrong."

William J.H. Boetcker

Read:
Proverbs, Chapter 7

April 8

> Praise be to the God and Father of our Lord Jesus Christ, the Father of compassion and the God of all comfort, who comforts us in all our troubles, so that we can comfort those in any trouble with the comfort we ourselves receive from God. *(2 Corinthians 1:3-4, NIV)*

What are we teaching people?

We're never too old to learn from others. Dorothy Law Nolte wrote this poem in 1972.

Children Learn What They Live

If children live with criticism, they learn to condemn.

If children live with hostility, they learn to fight.

If children live with ridicule, they learn to be shy.

If children live with shame, they learn to feel guilty.

If children live with encouragement, they learn confidence.

If children live with tolerance, they learn to be patient.

If children live with praise, they learn to appreciate.

If children live with acceptance, they learn to love.

If children live with approval, they learn to like themselves.

If children live with honesty, they learn truthfulness.

If children live with security, they learn to have faith in themselves and others.

If children live with friendliness, they learn the world is a nice place in which to live.

It's definitely great parenting advice, but it applies to everyone, no matter how old they are.

Read it again, and this time, replace *children* with *people*.

We never stop learning what we live—and we never stop teaching others with our actions.

What did you teach someone today?

Read:
Proverbs, Chapter 8

On this day in history

Notable events

In 1862, John D. Lynde patented the first aerosol dispenser or "improved bottle for aerated liquids."

In 2016, SpaceX successfully made the first soft return landing of a reusable Falcon 9 rocket booster on a robotic drone ship at sea.

Births

David Rittenhouse, American astronomer, inventor, scientific instrument craftsman, first director of the U.S. Mint, 1732

Larry David Norman, American musician, a pioneer of Christian rock music, 1947

Robert Kiyosaki, American investor, author (Rich Dad Company), 1947

Deaths

Elisha Otis, American industrialist, founder of the Otis Elevator Company, 1861

Frank Winfield Woolworth, American entrepreneur, operator of variety stores knowns as "five and dimes," and the founder of F. W. Woolworth Company, 1919

Benjamin Eisenstadt, American businessman, inventor, and philanthropist, designer of the modern sugar packet, developer of Sweet'N Low, and founder of Cumberland Packing Corporation, 1996

Jack Tramiel, American businessman, Holocaust survivor, founder of Commodore International, 2012

Thought for the day

"Fairy tales are more than true; not because they tell us that dragons exist, but because they tell us that dragons can be beaten."

G.K. Chesterton

I pray for those who need to forgive.

April 9

But because of his great love for us, God, who is rich in mercy, made us alive with Christ even when we were dead in transgressions—it is by grace you have been saved. And God raised us up with Christ and seated us with him in the heavenly realms in Christ Jesus, in order that in the coming ages he might show the incomparable riches of his grace, expressed in his kindness to us in Christ Jesus. *(Ephesians 2:4–7, NIV)*

Who is your customer?

There are two angles to the issue of knowing your customer: your *prospective* customers and your *actual* customers.

For your prospective customers, consider who has a need for your product or service, is likely to buy it, and can afford it? For B2C operations, you'll want to know consumer demographics—how old they are, where they live, how much money they make, how many children and pets they have. For B2B, you need details such as the industry, size of the company, location, number of employees, and so on.

For your actual customers, think about this: How closely do the people who are buying from you resemble the prospective customer your marketing plan is targeting? If there's a match, your marketing plan is working. If you see a significant difference between your target market and the customers you have, you need to figure out the problem in your marketing strategy. Why are your marketing efforts working on a group you're not targeting? And what do you need to change — your strategy or your target market?

Another element to toss into this equation is this: *How happy are you with your current customers?* Do you want more of them? Or would you rather have customers with different characteristics—those who will buy more, not be so price-sensitive, or that will be easier to serve?

You have to know who your customer is before you can decide whether to seek more customers who are similar or to put together a plan to go after a different customer group.

On this day in history

Notable events
In 1872, Samuel R. Percy patented dried milk.
In 1959, NASA introduced America's first astronauts.

Births
J. Presper Eckert, American electrical engineer and computer pioneer, 1919
Doug Ducey, American businessman (CEO of Cold Stone Creamery) and politician, 1964

Deaths
Eben Sumner Draper, American businessman (Draper Corporation) and politician, 1914
Frank Lloyd Wright, American architect, designer, writer, and educator, 1959
James Rouse, American businessman (The Rouse Company), real estate development, urban planner, philanthropist, 1996
Roger S. Nichols, American recording engineer, producer, and inventor (rubidium nuclear clock), 2011

Thought for the day

"Living each day as if it were our last, rather than converting us into hedonists, will make us appreciate how wonderful it is that we are alive and have the opportunity to fill this day with activity. This in turn will make us less likely to squander our days. As we think about and plan for tomorrow, remember to appreciate today."
William B. Irvine

I pray on the joy of 1 Kings 5:4.

Read:
Proverbs, Chapter 9

April 10

G odliness makes a nation great, but sin is a disgrace to any people.
(Proverbs 14:34, NLT)

Use your intuition

Intuition is the ability to understand something immediately, without the need for conscious reasoning. We all have it. Here's how to sharpen your natural intuitive skills.

Slow down. Our fast-paced lifestyles can drown out our intuition. Be intentional about taking some time away from the chaos, even if it just a brief solitary walk.

Listen to your gut. Most of the time, your gut feelings or inner voice will be right on target. Don't reject critical thinking; combine it with your intuition.

Develop empathic accuracy. Be intuitively aware of what other people are thinking and feeling.

Nurture your creativity. Intuition is a critical part of creativity; they go hand-in-hand.

Pay attention to your dreams. Dreams can be manifestations of intuition. Don't dismiss your dreams; analyze them and figure out how you can use them. *"For God speaks again and again, though people do not recognize it. He speaks in dreams, in visions of the night, when deep sleep falls on people as they lie in their beds." (Job 33:14-15, NLT)*

Ask good questions

When you ask good questions, you'll get good answers—well, maybe not always, but if your questions are sharp, clear, and specific, you're more likely to elicit the information you need.

I pray for the discernment to recognize toxic people and the strength to deal with them appropriately, even when that means walking away from them.

Today we observe
Global Work from Home Day

On this day in history
Notable events
- In 1849, Walter Hunt patented the safety pin and sold the rights to it for $400.
- In 1989, Intel Corp. launched the i486 microprocessor.
- In 2012, Apple, Inc., claimed a value of $600 billion, making it the largest company by market capitalization in the world.

Births
- William Booth, English Methodist preacher who, along with his wife, Catherine, founded the Salvation Army, 1829
- Joseph Pulitzer, Hungarian-American newspaper publisher and politician, established the Pulitzer Prize, 1847
- John D. Hertz, American businessman, racehorse owner/breeder, philanthropist; founder of the Yellow Cab Company and related businesses, 1879
- Wesley A. Clark, American physicist credited with designing the first modern personal computer, 1927
- Dolores Huerta, American labor leader and cofounder (with Cesar Chavez) of the United Farmworkers Association (which became the United Farm Workers), 1930

Deaths
- Samuel P. Massie, American chemist and educator, named one of the top 75 distinguished contributors to chemistry in history, 2005

Thought for the day

"I'm lazy. But it's the lazy people who invented the wheel and the bicycle because they didn't like walking or carrying things."
Lech Walesa

Read:
Proverbs, Chapter 10

April 11

> Should we offer him thousands of rams and ten thousand rivers of olive oil? Should we sacrifice our firstborn children to pay for our sins? No, O people, the Lord has told you what is good, and this is what he requires of you: to do what is right, to love mercy, and to walk humbly with your God. *(Micah 6:7-8, NLT)*

Back up your mailing list

Your customer mailing list is one of your most valuable assets. It's the foundation of your ability to communicate with the people you've identified as customers or potential customers.

Whether you market by email, direct (snail) mail, or a combination, think about this: What would it mean to your marketing plan specifically and your company overall if those files were deleted or corrupted?

Every operation is at risk of losing data by accident or an intentional malicious act. Create a system for regularly backing up your mailing lists that will keep the data safe and confidential.

For email lists: If you use an email service provider, periodically download all the data in your list and store it in a safe place in your own system. Most email service providers make this simple to do; just check their help section for instructions. If you have a smaller list you maintain within your email system, create a copy you can store in a separate place.

For snail mail lists: Create a backup and store it with your other critical company information. If you use a mail house to manage your list, insist that they periodically provide you with a current file that you can keep in your own system.

How often you back up your lists depends on how often you make changes to the data. Once you've determined how often you need to back up your mailing list data, decide who will be responsible for getting it done and how to make sure it happens as scheduled. Then hold that person accountable for this essential job responsibility.

Today we observe

International Be Kind to Lawyers Day

On this day in history

Notable events
In 1976, the Apple I computer, created by Steve Wozniak, was introduced.

Births
Hiram Bond Everest, American businessman, investor, inventor, and farmer, cofounder of the Vacuum Oil Company, 1830

Percy Lavon Julian, American research chemist and a pioneer in the chemical synthesis of medicinal drugs from plants, 1899

Deaths
James Anthony Bailey, American owner and manager of several 19th century circuses, including the Barnum & Bailey Greatest Show on Earth, 1906

Cecil Howard Green, British-born American geophysicist, electrical engineer, and electronics manufacturing executive; cofounder of Texas Instruments, 2003

Mitzi Shore, American comedy club owner, and founder of The Comedy Channel, 2018

Thought for the day

"There is no kind of ultimate goal to do something twice as good as anyone else can. It's just to do the job as best you can. If it turns out good, fine. If it doesn't, that's the way it goes."

Chuck Yeager

I am thankful that God cares for and blesses his children.

Read:
Proverbs, Chapter 11

April 12

> **D**o not be deceived; God is not mocked, for you reap whatever you sow. If you sow to your own flesh, you will reap corruption from the flesh, but if you sow to the Spirit, you will reap eternal life from the Spirit. So let us not grow weary in doing what is right, for we will reap at harvest time, if we do not give up. *(Galatians 6:7–9, NRSVue)*

Five ideas for blog content

Among all the new, jazzy content marketing tools that are available, blogs remain the foundation, the workhorse, the launchpad for everything else you do.

Important reasons to blog include:
- Search engine optimization (SEO)
- Reputation management
- Thought leadership
- Customer education
- Lead generation and list building

But even with AI, many bloggers find the biggest challenge is coming up with quality content—and content is what makes a blog effective.

Five ideas for generating blog content:

Answer the questions your customers are asking. Write blogs that respond to the questions and phrases your readers are searching on.

Do comparisons. Compare companies, products, opinions. Offer objective analysis that your readers can consider and will share.

Write about what's wrong with your industry and how to fix it. Don't attack anyone, but position yourself as a thought leader who cares about the industry and wants to see improvement.

Curate content. Share the valuable information you're seeing on other sites. Add your own thoughts and then link to the other content.

Invite guest bloggers. You don't have to create all the content on your blog. Guest bloggers will appreciate the exposure and expand your audience. Vet them carefully and only accept guest blogs that are relevant with links to quality sites.

Today we observe
Deskfast Day

On this day in history

Notable events

In 1892, George Canfield Blickensderfer patented the first portable, full-keyboard typewriter.

In 1955, the results of Jonas Salk's polio vaccine tests were announced and the vaccine was licensed the same day.

Births

Evelyn Berezin, American computer designer of the first computer-driven word processor, 1925

Deaths

Clara Barton, American nurse, founder of the American Red Cross, 1912

Franklin D. Roosevelt, 32nd U.S. President (longest-serving President), 1945

Philip K. Wrigley, American chewing gum manufacturer and MLB executive, son of William Wrigley Jr., 1977

Jerry Zucker, Israeli-born American businessman, investor, and philanthropist, president and CEO of the InterTech Group and the Polymer Group, 2008

Thought for the day

"High expectations are the key to everything."

— *Sam Walton*

I pray for forgiveness for the times I have done the right things but for the wrong reasons.

Read:
Proverbs, Chapter 12

April 13

You made all the delicate, inner parts of my body and knit me together in my mother's womb. Thank you for making me so wonderfully complex! Your workmanship is marvelous—how well I know it. You watched me as I was being formed in utter seclusion, as I was woven together in the dark of the womb. You saw me before I was born. Every day of my life was recorded in your book. Every moment was laid out before a single day had passed. *(Psalm 139:13–16, NLT)*

Reduce payroll costs without firing people

When you want to reduce payroll costs, the first thing that comes to mind is to cut staff. Before you start letting people go, consider these strategies:

Attrition. If you have time, let attrition reduce your staff. When people leave, whether for their own reasons or for cause unrelated to your goal of reducing staff, don't replace them. Create an orderly process through which you redistribute their workload.

Offer incentives for people to leave or retire. When people leave voluntarily, they leave happy, so you don't have to deal with disgruntled former employees or morale problems among remaining employees.

Reduce the work hours for employees. Cutting back on hours will let you cut back on wage costs. You may also ask salaried personnel to take a pay reduction. You may lose people who can't afford the lower income, but it will allow you to avoid layoffs in down cycles.

Furlough employees. This essentially amounts to forced unpaid vacations, perhaps for one day a week or one week a month. As with reducing work hours, some employees will appreciate the time off; others may look for work elsewhere—but it will be their choice.

I pray to appreciate everything God sends my way.

Read: Proverbs, Chapter 13

On this day in history

Notable events

In 1869, George Westinghouse patented the steam power brake.

In 1916, Funk Brothers Seed Co. of Bloomington, Illinois sold the first U.S. shipment of hybrid seed corn to Samuel Ramsay of Jacobsburg, Ohio for $15 a bushel.

Births

Thomas Jefferson, 3rd U.S. President, 1743

Frank Winfield Woolworth, American entrepreneur, operator of variety stores knowns as "five and dimes," and the founder of F.W. Woolworth Company, 1852

Alfred Mosher Butts, American architect and inventor of the board game Scrabble, 1899

Phyllis Fraser (also known as Phyllis Cerf Wagner), American socialite, writer, publisher, and actress, cofounder of Beginner Books, 1916

Jack Chick, American cartoonist and publisher (Chick Publications), best known for cartoon gospel tracts, 1924

Deaths

Elwood Haynes, American inventor, metallurgist, entrepreneur, and industrialist; designer of one of the earliest automobiles made in the U.S., 1925

Thought for the day

"Interestingly, koi, when put in a fishbowl, will only grow up to three inches. When this same fish is placed in a large tank, it will grow to about nine inches long. In a pond koi can reach lengths of eighteen inches. Amazingly, when placed in a lake, koi can grow to three feet long. The metaphor is obvious. You are limited by how you see the world."

Vince Poscente

April 14

> "But what about you?" he asked. "Who do you say I am?" Simon Peter answered, "You are the Messiah, the Son of the living God." Jesus replied, "Blessed are you, Simon son of Jonah, for this was not revealed to you by flesh and blood, but by my Father in heaven. *(Matthew 16:15–17, NIV)*

Money habits that pay off

Keep track of your finances. Be meticulous about knowing where your money comes from and where it goes.

Live below your means. Don't spend money on unnecessary items and don't indulge in luxuries unless you can truly afford them.

Have multiple streams of income. Don't rely on a single source of revenue, even if it's the revenue from your own business.

Invest in yourself. Prioritize your personal and professional development.

Take calculated risks. Weigh the risks against the potential rewards, mitigate the risks if possible, then make an informed decision.

Common business legal mistakes

Check your operating practices and be sure you're not making any of these common legal mistakes.
- Not using good written contracts.
- Ignorance of the law.
- Failing to maintain good business records.
- Not providing employees with clear policies and expectations.
- Getting involved in avoidable litigation.
- Ignoring intellectual property rights and issues.
- Not retaining an experienced lawyer when needed.

I pray to be perpetually curious and always learning.

Read: Proverbs, Chapter 14

Today we observe

International Moment of Laughter Day

On this day in history

Notable events

In 1896, John Harvey Kellogg received a patent for "flaked cereal, and process of making same."

In 1902, James Cash Penney opened his first store, the Golden Rule Store.

In 1912, the RMS *Titanic* hit an iceberg at 11:40 p.m.

In 1914, Stacy G. Carkhuff, U.S. head of Firestone Tire and Rubber Company, patented a non-skid tire pattern.

In 1960, American record company Motown was incorporated as Motown Record Corporation by Berry Gordy, Jr.

In 1994, Turner Classic Movies cable channel launched.

Births

Loretta Lynn, American country singer-songwriter, author, and businesswoman, 1932

Joseph Pedott, American advertising executive and entrepreneur (Chia Pet; the Clapper), 1932

Deaths

Louis Sullivan, American architect, called a "father of skyscrapers" and "father of modernism," 1924

Phil Katz, American computer programmer best known as the co-creator of the Zip file format for data compression, 2000

Thought for the day

"An education isn't how much you have committed to memory, or even how much you know. It's being able to differentiate between what you know and what you don't."

Anatole France

April 15

> I will turn your religious festivals into mourning and all your singing into weeping. I will make all of you wear sackcloth and shave your heads. I will make that time like mourning for an only son and the end of it like a bitter day. "The days are coming," declares the Sovereign Lord, "when I will send a famine through the land—not a famine of food or a thirst for water, but a famine of hearing the words of the Lord. People will stagger from sea to sea and wander from north to east, searching for the word of the Lord, but they will not find it. *(Amos 8:10-12, NIV)*

Market through writing

As a professional or businessperson, you can promote yourself, your products and your company through written content, such as:

- Books, including how-to, motivation and memoirs.
- Articles in trade journals and other business publications.
- Letters to the editor and op-ed pieces in your local newspaper or trade publications.
- Articles for websites, e-zines, and other online resources.
- Blogs.
- White papers and special reports.

Whatever you produce in the way of books, articles, and other materials should be written in a clear, cohesive, and engaging manner that reflects positively on you and your company.

Thought for the day

"It is a common experience that a problem difficult at night is resolved in the morning after the committee of sleep has worked on it."

John Steinbeck

I pray to always remember that nothing is too large or too small to take to God.

Grow your faith by rejecting prideful thinking.

Today we observe

Tax Day

On this day in history

Notable events

In 1817, the first American school for the deaf opened.

In 1865, U.S. President Abraham Lincoln died nine hours after being shot by John Wilkes Booth.

In 1892, General Electric Company was formed by a merger of Thomas Edison's General Electric Company with Thomson-Houston Electric Company; arranged by J.P. Morgan and incorporated in New York.

In 1912, RMS Titanic sank at 2:27 a.m. off Newfoundland after hitting an iceberg.

In 1924, Rand McNally published its first road atlas.

In 1955, Ray Kroc opened the first McDonald's fast food restaurant in Des Plaines, Illinois.

Births

Alfred S. Bloomingdale, American businessman, heir to the Bloomingdale's department store fortune, "father of the credit card," 1916

Kenneth Lay, American businessman, founder, CEO, and chairman of Enron, 1942

Deaths

Abraham Lincoln, 16th U.S. President (first U.S. President to be assassinated), 1865

John Jacob Astor IV, American business magnate, real estate developer, investor, writer, died in the sinking of the *Titanic*, 1912

Benjamin Guggenheim, American businessman, member of the Guggenheim family, died in the sinking of the *Titanic*, 1912

Read:
Proverbs, Chapter 15

April 16

He delivered us from the power of darkness and transferred us to the kingdom of the Son he loves, in whom we have redemption, the forgiveness of sins. *(Colossians 1:13-14, NET)*

Essential business travel tip: put yourself first

Certainly, you'll have to consider others when making your travel plans, but make your own health and comfort a top priority. If you're flying across several time zones, especially west-to-east, book a daytime arrival. Then head outside and do something active in the natural daylight—it will help you recover from jet lag faster.

It's natural to want to maximize your time when you're on the road, but you should include exercise and rest in your schedule. Plan a specific time each day or every other day to do your exercise routines. Give yourself ample breaks for downtime during the day.

Avoid going straight from a day of meetings to an important dinner; refresh yourself with a brief nap and a shower. Resist the temptation to over-indulge in unusual foods and limit alcohol consumption. End your evenings early enough to allow yourself time to relax and unwind before falling asleep.

Even though breakfast meetings can be productive, remember that getting up earlier than you're accustomed to can interfere with your sleep patterns and make you tired and dull for the rest of the day.

Thought for the day

"Whenever you're tempted to dwell in the past, repeat this single word: forward. Brainstorm one positive thought and action to use to keep you moving forward. When you're tempted to indulge in a negative, regressive behavior, swap it for one that will move you forward."

Karen Salmansohn

Today we observe
Wear Pajamas to Work Day
World Voice Day

On this day in history

Notable events

In 2015, Elizabeth Holmes, entrepreneur, founder and CEO of Theranos, was named one of Time's "100 Most Influential People;" she was later indicted on fraud charges and sentenced to more than eleven years in prison.

Births

Wilbur Wright, American aviation pioneer (Wright Brothers), 1867

John Bevins Moisant, American aviator, flight instructor, and businessman; cofounder of Moisant International Aviators, a flying circus, 1868

Ellis Marsalis Sr., American businessman, poultry farmer turned hotelier, Esso franchise owner, and civil rights activist, 1908

Edie Adams, American comedian, actress, singer, and businesswoman, 1927

Deaths

Thomas Blanchard, American inventor and pioneer of the assembly line style of mass production in the U.S., 1864

Arthur Chevrolet, Swiss-American racecar driver, automobile manufacturer, and race car development pioneer, 1946

Charles M. Geschke, American businessman, computer scientist, cofounder of Adobe, Inc., 2021

I am thankful for everyone who has ever prayed for me, whether or not I knew they were doing it.

Read:
Proverbs, Chapter 16

April 17

For the time will come when people will not put up with sound doctrine. Instead, to suit their own desires, they will gather around them a great number of teachers to say what their itching ears want to hear. They will turn their ears away from the truth and turn aside to myths. But you, keep your head in all situations, endure hardship, do the work of an evangelist, discharge all the duties of your ministry. *(2 Timothy 4:3-5, NIV)*

The emotional side of a disaster

Whether it's a major catastrophe or a minor incident, if an event was serious enough to warrant an insurance claim, it probably will have a psychological impact on you and your team. Dealing with your people is every bit as important as dealing with your insurance company.

Grieving the loss caused by a disaster is a natural process, and to ignore that can have a negative impact on your recovery. When a critical incident has taken place, you and your employees have been traumatized. While you have to attend to the business side of rebuilding, you also have to attend to the emotional wellbeing of the group.

Acknowledge that people may have strong feelings of grief, anger, fear and depression. Encourage an open discussion of those feelings to give individuals the opportunity to process what has happened. Talk about the future and communicate the status of the recovery openly. If your employees' jobs are secure, they need to know that; if the future looks shaky, they have a right to know that, too. The emotions people experience after work-related disasters may be similar to those felt when a close family member dies. Helping them deal with their feelings is not only compassionate but essential to the recovery of your company.

Consider bringing a professional in to help with trauma counseling. Some insurance policies will pay for critical incident debriefing.

Read:
Proverbs, Chapter 17

Today we observe

International Day of Mastering Conversations that Matter

On this day in history

Notable events

In 1930, DuPont scientist Elmer K. Bolton invented neoprene using Julius Nieuwland's divinyl acetylene.

In 1991, Dow Jones closed above 3,000 (3,004.46) for the first time.

Births

John Pierpont Morgan, Sr., American financier, investment banker and founder of J.P. Morgan & Co., 1837

Sidney R. Garfield, American medical doctor and pioneer of health maintenance organizations; cofounder of Kaiser Permanente healthcare system, 1906

Deaths

Benjamin Franklin, American polymath, writer, scientist, inventor, statesman, diplomat, publisher, printer, U.S. Founding Father (helped draft the Declaration of Independence and was one of its signers), 1790

Samuel Morey, American inventor (early internal combustion engines) and steamship pioneer, 1843

Frank E. Resnik, American businessman, CEO and chairman of Philip Morris USA, 1995

Thought for the day

"There is no such thing as 'your truth'. There is the truth and your opinion."

Ben Shapiro

I pray that I will be a positive influence in my workplace.

April 18

If then you have been raised with Christ, seek the things that are above, where Christ is, seated at the right hand of God. Set your minds on things that are above, not on things that are on earth. For you have died, and your life is hid with Christ in God. When Christ who is our life appears, then you also will appear with him in glory. *(Colossians 3:1-4, NIV)*

Managing your insurance

Insurance isn't something you can simply take care of once and then forget about. Do an annual review of both your needs and your coverage. Because the insurance industry is changing rapidly, this is a good time to ask your agent about new products that might be more appropriate for your organization.

Keep records of all your assets, not just your saleable inventory; you'll need them to document any claims. If your inventory fluctuates, perhaps due to seasonal or other reasons, consider insuring for the higher amounts. For some coverages, seasonal rates and limits are available. Also, some property coverages can be written on a reporting basis; for example, your inventory coverage could change as your inventory fluctuates. Talk to your agent to see what's most appropriate for your operation.

If you make changes to existing policies, follow up to make sure the necessary paperwork is completed. Even though your agent should handle these things for you, it's ultimately your responsibility to make sure the right insurance is in place.

Review your health and other benefits-related insurance to make sure it's meeting your employees' needs and is legally compliant. As employees' personal circumstances change, so will their insurance requirements. Consider adding or dropping various benefits based on the needs of your worker population.

Insurance companies often structure their policies differently, so if you change any of your insurers, study the new policy carefully to be sure you know what you're buying.

Don't sacrifice coverage for rates. Competitive rates matter, but so do performance and coverage in the event of a claim.

On this day in history

Notable events
In 1906, an earthquake and subsequent fire killed nearly 4,000 people and destroyed 75 percent of the city of San Francisco.

Births
Bernard Ogilvie Dodge, American botanist and pioneer researcher on heredity in fungi, 1872
Clifton Hillegass, creator and publisher of CliffsNotes, 1918
Andrew Yan-Tak Ng, British-American computer scientist and technology entrepreneur focusing on machine learning and artificial intelligence, 1976

Deaths
Albert Einstein, German-born theoretical physicist, 1955
Edgar F. "Ted" Codd, English computer scientist, inventor of the relational model for database management (while working for IBM), 2003
Joseph Lechleider, American electrical engineer, inventor (DSL/high speed internet technology), 2015

Thought for the day

"Don't try to figure out what other people want to hear from you; figure out what you have to say. It's the one and only thing you have to offer."

Barbara Kingsolver

I pray that the choices I make will be wise and in line with God's will for my life and business.

Read:
Proverbs, Chapter 18

April 19

> The name of the Lord is a strong fortress; the godly run to him and are safe. *(Proverbs 18:10)*

Sales tip: remember the influencers

Always remember the impact of decision-influencers—the people who don't make the actual purchase but who might make a difference in your results.

Receptionists and assistants are often very influential in terms of expressing their opinions about vendors. They can also be a tremendous source of information and support for you, so nurture those relationships in a sincere and non-patronizing way.

If the decision-maker won't be the ultimate user of your product, ask if you can meet with the staffers who will directly use what you're selling to do a needs analysis and show how your product works. If you get those people on your side, a great deal of your work is done.

Thought for the day

"Self-pity gets you nowhere. One must have the adventurous daring to accept oneself as a bundle of possibilities and undertake the most interesting game in the world—making the most of one's best."

Harry Emerson Fosdick

> Grow your faith by doing whatever it takes to keep your eyes on Jesus. Read the Bible and memorize scripture. Sing hymns and praise songs. Read devotions. Study the lives of other faithful Christians. When your attention falters, intentionally bring it back.

Today we observe

National Oklahoma City Bombing Commemoration Day

On this day in history

Notable events

In 1955, after six years of selling cars in the U.S., German automaker Volkswagen founded Volkswagen of America to standardize its dealer and service network.

In 1991, Greyhound Bus posted a $195 million loss for 1990.

Births

Jack Roush, American racing entrepreneur, his companies include Roush Fenway Keselowski Racing, Roush Industries, Roush Performance, and Roush CleanTech, 1942

Ole Evinrude, Norwegian-American entrepreneur, inventor of the first outboard motor with practical commercial application, 1877

Deaths

Charles Scribner II, American publisher, president of Charles Scribner's Sons, founding member of the American Publishers Association, 1930

Percy Lavon Julian, American research chemist and a pioneer in the chemical synthesis of medicinal drugs from plants, 1975

J. Peter Grace, American industrialist, president of the diversified chemical company W. R. Grace & Co. (founded by his grandfather), the longest serving CEO of a public company, 1995

Helen Robson Walton, American philanthropist, widow of Wal-Mart Stores, Inc., founder Sam Walton, 2007

Al Neuharth, American businessman, author, and founder of *USA Today*, 2013

I pray for teachers—those in the formal education system and those who teach in other settings.

Read:
Proverbs, Chapter 19

April 20

> For ever since the world was created, people have seen the earth and sky. Through everything God made, they can clearly see his invisible qualities—his eternal power and divine nature. So they have no excuse for not knowing God. *(Romans 1:20, NLT)*

Do you have a cannabis policy?

April 20 or 420 is also known as Weed Day, an unofficial celebration of marijuana. As an increasing number of states and communities decriminalize marijuana and medical use of the substance is on the rise, this is a good time to either create or review your cannabis policy.

Because laws and regulations are changing so rapidly, it's a good idea to get assistance from a qualified HR expert or attorney before changing or finalizing your policy.

You can incorporate cannabis into your drug and substance abuse policy, which should address issues including pre-employment drug testing, testing of current employees, expectations, and discipline. Your cannabis policy needs to balance your interest in maintaining a safe and lawful workplace with the realities of a society where cannabis use in various forms is growing in acceptance and practice.

Depending on your industry and working environment, you may want to distinguish between recreational and medical use of marijuana. Another issue to consider is the various ways medical cannabis is consumed (inhalation, sublingual, oral, topical, edibles, and suppository).

If you have a federal contract of $100,000 or more or a federal grant in any amount, you must implement a drug-free workplace program that includes a drug-free workplace policy, supervisor training, employee education, employee assistance, and drug testing.

In the absence of a specific policy, let employees know you will follow the law. Of course, employees should not be working while impaired by any substance, legal or not.

Today we observe

Volunteer Recognition Day

On this day in history

Notable events

In 2010, the Deepwater Horizon offshore oil drilling rig exploded, killing eleven and causing the largest marine oil spill in history.

Births

Charles Gordon Curtis, American engineer, inventor (Curtis steam turbine), and patent attorney, 1860

Robert G. Wilmers, American billionaire banker, chairman and CEO of M&T Bank, 1934

David Filo, American billionaire businessman, cofounder of Yahoo! Inc., 1966

Deaths

Jesse G. Vincent, American aircraft, marine, and automobile engine designer, chief engineer for Packard automobiles, 1962

Thought for the day

"Man often becomes what he believes himself to be. If I keep on saying to myself that I cannot do a certain thing, it is possible that I may end by really becoming incapable of doing it. On the contrary, if I shall have the belief that I can do it, I shall surely acquire the capacity to do it, even if I may not have it at the beginning."

Mahatma Gandhi

I pray that I may be a positive representative of my company.

Read:
Proverbs, Chapter 20

April 21

Invest in seven ventures, yes, in eight; you do not know what disaster may come upon the land. (Ecclesiastes 11:2, NIV)

Start a workplace book club

An effective way to get your employees on the same page is to start a company book club. It can introduce new ideas, help with skill development, and create a general culture of personal and professional growth.

Develop some guidelines before you announce the club, including:
- A general theme
- How books will be chosen and acquired
- Frequency (monthly, bimonthly, or quarterly)
- How to structure your discussions about the books

Make participation voluntary. Read books about your industry, technical skills your team needs, and soft skills that everyone can use. Switch around from new releases to business classics, and include authors from various backgrounds, races, and genders. As the leader, you can select the titles you'll read, but it's also a good idea to get input from the team.

Decide if you'll provide the books and in what format (print, digital, audio) or if employees must purchase or get them from the local library. Be sure to give participants plenty of time to read the book.

Allow between forty-five and ninety minutes for your discussions, and be sure everyone has a chance to contribute. Decide if you'll meet in person (maybe over lunch) or online. During the meeting, listen carefully to what everyone has to say about the book and implement new ideas when feasible and practical.

After the club is established, consider expanding to occasionally watching or listening to relevant webinars, podcasts, or TED talks instead of reading a book. You might also invite guest speakers to your meetings.

Today we observe
World Creativity and Innovation Day

On this day in history

Notable events

In 1857, Alexander Douglas patented a "new and improved" bustle (ladies' undergarment).

In 1878, the first U.S. firehouse pole (a three-inch diameter wooden pole) was installed in New York City by Captain David B. Kenyon; the first brass pole was installed in Boston, Massachusetts in 1880.

In 1967, General Motors (GM) celebrated the manufacture of its 100 millionth American-made car.

Births

Herbert Schlosser, American television executive, president of NBC (1974-1978), cofounder of A&E, played a key role in the creation of *Saturday Night Live*, 1926

Donald J. Tyson, American businessman, president and CEO of Tyson Foods, 1930

Deaths

Samuel Slater, English-American industrialist best known for bringing the Industrial Revolution to the U.S. from Great Britain, 1835

Mark Twain (Samuel Langhorne Clemens), American author, entrepreneur, publisher, and lecturer, 1910

Peter Ruckman, American pastor, author, and founder of the Pensacola Bible Institute, 2016

Thought for the day

"Prayer is as essential to the inner life as breath is to the body."

Don M. Aycock

I am thankful for feeling peace in the midst of turmoil.

Read:
Proverbs, Chapter 21

April 22

A new heart I will give you, and a new spirit I will put within you, and I will remove from your body the heart of stone and give you a heart of flesh. *(Ezekiel 36:26)*

The real cost of free

Who doesn't love a bargain? But free isn't always a bargain. Although it may sound good, "free" isn't always the best deal.

Remember, nothing is free. Everything has a cost.

Many companies offer versions of their products that they don't charge for. Of course, the company's strategy is usually to get users to upgrade from a limited-feature, no-support free version to a paid version. Free as a marketing strategy can be effective.

But if you're trying to build an online presence using free resources, you are making a huge mistake. Here's why:

Looking for free resources takes a tremendous amount of time. You can spend hours searching for a tool, service or image that you don't have to pay for. But how much is your time worth and how does that compare with how much you're saving?

You usually get what you pay for. You might get a free download, but you aren't going to get support, nor will you get the same level of features that paying customers receive.

Sometimes the cost for substantially higher quality is nominal. A paid version might cost a few dollars but deliver the features you want that will help you function more efficiently and generate more revenue.

Here's the most important reason focusing on getting things for free will hurt you:

It projects the image of someone who isn't successful or professional. It says you're either not serious about your business or you're not very good at what you do.

There's a real cost to free. Do you want to pay it?

Today we observe

Earth Day

In God We Trust Day

National IT Service Provider Day

On this day in history

Notable events

In 1897, the *Forward*, formerly known as *The Jewish Daily Forward*, published its first issue.

In 1991, Intel released the lower cost i486SX microprocessor.

Births

Donald E. Graham, majority owner and chairman of Graham Holdings Company, former publisher of *The Washington Post*, 1945

Carl Linder Jr., American businessman and philanthropist, founder of American Financial Group, 1919

Randall L. Stephenson, retired American telecommunications executive (AT&T), 1960

Sam Altman, American entrepreneur, investor, and programmer; cofounder of Loopt, CEO of OpenAI, 1985

Deaths

Richard M. Nixon, 37th U.S. President, 1994

Thought for the day

"There are generations yet unborn, whose very lives will be shifted and shaped by the moves you make and the actions you take."

Andy Andrews

I pray that I will recognize when I should persevere and when I should change course.

Read:
Proverbs, Chapter 22

April 23

God is our refuge and strength, an ever-present help in trouble. Therefore we will not fear, though the earth give way and the mountains fall into the heart of the sea, though its waters roar and foam and the mountains quake with their surging. *(Psalm 46:1-3, NIV)*

Lord I Want to be a Christian

African-American Spiritual

Lord, I want to be a Christian
in my heart, in my heart.
Lord, I want to be a Christian in my heart.
In my heart, in my heart,
Lord, I want to be a Christian in my heart.

Lord, I want to be more loving
in my heart, in my heart.
Lord, I want to be more loving in my heart.
In my heart, in my heart,
Lord, I want to be more loving in my heart.

Lord, I want to be more holy
in my heart, in my heart.
Lord, I want to be more holy in my heart.
In my heart, in my heart,
Lord, I want to be more holy in my heart.

Lord, I want to be like Jesus
in my heart, in my heart.
Lord, I want to be like Jesus in my heart.
In my heart, in my heart,
Lord, I want to be like Jesus in my heart.

Thought for the day

"Prayer is a strategic alliance with God. It is a good faith contract, a spiritual handshake agreement. Only faith and patience are required on our part."

Cher & Bil Horton

I pray for supervisors and managers who must deliver bad news to their teams.

Read:
Proverbs, Chapter 23

Today we observe

World Book and Copyright Day
National Take a Chance Day
National Email Day

On this day in history

Notable events
In 1985, Coca-Cola introduced New Coke, the unofficial name of a reformulation of the soft drink. It was renamed Coke II in 1990 and discontinued in 2002.
In 2005, the first video was uploaded to YouTube; it featured Jawed Karim, YouTube's cofounder, at the San Diego Zoo.

Births
James Buchanan, 15th U.S. President, 1791
Chuck Feeney, American businessman and philanthropist, cofounder of Duty Free Shoppers Group, 1931

Deaths
Julius Freed, American banker, mechanical engineer, and amateur pigeon racer, notable for his involvement in the creation of the beverage Orange Julius, 1952
Cesar Chavez, American labor leader, civil rights activist, cofounder of the National Farm Workers Association (which became the United Farm Workers labor union), 1993
Henry W. Bloch, American businessman and philanthropist, cofounder of the tax-preparation company H&R Block, 2019

Don't dwell on what you've lost; find joy in what you have.

April 24

> **B**ut you will not even need to fight. Take your positions; then stand still and watch the Lord's victory. He is with you, O people of Judah and Jerusalem. Do not be afraid or discouraged. Go out against them tomorrow, for the Lord is with you!" *(2 Chronicles 20:17, NLT)*

Accept responsibility

Accepting responsibility for your life puts you (and God) in control of your life. You accept what you do right, and you accept what you do wrong. You don't blame others for what happens. This gives you the freedom to follow God's plan without distraction.

An important distinction about this concept is this: Accepting responsibility is not the same as accepting blame. Responsibility looks to the future; blame looks to the past.

Asset protection vs. tax planning

An asset protection plan will almost never save you money on taxes. Asset protection and tax planning are two completely separate issues.

If someone promises you that an asset protection plan—particularly one that includes offshore trusts and other entities—can reduce your taxes, get everything in writing and verify it with a trusted and knowledgeable independent resource, because chances are you are in the early stages of a scam.

Don't let greed overcome your common sense. Asset protection means protecting your assets from predators. Tax planning means taking advantage of legal and ethical ways to reduce your tax liability.

Grow your faith by serving and caring for others.

On this day in history

Notable events
- In 1833, Jacob Ebert and George Dulty patented the first soda fountain.
- In 1913, the Woolworth Building opened in New York City; at 792 feet, it was the world's tallest building at the time.

Births
- Robert Bailey Thomas, American schoolteacher, bookbinder, and bookseller; creator and publisher of the Old Farmer's Almanac, 1766
- Larry Tesler, American computer scientist (invented copy, cut, paste), 1945

Deaths
- Eugene Stoner, American machinist and firearms designer most associated with the development of the ArmaLite AR-15, 1997
- Estee Lauder, American businesswoman and entrepreneur, cofounder (with her husband, Joseph Lauter) of her eponymous cosmetics company, 2004
- Warren Avis, American entrepreneur, founder of Avis Car Rentals, 2007

Thought for the day

"Ideals are like stars; you will not succeed in touching them with your hands. But like the seafaring man on the desert of waters, you choose them as your guides, and following them you will reach your destiny."

Carl Schurz

I am thankful for being proof that God performs miracles.

Read:
Proverbs, Chapter 24

April 25

By a new and living way which He inaugurated for us through the veil, that is, His flesh, and since we have a great priest over the house of God, let us draw near with a sincere heart in full assurance of faith, having our hearts sprinkled from an evil conscience and our bodies washed with pure water. *(Hebrews 10:20-22, LSB)*

Conscious and subconscious

The conscious mind is rational. It receives and analyzes information, then determines if any action needs to be taken. The subconscious mind makes sure we think and behave in a manner consistent with what the conscious mind has accepted as true. When the conscious mind accepts a thought, it's immediately communicated to the subconscious, which takes action.

We're naturally wired with a wide range of automatic functions. For example, consider breathing. We didn't have to be taught how to breathe, and we don't have to think about it for it to happen. However, if we do think about it, we can deliberately change our breathing pattern—we can take long, slow breaths or short, quick pants. Most of the time, we're better off if we just breathe naturally.

Then there are the things we learn that, once learned, our subconscious minds will manage. When babies are learning to walk, they have to think about what they're doing. Eventually, walking becomes automatic and requires virtually no thought. When you learned to drive a car, you thought about every step of the process. But after you mastered that skill, it became automatic. There are thousands of things you have learned to do, both physically and mentally, that took effort at first, but now you do them without any thought at all.

If you take the time and effort to teach yourself to be positive, to expect success, it will become automatic. It may feel a little awkward at first, but it will eventually become comfortable and reflexive, and it will drive your subconscious mind to take the appropriate actions in any situation.

Today we observe

National Telephone Day

International Financial Independence Awareness Day

International Noise Awareness Day

On this day in history

Notable events

In 1954, Bell Telephone Laboratories announced the first solar battery made from silicon.

Births

Charles F. Dowd, American co-principal of the Temple Grove Ladies Seminary (now Skidmore College), first person to propose time zones for U.S. railways, 1825

Arthur Chevrolet, Swiss-American racecar driver, automobile manufacturer, and race car development pioneer, 1884

Deaths

William Beaumont, U.S. Army surgeon who became known as the father of gastric physiology for his research on human digestion on Alexis St. Martin, 1853

Thought for the day

"Never stop investing. Never stop improving. Never stop doing something new. Make it your goal to be better each and every day, in some small way. Remember the Japanese concept of Kaizen. Small daily improvements eventually result in huge advantages."

Bob Parsons

I pray that all of my pursuits be honorable and pleasing to God.

Read:
Proverbs, Chapter 25

April 26

> But don't just listen to God's word. You must do what it says. Otherwise, you are only fooling yourselves. For if you listen to the word and don't obey, it is like glancing at your face in a mirror. You see yourself, walk away, and forget what you look like. But if you look carefully into the perfect law that sets you free, and if you do what it says and don't forget what you heard, then God will bless you for doing it. *(James 1:22-25, NLT)*

Be an active listener

Listening is one of the most powerful skills we can develop, and it's useful in all areas of life. Active listening helps avoid misunderstandings and reduces the potential for conflict. Use these tips to improve your communication and make the other person feel valued.

Face the speaker and make eye contact. Eye contact lets the speaker know you're paying attention—but don't stare. Break eye contact every five seconds or so by looking at one eye, then the other, then the mouth, and then glancing away briefly. Keep your posture open and lean slightly forward to show your interest.

"Listen" to non-verbal cues. Pay attention to facial expressions, tone of voice, gestures, and overall body language—those things will often tell you as much about what the speaker wants to convey as their words.

Show that you're listening. Nod your head, make appropriate facial expressions (smiles, frowns, etc.), and make acknowledging sounds (yes, uh-huh). Don't fidget or check the time.

Don't interrupt. Interrupting sends the message that you're not really interested in what they have to say.

Ask questions. Relevant questions asked at an appropriate time demonstrate that you've been listening and help clarify what's been said.

Paraphrase and summarize. This shows that you've been paying attention and confirms that you understood what was said. It also gives the speaker the opportunity to correct and clarify as necessary.

Today we observe

Get Organized Day

World Intellectual Property Day

On this day in history

Notable events

In 1983, Dow Jones Industrial Average broke 1,200 for the first time.

Births

Frederick Law Olmsted, American landscape architect (the father of American landscape design) and writer, 1822

James Rouse, American businessman (The Rouse Company), real estate development, urban planner, philanthropist, 1914

Preston Robert Tisch, American businessman, chairman and part owner of Loews Corporation, NFL team owner, 1926

Ted Stanley, American entrepreneur and philanthropist, cofounder of the Danbury Mint, 1931

Larry H. Miller, American entrepreneur (owner of more than 60 automotive dealerships and a variety of other ventures), philanthropist, and owner of NBA's Utah Jazz, 1944

Thought for the day

"It's not who you are that holds you back. It's who you think you're not."

Denis Waitley

I pray for peace as I wait through uncertain times.

Read:
Proverbs, Chapter 26

April 27

When the centurion and those with him who were guarding Jesus saw the earthquake and all that had happened, they were terrified, and exclaimed, "Surely he was the Son of God!" *(Matthew 27:54, NIV)*

Establish and honor quiet time

The world is noisier and more distracting than ever—and our need for quiet time is greater than ever. Workplace quiet time is a block of time with no physical or digital interruptions, a time when you can focus on your work without distractions that decrease productivity and increase the risk of error.

Companies that implement quiet time report almost immediate results in improved performance, reduced stress, increased creativity, sharper thinking, and greater engagement.

To build a culture that honors quiet time, begin with a dialog. Ask your team members the following questions and use the answers as a guideline for action. Make sure everyone, including the leader, participates.

How do I create noise and cause distractions for others? This isn't potentially punitive; it should be an honest self-examination to see what behaviors can be changed.

What do I find most distracting and disrupting? Emphasize that you don't want anyone casting blame; you're simply seeking to identify issues.

How can I help create quiet time others need? Encourage everyone to share ideas that can be adopted as group norms, such as periods of time without email or meetings, or when phones are put away, or when interruptions are not allowed.

I am thankful for the competitors who drive me to deliver higher quality.

Read:
Proverbs, Chapter 27

Today we observe

World Design Day

On this day in history

Notable events

In 1965, R. C. Duncan patented the Pampers brand disposable diaper.

In 2005, the Airbus A380, the world's largest passenger airliner, completed its first flight.

Births

Samuel Morse, American inventor and painter, inventor of a single-wire telegraph system and co-inventor of Morse code, 1791

Ulysses S. Grant, 18th U.S. President, 1822

Wallace Hume Carothers, American chemist, inventor (nylon), and leader of organic chemistry at DuPont, 1896

Jim Justice, American businessman (built a business empire with 94 companies) and politician, 1951

Deaths

Alfred E. Hunt, American metallurgist and industrialist, founder of the company that would eventually become Alcoa, 1899

Ruth Handler, American businesswoman and inventor (Barbie doll); cofounder of toy manufacturer Mattel, founder of Ruthton Corp., which designed and manufactured prosthetic breasts for women who had undergone mastectomies, 2002

Thought for the day

"You may think that taking a detour in life is a waste of time and energy, but you can also see the detour as a means of learning more about who you are and where you are heading in your life. Being off the beaten path may be disorienting and confusing at times, yet it challenges your creative spirit to discover new and different ways to get back home, into your heart; for your heart is your real home."

Andreas Moritz

April 28

Even fools are thought wise when they keep silent; with their mouths shut, they seem intelligent. *(Proverbs 17:28, NLT)*

Faith in the marketplace

When Jennifer O'Neal-Rojas decided to open a bookstore, she wanted to do more than sell books. "We wanted it to be a way to reflect God's light somehow," says the owner/manager of Walls of Books Oviedo (Oviedo, Florida). "Having your own business can be tough. If we don't have a higher purpose, it's kind of pointless. If whoever walks through the door can somehow feel God's love, even if they don't know who God is, then we're serving that purpose."

How O'Neal-Rojas shares God's love:

- The store's background music comes from Christian radio stations. Secular music is never played.
- The chalkboard sign in front of the store always includes Bible verses. It's a two-sided board; O'Neal-Rojas puts a different verse on each side. Customers often comment on the scripture and even take pictures of the sign.
- Bible tracts are left on a small table in the restroom and at the checkout counter. O'Neal-Rojas says the ones in the restroom are rarely taken, but they are moved and sometimes creased, so she knows they're being seen.
- A prayer request board lets customers post their concerns. When O'Neal-Rojas passes the board during the day, she pauses for a moment of prayer, and she often sees others doing the same.
- Her favorite Bible verse is included in her email signature block. The complete text of John 1:1 is written out below her company logo and shows up in every email she sends.
- Conversations about faith are welcome and encouraged. Whether it's between employees or in exchanges with customers, mentions of faith are never shut down.

Today we observe

Biological Clock Day
National Cubicle Day
Occupational Safety & Health Day
Workers Memorial Day

On this day in history

Notable events

In 1855, the first veterinary college in the U.S. was incorporated in Boston.

In 1967, behind schedule with deliveries of the DC-8 and DC-9 and close the bankruptcy, the Douglas Aircraft Company agreed to merge with the McDonnell Aircraft Corporation to form McDonnell Douglas.

Births

James Monroe, 5th U.S. President, 1758
Jessica Alba, American actress and businesswoman, cofounder of The Honest Company, Inc., 1981

Deaths

Arthur Leonard Schawlow, American physicist and co-inventor of the laser, 1999

Thought for the day

"Real intelligence is a creative use of knowledge, not merely an accumulation of facts. The slow thinker who can finally come up with an idea of his own is more important to the world than a walking encyclopedia who hasn't learned how to use information productively."

D. Kenneth Winebrenner

I pray that I never miss an opportunity to share my faith.

Read:
Proverbs, Chapter 28

April 29

> ❝He will wipe every tear from their eyes. There will be no more death' or mourning or crying or pain, for the old order of things has passed away." *(Revelation 21:4, NIV)*

Don't worry

Worry is fear caused by indecision and results in negative goal-setting. When you worry, you focus on what you *don't* want to happen and then turn that into a self-fulfilling prophecy because that's what you're thinking about and visualizing. It's been said that worrying is just praying for the wrong thing to happen. Here's how to deal with worry:

1. Clearly define what you are worried about. If you can figure out what you're really worried about, it will be easier to deal with the issue. Often, just the process of defining what you're worried about will resolve the situation.

2. Articulate what the worst possible outcome of the situation could be. In most cases, you'll realize that whatever the worst possible outcome is, it's not as bad as you thought. More importantly, the worst is not guaranteed to happen. Chances are, even if things don't go well, they won't be as bad as the worst possible outcome.

3. Resolve to accept that worst-case scenario if it should occur. Know what you'll do to deal with the situation if it happens—then stop thinking about it until and unless you need to.

4. Do everything possible to make sure that the worst-case scenario does not happen. This circles back to step one, because if you know what you're worried about, you can take the necessary steps to prevent it from happening.

Once you make a decision, don't worry—simply focus on making whatever you have decided a success. Purposeful action is the best antidote to worry.

Read: Proverbs, Chapter 29

Today we observe
National Supply Chain Day

On this day in history

Notable events
In 2004, the last Oldsmobile came off the assembly line at the Lansing Car Assembly plant in Michigan, signaling the end of the 106-year-old automotive brand.

Births
John Tyler, 10th U.S. President, 1790
William Randolph Hearst, Sr., American businessman, newspaper publisher, and politician, 1863
Harry Payne Whitney, American businessman and thoroughbred horse breeder, 1872
Jake Burton Carpenter, American snowboarder and inventor, founder of Burton Snowboards, 1954
Marc Randolph, American tech entrepreneur, author, speaker, cofounder and first CEO of Netflix, 1958

Deaths
Wallace Hume Carothers, American chemist, inventor (nylon), and leader of organic chemistry at DuPont, 1937
Bob Akin, American business executive, journalist, and champion sports car racing driver, 2002
Jean Nidetch, American businesswoman, entrepreneur, founder of Weight Watchers, 2015

Thought for the day

"It's not just other people we need to forgive. We also need to forgive ourselves. For all the things we didn't do. All the things we should have done."

Mitch Albom

I pray to be the example others should and will want to follow.

April 30

Do not quench the Spirit. Do not treat prophecies with contempt but test them all; hold on to what is good, reject every kind of evil. *(1 Thessalonians 5:19-22, NIV)*

How do you name your files?

A file naming protocol is the system you use for naming your digital files so they can quickly, easily, and accurately be identified and revisions can be tracked and preserved.

Good reasons for having a consistent file naming protocol:

Find your own files and know what they are. Have you ever spent time trying to locate a file because you couldn't remember what you named it or where you put it? Or seen a file and didn't know what it was? A good file naming protocol puts an end to that frustration.

Make sure others recognize your files. Let recipients of your files know what they contain without having to open them.

Track revisions and input from multiple sources. If you're collaborating with a team or your documents are going through a series of reviews from different people, a file naming protocol followed by everyone helps you keep track of comments, notes, and changes.

Your file naming protocol might vary depending on the nature of the file and how it will be used and distributed. Consider including:

- An organization identification (if the file will be distributed externally)
- Author (last name or initials is usually sufficient)
- Category (the type of document, such as blog, report, web copy, etc.)
- Subject (what the file is about)
- Draft or version number and/or date (so people know what the most recent incarnation is)
- Status designation (such as draft or final)

Explain the file naming system to everyone on the team, and remind them that they should update the file name when they change the file content.

Today we observe

National Prepareathon Day

On this day in history

Notable events

In 1904, the ice cream cone (introduced by Ernest A. Hamwi) made its debut at the St. Louis World's Fair. This was independent of the ice cream cone invented and patented in 1903 by Italo Marchiony in New York City.

In 1952, Mr. Potato Head became the first toy advertised on television.

In 1993, the World Wide Web (WWW) launched in the public domain.

Births

Roger L. Easton, American physicist and state representative who was the principal inventor and designer of the global positioning system (GPS), 1921

Deaths

George Sperti, American inventor (Preparation H, Sperti Ultraviolet Lamp, Aspercreme), 1991

Don't take criticism from someone you wouldn't go to for advice.

Thought for the day

"I would rather the man who presents something for my consideration subject me to a zephyr of truth and a gentle breeze of responsibility rather than blow me down with a curtain of hot wind."

Grover Cleveland

———— ————

I pray that when I am in pain, I let God be close to me instead of shutting him out.

Read:
Proverbs, Chapter 30

Christian Business Almanac

May

May is the fifth month of the Gregorian calendar. The ancient Greeks named this month after the goddess Maia, who was revered for her association with growth and fertility.

May birthstone
Emerald

May flower
Lily of the Valley

May is ...

- Building Safety Month
- Clean Air Month
- Exercise is Medicine Month
- Global Employee Health and Fitness Month
- Home Schooling Awareness Month
- International Business Image Improvement Month
- International Civility Awareness Month
- International Internal Audit Awareness Month
- Labor History Month
- Mental Health Awareness Month
- Motorcycle Safety Awareness Month
- National Bicycle Safety Month
- National Foster Care Month
- National Historic Preservation Month
- National Military Appreciation Month
- National Revise Your Work Schedule Month
- Small Business Month
- Teen CEO Month
- Teen Pregnancy Prevention Month
- World Trade Month

Mark your calendar for these May holidays and observances

First Thursday in May	National Day of Prayer
First Wednesday in May	National Skilled Trades Day
First Thursday in May	World Password Day
Second Wednesday in May	National Receptionists Day
Second Wednesday in May	National Night Shift Workers Day
Friday before Mother's Day	Child Care Provider Day
Friday before Mother's Day	National Military Spouse Appreciation Day
Second Sunday in May	Mother's Day
Saturday before Mother's Day	National Birth Mother's Day
The calendar week in which May 15 falls	National Police Week
Third Monday in May	Supply Chain Professionals Day
Third Wednesday in May	National Employee Health and Fitness Day
Third Friday in May	National Bike to Work Day
Third Friday in May	Virtual Assistants Day
Last Friday in May	National Heat Awareness Day
Last Monday in May	Memorial Day

Fun Facts about May

May is one of seven months with 31 days.

In any given year, no month ever begins or ends on the same day of the week as May does.

May 1

For as high as the heavens are above the earth, so great is his love for those who fear him; as far as the east is from the west, so far has he removed our transgressions from us. *(Psalm 103:11-12, NIV)*

Create a joyful workplace

There is tremendous value in a joyful workplace, including reduced turnover and increased productivity. Joyful, loyal employees create happy, loyal customers. And it all flows down to the bottom line in the form of greater profits.

You can create a joyful company whether you are the owner, a manager or even an entry-level employee. Joy is contagious. If you are joyful, if you are intentional about creating a joyful environment, the people around you will become joyful.

Some strategies you can apply to your business and incorporate into your culture include:

Live in the moment. Sometimes we get so focused on regretting the past and worrying about the future that we don't deal with the here and now. Savor living in the moment.

Practice forgiveness. Forgive employees, coworkers and competitors. Forgive yourself and encourage those you work with to forgive themselves.

Learn to see problems as gifts. Winston Churchill said, "The pessimist sees difficulty in every opportunity. The optimist sees the opportunity in every difficulty." Be an optimist. Look at the situation and ask: How can I make this work for me?

When you are intentional about creating joy for yourself and others, you'll see a ripple effect. One small act can reach an infinite number of people.

I pray for all the saints in my life.

Read:
Proverbs, Chapter 1

Today we observe
May Day
Law Day
Executive Coaching Day
CSS Reboot Day
Frequent Flyer Day
National Loyalty Day

On this day in history

Notable events

- In 1926, Ford Motor Company became one of the first U.S. companies to adopt a five-day, forty-hour week for workers in its automotive factories; the policy was extended to office workers the following August.
- In 1981, Radio Shack released Model III TRSDOS 1.3.
- In 1989, Disney's MGM Studio theme park opened to the public.
- In 2020, Tweets by Elon Musk saying Tesla's share price was too high wiped $14 billion off the carmaker's value.
- In 2023, Geoffrey Hinton, "the Godfather of AI," resigned from Google to speak out about the dangers of AI.

Births

- Rufus Porter, American painter, inventor, and founder of *Scientific American* magazine, 1792
- Oliver W. Hill, American civil rights attorney who helped end the "separate but equal" doctrine, 1907

Deaths

- T.R.M. Howard, American civil rights leader, entrepreneur (founded an insurance company, restaurant, hospital, construction firm, and farm), and surgeon, 1976

Thought for the day

"To accomplish great things, we must not only act, but also dream; not only plan, but also believe."

Anatole France

May 2

> If it is possible, as far as it depends on you, live at peace with everyone. Do not take revenge, my dear friends, but leave room for God's wrath, for it is written: "It is mine to avenge; I will repay," says the Lord. *(Romans 12:18-19, NIV)*

The difference between leadership and guidance

There is a distinction between leadership and guidance. We are called to lead, not guide. God guides.

Your king will lead you; the Lord himself will guide you. (Micah 2:13, NLT)

We live in a culture that values leaders and encourages the development of leadership skills. Strong leaders inspire people to act together toward achieving a common goal. Leaders are typically empathetic, strategic, and have the ability to persuade others.

God calls us to lead. He does not call us to guide. He guides.

While leaders may organize and direct, a guide shows us the way. While leaders get us enthused about the goal and about working together, a guide keeps us on the right path.

Whether you are a leader or a follower, let God guide you.

Negotiation tip

You're doing the negotiation dance and you're down to the lowest price you can accept, but the prospect is still haggling. Try sweetening the deal with a little humor.

Say something like, "My final offer is $2,000 and I'll throw in my coffee cup." Or some other silly item.

It's not about the bonus, it's about being playful and breaking the tension. And it just might be what it takes to close the deal.

Read:
Proverbs, Chapter 2

Today we observe

National Life Insurance Day

On this day in history

Notable events
- In 1885, the first issue of *Good Housekeeping* magazine was published.
- In 1887, Hannibal Goodwin patented celluloid photographic film.
- In 1981, Radio Shack re-released Model III TRSDOS 1.3 with two fixes.
- In 2023, Writers Guild of America voted to strike over pay and industry changes, bringing television production to a halt.

Births
- Elijah McCoy, Canadian-American engineer and inventor (lubrication systems for steam engines); the popular expression "the real McCoy" has been attributed to his oil-drip cup invention, 1844
- Ted Dabney, American electrical engineer and cofounder of Atari, Inc., 1937

Deaths
- William Mouton Marston (also known by the pen name Charles Moulton), American psychologist, co-inventor of an early prototype of the polygraph, self-help author, comic book writer (creator of the character Wonder Woman), 1947

Thought for the day

"Give me a stock clerk with a goal and I'll give you a man who will make history. Give me a man with no goals and I'll give you a stock clerk."

— *J.C. Penney*

I am grateful because I know that with Jesus, I am enough.

May 3

You must have the same attitude that Christ Jesus had. Though he was God, he did not think of equality with God as something to cling to. Instead, he gave up his divine privileges; he took the humble position of a slave and was born as a human being. When he appeared in human form, he humbled himself in obedience to God and died a criminal's death on a cross. *(Philippians 2:5-8, NLT)*

Before you buy online

Before you make a purchase from a website, read the terms and conditions and policies and procedures. Links to these pages are often found in the small print at the bottom of a website. The content on those pages can be interesting and important.

Those pages have been known to include statements about waiving legal rights if you buy from the website or non-disparagement provisions to stop customers from sharing negative product reviews.

But who has the time or inclination to read pages of legal jargon before you make a purchase? An alternative is to use your browser's find feature and search on words like arbitration, auto shipment (or just auto), comments, waive, legal, refund, and guarantee. Words like these can highlight areas of these pages that might raise some red flags. It's a quick and easy way to check out an online seller before you buy.

Treat decisions like tasks

We make thousands of decisions every day. Most are small without significant consequences—coffee or tea, soup or salad—but some are critical with the potential for major consequences.

Treat those important decisions like tasks. Put them on your to-do list. Allot the required amount of time to do necessary research and consultation and give it the same priority you would a meeting or appointment. Making important decisions is an important process. To achieve the best outcome, give it the respect it deserves.

Today we observe
National Public Radio Day
National Textile Day
Wordsmith Day
World Press Freedom Day

On this day in history

Notable events
- In 1901, the Great Jacksonville (Florida) Fire destroyed 2,368 buildings over 146 city blocks; seven people died.
- In 1973, the Sears Tower (now Willis Tower) in Chicago was topped out.
- In 1999, the Dow Jones Industrial Average closed above 11,000 (11,014.70) for the first time in its history.
- In 2020, investor Warren Buffett dumped his holdings in four major U.S. airlines, reflecting an increasingly bleak outlook for the industry.

Births
- David Koch, American businessman (Koch Industries), political activist, philanthropist, and chemical engineer, 1940
- Ron Popeil, American inventor and marketing personality who popularized the phrase, "But wait, there's more!", 1935

Thought for the day

"May my testimony be a source of strength, encouragement and hope as I continue to serve in the Kingdom of God."
Mark Goldstein

I pray for clarity.

Read:
Proverbs, Chapter 3

May 4

> "Bring all the tithes into the storehouse so there will be enough food in my Temple. If you do," says the Lord of Heaven's Armies, "I will open the windows of heaven for you. I will pour out a blessing so great you won't have enough room to take it in! Try it! Put me to the test! *(Malachi 3:10, NLT)*

Meeting management

Meetings can be one of the biggest time wasters in the business or nonprofit worlds. Use these tips to make yours productive:

Confirm that the meeting is necessary. Do you really need to have this meeting or can it be handled in another way, such as an email or video?

Be punctual. If you're leading the meeting, start it on time. If you're attending, be there on time.

Create and follow an agenda. Make it specific. Share it in advance with the participants. If someone brings up something that isn't on the agenda, save it for another time.

Delegate the preparation. Get the team involved by delegating various elements of preparing for the meeting.

Be sure everything is working. Check all your tech equipment in advance. If you're making a presentation, practice it ahead of time so it goes smoothly.

End with a call to action. Be sure participants know what they're supposed to do next.

Today we observe

Anti-Bullying Day

World Give Day

On this day in history

Notable events

In 1780, the American Academy of Arts & Sciences was founded.

Births

Horace Mann, American education reformer, abolitionist, and politician, 1796

Frank Conrad, American electrical engineer and inventor (holder of more than 200 patents), best known for radio development, including his work as a pioneer broadcaster, 1874

W. Clement Stone, American businessman, philanthropist, self-help book author, 1902

Maurice R. Greenberg, American business executive and former chairman and CEO of American International Group (AIG), 1925

Deaths

George T. Delacorte, Jr., American magazine publisher, founder of Dell Publishing, and philanthropist, 1991

Don Shula, American professional football player and coach, entrepreneur, 2020

Thought for the day

"Bowmen bend their bows when they wish to shoot: unbrace them when the shooting is over. Were they kept always strung they would break and fail the archer in time of need. So it is with men. If they give themselves constantly to serious work, and never indulge awhile in pastime or sport, they lose their senses and become mad."

Herodotus

Make a list of the things that make you happy.
Make a list of the things you do every day.
Compare the lists.
Adjust accordingly.

I am grateful for all the times I have been blessed by the strength and faith of other believers.

Read:
Proverbs, Chapter 4

May 5

A re not five sparrows sold for two pennies? Yet not one of them is forgotten by God. Indeed, the very hairs of your head are all numbered. Don't be afraid; you are worth more than many sparrows. *(Luke 12:6-7, NIV)*

Prevent cyberattacks

Cyberattacks cost the U.S. economy billions of dollars a year and pose a threat for individuals and organizations. These best practices can help prevent cyberattacks.

Train your team. Train all employees on basic internet usage best practices.

Secure your networks. Safeguard your internet connection by encrypting information and using a firewall. If you have a Wi-Fi network, make sure it is secure and hidden.

Use antivirus software and keep all software updated. Make sure all of your business' computers are equipped with antivirus software and are updated regularly. Update software associated with operating systems, web browsers, and other applications to help secure your entire infrastructure.

Enable Multi-Factor Authentication (MFA). MFA is a mechanism to verify an individual's identity by requiring them to provide more than just a typical username and password.

Monitor and manage Cloud Service Provider (CSP) accounts. Consider using a CSP to host your organization's information, applications, and collaboration services, especially if you're utilizing a hybrid work structure. Software-as-a-Service (SaaS) providers for email and workplace productivity can help secure data being processed.

Secure, protect, and back up sensitive data. Use secure payment processing systems; control physical access to your business computers; back up your data; and control data access.

I pray that my business skills help guide my faith journey.

Today we observe
Cinco De Mayo
National Silence the Shame Day
World Hand Hygiene Day

On this day in history

Notable events

In 1936, Edward A. Ravenscroft received a patent for a screw-on bottle cap with a pour lip.

In 1961, astronaut Alan Shepard Jr. became the first American in space; the Freedom 7 mission flight lasted 15 minutes, 28 seconds.

In 1986, Rock and Roll Hall of Fame Foundation announced Cleveland, Ohio, as the site of the Rock and Roll Hall of Fame Museum.

In 2003, LinkedIn, the business and employment-focused social media platform, was launched.

Births

John Batterson Stetson, American hat manufacturer, philanthropist, inventor of the cowboy hat, founder of John B. Stetson Company, 1830

Arthur Leonard Schawlow, American physicist and co-inventor of the laser, 1921

Deaths

Clifton Hillegass, creator and publisher of CliffsNotes, 2001

Irv Robbins, Canadian-born American businessman, cofounder of the Baskin-Robbins ice cream parlor chain, 2008

Thought for the day

"Be creative. Use unconventional thinking. And have the guts to carry it out."
Lee Iaccoca

Read:
Proverbs, Chapter 5

May 6

But seek first His kingdom and His righteousness, and all these things will be provided to you. "So do not worry about tomorrow; for tomorrow will worry about itself. Each day has enough trouble of its own. (*Matthew 6:33–34, NASB*)

Give thanks to God

Thank God for all the good things you have and the bad things you don't.

Though it seems trite and clichéd, you can always find something to be thankful for having and something to be thankful for not having—even when it seems like everything is going wrong in your life.

Never minimize your troubles. Just because someone has it worse than you doesn't mean you don't have some serious and real problems to deal with. But you still can find some things to be thankful for.

The easiest way to give thanks is to create a gratitude list. Review it and add something to it every day. If you can't think of anything new to add, repeat something. Going through your gratitude list every day delivers two important benefits: One, it causes you to pause and thank God and two, it reminds you of how much you have to be grateful for even when you're dealing with challenges.

While it's important to count your own blessings every day, resist the urge to count the blessings of others. That only leads to envy, and envy will keep you from having a joyful day. Pray for others but let them be responsible for keeping track of what they're thankful for. Remember, too, that everyone has their own perspective about what's going on in their lives. What is a blessing to one person might not be to someone else. So let others count their own blessings; they know far better than you what those blessings are.

I am grateful for everything—the good and the bad—that has brought me to where I am today.

Today we observe

National Tourist Appreciation Day

On this day in history

Notable events

In 1835, the first issue of the *New York Herald* was published.

In 1837, U.S. blacksmith John Deere created the first steel plow.

In 1851, Dr. John Gorrie patented a refrigeration machine.

In 1851, Linus Yale, Jr., patented the Yale cylinder lock.

Births

Amadeo Giannini, American banker, entrepreneur, financier, founder of the Bank of Italy which became Bank of America; credited as the inventor of many modern banking practices, 1870

Daniel Frank Gerber, American baby food manufacturer, 1898

John P. Allen, systems ecologist, engineer, metallurgist, inventor and director of research of Biosphere 2, 1929

Deaths

B. C. Forbes, Scottish-American financial journalist and author, founder of *Forbes* magazine, 1954

Donald Pritzker, American entrepreneur, businessman, president of Hyatt, 1972

Thought for the day

"It is inevitable that some defeat will enter even the most victorious life. The human spirit is never finished when it is defeated...it is finished when it surrenders."

Ben Stein

Read:
Proverbs, Chapter 6

May 7

A wise son brings joy to his father, but a foolish man despises his mother.
(Proverbs 15:20, NIV)

Put your work into perspective

In *Work as Worship: How Your Labor Becomes Your Legacy*, Mark Goldstein says,

"We all are in business, doing something. But that isn't the reason we were put on this planet. It's the foundation to allow us to make money, to buy houses, food, cars—to live. But that's just the temporal, that's how you exist. The real reason we're here is to be in a relationship with others, to connect God and man through being who we are in what we do.

"We shouldn't spend our time in jobs that we don't enjoy. We should choose work that excites us, that we are passionate about. We shouldn't choose a career because somebody else said we should do that or because it's expected of us. You should do what will make you happy, what will make you feel fulfilled, that will let you use the gifts God gave you."

Trust yourself

If you have an idea for a business, don't let other people's opinions and thoughts on the matter drown out your own voice. Just because somebody thinks your idea is wacky doesn't mean it is. Trust in yourself and your dream.

The worst that can happen is you'll spend some money (a few hundred or thousand, depending on what you do), and it goes nowhere. The best that can happen is that you'll be successful beyond your wildest dreams. Put God in charge and surround yourself with people who get it. They're out there, they understand, they're excited, and they'll support you.

I pray to be a beacon for those who need what I can give.

Today we observe

National Barrier Awareness Day

National Packaging Design Day

On this day in history

Notable events

In 1847, the American Medical Association was founded.

In 1998, Mercedes-Benz bought Chrysler for $40 billion and formed DaimlerChrysler in the then-largest industrial merger in history.

Births

Edwin H. Land, American scientist and inventor, best known as the cofounder of the Polaroid Corporation, 1909

Deaths

Alfred Gwynne Vanderbilt, American businessman and member of the Vanderbilt family, died in the sinking of the RMS *Lusitania*, 1915

John Henry Patterson, American industrialist and founder of National Cash Register Company (NCR), known for pioneering business practices such as constructing the first "daylight factory" buildings with floor-to-ceiling windows that let in light and fresh air, 1922

Ernest Winston Angley, American Christian evangelist, author, and television station owner, 2021

Thought for the day

"We all have our own life to pursue, our own kind of dream to be weaving, and we all have the power to make wishes come true, as long as we keep believing."

Louisa May Alcott

Read:
Proverbs, Chapter 7

May 8

Therefore, my dear brothers and sisters, stand firm. Let nothing move you. Always give yourselves fully to the work of the Lord, because you know that your labor in the Lord is not in vain. *(1 Corinthians 15:58, NIV)*

Cultivating creativity

We are all naturally creative, but for our creativity to be effective, it must be cultivated. We must choose to prioritize developing our creativity.

Creativity can be maximized by the structure you put around it. When you set up structures and processes in your life for the routine things, you make room for the ah-ha moments.

The creative process is chaotic. It's non-linear and non-structured. Be prepared for that—and be ready to grab the ideas when they happen.

Creativity is often a byproduct of what happens when we relate to each other, when we collaborate and expose each other to new ideas. That can happen by just slowing down and having a cup of coffee with someone, or saying, "How are you?" and really listening to the answer.

Creativity doesn't necessarily mean being a great artist. In our information economy, the value and quality of our ideas is gold, but we must be able to capture and convey them.

Thought for the day

"A man begins cutting his wisdom teeth the first time he bites off more than he can chew."

Herb Caen

I pray for confidence to know that I am good enough.

Read:
Proverbs, Chapter 8

Today we observe
Free Trade Day

On this day in history

Notable events

In 1901, the first stock market crash on the New York Stock Exchange occurred (Panic of 1901).

In 1912, film and television production and distribution studio Paramount Pictures was founded.

In 1959, Little Caesars Pizza was founded by Mike and Marian Ilitch in Garden City, Michigan.

In 1979, Radio Shack released TRSDOS 2.3.

Births

William Henry Vanderbilt, American railroad magnate and philanthropist who nearly doubled the Vanderbilt family fortune bequeathed to him by his father, Cornelius, 1821

Harry S. Truman, 33rd U.S. President, 1884

Washington Duke, an American tobacco industrialist who began his career as a subsistence farmer, namesake of Duke University, founder of W. Duke, Sons & Co., a tobacco manufacturer that would later be merged with other companies to form American Tobacco Company, 1905

John C. Bogle, American investor, business magnate, and philanthropist; founder and chief executive of The Vanguard Group, 1929

Jerry Moss, American recording executive, cofounder of A&M Records, 1935

Deaths

Frank L. Gillespie, American businessman, founder of Supreme Life Insurance Company, 1925

Harry Gordon Selfridge, American retail magnate, founder of London-based department store Selfridges, 1947

Roger L. Easton, American physicist and state representative who was the principal inventor and designer of the global positioning system (GPS), 2014

May 9

For this reason we also, from the day we heard about you, have not ceased praying for you and asking God to fill you with the knowledge of his will in all spiritual wisdom and understanding, *(Colossians 1:9, NET)*

Non-standard punctuation

Punctuation is important. It's the guideline readers need to accurately understand written content. Standard punctuation marks include the comma, period, question mark, exclamation point, colon, semicolon, quotation marks, and so on. But there are some non-standard punctuation marks you'll want to understand and maybe even use.

Here's a small sample:

The interrobang, invented by Martin Speckter, combines an exclamation point with a question mark to replace multiple punctuation marks when the writer wants to convey shock and confusion at the same time.

The SarcMark™, invented by Douglas and Paul Sak, is an open circle with a dot in it used to convey sarcasm.

The certitude point, invented by Herve Bazin, is an exclamation point with a line through it used to express total conviction in what you've written.

And then there's the doubt point, also invented by Herve Bazin, which is a blend of the letter Z and a question mark to show skepticism and disbelief.

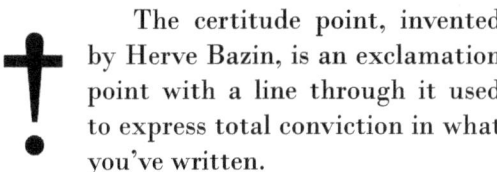

While you're waiting for God to open the door,
praise him in the hallway.

Read:
Proverbs, Chapter 9

Today we observe
Tear the Tags Off the Mattress Day

On this day in history
Notable events
- In 1914, U.S. President Woodrow Wilson proclaimed Mother's Day.
- In 2005, the liberal commentary website *The Huffington Post* was launched.

Births
- William Mouton Marston (also known by the pen name Charles Moulton), American psychologist, coinventor of an early prototype of the polygraph, self-help author, comic book writer (creator of the character Wonder Woman), 1893
- Henry J. Kaiser, American industrialist knows as the father of modern American shipbuilding, 1882

Deaths
- C. W. Post, American innovator, breakfast and cereal foods manufacturer, and pioneer in the prepared-food industry, founder of what is now Post Consumer Brands, 1914
- Cyrus S. Eaton, Canadian-American investment banker, businessman, and philanthropist, known for his occasionally ruthless financial manipulations and his passion for world peace, 1979
- Vidal Sassoon, British-American hairstylist, businessman, and philanthropist, 2012

Thought for the day
"Discipline is choosing between what you want now and what you want most."
Abraham Lincoln

I am grateful for God's faithfulness even when I don't understand.

May 10

> Remember the Lord your God. He is the one who gives you power to be successful, in order to fulfill the covenant he confirmed to your ancestors with an oath. *(Deuteronomy 8:18, NLT)*

Dealing with extortion

It's the stuff movies are made of: bomb threats, product tampering, sabotage, and kidnapping. You might think it will never happen to you because you're a small, relatively obscure company, but that could actually be what makes you an attractive target to an extortionist.

The first step in protecting your company from various forms of corporate terrorism is to understand that it can, indeed, happen to you. Possible scenarios include ransomware attacks that hold your electronic files hostage; an unhappy employee who threatens to release company secrets or plants a virus in your IT system; threats from a stranger or a fanatic to injure people or damage property if a ransom is not paid; product tampering; and threats to generate negative publicity if the company fails to take specific actions.

The next step is to develop a crisis management plan. Though you certainly can't plan for all contingencies, think in advance about what steps you'll take so you can react calmly and with a sense of purpose to resolve a situation. Decide who will be in charge of what, and plan for communicating with law enforcement, the media, your customers, and your employees. It's a good idea to meet with a crisis management consultant before anything happens. Establishing such a relationship in advance may cost a small amount of time and money, but it will be invaluable if a real need arises.

Consider, too, how you will handle the costs associated with an incident. Some of the expenses may be covered under your regular business insurance, or you may want to talk to your insurance agent about special policies.

Today we observe
National Golf Day
National Ship via Rail Day
National Small Business Day

On this day in history

Notable events

In 1869, the golden spike (a ceremonial 17.6-karat gold final spike) was driven by Leland Stanford at Promontory Summit, Utah Territory, to join the rails of the first transcontinental railroad across the U.S.

In 2019, Uber Technologies, Inc., became a public company via an IPO.

Births

David O. Selznick, American film producer, screenwriter, and film studio executive, 1902

Deaths

John Wesley Hyatt, American entrepreneur (founder of Hyatt Roller Bearing company), inventor (mainly known for simplifying the production of celluloid), holder of more than 200 patents, 1920

Carroll Shelby, American automotive designer, racing driver, and entrepreneur, 2012

Thought for the day

"I've been absolutely terrified every moment of my life and I've never let it keep me from doing a single thing that I wanted to do."

Georgia O'Keeffe

I pray for mothers and those who stand in the stead of mothers.

Read:
Proverbs, Chapter 10

May 11

I treasure your word in my heart, so that I may not sin against you.
(Psalm 119:11, NRSVue)

Do your content file names work for you?

If your content marketing strategy includes distributing information in digital format, the names of those files can be as much a marketing tool as the information itself.

When you're creating digital products to use as content marketing tools, use whatever internal file naming system works while the work is in progress. Once the piece is final and you're ready to distribute it, rename the file with your audience in mind.

A good file name will clearly identify the content (the title) and creator (either an individual or company), and won't include any work progress indicators (such as "draft" or "final").

Let's say you're offering an ebook, research paper or infographic as an incentive for people to subscribe to your mailing list. They sign up and download the file, which they save somewhere on their computer. Then later (hours, days or longer), they want to take a look at your information again. Will they be able to find it by the file name? Or suppose they open the folder your file is in looking for something else—will they be reminded of you when they see your file?

You work hard to create great content, so take the final step of renaming your content marketing files in a way that lets the user know what those files contain and where they came from.

I am grateful for the people in my life who help me keep it all together.

Read:
Proverbs, Chapter 11

Today we observe
World Ego Awareness Day

On this day in history

Notable events
In 1752, the first U.S. fire insurance policy was issued in Philadelphia.
In 1947, BF Goodrich announced the development of the tubeless tire.
In 1951, American engineer Jay Forrester applied for a patent for computer core memory.

Births
Robert E. Gross, American businessman, investor, president of Lockheed Aircraft Corporation (1934-1956), 1897
Ewart Abner, American record company executive, part owner and general manager of Vee-Jay Records, president of Motown Records (1973-1975), 1923
William P. Carey, American businessman and philanthropist, founder of W.P. Carey & Co., 1930

Deaths
John D. Rockefeller, Jr., American businessman, financier, and philanthropist, 1960

Thought for the day

"I don't need a friend who changes when I change and who nods when I nod; my shadow does that much better."
Plutarch

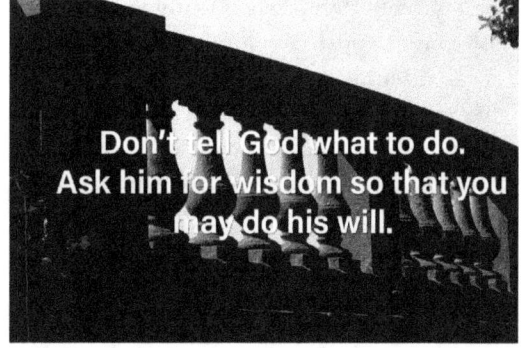

May 12

"Honor your father and mother"—this is the first commandment with a promise—"so that it may be well with you and you may live long on the earth." *(Ephesians 6:2-3, NRSVue)*

Techniques for rapid change

If you're not satisfied with your present circumstances, the only way to make them different is through change. And yet it is human nature to resist change. We prefer the familiar and comfortable to the unknown, even when the familiar and comfortable isn't satisfactory. Change often means giving something up to make room for something else, so we focus on the sacrifice instead of the gain.

If you struggle with the dichotomy of being dissatisfied with the status quo but reluctant to change, try these four techniques to change your mental programming quickly:

1. Write out your goals using precise language. Every day, copy your major goals over in a journal, reading them aloud as you write. As you do that, see a mental picture of yourself enjoying the goal.

2. Take time every day to relax in a private place. Breathe deeply, clear your mind of distractions, ask God to keep you focused, then read your major goals and repeat them out loud three to five times.

3. Use the programming technique employed by athletes. Before they begin a competitive event, they go through their entire routine in their minds, mentally doing every step of the process the way they want it to happen in reality. Mentally see yourself doing everything you need to do to create positive change in your life.

4. Mentally rehearse any non-recurring event of importance. Affirm a positive outcome by visualizing yourself completely relaxed and in control of the situation ahead of time.

Read: Proverbs, Chapter 12

Today we observe
National Hospital Day

On this day in history

Notable events

In 1995, the Dow Jones set a new record (4430.59) for the fifth straight day of the week.

In 2015, Verizon announced plans to buy AOL for $50 per share in a deal valued at $4.4 billion; the transaction was completed on June 23.

Births

Halsey William Wilson, American publisher of reference books (*Readers' Guide, Cumulative Book Index, Book Review Digest*), founder of H. W. Wilson Company, 1868

Mary Kay Ash, American businesswoman and founder of Mary Kay Cosmetics, Inc., 1918

Eugene Kleiner, Austrian-American engineer and venture capitalist, pioneer of Silicon Valley, one of the original founders of Fairchild Semiconductor, 1923

Deaths

Edmund C. Lynch, American stockbroker and financier, known for helping create, finance, and broker many U.S. large chain stores, cofounder of Merrill Lynch, 1938

Bette Nesmith Graham, American typist, commercial artist, and inventor (Liquid Paper), 1980

Thought for the day

"God's love isn't based on me. It's simply placed on me. And it's the place from which I should live... loved."

Lysa TerKeurst

I pray for direction as I prepare for eternity.

May 13

"For the Lord your God is living among you. He is a mighty savior. He will take delight in you with gladness. With his love, he will calm all your fears. He will rejoice over you with joyful songs." *(Zephaniah 3:17, NLT)*

How to help grieving employees

It's not realistic to expect that employees can leave the impact of personal tragedies at home. The effects of death, divorce, accidents, serious illness, or other personal crises frequently carry over into the workplace.

Companies can ease the stress of difficult situations by establishing procedures before they are needed. Many companies limit their written policies to guidelines on the amount of time off an employee may take when there is a death in the family. Other policies are typically unwritten and may vary, depending on the specific situation and the employee involved. The key is to remember that support at work is critical.

When an employee has a death in the family, notify close associates of the person affected first, then issue a simple memo to inform the rest of the staff. Send flowers and have an official representative at the funeral. The need for support doesn't end when the funeral is over. There may be some inconsistencies in the employee's work for as much as a year afterward. People who have experienced a loss may initially bury themselves in their work and be tremendously productive and then a few months later might show a sharp decline in performance. Before taking any disciplinary steps, consider the level the employee was working on prior to the loss and make any evaluations based on that. This approach should be used if the employee has experienced any type of personal crisis.

The practical side to this compassionate attitude is that the expense of replacing trained, experienced people is usually greater than the expense of helping them work through a difficult period in their lives.

Today we observe

Children of Fallen Patriots Day

Fair Trade Day

On this day in history

Notable events

In 1991, Apple released Macintosh operating System 7.0, codenamed "Big Bang" and "Furnishings 2000," retroactively referred to as Mac OS 7.

Births

Natalie Sara Massenet, British-American fashion entrepreneur, founder of Net-a-Porter, 1965

Deaths

Joseph Henry, American scientist, first secretary of the Smithsonian Institution, known for electromagnetic induction, inventor of a precursor to the electric doorbell and electric relay, 1878

Cyrus McCormick, American businessman and inventor (mechanical reaper), founder of McCormick Harvesting Machine Company, which later became part of International Harvester Company, 1884

Thought for the day

"I don't believe for a second that success is just about self-motivation. If that were all it took, all any of us would ever need is a little pep rally now and again and we'd soar to the stars. But after all the rah-rahs and the warm feelings wear off, it's ultimately about action."

Rob Walman

I am grateful for the sovereignty of God.

Read:
Proverbs, Chapter 13

May 14

> When we were utterly helpless, Christ came at just the right time and died for us sinners. Now, most people would not be willing to die for an upright person, though someone might perhaps be willing to die for a person who is especially good. But God showed his great love for us by sending Christ to die for us while we were still sinners. *(Romans 5:6-8, NLT)*

Don't make it obvious you're using an email template

Email templates are a tremendous productivity tool, but your readers shouldn't be able to tell that you're using a template.

Ask any woman who has ever shown up at a party and seen another woman wearing the same outfit how she feels. That's how you ought to feel if someone recognizes your templates because they've seen them used by another company.

Both free and paid email service providers offer users templates that make it easy to set up marketing messages, and those templates usually allow for substantial customization. Take the time to customize your emails with fresh, original images; your logo; a different font; and/or different colors. Consider rearranging the elements in the template for a distinct look.

You may have a wonderful message to share, but if your email looks the same as those that others are sending, your audience may never read it. Differentiate yourself visually as well as in your content.

Thought for the day

"Each of us has been put on earth with the ability to do something well. We cheat ourselves and the world if we don't use that ability as best we can."

Gracie Allen

I pray on the assurance of Psalm 91.

Read:
Proverbs, Chapter 14

Today we observe

The Stars and Stripes Forever Day

On this day in history

Notable events

In 1853, Gail Borden, land surveyor, newspaper publisher, and inventor, patented his process for condensed milk.

In 1948, the State of Israel was proclaimed.

Births

B. C. Forbes, Scottish-American financial journalist and author, founder of *Forbes* magazine, 1880

George Lucas, American filmmaker and businessman, 1944

Mark Zuckerberg, American business magnate, computer programmer, internet entrepreneur, and philanthropist, cofounder of Facebook and its parent company Meta Platforms, 1984

Deaths

Henry John Heinz, American entrepreneur, founder of H. J. Heinz Company, known for creating tomato ketchup, 1919

Ernst Alexanderson, Swedish-American electrical engineer, inventor (held 344 patents), and pioneer in radio and television development, 1975

Bill Lear, American inventor (developed the car radio and 8-track cartridge) and businessman, founder of Learjet, a business jet manufacturer, 1978

William Randolph Hearst, Jr., American businessman and newspaper publisher, 1993

> Grow your faith by getting sufficient rest. Jesus made time to rest; you should, too.

May 15

That night the Lord appeared to Solomon in a dream, and God said, "What do you want? Ask, and I will give it to you!" *(1 Kings 3:5, NLT)*

Support employees who travel on business

Business travel is challenging, tiring, and one of the biggest intrusions work makes on someone's personal life. Here's how to help employees who are on the road balance their work and personal responsibilities:

Provide a consultation and referral program. Employees may need assistance with a variety of service and information needs related to travel and caring for their families while they're gone. This is especially important for inexperienced travelers and employees who are primary caregivers for children and/or elderly dependents. If you have an inhouse travel expert, great. If not, ask your travel agent for help.

Offer dependent care vouchers. The cost of child care, elder care, and even pet care can make business travel a serious financial burden for employees. Consider a voucher program that reimburses workers for all or a portion of these extra costs.

Give as much notice as possible. While it may be impossible to totally avoid last-minute trips, the more advance notice you can give an employee about a trip, the easier it will be for them to prepare both professionally and personally.

Thought for the day

"Failure is good as long as it doesn't become a habit."

Michael Eisner

I pray to know the truth.

Read:
Proverbs, Chapter 15

Today we observe

National Chocolate Chip Day
Bring Flowers to Someone Day
International Family Day

On this day in history

Notable events

In 1911, the U.S. Supreme Court found Standard Oil Company of New Jersey in violation of the Sherman Act and divided the company into several geographically separate and eventually competing firms.

In 1951, AT&T became the first U.S. corporation to have a million stockholders after car salesman Brady Denton purchased seven shares worth $1,078.

In 1957, the longest Billy Graham evangelistic crusade began in Madison Square Garden in New York City and lasted 16 weeks.

In 2015, ride-hailing service Lyft announced new funding worth $150 million, including $100 million from billionaire investor Carl Icahn.

Births

Frank Heart, American computer engineer, influential in computer networking, 1929

Dave Brandon, American businessman, former CEO of Toys "R" Us and former president and CEO of Domino's, 1952

Noah Glass, American technology entrepreneur and software developer, cofounder of Twitter (now X) and Odeo, credited with coining the name Twitter, 1981

Deaths

Francis A. Schaeffer, American evangelical theologian, philosopher, author, and Presbyterian pastor, 1984

Edward J. Flanagan, Irish-American Catholic priest and founder of Boys Town, 1948

Donald F. Duncan, Sr., American entrepreneur and inventor, founder of Duncan Toys Company, known for marketing the Yo-Yo, 1971

Jerry Falwell, American Baptist pastor, televangelist, and conservative activist, 2007

May 16

> Whoever heeds discipline shows the way to life, but whoever ignores correction leads others astray. *(Proverbs 10:17, NIV)*

Practice freudenfreude

Freudenfreude is a relatively new term combining two German words: *freuden* (of joy) and *freude* (joy). It means taking joy in the successes and good fortunes of others.

It's essentially the opposite of schadenfreude, which is a German term that's been around for centuries that refers to taking pleasure in the misfortune of others.

On an intellectual level, you'd think this doesn't need a lot of discussion. Freudenfreude is good and schadenfreude isn't.

But, of course, it's not that simple.

When the coworker who has tormented you for years finally gets fired, it's hard not to experience at least some pleasure because they've finally gotten what they deserve. And when that same coworker snags the job of *your* dreams, feeling happy for them is probably way down on your list of emotions.

Avoiding schadenfreude and practicing freudenfreude takes a conscious effort, but it's worth it. Feeling joy boosts your immune system, fights stress and pain, promotes a healthier lifestyle, and supports longevity. So why not expand your feelings of joy by embracing freudenfreude?

Make the joyful feelings of others your own.

Thought for the day

"Productivity is never an accident. It is always the result of a commitment to excellence, intelligent planning, and focused effort."

Paul J. Meyer

I am grateful for the unexpected good things that happened to me yesterday.

Today we observe
International Day of Light

On this day in history

Notable events

In 1876, pharmacist Charles E. Hires presented Hires Root Beer, the first commercial brand of root beer, at the Centennial Exposition in Philadelphia.

In 1965, the Campbell Soup Company introduced SpaghettiOs under its Franco-American brand.

In 2020, 118-year-old American department store JCPenney filed for bankruptcy.

Births

Philip Danforth Armour, American meatpacking industrialist, founder of Armour & Company, 1832

Peter L. Jensen, Danish-American engineer, inventor, and entrepreneur, founder of Magnavox and Jensen Radio Manufacturing Company, 1886

Konrad Wachsmann, German-American modernist architect known for his contribution to the mass production of building components, 1901

Ivan Edward Sutherland, American computer scientist, internet pioneer, computer graphics pioneer, inventor of Sketchpad, 1938

Tucker Carlson, American conservative political commentator, author, cofounder of *The Daily Caller*, 1969

Deaths

Jim Henson, American puppeteer, animator, cartoonist, actor, inventor, and filmmaker, creator of the Muppets, 1990

H. B. Reese, American inventor and businessman, creator of Reese's Peanut Butter Cups, founder of H. B. Reese Candy Company, 1956

Mark McCormack, American lawyer, sports agent, writer, founder of International Management Group, now IMG, 2003

Read:
Proverbs, Chapter 16

May 17

Rejoice always, pray continually, give thanks in all circumstances; for this is God's will for you in Christ Jesus. *(1 Thessalonians 5:16-18, NIV)*

A Mighty Fortress is our God

Martin Luther, 1529
Trans. Frederick Henry Hedge, 1852

A mighty fortress is our God,
a bulwark never failing;
our helper he, amid the flood
of mortal ills prevailing.
For still our ancient foe
does seek to work us woe;
his craft and power are great,
and armed with cruel hate,
on earth is not his equal.

Did we in our own strength confide,
our striving would be losing,
were not the right Man on our side,
the Man of God's own choosing.
Dost ask who that may be?
Christ Jesus, it is he;
Lord Sabaoth his name,
from age to age the same;
and he must win the battle.

And though this world, with devils filled,
should threaten to undo us,
we will not fear, for God has willed
his truth to triumph through us.
The prince of darkness grim,
we tremble not for him;
his rage we can endure,
for lo! his doom is sure;
one little word shall fell him.

That Word above all earthly powers
no thanks to them abideth;
the Spirit and the gifts are ours
through him who with us sideth.
Let goods and kindred go,
this mortal life also;
the body they may kill:
God's truth abideth still;
his kingdom is forever!

Today we observe

World Information Society Day

On this day in history

Notable events

In 1993, Intel unveiled its new Pentium processor.
In 2009, the video game Minecraft was released to the public while in development.

Births

Horace Elgin Dodge, Sr., American automobile manufacturing pioneer, cofounder of Dodge Brothers Company, 1868
Frederick McKinley Jones, American inventor, entrepreneur, and engineer best known for his work in refrigeration technology, 1893
Colin Kroll, American entrepreneur, cofounder of the video hosting service Vine and trivia game app HQ Trivia, 1984

Deaths

Asa Packer, American businessman, railroad construction pioneer, founder of Lehigh University, 1879
John Deere, American blacksmith and manufacturer, founded Deere & Company, 1886

Thought for the day

"No one rises above who he or she has been without first having fallen down. The best time—in fact, the only time—to make a real change in your life is in the moment of seeing the need for it. He who hesitates always gets lost in the hundred reasons why tomorrow is a better day to get started."

Guy Finley

I pray for forgiveness for the times when I have been selfish and self-centered.

Read:
Proverbs, Chapter 17

May 18

But I am afraid that just as Eve was deceived by the serpent's cunning, your minds may somehow be led astray from your sincere and pure devotion to Christ. *(2 Corinthians 11:3, NIV)*

Who are you?

You are a child of God.

This very simple statement is, for many of us, an extremely difficult concept to grasp. But once you understand and accept it, once you know deep within yourself that you have a Heavenly Father who loves you mightily and wonderfully, you will live a life of fullness and peace, no matter what your circumstances.

Nothing else in our human experience compares to the love of a parent for a child. Creating another human being establishes a powerful bond, a love that is so deep and strong it must be experienced to be understood and believed. Yet as awesome as this parent/child love is, God's love for us is so much more because it's not restricted by our human limitations. Being a child of God means being loved unconditionally by a parent who is truly all-powerful. Earthly parents, in their humanity, are not perfect, but God is. God never gets tired, or grouchy, or loses his temper.

Of course, God is not our biological father; he is more like an adoptive father. We can put this in human terms by thinking of someone who chooses to adopt a child and loves that child with the same, or even greater, depth and breadth than a biological parent does. God chose us to be his children. As strong as any parent's love is, consider how much stronger is the love of God for us, his adopted children.

Excerpted from Finding Joy in the Morning: You can make it through the night

I am grateful for our freedoms.

Read: Proverbs, Chapter 18

Today we observe

International Museum Day

On this day in history

Notable events

In 1897, Dow Chemical was founded by Herbert Henry Dow in Midland, Michigan, as a one-product start-up.

In 1965, American engineer Ray Dolby founded Dolby Laboratories in London, England.

Births

Thomas Midgley Jr., American mechanical and chemical engineer who played a major role in developing leaded gasoline and some of the first chlorofluorocarbons (CFCs), both products that were later banned; his legacy is one of negative environmental impact and his death in 1944 was publicly reported as an accident but privately declared a suicide, 1889

Deaths

Elijah Craig, American Baptist preacher and entrepreneur, credited with the invention of bourbon whiskey, 1808

Mary McLeod Bethune, American educator (Bethune-Cookman University), philanthropist, humanitarian, civil rights activist, advisor to presidents, 1955

Thought for the day

"In short, I didn't become a Christian because God promised I would have an even happier life than I had as an atheist. He never promised any such thing. Indeed, following him would inevitably bring divine demotions in the eyes of the world. Rather, I became a Christian because the evidence was so compelling that Jesus really is the one-and-only Son of God who proved his divinity by rising from the dead. That meant following him was the most rational and logical step I could possibly take."

Lee Strobel

May 19

> "God's way is perfect. All the Lord's promises prove true. He is a shield for all who look to him for protection. For who is God except the Lord? Who but our God is a solid rock? God is my strong fortress, and he makes my way perfect. He makes me as surefooted as a deer, enabling me to stand on mountain heights. *(2 Samuel 22:31-34, NLT)*

What are you trying to teach me?

Of the businesses that suffered during the COVID-19 lockdowns, the restaurant industry was one of the most devastated. John Rivers, founder of the Florida-based 4 Rivers Smokehouse, says that what he asked God at the time, and what he encourages us to ask God all the time, is not, "Why are you doing this?" but "What are you trying to teach me?"

You'll hear a lot of voices; be sure the one you're listening to is God's.

Often what's stopping us can be the vehicle for movement. "The obstacle we face becomes the means to overcome the obstacle," he says. "What stands in the way becomes the way."

As crazy as it sounds, for the restaurants across Florida in the 4 Rivers chain, the pandemic itself provided the means to overcome the crushing impact of the pandemic. It wasn't business as usual—it quickly moved to business as better.

The company added virtual drive-thrus and expanded delivery. The creation of 4R Grocery helped customers acquire scarce supplies (in particular, toilet paper).

Rivers says business leaders need to let God write their business plans. "Set yourself to a purpose and let God ordain how to do it," he says.

He makes these four points:
- The willingness to stand apart is a requirement to the ability to stand above.
- If you've yet to fail, you've yet to try something worthy of your effort.
- Faith is the embrace of uncertainty.
- If your dream doesn't require a miracle, you aren't dreaming big enough.

Today we observe

National Endangered Species Day

Celebrate Your Elected Officials Day

On this day in history

Notable events

In 1857, the first U.S. patent for an "electromagnetic fire alarm telegraph for cities" was issued to William Francis Channing of Boston and Moses Gerrish Farmer of Salem, Massachusetts.

In 1906, the Federated Boys Clubs (now known as Boys & Girls Clubs of America) formed with 53 member organizations.

Births

Johns Hopkins, American merchant, investor, and philanthropist, 1795

Edmund C. Lynch, American stockbroker and financier, known for helping create, finance, and broker many U.S. large chain stores, cofounder of Merrill Lynch, 1885

Gary Kildall, American computer scientist and microcomputer entrepreneur, created CP/M operating system, founded Digital Research, Inc., 1942

Thought for the day

"I've learned from experience that the greater part of our happiness or misery depends on our dispositions and not on our circumstances."

Martha Washington

I pray that I will be open to stillness.

Read:
Proverbs, Chapter 19

May 20

T he Spirit clearly says that in later times some will abandon the faith and follow deceiving spirits and things taught by demons. *(1 Timothy 4:1, NIV)*

Why do business with other Christians?

When you're choosing what companies to buy from, does the faith of the owner(s) matter? Krystal Parker, president of the U.S. Christian Chamber of Commerce, says yes.

"We believe that Christians in business serve with excellence and ethics, so you're going to get great service and maybe above and beyond what you would expect with just another businessperson," Parker says.

Beyond the immediate benefit of a positive transaction is the multiplier effect. "When you do business with someone who shares your values, the dollars you spend with them not only support their business, but there's a multiplier effect of where they spend their money," Parker says. The profits from Christian businesses tend to support other businesses and causes that are compatible with Christian values. And you won't be supporting companies that support initiatives you disagree with.

Doing business with other Christians can help you strengthen both your faith and your respective companies.

"As Christians, we have to be wise about who we allow to speak into our lives. Yes, iron sharpens iron (Proverbs 27:17), but you don't want to be sharpened by just any businessperson," Parker says." As it says in Proverbs 13:20 (NRSV), 'Whoever walks with the wise becomes wise, but the companion of fools suffers harm.' Walk with other Christians so you can all increase in wisdom."

Being intentional about patronizing Christian businesses helps those organizations grow and increases their ability to serve and make a difference. Parker says, "We have to take back that economic mountain, that economic sphere of influence."

Today we observe
Weights and Measures Day

On this day in history
Notable events
In 1873, Levi Strauss and Jacob Davis obtained a U.S. patent on the process of putting rivets in men's work pants (the birth of blue jeans).
In 2013, Yahoo! purchased Tumblr for $1.1 billion.

Births
William Fargo, a pioneer American expressman who helped found the modern-day financial firms of American Express company and Wells Fargo, 1818
Bill Hewlett, American engineer and businessman, cofounder of Hewlett-Packard Company, 1913
Cindy McCain, American diplomat, businesswoman, and humanitarian, 1954

Deaths
Max S. Klein, American engineer and owner of Palmer Paint Company in Detroit Michigan, who (with commercial artist Dan Robbins) invented, developed, and marketed paint by numbers kits, 1993

Thought for the day

"Never let someone else determine God's will for your life. No one else can understand God's unique call on your life as clearly as you can."

Ray Pritchard

I pray for the students who are graduating and starting a new chapter in their lives.

Read:
Proverbs, Chapter 20

May 21

> "Surely God is my salvation; I will trust and will not be afraid, for the Lord is my strength and my might; he has become my salvation."
> *(Isaiah 12:2, NRSVue)*

Make the most of every dollar

Use these tips to maximize your finances.

Create a budget. Give yourself a roadmap for your income and expenses. Track your expenses. Prioritize the essentials and reduce discretionary spending. Then review and adjust as necessary.

Make smart spending decisions. Avoid impulse purchases and make conscious spending choices. Compare prices and features. Look for great deals on second-hand items. Borrow or rent instead of buying things you only need for a short time. Cancel unused subscriptions.

Save. Financial stability requires saving. Build a cash emergency fund and make automatic deposits into it. When you can, begin investing for greater financial growth.

Protect your money. Monitor your accounts for unusual or fraudulent activity. Create strong passwords. Watch for scams. Shred documents containing personal information.

Maximizing your finances doesn't mean deprivation or sacrifice, it means making good choices that align with your values and priorities.

Thought for the day

"Gratitude unlocks the fullness of life. It turns what we have into enough, and more. It turns denial into acceptance, chaos to order, confusion to clarity. It can turn a meal into a feast, a house into a home, a stranger into a friend. Gratitude makes sense of our past, brings peace for today, and creates a vision for tomorrow."

Melody Beattie

Today we observe

Eat More Fruits and Vegetables Day

National Memo Day

On this day in history

Notable events

In 1881, the American Red Cross was founded by Clara Barton.

In 1936, Du Pont began commercial production of Lucite, clear, non-conducting synthetic resin material (called Perspex and Plexiglass by other manufacturers).

Births

William C. Coleman, American businessman and politician, founder of the Coleman Company, a maker of camping equipment, 1870

Henry E. Warren, American entrepreneur, inventor (synchronous electric clock and 134 other inventions), founder of Warren Telechron Company, 1872

Glenn Curtiss, American aviation and motorcycling pioneer, inventor (hydroplane), a founder of the U.S. aircraft industry, 1878

Armand Hammer, American business magnate most closely associated with Occidental Petroleum, 1898

Deaths

Jane Addams, American social activist and reformer, social worker, author, women's suffrage leader, cofounder of the American Civil Liberties Union, first American woman to be awarded the Nobel Peace Prize, 1935

Mark R. Hughes, American entrepreneur, founder of Herbalife International, Ltd., 2000

I am thankful for everyone who has mentored me in small and large ways over the years.

Read:
Proverbs, Chapter 21

May 22

> I sought the Lord, and he answered me; he delivered me from all my fears. Those who look to him are radiant; their faces are never covered with shame. *(Psalm 34:4-5, NIV)*

To sell it, give it away

For many products, one of the most effective ways to sell is to give them away first. Especially if your product is subject to repeat purchases, providing consumers with a free sample may be exactly what it takes to turn them into loyal—and paying—customers.

Food products are a great example. How often have you been in a grocery store and made an unplanned purchase because you were given a tasty sample? Cosmetics, cleaning supplies, paper goods (both for the home and office), office supplies, and more can all be effectively sold through a sample program.

Samples can make customers more comfortable with their purchase decision, particularly when you have a premium-priced product. Use these tips to develop and measure a sample program:

- Calculate your cost per contact and cost per sale.
- Provide an adequate supply so the customer can fully evaluate the product.
- Be sure prospective customers know what to do with your product.
- If you're providing samples to a retailer for resale, include suggestions for displaying and demonstrating the product.
- Combine samples with other marketing techniques, such as coupons.

I pray to be open to what will bring true joy.

Read:
Proverbs, Chapter 22

Today we observe
National Maritime Day

On this day in history

Notable events

In 1849, Abraham Lincoln received a patent for a device to lift a boat over shoals and obstructions; he is the only U.S. President to patent an invention.

In 1900, the Associated Press organized in New York City as a nonprofit news cooperative.

In 1906, the Wright Brothers were granted a patent for their "flying machine."

Births

T. Boone Pickens, American business magnate and financier, author, chaired the hedge fund BP Capital Management, 1928

Deaths

Martin Gardner, American author and popular science and mathematics writer, and magician, authored the "Mathematical Games" column in Scientific American for twenty-five years, 2010

Thought for the day

"The problems of this world cannot possibly be solved by skeptics or cynics whose horizons are limited by the obvious realities. We need men who can dream of things that never were."

John F. Kennedy

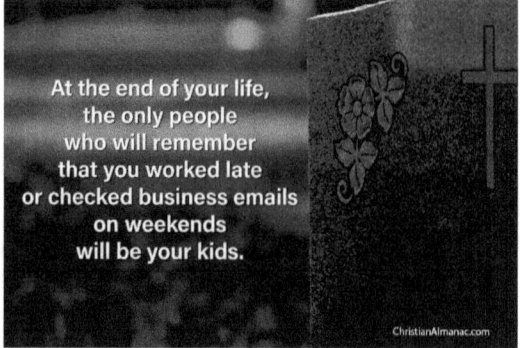

At the end of your life, the only people who will remember that you worked late or checked business emails on weekends will be your kids.

May 23

Then if my people who are called by my name will humble themselves and pray and seek my face and turn from their wicked ways, I will hear from heaven and will forgive their sins and restore their land. *(2 Chronicles 7:14, NLT)*

You look familiar

When someone tells you that you look familiar and asks how they know you, how do you respond? Because we want to be friendly and helpful, most of us will volunteer personal information as we try to figure out the connection, but doing that may put us at risk of identity theft.

The "you look familiar" line is a common social engineering trick. In the context of information security, social engineering is the use of deception to manipulate individuals into divulging confidential or personal information that may be used for fraudulent purposes.

Of course, not everyone who tells you that you look familiar is a fraudster looking to collect information. Sometimes you really do look familiar.

Use these techniques to engage with a stranger without revealing too much about yourself:

Ask the person's name. If they don't want to tell you their name, or they don't give you their full name, that's a red flag.

Turn their questions around. Answer in general terms and ask them the same question slightly rephrased.

Be vague. If they ask where you work, give them a city, not the name of the company.

Ask for a business card. Tell them you'll reach out if you can remember where you've met.

Consider the circumstances when deciding how much information to share. You should definitely be more cautious when someone you don't recognize approaches you in a public place than you would be if you're at an industry conference where it's likely that you really have met the person before.

On this day in history

Notable events

In 1785, Benjamin Franklin announced his invention of bifocals.

In 1892, Eastman Kodak Company was incorporated after the release of the Kodak camera.

Births

John Bardeen, American physicist, electrical engineer, co-inventor of the transistor, and only person to be awarded the Nobel Prize in Physics twice, 1908

Robert Moog, American engineer, electronic music pioneer, inventor of the Moog synthesizer, and founder of Moog Music, 1934

Deaths

Henry E. Huntington, American railroad magnate, real estate investor, and major booster for Los Angeles, 1927

John D. Rockefeller Sr., American business magnate and philanthropist, founder of the Standard Oil Company, 1937

Thought for the day

"People think focus means saying yes to the thing you've got to focus on. But that's not what it means at all. It means saying no to the hundred other good ideas that there are. You have to pick carefully. I'm actually as proud of the things we haven't done as the things I have done. Innovation is saying no to 1,000 things."

Steve Jobs

I am thankful for the positive reviews and recommendations my customers and clients share.

Read:
Proverbs, Chapter 23

May 24

S o, dear brothers and sisters, work hard to prove that you really are among those God has called and chosen. Do these things, and you will never fall away. *(2 Peter 1:10, NLT)*

Just say what you mean

Whether writing or speaking, your goal should be to communicate, not to impress.

In *Why Business People Speak Like Idiots: A Bullfighter's Guide*, Brian Fugere, Chelsea Hardaway and Jon Warshawksy wrote:

"When obscurity pollutes someone's communication, it's often because the author's goal is to impress and not to inform. The low road to impressing an audience is to make them feel inferior, by using words they won't understand."

You may know plenty of words your audience doesn't. But what does it accomplish if you fail to communicate your message?

Whether you're speaking or writing, the best way to impress your audience is to present your information in a way they can understand and use. Keep these tips in mind:

Make it a conversation. Don't lecture; have a discussion with a friend.

Avoid condescension. Don't talk down to anyone.

Elevate your audience, not yourself. Make your audience feel great about themselves—when they do, they'll feel the same way about you.

The people who are most impressive are usually the ones who aren't trying to impress. Be that person.

Today we observe
National Caterers Appreciation Day

On this day in history

Notable events

In 1844, Samuel Morse sent the world's first telegraph message: "What hath God wrought?"
In 1883, the Brooklyn Bridge opened.
In 1915, Thomas Edison introduced the telescribe, a machine he invented to record telephone conversations.

Births

Lillian Moller Gilbreth, American psychologist, industrial engineer, early pioneer in applying psychology to time-and-motion studies, 1878
H. B. Reese, American inventor and businessman, creator of Reese's Peanut Butter Cups, founder of H. B. Reese Candy Company, 1879
Samuel Irving Newhouse Sr., American broadcasting businessman, magazine and newspaper publisher, founder of Advance Publications, 1895
Florence Knoll Bassett, American architect, interior designer, furniture designer, and entrepreneur who revolutionized office design, 1917

Deaths

John Froelich, American inventor, invented the first gasoline-powered tractor that would go in forward and reverse, 1933
Louis Alan Hazeltine, American engineer, physicist, inventor (Neutrodyne circuit, Hazeltine-Fremodyne Superregenerative circuit), founder of Hazeltine Corporation, 1964

I pray that I may be strengthened by the faith of my fellow believers.

Read:
Proverbs, Chapter 24

Thought for the day

"Our Lord has written the promise of resurrection, not in books alone but in every leaf of springtime."

Martin Luther

May 25

Jesus was handed over to sinful men. God knew this and planned for it to happen. You had sinful men take Him and nail Him to a cross. But God raised Him up. He allowed Him to be set free from the pain of death. Death could not hold its power over Him. *(Acts 2:23–24, NLV)*

What makes a great newsletter?

Newsletters are powerful content marketing tools, but if you want yours to be effective, it should have these five elements:

1. Readable. Keep sentences and paragraphs short and use catchy headlines and section labels. Remember that busy people tend to scan rather than read every word. Make it easy for them to find what matters to them.

2. Tell stories. Go beyond your headlines and blurbs with stories. Storify your content to provide a richer, more engaging experience for your subscribers.

3. Focus on the reader. Deliver the information your audience wants, not canned marketing or branding messages.

4. Include clear calls to action. Be direct about what you're offering and include compelling calls to action that clearly tell subscribers what to do. Design your CTAs so they're easy to spot.

5. Eye-appealing, user-friendly design. The greatest content will get dumped if your newsletter is ugly, cluttered, or difficult to navigate. Choose simple, readable fonts and attractive colors. Your design should showcase your content, not distract from it. Remember that people read newsletters on their phones, so be sure yours is optimized for mobile.

Thought for the day

"Most people never get to see how brilliant they can be. They don't find teachers who believe in them."

Sean Maguire

Read:
Proverbs, Chapter 25

Today we observe

Geek Pride Day

National Missing Children's Day

On this day in history

Notable events

In 1927, Henry Ford announced the end of production of the Model T Ford.

In 1961, John F. Kennedy announced the U.S. goal of putting a man on the Moon before the end of the decade.

Births

Igor Sikorsky, Russian-American aviation pioneer in helicopters and fixed-wing aircraft, 1889

J. Peter Grace, American industrialist, president of the diversified chemical company W. R. Grace & Co. (founded by his grandfather), the longest serving CEO of a public company, 1913

Jeff Bewkes, American media executive, former president, CEO, and chairman of the board of Time Warner, 1952

Deaths

Madam C. J. Walker, African-American entrepreneur, philanthropist, and activist, founder of Madam C. J. Walker Manufacturing Company, recorded as the first female self-made millionaire in America in the *Guinness Book of World Records*, 1919

Payne Whitney, American businessman, investor, and philanthropist, 1927

Charles Momsen, American inventor and pioneer in submarine rescue, 1967

Malcolm McLean, American businessman, inventor of the modern intermodal shipping container, founder of McLean Trucking Company, Sea-Land Service, Inc., and Trailer Bridge, Inc., 2001

I am grateful that Jesus is always there to pick me up when I stumble.

May 26

He will love you and bless you and increase your numbers. He will bless the fruit of your womb, the crops of your land—your grain, new wine and olive oil—the calves of your herds and the lambs of your flocks in the land he swore to your ancestors to give you. *(Deuteronomy 7:13, NIV)*

Not everything will change

Successful business leaders are often asked what they think will change in the next ten years. That's important, but what's more important is what's *not* going to change. Think about what will be the same in the next decade.

Technology will advance, but human nature isn't likely to fundamentally change—which means that strong people skills will remain in high demand.

That's why you need to invest your time and energy in developing your own and your team's interpersonal skills. Skills that are in demand now and will continue to be in demand include:

Communication. We need to be able to understand and be understood, to speak clearly and to listen effectively.

Mental flexibility. Because change is inevitable, we need to be flexible, adaptable, and have the ability to learn.

Relationship-building. Establishing and maintaining relationships is a key element of success in any arena. Doing this requires empathy, humility, sociability, and trustworthiness.

Teamwork. The ability to collaborate is and will continue to be essential. This includes conflict resolution skills, the ability to motivate and empower others, and coaching skills.

Leadership. Effective leadership requires a wide range of skills and personality traits, including integrity, self-awareness, courage, respect, compassion, and resilience.

Grow your faith by focusing on the needs of others.

On this day in history

Notable events

In 1781, the Bank of North America incorporated in Philadelphia.

In 1896, the Dow Jones Industrial Average began with an average of twelve industrial stocks.

Births

David Edgerton, American entrepreneur and cofounder of Burger King, 1927

Deaths

Charles Horace Mayo, American medical practitioner and cofounder of the Mayo Clinic, 1939

Allan Lockheed (born Allan Loughead), American aviation engineer and businessman, founder of the Alco Hydro-Aeroplane Company, which became Lockheed Corporation, 1969

Ted Dabney, American electrical engineer and cofounder of Atari, Inc., 2018

Thought for the day

"Immanuel, God with us in our nature, in our sorrow, in our lifework, in our punishment, in our grave, and now with us, or rather we with Him, in resurrection, ascension, triumph, and Second Advent splendor."

Charles H. Spurgeon

I pray for those who must continue to work as they struggle through personal heartache.

Read:
Proverbs, Chapter 26

May 27

Now to him who is able to do immeasurably more than all we ask or imagine, according to his power that is at work within us, to him be glory in the church and in Christ Jesus throughout all generations, for ever and ever! Amen. *(Ephesians 3:20-21, NIV)*

Need a website?

If you need a website, you may think the first thing you should do is find a website designer or developer.

It's not.

Most website designers are techies who will do what you tell them to do. They may be great at the mechanics of building a website, setting up the navigation, making sure the site is mobile-responsive and so on, but if they don't understand your business and what you're trying to accomplish, the site isn't going to work for you.

What you need is someone who can share your vision, understand what it's going to take to make it a reality, and then have the resources to put all the pieces—including website design—together for you. Find a marketing consultant who understands your industry and your business to work with you to put together a total marketing plan.

You can find a marketing consultant by tapping into your network and asking for referrals. But a single recommendation is not enough. Check out their website, portfolio, and client list. Follow them on social media. Do they work with people like you? Have they actually done for others what you want them to do for you? If you can't tell, ask. Also, read their online client reviews. Just remember that not all reviews tell the full story; a one-off negative review may or may not be accurate or fair.

Once you've found someone you think may be able to help you, set up a meeting and interview them.

Read:
Proverbs, Chapter 27

Today we observe
Nothing to Fear Day

On this day in history

Notable events

In 1930, the 1,046-foot Chrysler Building in New York City, the tallest man-made structure at the time, opened to the public.

Births

Cornelius Vanderbilt, American business magnate who built his wealth in railroads and shipping, nicknamed "the Commodore," 1794

Sumner Redstone, American billionaire businessman, media magnate, founder and chairman of the second incarnation of Viacom, 1923

Deaths

Victor Kiam, American entrepreneur, owner and spokesman for Remington Products, owner of the New England Patriots football team, 2001

Ed Yost, American businessman (cofounder of Raven Industries) and inventor of the modern hot air balloon, 2007

Thought for the day

"There are countless ways of achieving greatness, but any road to achieving one's maximum potential must be built on a bedrock of respect for the individual, a commitment to excellence, and a rejection of mediocrity."

Buck Rodgers

I pray I am grateful for the times I have been able to be God's hands and feet in the world.

May 28

Trust in the Lord with all your heart; do not depend on your own understanding. Seek his will in all you do, and he will show you which path to take. *(Proverbs 3:5-6, NLT)*

Wisdom is the foundation of success

Wisdom is not just knowledge or understanding, it's the application of those in our lives, says Paul Louis Cole, president of the Christian Men's Network Worldwide and founding pastor of C3 Church in Dallas, Texas.

"The distinction between earthly and Godly wisdom is crucial. By digging into the Word of God, we cultivate Godly wisdom, a key to navigating life's twists and turns," Cole says. "Let's strive to seek Godly wisdom in our daily lives. It's not just about making smart choices; it's about shaping a life that aligns with God's principles and understanding."

Though wisdom doesn't guarantee material success, Cole says successful individuals, especially those who triumph in adversity, often share the trait.

"Wisdom is the key to navigating our chaotic world with clarity and purpose. Seek it earnestly," he says. "Build a foundation of wisdom that will sustain a structure of success."

Thought for the day

"In poverty and other misfortunes of life, true friends are a sure refuge. The young they keep out of mischief; to the old they are a comfort and aid in their weakness, and those in the prime of life they incite to noble deeds."

Aristotle

I am grateful that the Lord is so consistent in showing me his ways.

Today we observe
Amnesty International Day

On this day in history
Notable events
In 1892, the Sierra Club was formed in San Francisco.
In 1928, Dodge Brothers, Inc. and Chrysler Corporation merged.

Births
John Birch, U.S. Army intelligence officer, Baptist minister and missionary for whom the John Birch Society was named, 1918
Barney Rosset, pioneering American book and magazine publisher, founder of Grove Press and *Evergreen Review*, 1922

Deaths
Noah Webster, Jr., American lexicographer, textbook pioneer, English-language spelling reformer, editor, and author, 1843
Philip L. Carret, American investor and founder of Pioneer Fund, one of the first mutual funds in the U.S., 1998

Get your payment guaranteed

If you're extending credit to a small business that's incorporated or a partnership or LLC, have the owner(s) personally guarantee the obligation. This means that if the business fails to pay, you can collect from the owner.

If the owner is reluctant to make a personal guarantee, you may want to reconsider your decision to extend credit or at least reevaluate your terms. Also, consider this: if the business does run into cash flow problems, it's likely that the debts the owner will try to pay first are the ones for which his personal assets are on the line.

Read:
Proverbs, Chapter 28

May 29

Christ suffered for our sins once for all time. He never sinned, but he died for sinners to bring you safely home to God. He suffered physical death, but he was raised to life in the Spirit. *(1 Peter 3:18, NLT)*

Are you purpose-led or purpose-washing?

Consumers want more from brands in terms of purpose, but they often don't trust brands to deliver. There's a growing concern about companies purpose-washing, which is when they talk with purpose and use their marketing campaigns to reinforce that message but then don't follow through with any meaningful actions. In other words, purpose-led is genuine; purpose-washing is hypocritical.

Purpose-washing can seriously damage your company's credibility, cause your customers to feel misled and betrayed, and ultimately cost you business.

How do you stay purpose-led and avoid purpose-washing? Be sure your purpose
- is sincerely embedded in your company culture,
- is relevant and up-to-date, and
- creates real value.

Then show, don't tell. Demonstrate your commitment to your values and mission in everything your company does, no matter how visible. Make it meaningful and measurable. Be authentic and transparent.

We operate in a purpose economy. It's not just *what* you do, it's *why* you do it. But the what and why need to be in sync and go beyond a terrific marketing campaign.

Thought for the day

"Know that you serve through vocation. It's already happening! A lawyer helps her client through a time of great difficulty; a gardener creates beauty in the lives of those who see his work. What about the employer who provides jobs and the employees who make the employer's business a success?"

Donald Clinebell

Today we observe

National Paperclip Day

On this day in history

Notable events

In 1886, American pharmacist John Pemberton began advertising his patent medicine, Coca-Cola, in Atlanta, Georgia.

In 1919, Charles Strite filed his patent for the automatic pop-up toaster.

Births

John F. Kennedy, 35th U.S. President (fourth President to be assassinated), 1917

Peter Chernin, American businessman, film and television producer, and investor; founder of The Chernin Group, 1951

Deaths

William Arnold Anthony, American physicist, educator, and researcher; introduced and taught Cornell University's electrical engineering course, one of the first in the U.S., 1908

Should you sue?

You may have legitimate grounds to file a lawsuit, but should you? A good policy is to never litigate solely on principle. Only litigate when your business is going to be harmed or you can't get a dispute resolved any other way—and even then, carefully balance the cost of litigation with the potential benefit it will bring. Litigation is expensive and time-consuming, and the cost can take business under, even when the business is in the right. If you don't have the cash to fight a big fight, litigation is almost never the way to go.

I pray for peace.

Read:
Proverbs, Chapter 29

May 30

> Those who are wise shall shine like the brightness of the sky, and those who lead the many to righteousness, like the stars forever and ever.
> *(Daniel 12:3, NRSVue)*

Take a fresh look

Look at your world as though you'd never seen it before. You'll be surprised at how many things you'll notice that you've been overlooking.

Do this for a few minutes or a few hours. Drive down a street you travel often, looking at the landscape with fresh eyes. Look at your church through the eyes of a first-time visitor (without nitpicking all the little things that need correcting—focus on the good things you've been taking for granted). Take a fresh look at some of the people you deal with regularly—your spouse, family members, friends, and coworkers. Whatever your position, do your job as though it was your first day at the company.

You've heard the old saying that familiarity breeds contempt. That's not true. Familiarity is how we build relationships, establish intimacy, and learn to love. What actually breeds contempt is disrespect and dishonoring others. But sometimes—especially after we've become familiar with them—we take people and things for granted, we're not excited about them anymore. Looking at your world and the people in it through fresh eyes will show you things you've been missing and restore interest and excitement to your day.

Thought for the day

"Think back to the most important experiences of your life, the highest highs, the greatest victories, the most daunting obstacles overcome. How many happened to you alone? I bet there are very few. When you understand that being connected to others is one of life's greatest joys, you realize that life's best comes when you initiate and invest in solid relationships."

John C. Maxwell

Today we observe

National Creativity Day

On this day in history

Notable events

In 1906, Hersheypark, founded as a leisure park by Milton S. Hershey for the exclusive use of his employees, opened. Today, it's a family theme park open to the public.

Births

James McLamore, American entrepreneur, founder and first CEO of the Burger King fast food franchise, creator of the Whopper sandwich, 1926

Deaths

Milton Bradley, American business magnate, game pioneer and publisher, credited with launching the board game industry, 1911

Wilbur Wright, American aviation pioneer (Wright Brothers), 1912

Use basic sales techniques

Whether you're in sales or not, remembering and applying these basic sales techniques will keep your company on a growth path. Ask questions and listen carefully to the answers. Show how your product or service can meet the customer's needs and solve problems for them. See clients regularly and entertain them appropriately. Be sensitive to their requirements, even though you may find them frustrating. Most importantly, respond promptly when there's a problem.

I am thankful for my values, even though they sometimes mean I must make tough choices.

Read:
Proverbs, Chapter 30

May 31

So we do not lose heart. Though our outer self is wasting away, our inner self is being renewed day by day. For this light momentary affliction is preparing for us an eternal weight of glory beyond all comparison, as we look not to the things that are seen but to the things that are unseen. For the things that are seen are transient, but the things that are unseen are eternal. *(2 Corinthians 4:16-18, ESV)*

Create a direct mail strategy

The difference between direct mail and an email campaign is an email campaign is in essence free unless you annoy your audience and they unsubscribe. You can try different things with email and you don't have the same investment in postage, printing, and mailing that you do with direct mail. With direct mail, you have to be a little more cautious and thoughtful about what goes into your upfront planning.

As you develop your direct mail strategy, consider:
- What do you want to accomplish?
- How will you measure the impact of your efforts?
- Who is your audience?
- What sort of mailpiece will set the right tone for your goals?
- How often should you mail?

The biggest issue is likely your budget. Once you have an idea of how much you can spend, you can start looking at the specific components—printing costs, audience size, postage considerations.

Next you need to determine your message—that is, what you're trying to communicate and what you want the impression of your piece to be. Is there anything you know about your audience that will get them to open that envelope? That might be putting a familiar name on the envelop, or an offer, or a teaser that will be answered inside.

Then consider your list. Are you sending to a narrowly targeted group or a large geographic area? After that, you can get into the design of your mailpiece, blending that with your budget and goals.

Today we observe
National Save Your Hearing Day

National Speak in Complete Sentences Day

Web Designer Day

World No Tobacco Day

On this day in history

Notable events

In 1790, the first copyright law was enacted under the United States Constitution, protecting books, maps, and charts for only fourteen years.

In 1837, the Astor Hotel, which would later become the Waldorf-Astoria, opened in New York City.

In 1879, Madison Square Garden (named after James Madison) opened in New York City.

In 1934, the Barmen Declaration was published by a group of church leaders in Germany.

Births

Norman Vincent Peale, American Protestant clergyman, author of *The Power of Positive Thinking*, 1898

Thought for the day

"There are no easy answers but there are simple answers. We must have the courage to do what we know is morally right."
Ronald Reagan

I pray for those who are discouraged.

Read:
Proverbs, Chapter 31

Christian Business Almanac

June

June is named for the goddess Juno, the queen of the gods and the principal goddess of marriage who was associated with childbirth, motherhood, and fertility. The origin of the word June may also be related to the Roman word *juvenis* which means young people.

June birthstone
Pearl, moonstone, alexandrite

June flower
Rose and honeysuckle

June is ...

- Alzheimer's & Brain Awareness Month
- Audio Book Month
- Effective Communications Month
- Entrepreneurs Do It Yourself Marketing Month
- Family Month
- Humility Month
- National Disaster Preparedness Month for Animals
- National Fatherhood Month
- National Fireworks Safety Month
- National Home Ownership Month
- National Safety Month
- National Sun Safety Month
- PTSD Awareness Month
- Rebuild Your Life Month
- Skyscraper Month
- Stroke Awareness Month
- Zoo and Aquarium Month

Mark your calendar for these June holidays and observances

The day before Pentecost	National Christian T-Shirt Day
Second Sunday in June	National Children's Day
Second Tuesday in June	National Call Your Doctor Day
Second Tuesday in June	National Forklift Safety Day
Third Sunday in June	Father's Day
The Friday following Father's Day	National Take Your Dog to Work Day
Fourth Sunday in June	National Fatherless Children's Day
Last Thursday in June	National Work from Home Day
Last Thursday in June	National Handshake Day
Last Friday in June	National Safer Workplace Day
Last Friday in June	National Food Truck Day

Fun Facts about June

June was the fourth month of the year until Julius Caesar added two months to the year, which made June the sixth month.

The full moon in June is known as the strawberry moon.

No other month begins on the same day of the week as June.

Summer Solstice or the Longest Day is observed in the northern hemisphere on June 20, 21, or 22, depending on when the Sun reaches its northernmost point from the celestial equator.

June 1

Praise the Lord, my soul, and forget not all his benefits—who forgives all your sins and heals all your diseases, who redeems your life from the pit and crowns you with love and compassion, who satisfies your desires with good things so that your youth is renewed like the eagle's. *(Psalm 103:2-5, NIV)*

Keys to effective business writing

The goal of business writing, regardless of its form, is to communicate clearly, crisply, and effectively. These keys can be your foundation.

Have a purpose. Know the purpose of what you're writing and stay on point.

Know and respect your audience. Write in their language. Give them information they need or want to know. Don't waste their time.

Use an appropriate tone. Be professional but appropriate for the situation.

Format effectively. Whether it's an email, letter, report, or presentation, format your content with the audience in mind.

Be clear and concise. Use short sentences and plain language. Avoid jargon, fluff, and off-topic information. Eliminate unnecessary words.

Be accurate. All your information should be precise and correct. Check all your facts.

Be error-free. Use proper grammar and punctuation. Edit and proofread carefully.

Thought for the day

"When you're happy for yourself, it fills you. When you're happy for someone else, it pours over."

Sarah Addison Allen

I pray for direction in troubled times.

Read:
Proverbs, Chapter 1

Today we observe

National Say Something Nice Day

New Year's Resolution Recommitment Day

Atlantic hurricane season begins

On this day in history

Notable events

In 1911, the first U.S. group insurance policy was written in Passaic, New Jersey.

In 1974, the Heimlich maneuver for rescuing choking victims was published in the journal Emergency Medicine.

In 1980, CNN (Cable News Network), the world's first 24-hour television news network, made its debut from its headquarters in Atlanta, Georgia.

Births

Francis Edgar Stanley, American inventor, entrepreneur, photographer, cofounder of the Stanley Motor Carriage Company which built steam-powered automobiles, 1849

Freelan Oscar Stanley, American inventor, entrepreneur, hotelier, and architect, cofounder of the Stanley Motor Carriage Company which built steam-powered automobiles, 1849

Jeff Hawkins, American businessman, neuroscientist, and engineer; cofounder of Palm Computing (co-creator of the PalmPilot and Treo) and Handspring, 1957

Deaths

James Buchanan, 15th U.S. President, 1868

James Gordon Bennett, Sr., Scottish-born American businessman who was the founder, editor, and publisher of the New York Herald, 1872

Helen Keller, American author, disability rights advocate, political activist, and lecturer, 1968

Arthur Nielsen, American businessman, electrical engineer, and market research analyst, founder of the A.C. Nielsen Company, 1980

June 2

> But we have this treasure in clay jars, so that the extraordinary power belongs to God and does not come from us. *(2 Corinthians 4:7, NET)*

Any day can be your New Year's Day

You don't have to wait until January 1 of any year to start doing things to improve your life.

How often have you fallen into the December trap of doing too much of what you shouldn't and not enough of what you should with the promise of a New Year's resolution on the horizon?

Resolve right now to never do that again.

When it's time to make a change, make it. Don't make the change harder to accomplish by delaying it. Don't pay any attention to the calendar.

Any day can be your New Year's Day. Make it today—not tomorrow, not next week, and certainly not next year.

Start now.

High achievers are givers

High achievers are rarely selfish people. In fact, they tend to be very generous, because they know that, to use a cliché, what goes around, comes around—and it's usually multiplied by the time it comes back. The mindset of a high achiever includes an understanding and acceptance of these fundamentals:

- The beginning of true success and wealth is when you learn how to concentrate on what you can give and how you can serve.
- Be willing to go the extra mile and always do more than you are paid for. You will be rewarded.
- People who don't achieve are the ones who focus on what they can get, not what they can give.

Today we observe

American Indian Citizenship Day

On this day in history

Notable events
In 1835, P.T. Barnum and his circus began their first U.S. tour.

Births
Edwin J. Shoemaker, American businessman, inventor (original reclining chair), and philanthropist, cofounder of La-Z-Boy, known as the father of motion furniture, 1907

Deaths
Timothy Thomas Fortune, American orator, civil rights leader, writer, editor, and publisher, 1928

Robert Noyce, American physicist and entrepreneur, cofounder of Fairchild Semiconductor and Intel Corporation, 1990

Norton Simon, American industrialist (Hunt's Foods) and philanthropist, founder of Norton Simon Museum, 1993

Thought for the day

"Whatever you do, do it with all your might. Work at it, early and late, in season and out of season, not leaving a stone unturned, and never deferring for a single hour that which can be done just as well as now."

P. T. Barnum

I am grateful for the trust and loyalty of my clients and customers.

Read:
Proverbs, Chapter 2

June 3

I have fought the good fight; I have finished the race; I have kept the faith. From now on there is reserved for me the crown of righteousness, which the Lord, the righteous judge, will give me on that day, and not only to me but also to all who have longed for his appearing. *(2 Timothy 4:7-8, NRSVue)*

The benefit of the doubt

To give someone the benefit of the doubt means that you are going to believe them even though you might have some doubt—but no proof—about the truthfulness of what they said. Giving someone the benefit of the doubt means you are choosing to believe something good rather than something bad about the person when you don't have evidence for either case.

Should you always give people the benefit of the doubt? Of course not. In general, you wouldn't give the benefit of the doubt to someone who has a pattern of being untrustworthy. You should also consider how much is at stake. What are you putting at risk by taking the person at their word instead of insisting on proof? Don't override your intuition—if your gut is telling you no, listen to it.

But there are plenty of times when giving someone the benefit of the doubt throws open the doors to let joy in—not only in your life but in theirs as well.

Want people to listen? Publish!

Do you sometimes feel like you've got great ideas but no one will listen to them? One way to get people to pay attention and recognize your ability is to publish your thoughts. Being an author grants you automatic credibility, whether you write a book, a paper, a short article, or even social media posts.

On this day in history

Notable events
In 2017, the Amazing World of Dr. Seuss Museum opened in Springfield, Massachusetts.

Births
Ransom Eli Olds, American automotive industry pioneer after whom the Oldsmobile and REO brands were named, 1864

Charles R. Drew, American surgeon and medical researcher who developed large-scale blood banks early in World War II, 1904

Jay Van Andel, American businessman, cofounder of the Amway Corporation, 1924

Deaths
Amadeo Giannini, American banker, entrepreneur, financier, founder of the Bank of Italy which became Bank of America; credited as the inventor of many modern banking practices, 1949

Emmett J. Culligan, American businessman, Horatio Alger Award recipient, founder of Culligan, Inc., 1970

Robert Noyce, American physicist and entrepreneur, cofounder of Fairchild Semiconductor and Intel Corporation, 1990

J. Presper Eckert, American electrical engineer and computer pioneer, 1995

William E. Simon, American businessman, philanthropist, U.S. Secretary of the Treasury (1974-1977), president of the U.S. Olympic Committee (1981-1985), 2000

Thought for the day

"It had long since come to my attention that people of accomplishment rarely sat back and let things happen to them. They went out and happened to things."

Leonardo da Vinci

I pray for God to teach me more about him, his Word, and his character.

Read:
Proverbs, Chapter 3

June 4

After they prayed, the place where they were meeting was shaken. And they were all filled with the Holy Spirit and spoke the word of God boldly. *(Acts 4:31, NIV)*

What did you say?

Here's how to respond when someone who is hard of hearing asks you to repeat yourself: **Don't raise your voice, change your words.**

Let's say a wife asks her husband, "What do you want for dinner?"

He knows she said something and he might have understood two or three of the words, but not enough to know how to answer her, so he replies, "What?"

If she repeats the same words with more volume, there's a good chance he still won't understand—but he'll feel like she's yelling at him and possibly get defensive or angry.

If instead of repeating her first question, she rephrases it and says, "I'm planning what we're going to have for dinner. What are you in the mood for?", he might still miss some of the words, but there's a good chance he'll connect enough of what he heard from both questions and be able to answer her.

The result? Less frustration, better communication.

Of course, there are different types and degrees of hearing loss, and this technique won't work for all of them. But if you're close to someone whose hearing is deteriorating and you find yourself repeating things and raising your voice (yelling) without success, try rephrasing. It might make a huge improvement in your relationship.

I am grateful that God always wants what's best for me.

Read:
Proverbs, Chapter 4

Today we observe
National Safe Day

On this day in history

Notable events
In 1924, the ten millionth Ford was produced at the Highland Park plant.
In 1942, Capitol Records opened for business and presented the company's first free record to a Los Angeles disc jockey.
In 1973, a patent for the ATM was granted to Don Wetzel, Tom Barnes, and George Chastain.
In 1990, Greyhound Bus filed bankruptcy.

Births
John Blair Scribner, American magazine and book publisher (Charles Scriber's Sons), 1850
S. B. Fuller, American entrepreneur, publisher, founder of the Fuller Products Company, 1905
William M. Batten, American businessman, chairman and CEO of JCPenney Company (1964-1974), chairman of the New York Stock Exchange (1976-1984), 1909
Robert Fulghum, author (*All I Really Need to Know I Learned in Kindergarten*) and Unitarian Universalist minister, 1937

Deaths
Blanche Knopf, publisher, cofounder and president of Alfred A. Knopf, Inc., 1966
Bill France, Jr., American motorsports executive, CEO of NASCAR, 2007

Thought for the day

"Finish each day and be done with it. You have done what you could; some blunders and absurdities have crept in; forget them as soon as you can. Tomorrow is a new day; you shall begin it serenely and with too high a spirit to be encumbered with your old nonsense."

Ralph Waldo Emerson

June 5

> **"** Take care that you do not forget the LORD your God by failing to keep his commandments, his ordinances, and his statutes that I am commanding you today. *(Deuteronomy 8:11, NRSVue)*

Pray and give the credit to God

It's easy to get caught up in the busyness of business, but you can be more focused and productive when prayer and thanksgiving is an integral part of your operation.

Lois Rosenberry, president and CEO of Children's Discovery Center (Toledo, Ohio), begins every meeting with prayer—not just internal meetings, but even meetings with outsiders that are more secular in tone.

For example, Rosenberry's advisory board consists of a range of business leaders, not all of whom are Christians. "When I have my advisory board meetings, I always quote a scripture from proverbs that talks about the wisdom in counsel of others, and then we pray and ask for God's direction in making good decisions," she says.

Taking workplace prayer even further, Rosenberry instituted a monthly prayer ministry in the corporate office, led by one of her adult daughters who works for the company. A light lunch is provided and anyone who has a prayer need is welcome.

"God has given me a mission field right in my office," she says. "I'm seeing people wanting to know more about faith. And people I thought would never come to that meeting are coming and they're crying and being moved by it."

The other side of prayer is thanking God both publicly and privately for the results. As the recipient of numerous awards (including the Governor's Award for Excellence in Enterprise and Entrepreneur of the Year), Rosenberry says, "Every time I win an award, regardless of where it is, I remember to thank God, because I know he was the one who directed me."

On this day in history

Notable events
In 1947, in a speech at Harvard University, Secretary of State George Marshall proposed that European nations create a plan for their economic reconstruction and that the U.S. provide economic assistance. The Marshall Plan provided markets for American goods, created reliable trading partners, and supported the development of stable democratic governments in Western Europe.

Births
Robert Kraft, American businessman and sports executive, chairman and CEO of the Kraft Group, 1941

Mark Wahlberg, American actor, producer, businessman, rapper, 1971

Omeed Malik, investment banker, founder and CEO of Farvahar Partners, cofounder and president of 1789 Capital, 1979

Deaths
Mary Ann Shadd Cary, African-American activist, journalist, publisher, teacher, and lawyer, 1893

Ronald Reagan, 40th U.S. President, 2004

Thought for the day

"In times of change, learners inherit the earth, while the learned find themselves beautifully equipped to deal with a world that no longer exists."

Eric Hoffer

I pray for salespeople and the essential work they do for their companies.

Read:
Proverbs, Chapter 5

June 6

Such things were written in the Scriptures long ago to teach us. And the Scriptures give us hope and encouragement as we wait patiently for God's promises to be fulfilled. *(Romans 15:4, NLT)*

Taking responsibility when something goes wrong

The day before the invasion of Normandy, General Dwight D. Eisenhower gave a famous speech, telling the troops, "The eyes of the world are upon you."

He composed another speech that he never delivered—one in which he accepted responsibility if the invasion failed. On a piece of scrap paper, he wrote:

"My decision to attack at this time and place was based upon the best information available. The troops, the air, and the Navy did all that Bravery and devotion to duty could do. If any blame or fault attaches to the attempt it is mine alone."

When you're in charge and something goes wrong, take responsibility.

Thought for the day

"In matters of style, swim with the current; in matters of principle, stand like a rock."

Thomas Jefferson

I am grateful that God sees and cares for me.

Read:
Proverbs, Chapter 6

Grow your faith by making time for what is truly important in life: your health, your family, your relationship with Jesus Christ.

Today we observe
National Higher Education Day

On this day in history

Notable events

- In 1822, U.S. Army surgeon William Beaumont treated Alexis St. Martin, who had been shot in the stomach. Beaumont conducted digestion experiments through a hole in St. Martin's stomach, becoming known as the father of gastric physiology because of his groundbreaking research.
- In 1925, the Chrysler Corporation was officially formed by Walter P. Chrysler.
- In 1944, D-Day begins as the 156,000-strong Allied Expeditionary Force landed in Normandy, France, during World War II.
- In 2023, the PGA Tour, DP World Tour, and LIV Golf League agreed to unify to create a for-profit entity to be run by the PGA Tour and funded by Saudi Arabia's Public Investment Fund.

Births

- David T. Abercrombie, American topographer and expert in the outdoors, cofounder of Abercrombie & Fitch, 1867
- Donald F. Duncan, Sr., American entrepreneur and inventor, founder of Duncan Toys Company, known for marketing the Yo-Yo, 1892.
- Kirk Kerkorian, Armenian-American businessman, investor, and philanthropist; known as the father of the mega-resort, 1917

Deaths

- Louis Chevrolet, Swiss-American race car driver, mechanic, inventor, and entrepreneur, cofounder of the Chevrolet Motor Car Company, 1941
- James E. Casey, American businessman and founder of the American Messenger Company (today known as UPS), 1983
- J. Paul Getty, Sr., American-born British petroleum industrialist, founder of Getty Oil Company, 1976

June 7

> To the Jews who had believed him, Jesus said, "If you hold to my teaching, you are really my disciples. Then you will know the truth, and the truth will set you free." *(John 8:31-32, NIV)*

Start a workplace Bible study

The workplace is one of the biggest mission fields we have. Chances are, you're working side-by-side with people who need Jesus. Here are some tips on how to start and lead a Bible study at work:

Pray for your co-workers and get to know them. Get comfortable with them. Find out if they're people of faith, open to a conversation, or anti-religion.

Plan a place and time for your study. Is there a location in your workplace such as a breakroom or conference room where you can meet? A place near the office? Someone's home? Or online? You don't have to meet at your workplace. Choose a frequency and time that will work for the participants. Don't do it on company time unless you have permission.

Find a co-leader if you can. It's not essential, but it will help.

Start small. Don't worry if you begin with just a few people—that can actually be more productive than a larger group.

Choose a study and set a schedule. You can go through the Bible itself, you can focus on a topic, or you can use an organized study. Let people know how long it will take. "We will do this for six weeks and evaluate."

Lead by example. Be the model others seek. Don't monopolize the conversation; ask questions and encourage discussion.

Be prepared. Review what you'll be discussing in advance.

Don't judge or assume. Everyone in your group will likely be at a different place in terms of their faith walk.

Trust God with whatever happens. Just be faithful.

Today we observe
World Caring Day
World Food Safety Day

On this day in history

Notable events

In 1860, workmen began laying track for the Market Street Railroad in San Francisco.

In 1917, Melvin Jones and other Chicago businessmen held an organizational meeting to form the International Association of Lions Clubs.

Births

Vivien Kellems, American industrialist, inventor, and public speaker, known for her battle with the U.S. government over income tax withholding and other tax issues, 1896

Frederick Terman, American professor and academic administrator at Stanford University, credited (with William Shockley) as being the father of Silicon Valley, 1900

Virginia Apgar, American physician, obstetrical anesthesiologist, medical researcher, and inventor of the Apgar score, a way to quickly assess the health of newborns, 1909

Deaths

Richard March Hoe, American inventor and industrialist known for designing a rotary printing press that used a continuous roll of paper and revolutionized newspaper publishing, 1886

Bill France, Sr., American businessman, racing driver, NASCAR founder, 1992

Thought for the day

"Time is free, but it's priceless. You can't own it, but you can use it. You can't keep it, but you can spend it. Once you've lost it you can never get it back."

Harvey MacKay

Read:
Proverbs, Chapter 7

I pray for discipline.

June 8

But love your enemies, do good to them, and lend to them without expecting to get anything back. Then your reward will be great, and you will be children of the Most High, because he is kind to the ungrateful and wicked. *(Luke 6:35, NIV)*

Six essential communication qualities

"Poor communication is one of the leading causes of conflict in the marketplace," says Latondra Heaven, Kingdom-driven Leadership Strategist, Kingdom Reach Leadership, and co-president of the Central Florida Christian Chamber of Commerce. "It produces frustration, confusion, distress, and low morale."

Applying these six qualities to your communication will improve your relationships and help grow your business.

Clear. "Be clear in what you say, what you mean, and what you expect," Heaven says.

Complete. "Provide all the necessary information so they can fully understand what you're saying," she says.

Controlled. Heaven says, "Get to the point and keep your emotions out of it."

Consistent. Referring to scripture—"*In the multitude of words sin is not lacking, but he who restrains his lips is wise.*" (*Proverbs 10:19, NKJV*)—Heaven says, "Make up your mind what your message is, stick to it, and reinforce it."

Convicted. Let others know that you truly believe what you're saying.

Compassionate. "With Godly confidence comes the humility that helps you consider others, consider where they are, and how your communication affects their ability to perform at their best," she says.

Don't use foul or abusive language. Let everything you say be good and helpful, so that your words will be an encouragement to those who hear them. (Ephesians 4:29, NLT)

Read:
Proverbs, Chapter 8

On this day in history

Notable events
In 1912, Carl Laemmie incorporated Universal Pictures.
In 1869, Ives W. McGaffey patented the first vacuum cleaner, calling it a sweeping machine.

Births
Frank Lloyd Wright, American architect, designer, writer, and educator, 1867
Noel Wien, American pioneer aviator, founder of Wien Alaska Airways, 1899
Ye (Kanye West), American rapper, singer, songwriter, producer, and fashion designer, 1977

Deaths
Andrew Jackson, 7th U.S. President, 1845
Walter Hunt, American mechanical engineer and prolific inventor (safety pin, sewing machine), 1859
Erastus Corning, American businessman, investor, politician, and founder of Erastus Corning & Co., 1872
Abraham Maslow, American psychologist and creator of Maslow's hierarchy of needs, 1970
William G. McGowan, American entrepreneur and founder and chairman of MCI Communications, 1992
Pat Robertson, American media mogul, religious broadcaster, political commentator, Southern Baptist minister, 2023

Thought for the day

"If an egg is broken by outside force, Life ends. If broken by inside force, Life begins. Great things always begin from inside."

Jim Kwik

I am thankful for beautiful sunrises and sunsets.

June 9

A river brings joy to the city of our God, the sacred home of the Most High. God dwells in that city; it cannot be destroyed. From the very break of day, God will protect it. *(Psalm 46:4-5, NLT)*

Take that meeting outside

Looking for a new place to hold your next company meeting? Try going outside.

A work session at a local park with plenty of fresh air and sunshine may be just what your staff needs to relax, get the creative juices flowing, and increase their productivity. But don't just grab a few cans of soft drinks and some carry-out food; an outdoor meeting takes as much, if not more, planning than one held inside. Some advice:

Reserve a spot with shelter. True, the goal is to be outside, but you also want protection from too much sun and the possibility of rain. Reservations also ensure that your location of choice will be available.

Find out what else is going on. Be sure that other events scheduled for the same day won't distract your group. Consider what other ambient noises and nearby activities might affect your meeting.

Arrange a comfortable work area. Does the park have tables? Do you need to bring chairs or blankets? Be sure the restrooms are clean, conveniently located, and stocked with necessities.

Take advantage of recreational offerings. Plan your agenda so participants can use the park's amenities at breaks or after the meeting.

Plan food carefully. Consider using a caterer. Make lists so you don't forget anything, and have plenty of coolers and ice on hand so food won't spoil.

I pray for my support team.

Read:
Proverbs, Chapter 9

On this day in history

Notable events

In 1902, the first U.S. automat restaurant (a coin-operated cafeteria) opened in Philadelphia.

In 1931, Robert Goddard patented the first rocket-powered aircraft design.

In 1943, the Current Tax Payment Act required employers to withhold taxes from employees' wages and remit them quarterly.

Births

Samuel Slater, English-American industrialist best known for bringing the Industrial Revolution to the U.S. from Great Britain, 1768

Ted Stepien, American businessman (founder of Nationwide Advertising Service), entrepreneur, and NBA team owner, 1925

Deaths

Edward Asahel Birge, American professor and administrator at the University of Wisconsin-Madison, pioneer in the study of limnology, 1950

Thought for the day

"There's always going to be bad stuff out there. But here's the amazing thing—light trumps darkness, every time. You can stick a candle into the dark, but you can't stick the dark into the light."

Jodi Picoult

Nothing is more joyful than experiencing God in prayer.

June 10

> **D**on't you realize that all of you together are the temple of God and that the Spirit of God lives in you? *(1 Corinthians 3:16, NLT)*

Is it time to fire that customer?

Some customers just aren't worth it, but how do you deal with such a situation? The first step is recognizing that the relationship needs to end. Some of the signs include:

- The client doesn't respect or appreciate your work.
- They make excessive demands on your company and staff.
- They are not fair-minded in either their expectations or what they are willing to pay.
- They want work done cheaply and under unrealistic deadlines.
- They don't want you to make a profit.
- They pay bills slowly, or sometimes not at all.
- They push you to the limit in all areas, taking advantage at every turn.
- They see you as a disposable vendor, not a valued partner.

It's always a good idea to try to fix the problem before you simply drop the customer. Put the offending party or parties on notice. Talk to them. Outline what the problems are, what the possible solutions are, and ask for their cooperation to help reach those solutions. Be sure to document these efforts so you can refer to them later, if necessary.

If your attempts to make the relationship mutually productive don't work, it may be time to move on.

Calculate what you will lose in gross revenue, and decide if your business can stand the financial hit. If it can, use the time you had been spending on that client to focus on more profitable clients and prospect for new business. If it can't, put up with the current problem until you can replace that client's vital gross revenues with one or more new clients.

Today we observe

National Ballpoint Pen Day

On this day in history

Notable events

In 1935, Dr. Robert H. Smith from Akron and Bill Wilson from New York city formed Alcoholics Anonymous.

In 1963, the Equal Pay Act was signed into law by President John F. Kennedy.

In 1996, Intel released the 200mhz Pentium chip.

Births

John Jacob Astor III, American businessman, financier, philanthropist, and soldier during the Civil War, 1822

Ruth Bell Graham, Chinese-born American Christian author, wife of evangelist Billy Graham, 1920

Sundar Pichai, Indian-born American business executive, CEO of Alphabet, Inc. and its subsidiary, Google, 1972

Deaths

Mary Maxwell Gates, American banker, civic activist, nonprofit executive, teacher, and mother of Bill Gates, 1994

Jeanne Bice, American entrepreneur, businesswoman, television personality, and founder of the Quacker Factory clothing line, 2011

Thought for the day

"Trust yourself. If you can't trust yourself, how can anyone else trust you? How can you trust anyone else?"

Jacquelyn Lynn

I am thankful for my senses.

Read:
Proverbs, Chapter 10

June 11

Good people leave an inheritance to their grandchildren, but the sinner's wealth passes to the godly. *(Proverbs 13:22, NLT)*

Give yourself credit

It's easy to beat ourselves up when we make a mistake, miss a goal, or fail at something we really wanted to achieve. When your self-talk starts heading in that direction, stop. Give yourself credit.

Give yourself credit for everything you've overcome in your life—all the challenges, all the obstacles, all the trials.

Give yourself credit for all the things you've done for others—all the favors you did, all the gifts you gave, all the pleasant words you took the time to say.

Give yourself credit for the things you've achieved—the projects you finished, the successful investments you've made, the goals you reached or exceeded.

Give yourself credit for the things you do well—the things that give you satisfaction, the things that others praise you for, the things that you've practiced and advanced your skill level.

Give yourself credit for making a difference—for the times you caught someone else before they could fall, for the times you served in a way no one else did or could, for the times you stepped up and took action.

Give yourself credit for having taken chances—for the chances that didn't work out, for the chances that did, for the chances that worked out better than you hoped.

Give yourself credit for little things and big things.

Go back as far as you can remember and write all your credits in a journal so you can remind yourself of them when you need to.

No one is successful one hundred percent of the time. That's okay. Don't let failure stop you from trying again. Let the lessons from your past strengthen you as you deal with the present and prepare for the future.

Give yourself credit.

On this day in history

Notable events

In 1816, the Gas Light Co. of Baltimore was founded.

In 1935, Edwin Armstrong gave the first public demonstration of FM broadcasting in the U.S.

In 1998, Compaq Computer paid $9.6 billion for Digital Equipment Corporation; it was the largest high-tech acquisition at the time.

Births

Paul Mellon, American philanthropist and owner/breeder of thoroughbred racehorses, 1907

Deaths

Henry Clay Folger Jr., American businessman, president and later chairman of Standard Oil of New York, founder of the Folger Shakespeare Library, 1857

Daniel Carter Beard, American illustrator, author, social reformer, founder of Sons of Daniel Boone, which later merged with the Boy Scouts of America, 1941

Thought for the day

"Regardless of how you feel inside, always try to look like a winner. Even if you are behind, a sustained look of control and confidence can give you a mental edge that results in victory."

Arthur Ashe

I pray for those who are ill, that they may be strengthened and comforted as they deal with their conditions.

Read:
Proverbs, Chapter 11

June 12

For every creation of God is good and no food is to be rejected if it is received with thanksgiving. For it is sanctified by God's word and by prayer. *(1 Timothy 4:4–5, NET)*

Be ready for success

Companies that experience rapid and unexpected growth often stumble. Don't let a wave of growth knock you down.

Know what growth looks like. To prepare for something, you have to know what it is and how you'll recognize it.

Maintain relationships with your funding sources and do regular cash flow projections. The faster you grow, the more cash you're likely to need to fund that growth.

Get comfortable in the spotlight. Successful owners of growing companies are almost always in the spotlight to some degree. Be prepared for a level of attention that you probably haven't received before.

Hire people for where you want to be, not where you are. The team that can successfully run a $1 million company is not the same team that can run a $100 million company. If your goal is growth, hire people who can perform in the size company you want to be—they'll help you get there.

Put the right people in the right places. Getting the right people in the right jobs is absolutely critical for sustained growth.

Take care of your people. You may be the driving force behind your company, but your employees are what keep you successful. Recognize and reward that. Also take care of your suppliers, your professional advisors, and anyone else who impacts your operation.

Listen to the experts. Identify the experts you need, listen to them, learn from them and let them help smooth out your learning curves.

Stay close to your customers. Know what they need and want, and do everything you can to provide it.

Focus on your core business and don't get distracted. Stick to the business your company knows best.

Today we observe
Child Labor Day

On this day in history

Notable events

In 1849, Lewis Haslett of Louisville, Kentucky, patented the gas mask.

In 1934, the Air Mail Act of 1934 reintroduced competitive bidding as a means for commercial airlines to procure mail contracts and caused the separation of passenger service airlines from aircraft manufacturers.

In 2009, the transition for full-power TV stations in the U.S. from analog to exclusively digital broadcasting was completed.

Births

David Rockefeller, American investment banker, chairman and chief executive of Chase Manhattan Bank, 1915

George H.W. Bush, 41st U.S. President, 1924.

Blake Ross, American software developer, co-creator of the Mozilla Firefox internet browser, 1985

Thought for the day

"We cannot control the parade of negative thoughts marching through our minds. But we can choose which ones we will give our attention to. Picture your thoughts as people passing by the front of your home. Just because they're walking by doesn't mean you have to invite them in."

Gladys Edmunds

I am thankful for good neighbors.

Read:
Proverbs, Chapter 12

June 13

The Lord does not delay His promise, as some understand delay, but is patient with you, not wanting any to perish but all to come to repentance. *(2 Peter 3:9, HCSB)*

Be sure you can do what you claim

When it comes to marketing, some businesses are extremely regulated and others aren't, but that doesn't mean you can say whatever you want if you can't back it up.

Puffery, which is an exaggeration or statement that no reasonable person would believe is factual, is legally okay, but use it cautiously. For example, a dry cleaner could say, "We offer the best spot treatment in town," and that's okay. But if you say, "We guarantee we will remove blood, grass, and ink stains," you'd better be able to do it.

If your claim is specific, it must be accurate. If what you say can't be backed up, you could get in trouble.

There's a line you can't cross in making claims, and that's when they are specific and can't be proved. Case studies go a long way in providing backup for your claims. You can use them to show that, when used a certain way, then yes, our product does what we say it does. But even with case studies, you should have disclaimers that say, "Under these circumstances, our product has been shown to [do whatever you claim]. Your results may be different."

It's a good idea to keep your claims general, such as "Our product may help …" instead of "Our product cures …" Don't make specific claims that you can't prove. And even if you make broad claims, they still need to be substantiated because you are liable for what you claim.

Today we observe
National Productive Business Civility Day

On this day in history
Notable events
In 1920, the U.S. Post Office ruled children may not be sent by parcel post.
In 2022, a Google engineer said one of the firm's artificial intelligence systems might have its own feelings and its wants should be respected. Google rejected the claims and placed the engineer on paid leave.

Births
William Austin Burt, American inventor (typographer, solar compass), legislator, surveyor, and millwright, 1792
Bradley A. Fiske, American naval officer, author, and inventor of more than 130 electrical and mechanical devices including the rangefinder, 1854
Ken Behring, American real estate developer, builder, entrepreneur, and NFL team owner, 1928
Mary-Kate Olsen, Ashley Olsen, also known as the Olsen twins, American fashion designers and former actresses, 1986

Deaths
Jimmy Dean, American singer, actor, and businessman, creator of the Jimmy Dean sausage brand, 2010

Thought for the day
"In God's eyes, addictions are avenues for salvation. They provide the impetus I need to finally surrender my life to God. My addiction is 'exhibit A' among my proofs for why I can't manage the job of being my own savior."

Mark E. Thibodeaux

I pray for fathers and those who stand in the stead of fathers.

Read:
Proverbs, Chapter 13

June 14

> And I saw that there is an advantage in wisdom over simpleminded folly as light has an advantage over darkness. *(Ecclesiastes 2:13, LSB)*

We all have our work to do

In *Work as Worship: How Your Labor Becomes Your Legacy*, Mark Goldstein says,

"When it comes to doing God's work and our mission field, an organization's receptionist is just as impactful as the well-known evangelist or the corporate executive. But receptionists often don't get the recognition they deserve. They have just as much relevance, they have just as strong of a story, and they are as blessed gift-wise with the overt and covert gifts as anyone, anywhere. It's okay for us to say, 'Lord, give me your eyes and ears, let me be the hands and feet to do what you've called me to do, where you've called me to do it.'"

Peace Prayer of Saint Francis of Assisi

Lord, make me an instrument of your peace:
   where there is hatred, let me sow love;
   where there is injury, pardon;
   where there is doubt, faith;
   where there is despair, hope;
   where there is darkness, light;
   where there is sadness, joy.
O divine Master, grant that I may not so much seek to be consoled as to console,
   to be understood as to understand,
   to be loved as to love.
   For it is in giving that we receive,
   it is in pardoning that we are pardoned,
   and it is in dying that we are born to eternal life.

   Amen.

I am thankful for all the people who care about me.

Today we observe

U.S. Flag Day

World Blood Donor Day

On this day in history

Notable events

In 1951, the first UNIVAC 1 computer (first American computer designed for business and administrative use) entered service at the U.S. Census Bureau.

In 1954, President Dwight Eisenhower signed a bill to add the phrase "under God" into the U.S. Pledge of Allegiance.

Births

John Bartlett, American writer and publisher (*Bartlett's Familiar Quotations*), 1820

E. Cuyler Hammond, American biologist and epidemiologist, one of the first researchers to establish a link between smoking and lung cancer, 1912

John F. MacArthur, American Reformed Baptist pastor, author, radio and television host, 1939

Donald J. Trump, 45th U.S. President, 1946

Bob Frankston, American software engineer and businessman, co-creator (with Dan Bricklin) of the VisiCalc spreadsheet program, cofounder of Software Arts, 1949

Deaths

Ruth Bell Graham, Chinese-born American Christian author, wife if evangelist Billy Graham, 2007

Thought for the day

"Real difficulties can be overcome. It is only the imaginary ones that are unconquerable."

Theodore N. Vail

Read:
Proverbs, Chapter 14

June 15

As you therefore have received Christ Jesus the Lord, continue to walk in him, rooted and built up in him and established in the faith, just as you were taught, abounding in thanksgiving. *(Colossians 2:6-7, NRSVue)*

Complacency can kill a company

When everything is going well, it's easy to get complacent. But when you get complacent, that's when things will stop going well.

Try these strategies to keep your business from becoming stagnant.

Market research. You've probably already done it, but can you use that information in a different way? Maybe to reach a new audience or to better understand what differentiates you?

Get uncomfortable. When your business is running smoothly, it's an ideal time to step out of your comfort zone. Take a risk much like you did when you started.

Improve customer service. It may already be good or great, but figure out what you can do to make it even better.

Study your competitors. Do a SWOT (strengths, weaknesses, opportunities, and threats) analysis of your competition. Develop ways to combat their strengths and capitalize on their weaknesses.

Stay current on trends. Pay attention to trends within your industry and those outside it that could still affect your business.

Automate. What are you still doing manually that could be automated?

Boost your cybersecurity. Are you as secure as you think you are? Probably not. Do an analysis and update your plan.

What's bothering you the most right now? Will it matter in a year from now? If not, let it go. If it will, pray. Ask God to guide you to a resolution. Then let it go.

Today we observe
World Elder Abuse Awareness Day

Nature Photography Day

On this day in history

Notable events

In 1844, the Goodyear Company patented the vulcanization of rubber.

Births

William Butler Ogden, American real estate investor, railroad executive, politician (first mayor of Chicago), and philanthropist, 1805

Marshall Field IV, publisher, businessman, owner of the Chicago Daily News, 1916

Deaths

James K. Polk, 11th U.S. President, 1849

Charles Francis Brush, American engineer, inventor (arc lamp), entrepreneur, and philanthropist, 1929

George W. Fuller, American sanitary engineer responsible for important innovations in water and wastewater treatment, 1934

Kirk Kerkorian, Armenian-American businessman, investor, and philanthropist; known as the father of the mega-resort, 2015

Thought for the day

"Because of the empty tomb, we have peace. Because of His resurrection, we can have peace during even the most troubling of times because we know He is in control of all that happens in the world."

Paul Chappell

I pray for the entry-level workers, for those who are just getting started in their careers.

Read:
Proverbs, Chapter 15

June 16

One Lord, one faith, one baptism; one God and Father of all, who is over all and through all and in all. *(Ephesians 4:5-6, NIV)*

What's really stopping you from getting what you want?

You have a big but vague goal. What's stopping you from reaching it?

To find out, you need to drill down to some very focused questions.

Let's say your goal is to get more customers. But to ask, "How do I get more customers?" is so broad it's useless.

Instead of "how do I get," ask, "What's stopping me from getting more customers?"

If your answer is that you don't know who your potential customers are, your next question should be, "What's stopping me from finding out who my potential customers are?" If you don't know how to reach them, your question should be, "What's stopping me from finding out how to reach my potential customers?"

If you don't have access to certain market data, what's stopping you from getting it?

Instead of trying to figure out how to do something, ask yourself what's stopping you from doing it. Then deal with that and watch the results.

Thought for the day

"Innovation is the specific tool of entrepreneurs, the means by which they exploit change as an opportunity for a different business or a different service. It is capable of being presented as a discipline, capable of being learned, capable of being practiced. Entrepreneurs need to search purposefully for the sources of innovation, the changes and their symptoms that indicate opportunities for successful innovation. And they need to know and to apply the principles of successful innovation."

— Peter F. Drucker

On this day in history

Notable events

In 1903, Henry Ford and other prospective stockholders in the Ford Motor Company met to sign the official paperwork required to create a new corporation.

In 1903, Pepsi-Cola became an official trademark.

In 1930, Trans World Airlines (TWA) was founded as Transcontinental & Western Air.

In 1977, Oracle Corporation was founded by Larry Ellison and Bob Miner as Software Development Laboratories.

In 2017, Amazon announced it was buying Whole Foods for $13.7 billion.

Births

Nelson Doubleday, American book publisher, president of Doubleday Company (1922-1946), 1889

Katharine Graham, American newspaper publisher (*The Washington Post*), 1917

August Busch III, American businessman, president (1974-2002) and CEO (1975-2002) of the Anheuser-Busch Companies, Inc., 1937

Deaths

Ezra Fitch, American real estate developer and hobbyist outdoorsman who bought into and later fully owned the company that became Abercrombie & Fitch, 1930

Elmer Ambrose Sperry, American entrepreneur and inventor, founder of Sperry Gyroscope company, known as the father of modern navigation technology, 1930

John S. Knight, American newspaper publisher and editor, cofounder of Knight Ridder newspapers, 1981

I am thankful for the disappointments that helped me see another path and grow as a person.

Read:
Proverbs, Chapter 16

June 17

If you make the Lord your refuge, if you make the Most High your shelter, no evil will conquer you; no plague will come near your home. For he will order his angels to protect you wherever you go. *(Psalm 91:9-11, NLT)*

It's okay to say, "I don't know what to say."

We've all been in situations where we didn't know what to say—situations that range from hearing bad news to being the target of a rude comment or question.

So what should you say when you don't know what to say?

One response, of course, is to say nothing. That can sometimes be powerful and effective.

It's better to remain silent and be thought a fool than to speak and remove all doubt.

We've all heard some version of that maxim, which has been attributed to many sages over the years. Even King Solomon included it in the book of Proverbs.

Even fools are thought wise when they keep silent; with their mouths shut, they seem intelligent. (Proverbs 17:28, NLT)

Sometimes total silence doesn't work, and you must speak. In that case, it's fine to tell the truth and say, "I don't know what to say."

And then be quiet. Don't feel like you have to fill the silence—that's when you're likely to say something you'll regret. Let the other person talk and use that as a guide for what, if anything, you should say next.

Remember, honesty is the best policy (another maxim that's been attributed to many). If you don't know what to say, say so—and then be quiet.

Thought for the day

"Speak little; do much. Well done is better than well said."

Benjamin Franklin

Today we observe

Global Garbage Man Day and beginning of Waste & Recycling Workers Week

On this day in history

Notable events

In 1863, Travelers Insurance Company in Hartford, Connecticut received its official state charter.

In 1946, the first commercially operated mobile telephone network for private subscribers was opened by AT&T and its associate company Southwestern Bell in St. Louis, Missouri.

In 1963, the U.S. Supreme Court ruled that legally or officially mandated Bible reading or prayer in public schools is unconstitutional.

Births

Eben Sumner Draper, American businessman (Draper Corporation) and politician, 1858

Ruth Wakefield, American inventor and creator of the Toll House Cookie, the first chocolate chip cookie, 1903

Mercer Reynolds, American businessman and cofounder of the investment firm Reynolds, DeWitt & Co., 1945

Is your contact form working?

If you have a contact form on your website (and you should!), check it regularly to be sure it's working. Don't risk not receiving a message from a customer who needs help or a prospective customer trying to reach you for information. At least once a month, go outside your system and send yourself a test message.

I pray that I care more about God's opinion of me than of any person's opinion of me.

Read:
Proverbs, Chapter 17

June 18

Therefore, since we are surrounded by such a huge crowd of witnesses to the life of faith, let us strip off every weight that slows us down, especially the sin that so easily trips us up. And let us run with endurance the race God has set before us. We do this by keeping our eyes on Jesus, the champion who initiates and perfects our faith. Because of the joy awaiting him, he endured the cross, disregarding its shame. Now he is seated in the place of honor beside God's throne. *(Hebrews 12:1-2, NLT)*

Training senior workers

Workers over 65 can be a rich and reliable labor resource. What do you need to know about training and integrating them into your organization?

Get rid of your own stereotypes. Older people are not automatically senile, stubborn, and set in their ways—in fact, many actually "get it" faster than their younger counterparts.

Don't teach them what they already know. Seniors have a lot of basic jobs skills, such as getting to work on time, treating customers and others with courtesy and respect, and the importance of doing quality work. You don't need to teach them those things.

Give them the time they need to learn. Older people may need more time to learn a new task or skill, but with that additional time, they can learn to perform new tasks with fewer mistakes than young workers.

Create an effective learning environment. Senses, particularly sight and hearing, tend to dim with age. Be sure your training facility has adequate lighting and good acoustics, and that background noise is kept to a minimum. Provide frequent breaks for using restrooms or just moving around.

Don't assume seniors will resist change and technology. Most seniors will enthusiastically embrace new technology if they are provided with adequate training.

For assistance with setting up training programs for seniors, contact your local agency on aging, your public school systems' adult education department, or local senior citizens centers.

Today we observe
International Panic Day

On this day in history

Notable events
In 1948, Columbia/CBS introduced the 33$\frac{1}{3}$ rpm LP record.

Births
Edward Willis Scripps, American newspaper published and cofounder of the E. W. Scripps Company and United Press Associations (later United Press International), 1854

Henry Clay Folger, Jr., American businessman, president and later chairman of Standard Oil of New York, founder of the Folger Shakespeare Library, 1857

Hugh McColl, American banker and former chairman and CEO of Bank of America, 1935

William Randolph Hearst III, American businessman, publisher, and philanthropist, 1949

Deaths
Ralph J. Roberts, American businessman and founder of Comcast, 2015

Stockton Rush, American businessman, engineer, cofounder and CEO of OceanGate, 2023

Thought for the day

"Christianity is not a playground. It's a battleground."

Craig Groeschel

I am thankful for the farmers who grow our food.

Read:
Proverbs, Chapter 18

June 19

T hen the Lord answered me and said: Write the vision; make it plain on tablets, so that a runner may read it. *(Habakkuk 2:2, NRSVue)*

You need a great profile picture

Your profile picture is one of the most important elements of your online presence.

What does it say about you? Does it reflect your brand? Does it inspire confidence in prospective clients?

Here's how to get a great profile picture:

Avoid selfies and snapshots. Your profile picture needs to look professional, and that means hiring a professional photographer to do it.

Choose the right photographer. Your photographer should put you at ease, and understand that they're trying to capture your personality, not just doing a bland headshot.

Prepare for the photo shoot. Get your hair done. Consider having a make-up artist help you look your best. Put some thought into your wardrobe selection. Consider inviting a friend you enjoy being around to go with you.

Have fun during the shoot. Get comfortable. Try some different poses that might capture your personality in a way you hadn't thought of before. Most important, laugh.

Get help choosing the best photos. Most of us don't like the way we look in pictures, so get someone you trust to help you select the shots that will work for you.

Be realistic when it comes to editing your pictures. Photographers can edit out blemishes and whiten your smile a bit, but don't let them edit your picture to the point that you're unrecognizable.

Once you get a fabulous profile picture, update it every few years. You don't want people to be shocked when they see you in person because you've changed significantly since your profile picture was taken. If your picture is two or three years old, it's probably time for a new one.

Today we observe

Juneteenth

National Take Your Cat to Work Day

National Watch Day

On this day in history

Notable events

In 1865, Union General Gordon Granger declared that slaves in Texas were free.

In 2018, the ten millionth U.S. patent was granted to inventor Joseph Marron and patent assignee Raytheon Company for a "Coherent LADAR Using Intra-Pixel Quadrature Detection," which improves laser detection and ranging.

Births

William H. Webb, American shipbuilder and philanthropist, called America's first true naval architect, 1816

Ray Noorda, American electrical engineer, businessman, CEO of Novell, Inc., known as the father of computer networking, 1924

Thomas Breitling, American entrepreneur, cofounder of Travelscape, president of Breitling Ventures, 1969

Deaths

Thomas J. Watson, American businessman, chairman and CEO of IBM (1914-56), 1956

Thought for the day

"At least three times every day take a moment and ask yourself what is really important. Have the wisdom and the courage to build your life around your answer."

Lee Jampolsky

I am thankful for the opportunity to represent God in the world.

Read:
Proverbs, Chapter 19

June 20

I keep asking that the God of our Lord Jesus Christ, the glorious Father, may give you the Spirit of wisdom and revelation, so that you may know him better. *(Ephesians 1:17, NIV)*

Could your product become obsolete?

You never know when a change in your industry or a technological advance will make your current product or service obsolete. That's why you need to expand your product line. The more products and services you have, the easier it will be for you to survive discontinuing one or more of them.

Think 8-track tapes, even cassette tapes. Think BetaMax, VHS tapes, and now even DVDs. What's the market for those products today? Essentially zero.

Remember the Sony Walkman? Who uses a portable cassette player anymore? It's all smartphones playing digital files, not tapes.

If you're old enough to remember when fax machines were introduced, you'll recall how exciting it was to transmit documents in just minutes over telephone lines. Yet fax use was slashed by various types of electronic transmission because it's faster and paperless. While there are still a few fax machines in use, the technology is certainly moving toward obsolescence.

Be prepared for your product to become obsolete. It can and probably will happen.

Thought for the day

"If you pray more you will pray better. Take the help of all your senses to pray."
Saint Mother Teresa of Calcutta

Grow your faith by replacing feelings of envy with gratitude.

Today we observe
Ugliest Dog Day

World Productivity Day

On this day in history

Notable events

In 1840, Samuel F. B. Morse was granted a patent for "improvement in the mode of communicating information by signals by the application of electromagnetism," an electric telegraph system that led to the creation of Morse Code.

In 2017, Uber founder Travis Kalanick resigned as CEO after a shareholder revolt.

In 2019, Slack Technologies went public on the New York Stock Exchange. Salesforce acquired Slack in 2021.

Births

George T. Delacorte, Jr., American magazine publisher, founder of Dell Publishing, and philanthropist, 1894

Lloyd Hall, American chemist and inventor who contributed to the science of food preservation, 1894

Edgar Bronfman, Sr., Canadian-American businessman (president, treasurer and CEO of Seagram) and philanthropist, 1929

Deaths

Howard Deering Johnson, American entrepreneur, businessman, and founder of the Howard Johnson's chain of restaurants and motels, 1972

Jack Kilby, American electrical engineer, inventor, Nobel Prize winner, co-inventor of the handheld calculator and thermal printer, 2005

I pray for resilience and the ability to bounce back after difficult times.

Read:
Proverbs, Chapter 20

June 21

May God himself, the God of peace, sanctify you through and through. May your whole spirit, soul and body be kept blameless at the coming of our Lord Jesus Christ. The one who calls you is faithful, and he will do it. *(1 Thessalonians 5:23–24, NIV)*

All Things Bright and Beautiful

Cecil Frances Alexander, 1848

Refrain:
All things bright and beautiful,
all creatures great and small,
all things wise and wonderful,
the Lord God made them all.

Each little flow'r that opens,
each little bird that sings,
God made their glowing colors,
God made their tiny wings. *[Refrain]*

The purple-headed mountain,
the river running by,
the sunset and the morning
that brightens up the sky. *[Refrain]*

The cold wind in the winter,
the pleasant summer sun,
the ripe fruits in the garden:
God made them every one. *[Refrain]*

God gave us eyes to see them,
and lips that we might tell
how great is God Almighty,
who has made all things well. *[Refrain]*

Thought for the day

"I believe life is a series of near misses. A lot of what we ascribe to luck is not luck at all. It's seizing the day and accepting responsibility for your future. It's seeing what other people don't see and pursuing that vision."

Lewis Grizzard

Read:
Proverbs, Chapter 21

On this day in history

Notable events
In 1834, American inventor and businessman Cyrus McCormick was granted a patent for his reaping machine.
In 1879, Frank Winfield Woolworth opened his first successful Woolworth's Great Five Cent Store in Lancaster, Pennsylvania.

Births
Daniel Carter Beard, American illustrator, author, social reformer, founder of Sons of Daniel Boone, which later merged with the Boy Scouts of America, 1850
Charles Momsen, American inventor and pioneer in submarine rescue, 1896
Pierre Omidyar, French-born Iranian-American technology entrepreneur, software engineer, philanthropist, founder of eBay, 1967

Deaths
Leland Stanford, American business tycoon (Southern Pacific Railroad) and founder of Stanford University, 1893
Earl William "Madman" Muntz, American businessman and engineer, television commercial pioneer, creator of the Muntz Stereo-Pak, invented the practice known as Muntzing (simplifying otherwise complicated electronic devices), 1987

I pray on the comfort of 2 Chronicles 20:15.

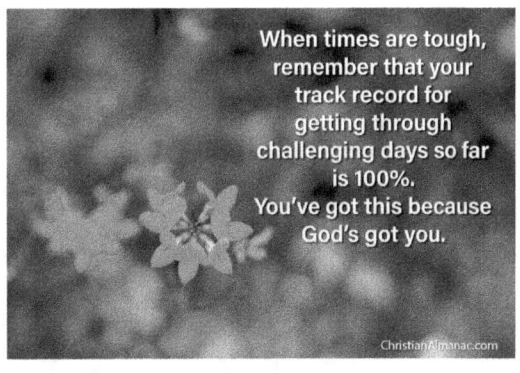

June 22

There is a time for everything, and a season for every activity under the heavens: a time to be born and a time to die, a time to plant and a time to uproot, a time to kill and a time to heal, a time to tear down and a time to build, a time to weep and a time to laugh, a time to mourn and a time to dance, a time to scatter stones and a time to gather them, a time to embrace and a time to refrain from embracing, a time to search and a time to give up, a time to keep and a time to throw away, a time to tear and a time to mend, a time to be silent and a time to speak, a time to love and a time to hate, a time for war and a time for peace. *(Ecclesiastes 3:1-8, NIV)*

What's your spiritual growth plan?

In the marketplace, we do a lot of planning. We have business plans, marketing plans, production plans, financial plans, and more. But none of those plans is as important as our own personal spiritual growth plan.

Use these steps to develop your spiritual growth plan.

Define spiritual growth. Understand what spiritual growth is beyond the superficial warm and fuzzy to what it really means to be a spiritually mature Christian.

Set goals. What are you going to do to achieve spiritual growth? Write that down. Be specific and include deadlines.

Identify your resources. Growing spiritually is not a solitary exercise. Who (other people) and what (books, studies, etc.) will you use to help?

Evaluate your progress. Regularly return to your goals and see how you're doing. Make adjustments and add new goals as necessary.

Model your growth and mentor others. Be a model of someone who is growing spiritually for others to emulate. Spiritual growth can be contagious—let others catch it from you. Take that down to a finer level by becoming a mentor to someone who is also seeking spiritual growth.

Commit to your plan and make it a priority. Give your spiritual growth the attention and precedence it deserves.

Today we observe
Positive Media Day

On this day in history

Notable events
In 1984, Virgin Atlantic Airways began operations.

Births
Richard Gurley Drew, American inventor who invented masking tape and cellophane tape, 1899

Deaths
David O. Selznick, American film producer, screenwriter, and film studio executive, 1965
Joseph Pedott, American advertising executive and entrepreneur (Chia Pet; the Clapper), 2023

Thought for the day

"I've always found that anything worth achieving will always have obstacles in the way and you've got to have that drive and determination to overcome those obstacles on route to whatever it is that you want to accomplish."

Chuck Norris

I am thankful for my enemies and what they teach me.

Read:
Proverbs, Chapter 22

June 23

My old self has been crucified with Christ. It is no longer I who live, but Christ lives in me. *(Galatians 2:20, NLT)*

A creative source of content ideas

One of the biggest challenges content marketers face is coming up with fresh material.

A great way to get ideas is to listen to what people around you are saying when you're in public places. In other words, eavesdrop.

If people are talking openly about something, it's obviously important to them. And if you hear two or three people discussing a topic, chances are that it's an issue for plenty of others as well.

When you're standing in line, commuting on a bus or train, in an elevator, at school, in the grocery store—wherever you are that you can overhear people talking with one another, pay attention to what they're saying.

Don't do anything illegal or immoral. Don't plant bugs or do anything else that would invade anyone's privacy. But when people talk in public places, they have no expectation of privacy, and they probably don't care that a stranger might overhear them.

It might not be appropriate for you to join their conversation (although sometimes it could be—use your own judgment there), but you may have information to share on the topic that would be of value to a wider audience. So when you hear something interesting, especially something that relates to your business or is a problem your product can solve, use that as the foundation for a blog, special report, ebook, or other information product. Write in a way that doesn't include anything that could identify the individuals involved.

Read: Proverbs, Chapter 23

Today we observe

International Olympic Day

Let it Go Day

National Family Owned & Operated Businesses Day

National Typewriter Day

On this day in history

Notable events

In 1964, Jack S. Kilby received a U.S. patent for his invention of "Miniaturized Electronic Circuits," now known as integrated circuits.

Births

Willie Mae Ford Smith, American musician and Christian evangelist instrumental in the development and spread of gospel music in the U.S., 1904

Art Modell, American businessman, entrepreneur, and NFL team owner, 1925

Vint Cert, American internet pioneer, led the engineering of MCI Mail (the first commercial email service connected to the internet), recognized (with Bob Kahn) as one of the fathers of the internet, 1943

Charles Lewis, Jr., American businessman, promoter, entertainer, and founder of the Tapout clothing line, 1963

Deaths

Jonas Salk, American medical researcher and virologist who created the polio vaccine, 1995

Dick Van Patten, American actor, comedian, businessman, and animal welfare advocate, 2015

Thought for the day

"Clarity about what matters provides clarity about what does not."

Cal Newport

I pray for mercy.

June 24

> Don't love money; be satisfied with what you have. For God has said, "I will never fail you. I will never abandon you." *(Hebrews 13:5, NLT)*

Get rid of something you don't need

Most of us have too much stuff. Even people who don't have a lot are likely to have things they don't need that are cluttering up their homes, offices, and lives. We know we need to declutter but we don't have time, and the task is too overwhelming.

You don't need to clean out your entire garage or closet or storage area. You don't need to set aside hours or even days to sort, purge, and organize.

Just get rid of *one thing* that you don't need.

Don't spend a lot of time thinking about it. Look around until you see something you haven't used in a while and may never use again.

Give it to someone, donate it to charity, or simply throw it away. But get rid of it. Then savor the feeling of satisfaction and freedom that comes from letting go of something that didn't need to be taking up space in your world.

Challenge yourself every day: How much love and kindness can you share? How will you do it?

Thought for the day

"Show kindness whenever possible. Show it to the people in front of you, the people coming up behind you, and the people with whom you are running neck and neck. It will vastly improve the quality of your own life, the lives of others, and the state of the world."

Ann Patchett

Today we observe
Upcycling Day

On this day in history

Notable events
- In 1884, the East Cleveland Street Railway Company in Cleveland, Ohio, began operating the first U.S. commercial electric streetcar line.
- In 1902, what would eventually become Target Corporation was founded by George Dayton as Goodfellow Dry Goods in Minneapolis.

Births
- Éleuthère Irénée du Pont, French-American chemist and industrialist, founded the gunpowder manufacturer E. I. du Pont de Nemours and Company (the original DuPont company), 1771
- Thomas Blanchard, American inventor and pioneer of the assembly line style of mass production in the U.S., 1788
- Gustavus Franklin Swift, American founder of the meatpacking firm Swift & Company, 1839
- Roy O. Disney, American businessman and cofounder of The Walt Disney Company, 1893
- William B. Ziff, Jr., American publishing executive and author, CEO of Ziff Davis Inc., 1930

Deaths
- Grover Cleveland, 22nd and 24th U.S. President, 1908
- Paul Winchell, American ventriloquist, comedian, actor, humanitarian, and inventor (artificial heart), 2005
- Frank Heart, American computer engineer, influential in computer networking, 2018

I am thankful for art.

Read:
Proverbs, Chapter 24

June 25

For the Lord is our judge, the Lord is our lawgiver, the Lord is our king; it is he who will save us. *(Isaiah 33:22, NIV)*

Build on honor and integrity

Trust is hard to earn, easy to lose, and once lost, extremely difficult, if not impossible, to regain. Consumer skepticism is sending business owners and managers a clear message: organizations must maintain the trust of their customers, employees, suppliers, and communities if they hope to succeed. Doing that requires honor and integrity.

Business owners, managers, and employees are faced daily with ethical dilemmas for which there are often no easy answers. Complicating the issue is that not all the companies you compete against adhere to the same high standards. It's a good idea to articulate your company's values and ethics in a policy statement, and use that statement both as an operations guide and a marketing tool. A clear statement removes any doubt as to what is considered right and wrong.

When it comes to your employees, deal swiftly and decisively with any violation of your values statement, but temper your action with understanding. Consider the true motivation behind the behavior when deciding what action to take. Was the person's behavior thought-out and intentional, or were they trying to do the right thing but made a mistake in the process? In the case of the former, that's probably someone you don't want in your company. In the case of the latter, some counseling and education should prevent the mistake from being repeated.

When your organization experiences an ethical lapse, it's not the end of the world. Recovery is possible. Begin by admitting what you've done to the affected parties. Take responsibility, put a plan in place to correct the situation, and learn from what happened.

Today we observe

International Day of the Seafarer
Color TV Day
Please Take My Children to Work Day

On this day in history

Notable events

In 1633, Massachusetts Bay Colony Governor John Winthrop introduced the fork (then known as a split spoon) to American dining. The clergy called it evil, saying the only thing worthy of touching God's food was fingers.

In 1951, CBS broadcast the first color television show, a musical variety special, but it couldn't be seen on black and white TV sets.

In 1981, Microsoft restructured to become an incorporated business in its home state of Washington.

Deaths

Fred Trump, Sr., American real estate developer and businessman, father of Donald Trump, 1999

Richard B. Sellars, American business executive (chairman and CEO of Johnson & Johnson), philanthropist, 2010

Ken Behring, American real estate developer, builder, entrepreneur, and NFL team owner, 2019

Thought for the day

"Even if you are on the right track, you will get run over if you just sit there."
Will Rogers

I pray that I will be remembered as a Jesus follower.

Read:
Proverbs, Chapter 25

June 26

For God has not given us a spirit of fear and timidity, but of power, love, and self-discipline. *(2 Timothy 1:7, NLT)*

Surviving failure

Failure is inevitable and it's never fun. But it's survivable and—more important—it's the key to success. Here's how to deal with failure:

Accept your feelings. Your feelings are your feelings—it's good to own them. When you fail, you likely feel sad, embarrassed, anxious, angry, or stressed. It doesn't feel good, but you need to accept how you feel.

Practice healthy coping and avoid unhealthy distractions. Indulge yourself in beneficial activities—call a friend, exercise, take a long bubble bath. Avoid unhealthy activities such as minimizing your pain or trying to mask your feelings with food, drugs, or alcohol.

Learn from what happened. As quickly as you can, redirect your negative feelings and figure out the lessons from your failure. What did you do wrong and what can you do differently?

Get away from the situation. If you can, get out of where you are now and into a new place, even if it's just temporary.

Don't isolate yourself. You may be tempted to hide after a failure, but don't. Surround yourself with positive people who will lift you up.

Don't give up. Just because what you tried didn't work doesn't mean another strategy won't. Figure out a different way.

Thought for the day

"We delight in the beauty of the butterfly, but rarely admit the changes it has gone through to achieve that beauty."
Maya Angelou

I am thankful for imagination—mine and others'.

Today we observe
Forgiveness Day
National Barcode Day
World Refrigeration Day

On this day in history

Notable events
In 1797, Charles Newbold was awarded a patent for the cast-iron plow; unfortunately, farmers feared the iron would poison their soil.
In 1919, the *New York Daily News* was founded as the *Illustrated Daily News*, the first U.S. daily printed in tabloid format.
In 1934, the Federal Credit Union Act enabled credit unions to be organized throughout the U.S. under charters approved by the federal government.

Births
Alonzo Herndon, American businessman and entrepreneur; born into slavery, he became one of the first millionaires in the U.S., 1858
Bill Lear, American inventor (developed the car radio and 8-track cartridge) and businessman, founder of Learjet, a business jet manufacturer, 1902
Milton Glaser, American graphic designer (the I Love New York logo), cofounder of Push Pin Studios and *New York* magazine, 1929
Orin C. Smith, American businessman, president and CEO of Starbucks Corporation (2000-2005), 1942

Deaths
David Rittenhouse, American astronomer, inventor, scientific instrument craftsman, first director of the U.S. Mint, 1796
Walter Ralston Martin, American Baptist minister, author, founder of the Christian Research Institute, 1989
Liz Claiborne, American fashion designer and entrepreneur, 2007
Milton Glaser, American graphic designer (the I Love New York logo), cofounder of Push Pin Studios and *New York* magazine, 2020

Read:
Proverbs, Chapter 26

June 27

> "My wayward children," says the Lord, "come back to me, and I will heal your wayward hearts." "Yes, we're coming," the people reply, "for you are the Lord our God. *(Jeremiah 3:22, NLT)*

We're not in this alone

Have you ever thought about the people you know who consistently show strength and resilience in the face of seemingly insurmountable challenges? About the people who somehow manage to enjoy incredible peace during some of life's toughest times? About how they do it and what they have in common?

Though it is human nature to want to be in complete control of the situations and circumstances we must deal with, life is not something we are made to handle alone. No matter what's happening, good or bad, we need God and each other. We were created to be part of God's family, dependent on God and on others.

That dependency is a magnificent two-way street. We are not just receivers of God's grace, mercy and wisdom, we are His wonderful hands in this world—hands that are used to give and receive in beautiful interconnectivity.

If we try to do things on our own, we will not only fail in the end, we will be miserable along the way. That we are dependent on God is not a burden, it's not a crutch, it's something to be celebrated. Accepting and celebrating our dependence on God and one another is the key to knowing peace in this chaotic world.

When you understand that, accept it and live it, it won't matter how out-of-control the world gets because you know God is in control and you'll be at peace.

I pray for discernment and the ability to recognize the lies the devil is telling me.

Read:
Proverbs, Chapter 27

Today we observe

Micro-, Small and Medium Sized (MSMEs) Enterprises Day

On this day in history

Notable events

In 1962, Ross Perot founded Electronic Data Systems, an American multinational information technology equipment and services company that was acquired by Hewlett-Packard in 2008.

In 1972, Nolan Bushnell and Ted Dabney founded Atari, Inc., and released Atari's first product, Pong, five months later.

In 2003, registration for the U.S. National Do Not Call Registry began.

Births

Harriet Hubbard Ayer, American cosmetics entrepreneur and journalist, 1849

Helen Keller, American author, disability rights advocate, political activist, and lecturer, 1880

Juan Terry Trippe, American commercial aviation pioneer, entrepreneur, and founder of Pan American World Airways, 1899

Ross Perot, American business magnate, politician, and philanthropist, 1930

Deaths

Mary Elizabeth Anderson, American real estate developer, rancher, viticulturist, and inventor of the windshield wiper, 1953

John T. Walton, American businessman and philanthropist, son of Walmart founder Sam Walton, 2005

Thought for the day

"Ordinary people believe only in the possible. Extraordinary people visualize not what is possible or probable, but rather what is impossible. And by visualizing the impossible, they begin to see it as possible."

Cherie Carter-Scott

June 28

Then turning to the disciples he said privately, "Blessed are the eyes that see what you see! For I tell you that many prophets and kings desired to see what you see, and did not see it, and to hear what you hear, and did not hear it." *(Luke 10:23-24, ESV)*

Staying optimistic

The world is in turmoil and it's easy to be overtaken by pessimism. But optimists have an edge—they enjoy increased physical, mental, and emotional health. They manage stress better. They're better problem-solvers, more motivated, and generally happier. So how can you stay optimistic? Some tips:

Use positive self-talk. Reject your inner critic. Speak to yourself in positive terms.

Focus on your successes. Things may seem crazy, but you've accomplished some great things.

Stay in the present. Don't worry about the future, just deal with the here and now.

Let the past go. Don't waste time on regrets; learn and move on.

Be grateful. When negativity threatens, stop and think about all you have to be grateful for.

Challenge your negative thoughts. When a negative thought enters your mind, reframe it and turn it into something positive.

Be an example. Optimism is learned and it's a teachable skill, so be the example for people you care about—family members, friends, and colleagues.

Commit a random act of kindness. Go out and do something nice for someone who isn't expecting it.

Make optimism a choice. It takes practice, but it can be done.

Today we observe

National Insurance Awareness Day

National Logistics Day

On this day in history

Notable events

In 1935, the U.S. Treasury announced its intention to build a gold depository on the grounds of Fort Knox to move gold reserves away from coastal cities to areas less vulnerable to foreign military invasion.

Births

Robert Ledley, professor, author, pioneered the use of electronic digital computers in biology and medicine, inventor (whole-body CT scanner), 1926

Klaus Schmiegel, German-American chemist and inventor best known for his work in organic chemistry which led to the invention of Prozac, 1939

Elon Musk, South African-born American business magnate, inventor, investor, philanthropist, 1971

Rob Dyrdek, American entrepreneur, actor, producer, former professional skateboarder, 1974

Deaths

James Madison, 4th U.S. President, 1836

Vannevar Bush, American engineer, inventor, and science administrator who headed the U.S. Office of Scientific Research and Development during World War II; founder of the company that became Raytheon Company; known for his work on analog computers, 1974

I am thankful for life's simple pleasures and the small blessings that are so easily overlooked.

Read:
Proverbs, Chapter 28

Thought for the day

"We can throw stones, complain about them, stumble on them, climb over them, or build with them."

William Arthur Ward

June 29

God created humankind in his own image, in the image of God he created them, male and female he created them. *(Genesis 1:27, NET)*

Ghosted? It's not about you

Ghosting is quietly and abruptly disappearing from someone's life, essentially becoming invisible. The person doing the ghosting stops communicating with no explanation, leaving the person being ghosted wondering what happened. When we've been ghosted, we feel rejected—and it hurts.

We typically hear about ghosting in the context of romantic relationships, but it happens with platonic and even business relationships, too.

When we've been ghosted, we tend to focus on what we could have done that chased the other person away. We spend a lot of time trying to figure out what happened, what changed, and what we can do to fix it. But the reality is when someone ghosts us, it's usually not about us—it's about them. It's their action based on their decision, and we may never know why.

How to ease the pain of being ghosted:

Know that you didn't fail. Being ghosted says more about the other person than it does about you. You are responsible for your behavior; they are responsible for theirs. That their behavior is rude and hurtful is a reflection on them, not you.

Forgive them. Ghosting is disrespectful and cruel. The reasons people ghost will vary—maybe they didn't have the courage to tell the truth about something or maybe they're simply unreliable. Whatever the reason, the deed and damage are done, so forgive them for hurting you.

Pray for them. It's never easy to pray for someone who has hurt you and made you angry. Do it anyway. It's hard to stay angry with someone you're praying for.

Let them go. You can't stay in a relationship the other person has left—and if they've ghosted you, they're gone. Accept it and move on.

Today we observe
National Camera Day

On this day in history

Notable events

In 1906, the Hepburn Act, a U.S. federal law that expanded the jurisdiction of the Interstate Commerce Commission, became effective.

In 1956, Congress passed the Federal Highway Act, which authorized the construction of the Interstate Highway System.

In 2009, financier Bernie Madoff was sentenced to 150 years in prison for conducting the largest known Ponzi scheme in history. He died in prison in 2021.

Births

William James Mayo, physician and surgeon, cofounder of the Mayo Clinic, 1861

Paul Galvin, American businessman and cofounder of Motorola, 1895

Deaths

John B. Gorrie, Nevisian-born American physician and scientist, credited as the inventor of mechanical refrigeration, 1855

Thought for the day

"All the woulda-coulda-shouldas layin' in the sun, talkin' 'bout the things they woulda-coulda-shoulda done... But all those woulda-coulda-shouldas all ran away and hid from one little did."

Shel Silverstein

I pray for journalists.

Read:
Proverbs, Chapter 29

June 30

The Lord is close to the brokenhearted and saves those who are crushed in spirit. The righteous person may have many troubles, but the Lord delivers him from them all; *(Psalm 34:18-19, NIV)*

Marketing partnerships

Team with non-competing businesses that share your market to offer mutually beneficial promotions. By partnering, companies can share marketing costs and reach a greater number of potential customers for less money.

Partnering opportunities are limited only by your imagination. Take a look at your customers and think about what else they purchase—it doesn't necessarily have to be directly related to your business. A house painter could team up with a fence company; a pest control service could partner with a security service (keeping all types of nasty intruders away); a bookkeeping service and a virtual assistant service will likely find some common clients; a restaurant located near an automotive service center could offer a free beverage to customers waiting for their cars to be repaired.

Though high-profile partners have a strong appeal, it's not essential that your partner be a household name. At the same time, don't be afraid to approach a large corporation with a partnering proposal; big companies are always on the lookout for low-cost ways to increase business. Finally, don't limit yourself to just one partner; wisely-selected multiple partners can further reduce your costs and increase your results.

Make sure that the program is indeed a partnership, with all parties investing and benefiting with relative fairness, and all operating with complete integrity.

I am grateful that God has made me an ambassador of his redemption story.

Today we observe
Social Media Day

On this day in history

Notable events

In 1896, William S. Hadaway patented an electric stove.

In 1906, President Theodore Roosevelt signed the Pure Food and Drug Act and the Meat Inspection Act, which passed Congress in large part due to revelations in Upton Sinclair's novel, *The Jungle*, and other exposé journalism.

In 2023, the U.S. Supreme Court found in favor of a website designer, ruling that the state of Colorado cannot compel the designer to create work that violates her values (303 Creative LLC v. Elenis).

Births

Ed Yost, American businessman (cofounder of Raven Industries) and inventor of the modern hot air balloon, 1919

Tom Frost, rock climber, photographer, inventor, climbing equipment manufacturer (Patagonia, Inc.), 1936

Deaths

Lee de Forest, American inventor, entrepreneur, and early pioneer in electronics whose inventions helped start the Electronic Age, 1961

Harvey W. Wiley, American chemist who advocated for the passage of the Pure Food and Drug Act of 1906, 1930

Thought for the day

"If you wish to travel far and fast, travel light. Take off all your envies, jealousies, unforgiveness, selfishness, and fears."

Glenn Clark

Read:
Proverbs, Chapter 30

Christian Business Almanac

July

July is the seventh month of the year in the Julian and Gregorian calendars. It was named by the Roman Senate in honor of Julius Caesar who was born in this month.

July birthstone
Ruby, onyx

July flower
Larkspur, water lily

July is ...
- Air Conditioning Appreciation Month
- Freedom from Fear of Speaking Month
- Independent Retailer Month
- National Black Family Month
- National Carpet Cleaning Month
- National Cellphone Courtesy Month
- National Cleft & Craniofacial Awareness & Prevention Month
- National Hot Dog Month
- National Ice Cream Month
- National Sandwich Generation Month
- Sarcoma and Bone Cancer Awareness Month
- UV Safety Awareness Month
- Wild About Wildlife Month

Mark your calendar for these July holidays and observances

Third Saturday in July	Toss Away the "Could Haves" & "Should Haves" Day
Third Monday in July	National Get Out of the Doghouse Day
Third Monday in July	Global Hug Your Kids Days
Third Wednesday in July	Take Your Poet to Work Day
Third Thursday in July	Get to Know Your Customers Day
Third Friday in July	National Park & Recreation Professionals Day
Fourth Saturday in July	National Day of the Cowboy
Fourth Saturday in July	National Drowning Prevention Day
Fourth Sunday in July	National Parents Day
Fourth Sunday in July	World Day for Grandparents & the Elderly
Fourth Thursday in July	National Refreshment Day
Last Thursday in July	National Intern Day
Last Friday in July	System Administrator Appreciation Day
Last Friday in July	I Love My Credit Union Day
Last Friday in July	Talk in an Elevator Day
Last Friday in July	National Get Gnarly Day
Last Saturday in July	National Self Storage Day

Fun Facts about July

Before being named July, this month was called Quintilis; it was the fifth month of the calendar that started with March.

July is one of seven months that has 31 days.

July is known for its abundance of seasonal fruits and vegetables in many parts of the world.

July 1

> The thief comes only to steal and kill and destroy; I have come that they [my people] may have life, and have it to the full. *(John 10:10, NIV)*

Going through trials

Kim M. Clark says she didn't receive a "Get Out of Trials Free" card when she became a Christian. In *Deep Waters: Lift Your Gaze*, she writes:

"Unfortunately, whether we like it or not, trials are unavoidable during our lifetime. In hindsight, it seems we learn the most during our inescapable times of suffering. Trials are our greatest teachers. For me, the most interesting part is that God, in his infinite wisdom, allows us to be tested. We must decide if we will be a receptive or defiant student. And God is usually the quietest when we are going through a trial—just like a teacher giving a test and waiting to see if we'll apply what we have learned."

Thought for the day

"One of the secrets of a long and fruitful life is to forgive everybody everything every night before you go to bed."

Bernard Baruch

> Grow your faith by reflecting on the challenges Jesus faced: His life was short. He was mocked by many. He never married or experienced the joy of having children. He didn't earn a lot of money. But he knew God's plan. Just as God had a plan for Jesus, he has a plan for you—and it's bigger than any challenge you may face in this world.

Today we observe

National Postal Workers Day
American Zoo Day
National Hazard Awareness Day

On this day in history

Notable events

In 1836, U.S. Congress authorized the acceptance of a bequest from James Smithson, a British scientist who left his estate to the United States to found "at Washington, under the name of the Smithsonian Institution, an establishment for the increase and diffusion of knowledge."

In 1879, Charles Taze Russell published the first edition of *The Watchtower*.

Births

William Strunk, Jr., American professor of English and author of The Elements of Style, 1869

Estee Lauder, American businesswoman and entrepreneur, cofounder (with her husband, Joseph Lauter) of her eponymous cosmetics company, 1908

Deaths

Charles Goodyear, American self-taught chemist and manufacturing engineer who developed vulcanized rubber (the Goodyear Tire and Rubber Company was named after but not founded by him), 1860

Allan J. Pinkerton, Scottish-American cooper, detective, and spy known for creating the Pinkerton National Detective Agency, 1884

R. Buckminster Fuller, American architect, systems theorist, writer, designer, inventor, and futurist, 1983

I am thankful for music and the joy it brings.

Read:
Proverbs, Chapter 1

July 2

Even youths grow tired and weary, and young men stumble and fall; but those who hope in the Lord will renew their strength. They will soar on wings like eagles; they will run and not grow weary, they will walk and not be faint. *(Isaiah 40:30-31, NIV)*

Be a media resource

Local reporters are always looking for ways to put a local spin on a national news event. You can get some great exposure for yourself and your company by positioning yourself as an expert in your industry or profession with local and regional media.

Let them know you are an easily accessible source whenever they need a comment on any aspect of your business. When they interview you, don't try to sell your product or service; just share your expertise, and the reporter will include your title and company with the story when it's published or aired.

Speak candidly about the issue, be clear and concise, and—most importantly—be available on short notice.

Thought for the day

"I love those who can smile in trouble, who can gather strength from distress, and grow brave by reflection. 'Tis the business of little minds to shrink, but they whose heart is firm, and whose conscience approves their conduct, will pursue their principles unto death."

Leonardo da Vinci

I pray for doctors, nurses, and other medical care providers.

Shareable Saturday

An inspirational thought, brief video, and more delivered to your inbox weekly.

Today we observe

Freedom from Fear of Public Speaking Day

Made in the USA Day

National Air Conditioning Appreciation Day

On this day in history

Notable events

In 1505, after a lightning bolt struck near him during a thunderstorm, Martin Luther vowed to become a monk.

In 1881, U.S. President James Garfield was shot in a Washington railroad station; he died on September 19.

In 1962, Sam Walton opened the first Walmart store in Rogers, Arkansas.

In 1964, the Civil Rights Act of 1964, a landmark civil rights and labor law in the U.S., became effective.

Births

Barry Gray, American radio personality known as the father of talk radio, 1916

Dave Thomas, American businessman, philanthropist, fast-food tycoon, founder of Wendy's, 1932

Deaths

John Fitch, American inventor, clockmaker, entrepreneur, and engineer, 1798

Stephen Moulton Babcock, American agricultural chemist, best known for the Babcock test, used to determine butterfat content in milk and cheese processing, 1931

Julia Montgomery Walsh, American businesswoman and stockbroker, 2003

Douglas Engelbart, American engineer and inventor known for the creation of the computer mouse, the development of hypertext, and networked computers, 2013

Lee Iacocca, American automobile executive and author, 2019

Read:
Proverbs, Chapter 2

July 3

Endure hardship as discipline; God is treating you as his children. For what children are not disciplined by their father?
(Hebrews 12:7, NLT)

Success tips

Learn from everything you do. No matter how menial or grand, there are lessons in everything.

Embrace your mistakes. Let your mistakes show you what you need to improve. Keep making mistakes and keep improving—just don't keep making the same mistakes.

Be a problem-solver. If something isn't working, figure out how to fix it—even if it's not your problem.

Listen to understand. It's not enough to simply hear what people are saying, you need to understand what they want and need.

Don't accept limits. Don't get boxed in by someone else's restrictions.

Build trust. Operate with integrity in everything you do.

Develop a strong work ethic. Don't stop until the job is done.

Are you adding value?

Success takes more than showing up with your talent. In any organization, talent and skill are important. You have to have the ability to do the work, to produce. But success requires more—you also have to add value.

Always be looking for ways to add value to your organization, whether or not it's in your job description. Be a mentor. Offer to help when you don't have to. Be a source of positive energy. Be someone others can count on. Add value by going beyond what's expected of you.

Read:
Proverbs, Chapter 3

On this day in history

Notable events
In 1985, CBS announced a 21 percent stock buy-back to thwart Ted Turner's takeover.

Births
Samuel P. Massie, American chemist and educator, named one of the top 75 distinguished contributors to chemistry in history, 1919

Deaths
Hetty Green, American businesswoman and financier known as the richest woman in America during the Gilded Age and often unfairly referred to as the Witch of Wall Street, 1916

Arthur Hawley Scribner, American magazine and book publisher, president of Charles Scribner's Sons, 1932

Thought for the day

"I find the great thing in this world is not so much where we stand, as in what direction we are moving—we must sail sometimes with the wind and sometimes against it—but we must sail, and not drift, nor lie at anchor."

Oliver Wendell Holmes, Jr.

I am thankful for seasons—the seasons of the year and the seasons of life.

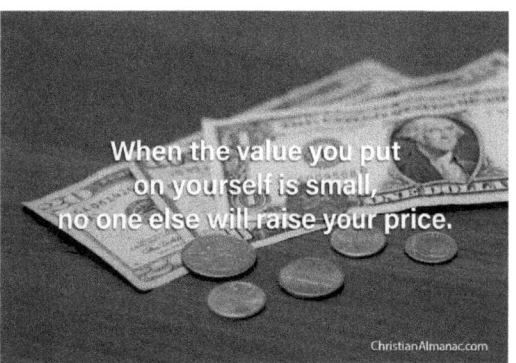

When the value you put on yourself is small, no one else will raise your price.

July 4

For freedom Christ has set us free. Stand firm, therefore, and do not submit again to a yoke of slavery. (Galatians 5:1, NRSVue)

Amazing Grace

Stanzas 1-4, John Newton, 1779
Stanza 5, A Collection of Sacred Ballads, 1790

1 Amazing grace, how sweet the sound,
that saved a wretch like me!
I once was lost, but now am found,
was blind, but now I see.

2 'Twas grace that taught my heart to fear,
and grace my fears relieved;
how precious did that grace appear
the hour I first believed!

3 Through many dangers, toils and snares
I have already come:
'tis grace has brought me safe thus far,
and grace will lead me home.

4 The Lord has promised good to me,
his word my hope secures;
he will my shield and portion be
as long as life endures.

5 When we've been there ten thousand years,
Bright shining as the sun,
We've no less days to sing God's praise
Than when we'd first begun.

Thought for the day

"The spirited horse, which will of itself strive to win the race, will run still more swiftly if encouraged."

Ovid

I am thankful for our liberty.

Read:
Proverbs, Chapter 4

Today we observe

U.S. Independence Day

On this day in history

Notable events

In 1776, the Second Continental Congress unanimously adopted the Declaration of Independence.

In 1828, construction began on the Baltimore & Ohio (B&O) Railroad, the first U.S. railway chartered for the commercial transportation of freight and passengers.

In 1881, Tuskegee University, formerly known as Tuskegee Institute, was founded.

Births

Hiram Walker, American entrepreneur, founder of Hiram Walker and Sons Ltd. Distillery, 1816

James Anthony Bailey, American owner and manager of several 19th century circuses, including the Barnum & Bailey Greatest Show on Earth, 1847

Calvin Coolidge, 30th U.S. President, 1872

Rube Goldberg, American cartoonist, author, engineer, and inventor, known for cartoons depicting complicated gadgets performing simple tasks in indirect, convoluted ways, 1883

Leona Roberts Helmsley, American businesswoman, hotelier, real estate investor, known as the Queen of Mean, 1920

Al Davis, American football coach, executive, NFL team owner, 1929

George Steinbrenner, American businessman, principal owner and managing partner of MLB's New York Yankees, 1930

Deaths

John Adams, 2nd U.S. President (served as the first Vice President under George Washington), 1826

Thomas Jefferson, 3rd U.S. President, 1826

James Monroe, 5th U.S. President, 1831

Harold Stirling Vanderbilt, American railroad executive, yachtsman, bridge player, 1970

Nathaniel C. Wyeth, American mechanical engineer and inventor best known for the plastic soda bottle, 1990

July 5

Worry weighs a person down; an encouraging word cheers a person up.
(Proverbs 12:25, NLT)

Tips for effective planning

Set aside time for planning every day. Even with your major plan in place, you need to spend a few minutes every day reviewing your plan and updating as necessary.

Task batch. Whenever you can, group similar tasks together and work on them at the same time. You'll improve focus, increase productivity, and reduce stress.

Set clear goals. Have both short- and long-term goals so you have a sense of direction and purpose.

Know your dependencies. Be aware when two tasks depend on one another's progress. For example, if you can't start Task B until you've completed Task A, you can keep that in mind when you're scheduling work so you don't get stuck or waste time.

Identify and establish priorities. As you plan your work, know what's urgent so it can be done first.

Prioritize tasks and set milestones. When the significance of each task is clear, you can efficiently allocate resources and time. Setting milestones helps you stay on track, maintain momentum, and celebrate your progress.

Use tools. You have a plethora of tools and software to assist in planning and task management. Find what works for you and your team.

Learn your patterns. We all have unique work patterns; learn what yours are so you can schedule your time to be naturally productive.

Review and revise as needed. Plans are living documents and may periodically need to be adjusted. Stay agile, flexible, and moving toward your goals.

Read:
Proverbs, Chapter 5

Today we observe
National Workaholics Day
Mechanical Pencil Day

On this day in history

Notable events
In 1937, Hormel Foods Corporation introduced Spam, a trademarked meat product consisting primarily of ground pork and ham.
In 1994, Jeff Bezos founded Amazon.
In 2023, Meta Platforms launched Threads, an online social media and social networking service.

Births
P. T. Barnum, American showman, businessman, politician, and founder of the Barnum & Bailey Circus, 1810
Mary Maxwell Gates, American banker, civic activist, nonprofit executive, teacher, and mother of Bill Gates, 1929
Susan Wojcicki, American business executive, CEO of YouTube (2014-2023), who was involved in the creation of Google in 1998 when she rented out her garage as an office to the company's founders, 1968

Deaths
Kenneth Lay, American businessman, founder, CEO, and chairman of Enron, 2006
Chester Greenwood, American engineer, inventor (earmuffs), and manufacturer, 1937

Thought for the day

"Every great dream begins with a dreamer. Always remember, you have within you the strength, the patience, and the passion to reach for the stars to change the world."

Harriet Tubman

I am thankful for the opportunities that have come to me when I wasn't looking for them.

July 6

But now you are free from the power of sin and have become slaves of God. Now you do those things that lead to holiness and result in eternal life. *(Romans 6:22, NLT)*

Manage your image library

If you don't want to invest in a digital asset management (DAM) system (which can be expensive and have a steep learning curve), use these tips to manage your own image library.

Set up folders by category. Don't just put everything in one folder. Instead, think about the types of images you'll be creating and organize subfolders under your main Images folder. Some suggestions for folder names/categories:

- Blog callouts
- Blog illustrations
- Facebook inspirational quotes
- Twitter inspirational quotes
- Product promotions

Do your best to anticipate the types of images you'll have so you can set up folders ahead of time, but remember you can always add more folders later.

Name the files descriptively. Name your image files so they are identifiable to search engines as well as your human audience, and include an internal file identifier.

You may want to include some keywords in the file name to make it easier for you to search by subject. If you update an image and don't delete the original, add a date or version indicator in the file name so you don't accidentally use an outdated image.

Tag the image files. To avoid creating file names that are too long and unwieldy, add tags to your images by editing the properties. You and the search engines can search on the tags.

I pray for the Lord to continue to show me his ways.

Today we observe

Virtually Hug A Virtual Assistant Day
Treat Your Webmaster or Webmistress Day
World Chocolate Day

On this day in history

Notable events

In 1858, Lyman Blake received a patent for his invention of a machine for sewing the soles of shoes to the vamp of the shoe.

In 2000, real estate developer Stan Kroenke announced the acquisition of the Denver Nuggets, Colorado Avalanche, and the Pepsi Centre for $450 million from the Ascent Entertainment Group.

Births

Harry Ford Sinclair, American industrialist, founder of Sinclair Oil, 1876

Harold Stirling Vanderbilt, American railroad executive, yachtsman, bridge player, 1884

Conrad "Nicky" Hilton, Jr., American socialite, hotel heir, and businessman, 1926

George W. Bush, 43rd U.S. President, 1946

Deaths

Thomas Davenport, American blacksmith and inventor who constructed the first American DC electric motor, 1851

Olive Ann Beech, American aerospace businesswoman, cofounder of the Beech Aircraft Corporation, known as the first lady of aviation, 1993

Thought for the day

"One of the greatest discoveries a man makes, one of his great surprises, is to find he can do what he was afraid he couldn't do."

Henry Ford

Read:
Proverbs, Chapter 6

July 7

And now, dear brothers and sisters, one final thing. Fix your thoughts on what is true, and honorable, and right, and pure, and lovely, and admirable. Think about things that are excellent and worthy of praise. Keep putting into practice all you learned and received from me—everything you heard from me and saw me doing. Then the God of peace will be with you. *(Philippians 4:8-9, NLT)*

Your business is a ministry

When it comes to ministries, conventional wisdom tends to separate faith-based organizations and for-profit businesses. Krystal Parker, president of the U.S. Christian Chamber of Commerce, says any business can—and should—be a ministry.

"Your business is a ministry, it's a tool to reach people for the Kingdom," she says. She offers these suggestions for operating a for-profit enterprise as a ministry:

Understand the Great Commission. Jesus said to "Go into the world and preach the gospel to all creation" *(Mark 16:15, NIV)* and to "make disciples of all nations" *(Matthew 28:19, NIV)*. "First and foremost, we're responsible for that," Parker says. "Don't believe the lie that the only place you can share the gospel is in church."

Make God the CEO. "Don't just make deals and do things on your own, seek the guidance and wisdom of the Holy Spirit in everything," Parker says.

Walk the talk. Operate with integrity and ethics, treat your employees well, be fair in all your business dealings.

Do good things in the world. "Business is not about amassing wealth and getting richer, it's about doing good things," Parker says. Give to causes that are aligned with your values, give employees time to serve in the community, and find other ways to model your faith through your company.

What's not on this list? "Notice that I didn't say talk to everybody about Jesus Christ and hit them over the head with the Bible," Parker says. "You can certainly do that, but you'll be more effective by creating an environment filled with love."

On this day in history

Notable events

In 1928, the first automatically sliced commercial loaves of bread were put on the shelves of grocery stores in Chillicothe, Missouri.

In 1936, American businessman Henry F. Phillips received a patent for a crosshead screw and screwdriver (invented by John P. Thompson, who sold his design to Phillips in 1935).

Births

Charles Tindley, American Methodist minister and gospel music composer, 1851

Deaths

Henry Eyster Jacobs, American religious educator, Biblical commentator, and Lutheran theologian, 1932

Thought for the day

"You can tell more about a person by what he says about others than you can by what others say about him."

Audrey Hepburn

Three ways to grow a business:

1. Increase the number of customers.
2. Increase the average transaction value.
3. Increase the frequency of repurchase.

I pray for those struggling with addiction.

Read:
Proverbs, Chapter 7

July 8

"Because of God's tender mercy, the morning light from heaven is about to break upon us, to give light to those who sit in darkness and in the shadow of death, and to guide us to the path of peace." *(Luke 1:78-79, NLT)*

Dealing with rejection

Rejection hurts. Whether it's personal or business, rejection causes a physical sensation that can be agonizing. But it's a part of life, so how do you deal with it?

Accept what happened. Don't deny it. Acknowledge the rejection and the feelings that come with it.

Process your feelings. Understand your emotions and work toward managing them in a positive way. Don't hurt others because you've been hurt.

Be kind to yourself. Do what you need to look after your own well-being.

Rally whatever support you can. Turn to friends and family for support. Don't isolate yourself.

Figure out what to do next. The circumstances of the rejection will guide your next steps. Was it job related, and now you need to plan a new career move? Was it romantic, and now you need to navigate a change in relationship status? Define the problem, consider your options, then choose what's best.

Grow from the experience. What can you learn from the situation that you can use in the future?

Optimism is essential, but it doesn't replace planning and preparation. You need a good plan that not only covers things when they go right, but has contingencies for when they go wrong.

Read:
Proverbs, Chapter 8

On this day in history

Notable events

In 1741, American theologian Jonathan Edwards preached his famous and influential sermon "Sinners in the Hands of an Angry God" in Enfield, Connecticut.

In 1889, the first issue of *The Wall Street Journal* was published.

Births

John Stith Pemberton, American pharmacist best known as the inventor of Coca-Cola, 1831

John D. Rockefeller, Sr., American business magnate and philanthropist, founder of the Standard Oil Company, 1839

Nelson Rockefeller, American businessman and politician (governor of New York and 41st U.S. vice president), 1908

Deaths

Elihu Yale, British-American colonial administrator and philanthropist; primary benefactor of Yale College (now Yale University), which was named in his honor, 1721

Alex d'Arbeloff, Georgian-American entrepreneur, cofounder of Teradyne (manufacturer of automatic test equipment), 2008

Thought for the day

"I think if I've learned anything about friendship, it's to hang in, stay connected, fight for them, and let them fight for you. Don't walk away, don't be distracted, don't be too busy or tired, don't take them for granted. Friends are part of the glue that holds life and faith together. Powerful stuff."

Jon Katz

I am grateful that God doesn't give up on me even when I'm doubting.

July 9

> ❝ Do not store up for yourselves treasures on earth, where moths and vermin destroy, and where thieves break in and steal. But store up for yourselves treasures in heaven, where moths and vermin do not destroy, and where thieves do not break in and steal. *(Matthew 6:19-20, NIV)*

How to make good decisions

A systematic approach to decision-making can increase the chances that you'll make good decisions and do it more easily. Use these steps:

Clarify the issue. What's at stake? Why is it important and what are the possible outcomes? What do you want to accomplish?

Gather information. Do your research to determine what your options are. Have you faced anything similar to this before? What did you do then? What have others done in this situation?

Evaluate the options. Identify all the options that could work and evaluate them. What will they cost to implement? What are the likely results?

Make the decision and act on it. Choose the best option and take action.

Review the results. What happened? What went well and what could have gone better? What did you learn for next time?

Schedule rest and relaxation

Rest and relaxation are difficult to define because they are different for everyone, but they're important. The benefits of daily rest and relaxation include:
- Reduced stress and anxiety
- Improved mood
- Lower blood pressure
- Chronic pain relief
- Improved immune health
- Stronger cardiovascular system

We make time every day to work and do essential activities such as eating, grooming, and caring for our families. Give rest and relaxation the same priority.

On this day in history

Notable events

In 1878, American inventor Henry Tibbe received a patent for his process of fireproofing the traditional corncob pipe.

Births

Jacob Perkins, American inventor, mechanical engineer, and physicist, known as the father of the refrigerator, 1766

Thomas Davenport, American blacksmith and inventor who constructed the first American DC electric motor, 1802

Elias Howe, Jr., American engineer and inventor best known for the creation of the modern lockstitch sewing machine, 1819

Daniel Guggenheim, American mining magnate and philanthropist, 1856

Deaths

Zachary Taylor, 12th U.S. President, 1850

King C. Gillette, American businessman and inventor of inexpensive and disposable safety razor blades, 1932

Eileen Ford, American model agency executive and cofounder of Ford Models, 2014

Ross Perot, American business magnate, politician, and philanthropist, 2019

Thought for the day

"When you hold resentment toward another, you are bound to that person or condition by an emotional link that is stronger than steel. Forgiveness is the only way to dissolve that link and get free."

Catherine Ponder

I am thankful for the bad things that did not happen.

Read:
Proverbs, Chapter 9

July 10

But you, Lord, are a shield around me, my glory, the One who lifts my head high. *(Psalm 3:3, NIV)*

Preventing problems

Rather than sharpening your problem-solving skills, concentrate on problem prevention. A proactive perspective of anticipating problems and taking steps to prevent them is far more beneficial than patching things up after the fact. Some thoughts:

Have good intuition and be pessimistic enough to imagine possible negative outcomes. Continually size up situations and consider possible outcomes, both positive and negative. Pay attention to your hunches and work on developing your intuition.

Visualize worst-case scenarios. Think about problems before they occur and plan for how you'll deal with them. This is not an exercise in negativity, but rather preparing in advance for dealing with manageable problems so they don't turn into major disasters.

Pay attention to early warning signals. Look for little signs that could mean troubles ahead. If you're feeling anxious, figure out why. If sales dip, even slightly, be sure you understand the reason.

Avoid bad decision-making. The most common error in decision-making is to accept the first good solution that comes along, rather than taking the time to find the best alternative. Never make decisions when you're emotional; delay action for a day or so until you've calmed down and can think clearly.

Thought for the day

"I believe the power to make money is a gift of God...to be developed and used to the best of our ability for the good of mankind."

John D. Rockefeller

On this day in history

Notable events
In 1866, Edson P. Clark patented an indelible pencil.

Births
Adolphus Busch, German-born cofounder of Anheuser-Busch (with his father-in-law, Eberhard Anheuser), philanthropist, 1839
Nikola Tesla, Serbian-American physicist, electrical engineer, and inventor, 1856
Mary McLeod Bethune, American educator (Bethune-Cookman University), philanthropist, humanitarian, civil rights activist, advisor to presidents, 1875
Owen Chamberlain, American physicist known for particle physics, Nobel Prize winner, 1920
Edward Lowe, American businessman and entrepreneur, noted for the invention of cat litter, 1920
Herbert Boyer, American biotechnologist, researcher, and entrepreneur, cofounder of the biotechnology giant Genentech, 1936

Deaths
John D. Rockefeller III, American billionaire and philanthropist, 1978

I pray that the Lord will keep my eyes open to those who wish to harm or betray me.

Read:
Proverbs, Chapter 10

We are not generous to gain blessings. We are generous because we are blessed.

July 11

Likewise, the tongue is a small part of the body, but it makes great boasts. Consider what a great forest is set on fire by a small spark. The tongue also is a fire, a world of evil among the parts of the body. It corrupts the whole body, sets the whole course of one's life on fire, and is itself set on fire by hell. *(James 3:5-6, NIV)*

How to pray for others

When you're concerned about people, you want to pray for them, but you may feel at a loss for words or focus. These tips might help:

Ask the person you're praying for. Tell them they're in your prayers and ask if there's anything specific they would like you to pray for.

Ask God to tell you what to pray. Then have the clarity and courage to pray what he puts on your heart.

Find a scripture that's appropriate. Pray those verses to God on behalf of whom you're praying for.

Pray for God to bring others into the lives of the people you're praying for who can be the answer to your prayers. Be willing to be the answer yourself.

Thank God for the people you're praying for and for the opportunity to lift them up. Thank him for working in their lives and yours.

When you don't know, say so

Don't be afraid to admit you don't know something. Maybe you're in a meeting and people are using terms you don't understand—speak up and get clarity before you get lost. Maybe someone asks a question you don't have the answer to—don't try to bluff, tell them you'll have to research and get back to them. We can't know everything. Admitting what you don't know takes courage and wisdom.

I pray that everyone on my team contributes to our work in a positive way.

On this day in history

Notable events

In 1962, Telstar 1 relayed its first non-public transatlantic television pictures.

Births

John Quincy Adams, 6th U.S. President, 1767

John Wanamaker, American merchant (operated on the then-revolutionary principle of "one price and goods returnable"), philanthropist, and religious, civic, and political figure, 1889

Frank Rosenblatt, American psychologist notable in the field of artificial intelligence, called the father of deep learning, 1928

Deaths

Owen D. Young, American industrialist, businessman, lawyer, diplomat, known for the plan to settle Germany's World War I reparations and for the creation of Radio Corporation of America (RCA), 1962

Frank Rosenblatt, American psychologist notable in the field of artificial intelligence, called the father of deep learning, 1971

Gary Kildall, American computer scientist and microcomputer entrepreneur, created CP/M operating system, founded Digital Research, Inc., 1994

Ed Mirvish, American-Canadian businessman, philanthropist, and theatrical impresario, known for his flagship business, Honest Ed's, and as a patron of the arts, 2007

Thought for the day

"Sooner or later, even the upbeat soul gets beat up by life. We need a higher power, a deeper strength, a wider mercy, and a mightier word."

Robert J. Morgan

Read:
Proverbs, Chapter 11

July 12

> **B**ut encourage one another daily, as long as it is called "Today," so that none of you may be hardened by sin's deceitfulness. *(Hebrews 3:13, NIV)*

When disaster happens

When a natural disaster, accident, or criminal act causes property damage to your business, it's essential to control the damage and avoid a response that would make the situation worse. Take immediate steps to protect your undamaged property and salvage whatever damaged items you can.

Verify the safety of the building before entering. Be sure emergency services personnel have deemed it safe for you to enter the building before you do so.

Make the necessary notifications, including contacting your insurance carrier, employees, customers, and suppliers. Take photographs and videos of the damage.

Find a place to operate if the damage prevents you from using your facility. If you have landlines, contact your telephone company to arrange for calls to be routed to a location where they can be answered.

Prevent further damage. Take whatever immediate steps are necessary to prevent further property damage, such as shutting off water and electricity, boarding up broken windows, covering damaged roofs with tarps, and doing preliminary emergency cleanup.

Contact a qualified professional restoration contractor. Be sure to tell the contractor what sort of business property—such as paper and electronic files, business equipment, inventory, etc.—you are attempting to salvage. Disaster restoration takes special skills and knowledge; get bids from several professionals before making a final selection. This will not take as long as you might think. Because immediate response is critical, professional restoration companies will usually have someone on site within one to two hours and be prepared to start work right away.

On this day in history

Notable events
In 1859, William Goodale received a patent for his paper bag manufacturing machine.

Births
George Eastman, American entrepreneur, inventor and founder of Eastman Kodak Company, 1854

Louis B. Mayer, Canadian-American film producer, cofounder of Metro-Goldwyn-Mayer (MGM), 1884

R. Buckminster Fuller, American architect, systems theorist, writer, designed, inventor, and futurist, 1895

Deaths
Cyrus West Field, American businessman and financier, cofounder of the Atlantic Telegraph Company, credited with getting the first telegraph line across the Atlantic Ocean completed, 1892

Charles Rolls, British automotive and aviation pioneer, cofounder of Rolls-Royce, first Briton to be killed in a plane crash, 1910

Ole Evinrude, Norwegian-American entrepreneur, inventor of the first outboard motor with practical commercial application, 1934

Amar Bose, American entrepreneur, electrical and sound engineer, founder of Bose Corporation, 2013

Thought for the day

"The older I get, the greater power I seem to have to help the world; I am like a snowball—the further I am rolled the more I gain."

Susan B. Anthony

I pray on the promise of Psalm 121:1-2.

Read:
Proverbs, Chapter 12

July 13

> **B**ut who am I, and who are my people, that we could give anything to you? Everything we have has come from you, and we give you only what you first gave us! *(1 Chronicles 29:14, NLT)*

Who owns your company?

You may be the owner of your company on all the legal documents, but who is the real owner? "We need to shift our perspective from an owner to a steward," says Michelle Ogden, founder and CEO of Ogden Wealth, LLC (Maitland, Florida).

"When you wholeheartedly know that God owns not just the business but he owns you as well, and you believe that and operate your business from the perspective of a steward and seek first the Kingdom—I'm not saying you will not have trials, but you will not go through them alone."

Ogden says we should surround ourselves with like-minded business owners as resources for when we need advice and prayer, "but don't just run to others, run to God and he will point you to whom you should talk to."

If we believe that God owns the company, it makes sense that we would always consult him first.

"It is not until we fear God enough that we consult him first," Ogden says. "This is reverential fear. We need to respect God's power and authority—not because he's angry with us, but because we desire to please him. Shift your mindset from that of owner to steward and consult God on everything."

Thought for the day

"The important thing is not being afraid to take a chance. Remember, the greatest failure is to not try. Once you find something you love to do, be the best at doing it."

Debbi Fields

Today we observe

Job Satisfaction Day

Fool's Paradise Day

On this day in history

Notable events

In 1836, U.S. patent #1 (after 9,957 unnumbered patents) was issued for locomotive wheels.

In 1955, industrialist Cyrus Eaton first offered to finance and host a conference for scientists to assess the dangers of weapons of mass destruction; the invitation wasn't taken up until 1957.

In 1978, Ford Motor Company chairman Henry Ford II fired Lee Iacocca as Ford's president.

In 2008, brewing company InBev announced a deal to buy Anheuser-Busch for almost $52 billion.

Births

John Jacob Astor IV, American business magnate, real estate developer, investor, writer, died in the sinking of the *Titanic*, 1864

Edward J. Flanagan, Irish-American Catholic priest and founder of Boys Town, 1886

Charles Scribner IV, American publisher, head of Charles Scriber's Sons publishing company, 1921

Deaths

George Steinbrenner, American businessman, principal owner and managing partner of MLB's New York Yankees, 2010

Theodore Henry Stanley, American anesthesiologist and medical entrepreneur, known for creating the fentanyl lollipop, 2017

I pray for faith and wisdom.

Read:
Proverbs, Chapter 13

July 14

> This means that anyone who belongs to Christ has become a new person. The old life is gone; a new life has begun! And all of this is a gift from God, who brought us back to himself through Christ. And God has given us this task of reconciling people to him. *(2 Corinthians 5:17-18, NLT)*

Charge for value, not time

Do you bill by the hour? How does what you bill compare to the value of what you provide?

Technology in general and artificial intelligence (AI) in particular have made it possible to do in minutes what used to take hours, even days. If you're billing by the hour, you're losing a lot of money.

It's time to pivot to value-based billing. Charge based on what the product or service is worth, not how long it took you to provide it.

If an attorney gives you advice that keeps you from getting sued, how much is that worth? It might have taken them 15 minutes to tell you what to do, but you avoided tens of thousands of dollars in legal fees.

If a marketing firm launches a campaign that generates a ten percent increase in sales, how much is that worth? Does how long it took them to do it make any difference in the results you saw?

Now look at what you do. If you're billing by the hour, how much knowledge and speed are you bringing to the table? What's that worth?

Charge for value, not time.

Thought for the day

"When one finds oneself in a hole of one's own making, it is a good time to examine the quality of the workmanship."

John Renmerde

Grow your faith through study and lifelong learning.

Today we observe

Shark Awareness Day

National Tape Measure Day

On this day in history

Notable events

In 1853, the first U.S. World's Fair opened in New York.

Births

Frederick Louis Maytag I, American businessman, founder of the Maytag Company, 1857

William Hanna, American animator and cofounder of Hanna-Barbera, 1910

Gerald R. Ford, 38th U.S. President, 1913

Frances Lear, American activist, author, magazine publisher, 1923

Esther Dyson, Swiss-born American investor, journalist, author, and philanthropist, 1951

Deaths

William Still, African-American businessman, writer, historian, abolitionist, conductor of the Underground Railroad, 1902

Charles A. Coffin, American businessman, cofounder and first president of General Electric Company, 1926

Raymond Loewy, French-born American industrial designer known as the father of streamlining and the father of industrial design, 1986

Richard McDonald, American entrepreneur, cofounder (with his brother Maurice McDonald) of McDonald's fast food restaurants, 1998

Dorothy Lee Bolden, domestic worker, founder of the National Domestic Workers Union of America, 2005

I am thankful for a good night's rest.

Read:
Proverbs, Chapter 14

July 15

> "I am the Lord, the God of all mankind. Is anything too hard for me?
> *(Jeremiah 32:27, NIV)*

Negotiating techniques

Try these strategies to reach winning deals.

Be charming. Open with a sincere compliment to establish respect and set a constructive tone.

Do your homework. Find out as much as you can about the person and company you're negotiating with so you can personalize your presentation and focus on what matters to them.

Show your vulnerability. Do this in a controlled way, but reveal just enough of yourself so that you're viewed as a partner rather than an opponent.

Be quiet. Once you've made your presentation and asked for the business, stop talking. Say nothing until your prospect does, no matter how long it takes or how uncomfortable the silence gets.

Working for the perfect boss

When we work for people, we may or may not always do our best. We may be willing to accept "good enough" instead of excellent.

As Christians, we work for the Lord, which means we are working for the perfect boss—the boss who is absolutely perfect, who never makes a mistake, who always knows what to say and do, and who wants our very best. When we care more about pleasing God with our work, it's likely that people will also be pleased.

Thought for the day

"[I]f we never pray for people to be healed, we have no reason to expect that the Spirit will use us to see people healed."
Andrew K. Gabriel

Today we observe
National Give Something Away Day

On this day in history

Notable events

In 1907, the Publishers Press Association, the Scripps-McRae Press Association, and the Scripps News Association consolidated under the name of United Press Associations, which became United Press International in 1958.

In 1916, timber merchant William Edward Boeing incorporated the Pacific Aero Products Company to manufacture airplanes; less than a year later, the company name was changed to Boeing Airplane Company.

In 1929, the first airport hotel opened in Oakland, California; the facility included 37 rooms, a restaurant, a barbershop, and a ticket office.

In 2006, Twitter launched.

Births

Arianna Huffington, Greek-American author and businesswoman, cofounder of *The Huffington Post*, founder and CEO of Thrive Global, 1950

Maggie L. Walker, African-American businesswoman, teacher, bank founder, and publisher, 1864

Deaths

William Painter, American mechanical engineer, inventor (the crown cork bottle cap and bottle opener), and founder of Crown Holdings, Inc., 1906

Dennis Murphy, sports entrepreneur, founder of World Team Tennis and Roller Hockey International, cofounder of World Hockey Association and American Basketball Association, 2021

I pray for those who are suffering.

Read:
Proverbs, Chapter 15

July 16

When the Spirit of truth comes, he will guide you into all truth. He will not speak on his own but will tell you what he has heard. He will tell you about the future. *(John 16:13, NLT)*

Tell a story

The next time you have to present data, make it relatable and memorable by sharing a story that illustrates the impact of the facts and features. If possible, use real names and detailed descriptions so your audience can connect with your message in a personal way.

Be a better thinker

Just as physical exercise helps keeps our bodies in shape and performing well, mental exercise keeps our minds sharp. Thinking is a skill which can be practiced and developed just as any other skill. Here's how to hone your thinking skills.

Ask questions—lots of them. Come at issues from a multitude of angles. Don't just wonder why and move on, get an answer.

Be skeptical. Don't accept things at face value—go deeper to truly understand and uncover the truth.

Read. Expose yourself to a variety of thinkers by reading diverse, challenging material, both fiction and non-fiction.

Learn from people. Learn something from every encounter.

Discard labels. Don't let labels inhibit your thinking; reach your own conclusions.

Think about thinking. Practice self-reflection through journaling or working with a thinking buddy.

Thought for the day

"Belonging starts with self-acceptance ... Believing that you're enough is what gives you the courage to be authentic."

Brene Brown

Today we observe

Artificial Intelligence Appreciation Day

National Change Your Font Day

On this day in history

Notable events

In 1935, the first parking meters were installed in the Oklahoma City business district to solve the problem of downtown workers parking on streets and leaving few spaces for shoppers and visitors.

Births

Mary Baker Eddy, American religious leader, author, and publisher, founder of The Church of Christ, Scientist and *The Christian Science Monitor* plus three religious magazines, 1821

Orville Redenbacher, American food scientist and businessman, 1907

Dan Bricklin, American businessman and engineer, co-creator (with Bob Frankston) of the VisiCalc spreadsheet program, founder of Software Garden, Inc. and Trellix, 1951

Larry Sanger, American internet project developer and philosopher, cofounder of Wikipedia, 1968

Deaths

Ellen G. White, American author and cofounder of the Seventh-day Adventist Church, 1915

John F. Kennedy, Jr., American attorney and magazine publisher, 1999

Robert H. Brooks, American businessman, restaurateur, executive, founder of Naturally Fresh, Inc., creator of Hooters of America, 2006

I am thankful for those who bring different perspectives and new ideas into my life.

Read:
Proverbs, Chapter 16

July 17

Then he came up and touched the bier, and those who carried it stood still. He said, "Young man, I say to you, get up!" So the dead man sat up and began to speak, and Jesus gave him back to his mother. *(Luke 7:14–15, NET)*

Spiritual courage

In *Who You Are When No One's Looking*, Bill Hybels has this to say about spiritual courage:

"Early in my ministry I heard people say that Christianity is for weak people, cowards and quiche eaters. I happened to like quiche, but I didn't take offense.

"It's an accusation I always found fascinating because in my experience the exact opposite is true. It takes immense courage to live as a Christian, not to mention immense courage to become one. According to Scripture, in order to become a Christian you have to own up to your sin before a holy and righteous God. When I talk with people about Christianity, I tell them, 'You've got to repent before a holy God. You have to tell him the truth about yourself—that you've lied, you've hurt people, you've cheated, that you've been greedy, dishonest, unfaithful to your spouse, self-centered.' Their response is usually accompanied by terror in their eyes. Why? Because who in a right mind wants to be that open and vulnerable—especially with God? ...

"As I say, it takes courage to become a Christian. What's more, it takes courage to then truly live like one."

Thought for the day

"You build on failure. You use it as a stepping stone. Close the door on the past. You don't try to forget the mistakes, but you don't dwell on it. You don't let it have any of your energy, or any of your time, or any of your space."

Johnny Cash

Read:
Proverbs, Chapter 17

Today we observe

World Emoji Day

World Day for International Justice

On this day in history

Notable events

In 2015, eBay and PayPal separated into independent publicly traded companies.

Births

John Jacob Astor, German-American businessman, merchant, real estate mogul, and investor, 1763

Deaths

Eugene Meyer, American banker, businessman, financier, and newspaper publisher (*The Washington Post*), 1859

Katharine Graham, American newspaper publisher (*The Washington Post*), 2001

Purchasing advice

Never rely on a single vendor for critical supplies. Keep in contact with other vendors and watch for new ones. It's a good idea to be on good terms with more than one supplier. If your primary supplier ever fails to ship on time, suspends operations because of a natural disaster, or starts offering poor service, you'll already know of and have a relationship with other sources to use as a backup. Don't be secretive about these multiple relationships—letting suppliers know that you have alternatives will keep them on their toes and motivate them to provide you with their best service.

I pray for the light of the Lord to shine through me.

July 18

Therefore, since we have been made right in God's sight by faith, we have peace with God because of what Jesus Christ our Lord has done for us. Because of our faith, Christ has brought us into this place of undeserved privilege where we now stand, and we confidently and joyfully look forward to sharing God's glory. *(Romans 5:1-2, NLT)*

Our goals must be in harmony with our values

You will find it extremely difficult, if not impossible, to achieve goals that are not in harmony with your other goals and your fundamental values.

For example, you can't achieve a financial goal of wealth if you have a personal goal of spending all your time reading novels on the beach. You can't achieve a self-improvement goal of learning to snow ski if you also have a personal goal of living full-time on a tropical island.

You aren't likely to achieve a goal of becoming a philanthropist if you don't genuinely enjoy and believe in giving to others. You aren't likely to achieve a goal that will require hard work if you aren't willing to work hard.

But if you have a goal of monetary wealth so you can engage in philanthropy and you're willing to work hard to achieve it, those goals and values are in alignment and your chances of success are much greater.

As you set your goals, be sure your goals are in accord with one another and your values.

Thought for the day

"Some people believe holding on and hanging in there are signs of great strength. However, there are times when it takes much more strength to know when to let go and then do it."

Ann Landers

Read:
Proverbs, Chapter 18

Today we observe
Perfect Family Day

On this day in history
Notable events
In 1968, Intel Corporation was established in Mountain View, California, when Robert Noyce and Gordon Moore decided to form a new company that would let them pursue innovation on their own terms.

Births
Jerome H. Lemelson, American engineer, inventor, and holder of more than 600 patents, 1923

Jerry Richardson, American businessman, football player, founder of the Carolina Panthers, philanthropist, 1936

Richard Branson, British business magnate, founder of the Virgin Group, 1950

Deaths
Horatio Alger, American clergyman and author for whom the Horatio Alger Association of Distinguished Americans was named, 1899

Mollie Parnis, American fashion designer known for designing clothes worn by many First Ladies, 1992

I am thankful for the technology that allows me to run my company efficiently and effectively.

July 19

> Wash and make yourselves clean. Take your evil deeds out of my sight; stop doing wrong. Learn to do right; seek justice. Defend the oppressed. Take up the cause of the fatherless; plead the case of the widow. *(Isaiah 1:16–17, NIV)*

Effective career-boosting tactics

Know how you define success. Don't be distracted by what other people are doing. Know what success means to you and stay focused on that.

Say no often so you can say yes to what matters. Bright shiny objects can be distracting. Similarly, you likely have plenty of people trying to get you to say yes to their exciting thing even though it's not in your plan. Only say yes if doing so is clearly in line with your goals.

Focus on what you can control. Don't waste time speculating on or regretting things that are out of your control. Invest in what you can control and let your results keep you motivated.

Stay curious and keep learning. Approach challenges with an open mind and be willing to consider new perspectives and solutions. Make learning new things a daily activity and lifelong commitment.

Get and be a mentor. Find a mentor—or mentors—who have the resources to help you. Be a mentor to others who are following your path.

Take initiative. Demonstrate your drive and ambition by seeking out opportunities rather than waiting for them to come to you.

Grow stronger every day. Whatever happens, let it strengthen you and make you better.

I am thankful for my inner child.

Read:
Proverbs, Chapter 19

On this day in history

Notable events

In 1848, the Seneca Falls Convention, the first American women's rights convention, convened in the Wesleyan Chapel in Seneca Falls, New York.

Births

Samuel Colt, American inventor, industrialist, and businessman who established Colt's Patent Fire-Arms Manufacturing company (now Colt's Manufacturing Company) and made the mass production of revolvers commercially viable, 1814

Charles Horace Mayo, American medical practitioner and cofounder of the Mayo Clinic, 1865

Percy Spencer, American physicist and inventor known for inventing the microwave oven, 1894

Howard Schultz, American businessman (Starbucks) and author, 1953

R. J. Williams, American media and internet entrepreneur (founder of media company Young Hollywood), former child actor, 1978

Deaths

George Parker, American inventor and industrialist, founder of Parker Pen Company, 1937

Noel Wien, American pioneer aviator, founder of Wien Alaska Airways, 1977

Thought for the day

"Only when people remember the good others have done for them will they have gratitude. Unfortunately, most people remember the bad people have done to them far longer than the good. Or to put it another way, gratitude takes effort; resentment is effortless."

Dennis Prager

July 20

> "He himself bore our sins" in his body on the cross, so that we might die to sins and live for righteousness; "by his wounds you have been healed."
> *(1 Peter 2:24, NIV)*

Create videos your viewers will watch, like, and share

Use these tips to create videos that will achieve your goals:

Be concise. Tell your story in as few words as possible. Be comprehensive but brief.

Get to the point. Do something in the first 5-10 seconds to let viewers know the rest of your video is worth their time. If you don't, they'll click away.

Keep them short. You'll have more success with a series of short videos than with fewer longer ones.

Include a call to action. Be sure you let your viewers know what you want them to do at the end of your video.

Don't let the background distract your viewers. Choose a background that's appropriate for your content but that won't compete with you for your viewers' attention.

Use visuals and motion. Video is visual—give your viewers something to see that will capture their interest

Use a script. Unless you're an expert speaker, use a script to help you cover everything you need to say without rambling or using an excessive amount of filler words. A teleprompter will let you read your script while looking into the camera.

Speak conversationally. Visualize a friend or family member and talk to that person.

Cut out your mistakes. Use a video editor to remove your flubs and misspeaks.

Don't worry about going viral. In most cases, the number of views your video gets is less important than who is watching and whether they take the desired action. Focus on creating a quality video with valuable content.

Today we observe

Deepfake Awareness Day

Space Exploration Day

On this day in history

Notable events

In 1970, the six-story, 90-ton, tin-clad novelty building known as Lucy the Elephant was moved to its current location in Margate, New Jersey. It was designated as a National Historic Landmark in 1974.

Births

John G. Shedd, American businessman and philanthropist, second president and board chair of Marshall Field & Company, 1850

Mike Ilitch, entrepreneur, cofounder (with his wife Marian) of Little Caesars Pizza, and professional sports team owner, 1929

Jeanne Bice, American entrepreneur, businesswoman, television personality, and founder of the Quacker Factory clothing line, 1939

Deaths

John W. Galbreath, American real estate developer, former owner of the Pittsburgh Pirates, and sportsman, 1988

Thought for the day

"People travel to wonder at the height of the mountains, at the huge waves of the seas, at the long course of the rivers, at the vast compass of the ocean, at the circular motion of the stars, and yet they pass by themselves without wondering."

St. Augustine

I pray for my community.

Read:
Proverbs, Chapter 20

July 21

Finally, dear brothers and sisters, we ask you to pray for us. Pray that the Lord's message will spread rapidly and be honored wherever it goes, just as when it came to you. *(2 Thessalonians 3:1, NLT)*

Fearing God isn't a bad thing

If you've ever heard the phrase, "I'll put the fear of God into you," you know it's not meant as a nurturing, comforting promise.

Merriam-Webster defines the idiom as *to frighten (someone) very badly*.

It's sad to hear Christianity distorted like that.

When referring to God, the word fear doesn't mean to be afraid. Do an internet search on "fear of God" and you'll get millions of results that include learned theologians explaining that it means respect, awe, reverence, and obedience to God.

The fear of the Lord is the beginning of wisdom, and knowledge of the Holy One is understanding. (Proverbs 9:10, NIV)

Wisdom doesn't come from being afraid or intimidated.

When we truly fear God in the biblical sense, when we respect him, love him, and are faithful to him, we are not afraid in the face of evil, hardship, and sin. We are fearless.

But does fear—that is, the feeling that something is dangerous and likely to cause pain—occasionally creep in? Yes.

And then we're reminded:

The Lord himself goes before you and will be with you; he will never leave you nor forsake you. Do not be afraid; do not be discouraged." (Deuteronomy 31:8, NIV)

So relax and let go of the human emotion God doesn't want you to feel and embrace the peace he gives us.

I praise you because I am fearfully and wonderfully made; your works are wonderful, know that full well. (Psalm 139:14, NIV)

No one has to put the fear of God in Christians. It's already there.

Today we observe

National Be Someone Day

On this day in history

Notable events

In 1962, Telstar 1 relayed the first publicly available live transatlantic television signal.

In 1989, Eastern Airlines filed a formal reorganization plan in federal bankruptcy court, vowing to repay its debts.

Births

Allan J. Pinkerton, Scottish-American cooper, detective, and spy known for creating the Pinkerton National Detective Agency, 1819 (some documents say August 25)

Roy Neuberger, American financier (cofounder of investment firm Neuberger Berman) and art patron, 1903

Deaths

Alonzo Herndon, American businessman and entrepreneur; born into slavery, he became one of the first millionaires in the U.S., 1927

Morris Michtom, Russian-born American businessman and inventor, created the teddy bear, cofounder of the Ideal Novelty and Toy Company, 1938

John Garnet Carter, American entrepreneur and inventor, the first to patent a version of miniature golf, 1954

Thought for the day

"An idea can turn to dust or magic, depending on the talent that rubs against it."
Bill Bernbach

I am thankful for the clear order of the universe that proves the existence of God.

Read:
Proverbs, Chapter 21

July 22

Whatever you are doing, work at it with enthusiasm, as to the Lord and not for people, because you know that you will receive your inheritance from the Lord as the reward. Serve the Lord Christ.
(Colossians 3:23-24, NET)

The power of God in us

In *Live a Life that Matters for God*, Jack Alan Levine writes this about God's power:

"It's the Word of God that speaks, that brings Spirit and life. It's the Word of God that's alive—not my word, but God's word, not my power but God's power working in us and through us to accomplish the will of God (the good works that God prepared in advanced for me to do, Ephesians 2:10). It's the power of God that super charges the Word spiritually in your heart and draws you to the Holy Spirit and excites you in the Holy Spirit. It's the power of God in us and in our life that equips us to do great things. It's the power of God and it's alive and working in your life today through the Holy Spirit of God deposited in your heart at salvation.

"God has the power to forgive. God has the power to heal. God has the power to love. God has the power to restore. God has the power to magnify. God has the power to enlarge. It's supernatural power. It's the same power that when people had nothing to eat, Jesus used to break two loaves and some fish and fed five thousand people with it. It's the same power that allowed Jesus to turn water into wine. It's the same power the Jesus used to raise Lazarus from the dead. It's the same power that raised Jesus from the grave. It's that same power that comes into every believer of Jesus Christ. But you've got to take it and more importantly you've got to use it."

I pray for the tools I need to be an effective part of God's plan for the world.

Today we observe

World Brain Day

Pi Approximation Day

On this day in history

Births

James Geddes, American civil engineer, lawyer, and politician who played a leading role in the construction of the Erie Canal, 1763

Deaths

Cassius Marcellus Clay, American planter, politician, military officer, and abolitionist, 1903

William Kissam Vanderbilt I, American businessman, philanthropist, and horse breeder; born into the Vanderbilt family, he managed the family's railroad investments, 1920

Reginald Fessenden, Canadian-American inventor who received hundreds of patents, with the most notable related to radio and sonar, 1932

Thought for the day

"Let us cry for the spilt milk, by all means, if by doing so we learn how to avoid spilling any more. Let us cry for the spilt milk, and remember how, and where, and why, we spilt it. Much wisdom is learnt through tears, but none by forgetting our lessons."

Maria Amparo Ruiz de Burton

> Grow your faith by specifically praying for someone you don't like.

Read: Proverbs, Chapter 22

July 23

A**nd we all, with unveiled face, beholding the glory of the Lord, are being changed into his likeness from one degree of glory to another; for this comes from the Lord who is the Spirit.** *(2 Corinthians 3:18, RSV)*

How positivity relates to health

Can a positive mindset be a catalyst for a healthier, more fulfilling life? Restorative Health Mentor Mike Beverly says yes.

In his newsletter *Health Hacks*, Beverly explains the first step of how positive thinking impacts health: our thoughts can cause chemical reactions in the brain.

"Neurotransmitters like dopamine and serotonin, often referred to as the 'feel-good' chemicals, flood the system, fostering happiness and alleviating stress," Beverly says. "The reduction in stress is not merely a subjective feeling; it translates into lower cortisol levels, which, in turn, contributes to improved overall well-being. Additionally, positivity has been scientifically linked to bolstering the immune system, providing the body with enhanced defense mechanisms against various illnesses."

Beverly says a positive mindset starts with gratitude. "Gratitude practices emerge as powerful tools in cultivating positivity. Regularly expressing thankfulness redirects focus from challenges to blessings, fostering a positive perspective.

"Mindfulness and meditation, acknowledged for their stress-relieving properties, contribute to a present-focused mindset, facilitating better stress management. Surrounding oneself with positivity, whether through uplifting content, supportive social circles, or nurturing environments, reinforces and sustains a positive outlook. Actively challenging negative thoughts and incorporating positive affirmations gradually reshapes cognitive patterns, facilitating lasting mindset shifts."

Read:
Proverbs, Chapter 23

Today we observe
National Care for Your Coworker Day

On this day in history
Notable events
In 1829, William Austin Burt patented the first typewriter (then called the typographer).

Deaths
Isaac Singer, American inventor, actor, and businessman, founder of what became one of the first American multinational businesses, the Singer Sewing Machine Company, 1875
Ulysses S. Grant, 18th U.S. President, 1885
Glenn Curtiss, American aviation and motorcycling pioneer, inventor (hydroplane), a founder of the U.S. aircraft industry, 1930
Mary Church Terrell, American educator, political activist, and first president of the National Association of Colored Women, 1954

Thought for the day

"If your parents ever measured you as a child, they had you stand against a wall, and made a little pencil mark on the wall to show your growth. They did not measure you against your brother, or the neighbor's kids, or kids on TV. When you measure your growth, make sure to only measure your today self by your past self. If you compare your relationships, your success, or your anything against anyone else, you are not being fair to you. Everyone has a different path, a different pace, and different challenges to face along the way."

Doe Zantamata

I am thankful that even when I'm in the midst of pain, heartbreak, and grief, I can depend on God's faithfulness.

July 24

> "If you keep quiet at a time like this, deliverance and relief for the Jews will arise from some other place, but you and your relatives will die. Who knows if perhaps you were made queen for just such a time as this?" (Esther 4:14, NLT)

Do your customers feel good about associating with you?

Consumers make buying decisions for a wide range of reasons. One that isn't talked about often but is still important is how they feel about associating with a particular brand. As brands feel compelled to make social statements, this issue is gaining traction.

Certainly you have to begin with a quality product or service at a price people are willing to pay. But you also need to make your customers feel good about connecting with you. This usually comes when you and your customers have shared values.

Customers are often motivated to be loyal to brands that are associated with causes they support and that have a positive social impact.

You must be authentic about the cause you stand for. Don't choose something because it's a current hot topic—customers will figure that out quickly and will ditch you with equal speed.

Expect that some customers will reject you because of your values, and that's okay. You'll be able to grow a stronger, more sustainable business with customers who share your values and are proud to associate with you.

Do you make it a priority to spend quality time with people you care about? Then spend quality time with God.

I pray for service providers.

Read:
Proverbs, Chapter 24

Today we observe
International Self-Care Day

On this day in history
Births
Amelia Earhart, American aviation pioneer, writer, first female aviator to fly solo across the Atlantic ocean, 1897
Ed Mirvish, American-Canadian businessman, philanthropist, and theatrical impresario, known for his flagship business, Honest Ed's, and as a patron of the arts, 1914

Deaths
Martin Van Buren, 8th U.S. President (first President to be born as a U.S. citizen), 1862
Robert Ledley, professor, author, pioneered the use of electronic digital computers in biology and medicine, inventor (whole-body CT scanner), 2012

Thought for the day

"In addition to ignoring the issues faced by businesspeople, seminars offer little analysis of or appreciation for the moral roots of the modern corporation, the concept of business as a calling, or multiple tasks that business performs for society and the common good."

David W. Miller

Tell a story

The next time you have to present data, make it relatable and memorable by sharing a story that illustrates the impact of the facts and figures. If possible, use real names and detailed descriptions so your audience can connect with your message in a personal way.

July 25

> Therefore consider carefully how you live—not as unwise but as wise, taking advantage of every opportunity, because the days are evil. For this reason do not be foolish, but be wise by understanding what the Lord's will is. *(Ephesians 5:15-17, NET)*

Small steps to big results

You've made the decision and the commitment, and now you're ready to start. Use these tips to increase your chances of self-improvement success.

Be specific and focused. Instead of "get organized," be precise. Maybe you're going to clean off the top of your desk or institute a new filing system. Those are more achievable goals than vague, open-ended resolutions.

Take baby steps. Small changes produce big results over time. Don't try to do it all at once.

Find and use technology that works for you. Smartphone apps can be great support tools.

Pay yourself first. We tend to think of this when it comes to saving money, but it's a good approach when it comes to meeting our goals. Work toward your goals first before you do other things.

Get rid of as many obstacles as you can. If you're going to exercise, choose a gym that's convenient and put your workout gear out the night before so it's ready in the morning. If you're going to take a class, choose a time and location that works with your other responsibilities.

Practice habit-stacking. Identify a positive habit you have and stack a new behavior on top. For example, for most of us, checking emails first thing in the morning is a habit. Instead of diving into work after that, add a new habit of doing a quick review of your plan for the day and optimize your task list. Or when you have a cup of coffee, also have a glass of water.

Be kind to yourself. Don't beat yourself up when you don't hit every goal exactly on target. Make whatever adjustments you need to and keep going.

Today we observe

National Hire a Veteran Day

On this day in history

Notable events

In 1854, American inventor Walter Hunt received a patent for his paper shirt collar.

Births

Frank J. Sprague, American inventor who contributed to the development of the electric motor, electric railways, and electric elevators, 1857

Mitzi Shore, American comedy club owner and founder of The Comedy Channel, 1930

Deaths

Malcolm Baldrige, Jr., American businessman and U.S. Secretary of Commerce (1981-1987), quality proponent for whom the Malcolm Baldrige National Quality Award was named, 1987

Charles Stark "Doc" Draper, American scientist and engineer, known as the father of inertial navigation, 1987

Tracy Hall, American physical chemist and early pioneer in the research of synthetic diamonds, 2008

Thought for the day

"I don't wait for moods. You accomplish nothing if you do that. Your mind must know it has got to get down to work."

Pearl S. Buck

I am thankful for the many ways I can serve the Lord through serving others.

Read:
Proverbs, Chapter 25

July 26

He said to his disciples, "The harvest is great, but the workers are few. So pray to the Lord who is in charge of the harvest; ask him to send more workers into his fields." *(Matthew 9:37-38, NLT)*

The power of coopetition

Can you really cooperate with your competitors? Yes, and it can be a powerful way for you both to maximize opportunities and profits, and grow your respective businesses. Technology companies do it all the time.

According to Investopedia, coopetition is the act of cooperation between competing companies; businesses that engage in both competition and cooperation are said to be in coopetition.

Certain businesses gain an advantage by using a judicious mixture of cooperation with suppliers, customers, and firms producing complementary or related products.

Coopetition requires a large degree of transparency (while still protecting sensitive information not related to the collaboration), trust, effective communication, comprehensive, carefully-structured agreements that protect all parties and keep everyone legally compliant.

Coopetition can lead to the expansion of the market and the formation of new business relationships. It can help you and your partners save time and money through sharing resources. It can create opportunities that might not have otherwise existed. It can breed innovation and break through stagnant product offerings.

If you have a competitor with whom you share customers, suppliers, and/or competitors, you may want to explore coopetition possibilities. Be bold and creative. How can you make it work in your industry or niche?

Today we observe
All or Nothing Day

On this day in history

Notable events

In 1775, the U.S. postal system was established by the Second Continental Congress with Benjamin Franklin as its first postmaster general.

In 1990, the Americans with Disabilities Act (ADA) was signed into law.

Births

Scott Cook, American billionaire businessman who cofounded Intuit, 1952

Deaths

Fred Duesenberg, German-American automobile and engine designer, manufacturer, and racer, credited with introducing an eight-cylinder engine and four-wheel hydraulic brakes, cofounder of the Duesenberg Motor Company, 1932

Charles Tindley, American Methodist minister and gospel music composer, 1933

George Gallup, American pioneer of survey sampling techniques and inventor of the Gallup poll, 1984

William A. Mitchell, American food chemist and inventor (received over 70 patents) who was the key inventor behind Pop Rocks, Tang, Cool Whip, and powdered egg whites, 2004

Bill English, American computer engineer who helped develop the computer mouse and the NLS computer system, 2020

Thought for the day

"Discipline and freedom are not mutually exclusive but mutually dependent because otherwise, you'd sink into chaos."
Paulo Coelho

Read:
Proverbs, Chapter 26

I pray for God's will to be done.

July 27

Be still in the presence of the Lord, and wait patiently for him to act. Don't worry about evil people who prosper or fret about their wicked schemes. *(Psalm 37:7, NLT)*

Strengthen your prayer life

Know whom you're talking with. Address whom you're praying to by name.

Have a prayer place and position. Physically set your scheduled prayer time apart.

Express your gratitude. Begin and end with thanks and praise.

Ask for God's will. In an uncertain world, you may not always know what to ask for, but God knows what you need.

Speak your needs. God wants you to bring your needs to him, to ask him for his blessings and gifts.

Don't limit your requests. Pray for small things, pray for big things. Be bold in your petitions and God will boldly respond.

Confess and ask for forgiveness. Acknowledge and confess your sins and ask God to forgive you.

Pray with a partner. Ask one or more friends to be prayer partners you can call to pray with you when you have an urgent need.

Pray the Scriptures. Praying God's Word back to him is one of the most powerful prayers you can make.

Keep a prayer journal. Write your prayers down.

Pray before projects, meetings, and important events. Whatever you're doing, set the tone by inviting God into it.

Look for answers. Be alert to the ways God is answering your prayers.

Be persistent. Don't just ask once; pray the same prayer over and over.

Pray any time, anywhere. When you need to pray, no matter where you are, stop and do it.

Read:
Proverbs, Chapter 27

Today we observe

Cross Atlantic Communication Day

On this day in history

Notable events

In 1909, Orville Wright successfully tested the Wright Military Flyer, the world's first military airplane, satisfying the Army's endurance and passenger carrying requirements.

Births

Allen K. Breed, American inventor, entrepreneur, and pioneer in the automotive industry's acceptance of airbags, 1927

Deaths

Garrett Morgan, American inventor (gas mask, traffic signal), 1963

Frank Zamboni, American entrepreneur, engineer, and inventor of the Zamboni Ice Resurfacer, 1988

Always begin with prayer

Whatever you do, begin with prayer.

God loves when his people come together in prayer, when they turn to his promises for their needs, when they pray boldly and confidently. Prayer guides and protects us in all of our endeavors, so begin them all in prayer.

Thought for the day

"If you can't fly then run, if you can't run then walk, if you can't walk then crawl, but whatever you do you have to keep moving forward."

Martin Luther King Jr.

I am thankful for those who care enough to pray for me.

July 28

Then Israel said to Joseph, "Behold, I am about to die, but God will be with you and will bring you back to the land of your fathers. *(Genesis 48:21, LSB)*

Are we living in the end times?

The world is a crazy place these days. So much evil, so much strife, so many natural disasters.

According to surveys, an increasing number of people believe we are living in the end times as prophesied in the Bible.

But are we?

However, no one knows the day or hour when these things will happen, not even the angels in heaven or the Son himself. Only the Father knows. (Matthew 24:36, NLT)

If we are in the end times, does it matter? Will it change anything about the way you live? If it would, you need to take a serious look at what you're doing and how you're living.

You also must be ready all the time, for the Son of Man will come when least expected. (Matthew 24:44, NLT)

Scripture is specific: We are not to speculate about when Jesus will return. We are to live each day prepared for it to happen—and prepared for it to not happen.

Throughout recorded history, people have been able to point to certain events as foreshadowing the end times. And yet, we're still here—not because of a flaw in the prophesies, but because of God's timing.

But you must not forget this one thing, dear friends: A day is like a thousand years to the Lord, and a thousand years is like a day. (2 Peter 3:8, NLT)

Yes, the world is a crazy place these days, full of evil, strife, and natural disasters. But it's always been that way. And it's also full of good, of love and service, of daily miracles and joy.

If knowing Jesus' return is imminent would cause you to make positive changes in your life, make those changes now. Your life will be better for it, no matter how much time you have.

Today we observe

World Nature Conservation Day

On this day in history

Notable events

In 1945, Betty Lou Oliver survived falling 75 stories (world record for longest survived elevator fall) after fog caused a U.S. bomber plane to crash into the 79th floor of the Empire State Building, breaking the cables supporting the elevator she was operating.

Births

Otto Frederick Rohwedder, American engineer, jeweler, and inventor (first automatic bread-slicing machine for commercial use), 1880

Earl Tupper, American businessman and inventor, founder of Tupperware Corporation, 1907

Deaths

William James Mayo, physician and surgeon, cofounder of the Mayo Clinic, 1939

Ron Popeil, American inventor and marketing personality who popularized the phrase, "But wait, there's more!", 2021

Thought for the day

"The more intensely we feel about an idea or a goal, the more assuredly the idea, buried deep in our subconscious, will direct us along the path to its fulfillment."

Earl Nightingale

I pray to not gloat or take satisfaction when bad things happen to people I don't like.

Read:
Proverbs, Chapter 28

July 29

Do your best to present yourself to God as one approved, a worker who has no need to be ashamed, rightly handling the word of truth. *(2 Timothy 2:15, ESV)*

Make your mentor appreciate *you*

When John Crossman, founder of Crossman Career Builders (Winter Park, Florida), talks about mentoring, he talks about charity (giving without receiving) and relationships (which are built on giving *and* receiving). And then he gets to the punch line: When you're advancing your career, do you want your connection with your mentors to be a charity-relationship or a relationship-relationship?

"Sometimes people say, 'I want a senior person to pour into me and I'm just going to take that and go do my thing.' That will work for a little bit, but it won't last," he says. "If you see a senior person and you think, 'I want them to pour into me,' then find ways to pour into them. That will last forever."

So what can someone younger, less-experienced, and less-connected do for that senior person? Crossman suggests:

- Write a handwritten note expressing gratitude, offering encouragement, or sharing a piece of information.
- Actively connect with the person and their company on social media, and leave positive comments and reviews.
- Notice what they've done in the community and let them know you appreciate it, even if you're not a direct beneficiary.
- Congratulate them on their achievements.
- Remember their birthday or anniversary with a card or note.
- Be supportive if they're having difficulties—don't disappear when a mentor is going through a tough time.

None of these things takes a lot of time, costs a significant amount of money, or requires an expansive network, but they have a powerful impact that can last a lifetime.

On this day in history

Notable events

In 1909, the newly formed General Motors Corporation acquired the Cadillac Automobile Company for $4.5 million.

In 1958, the U.S. Congress passed legislation establishing the National Aeronautics and Space Administration (NASA).

Births

Walter Hunt, American mechanical engineer and prolific inventor (safety pin, sewing machine), 1796

Vladimir Kosma Zworykin, Russian-American inventor, engineer, and pioneer of television technology, 1888

Charles R. Schwab, American investor and financial executive, founder of Charles Schwab Corporation, 1937

Virginia Marie "Ginni" Rometty, American business executive (served as chairman, president and CEO of IBM), 1957

Deaths

Vladimir Kosma Zworykin, Russian-American inventor, engineer, and pioneer of television technology, 1982

Richard L. Simon, American book publisher, cofounder of Simon & Schuster, 1960

Thought for the day

"Forgiveness is the key that unlocks the door of resentment and the handcuffs of hate. It is a power that breaks the chains of bitterness and the shackles of selfishness."
William Arthur Ward

I am thankful for the gift of imagination and the potential it provides.

Read:
Proverbs, Chapter 29

July 30

> **D**evote yourselves to prayer with an alert mind and a thankful heart.
> *(Colossians 4:2, NLT)*

Recommend, don't just refer

Making referrals is easy. Providing recommendations takes more effort.

When you make a referral, you are introducing two people who may want to do business with each other, and what happens next is up to them. When you make a recommendation, you're putting your reputation on the line. In *Work as Worship: How Your Labor Becomes Your Legacy*, Mark Goldstein explains it this way:

"Referrals are great. A recommendation is much stronger. For example, a guy comes to me and says, 'Hey, Mark, do you know a barber I can go to?' I might say, 'Yeah, there's a barbershop in the shopping center I drive by every day. I don't know anything about it, but you could check it out.' That's a referral.

"But if the guy asks about a barber and my response is, 'The best in the area is right up the street in that shopping center. His name is Phil. He's been cutting hair for years, he's been doing mine for ages, and you'll absolutely love him.'

"*That's* a recommendation. You've put some skin in the game.

"We will only recommend people we trust, and we only trust people we know. We're not going to take a chance on burning relational collateral by recommending somebody who is going to disprove what we said, who is going to not show up or is going to do a lousy job. That makes us look bad.

"When you meet people, don't just qualify them as prospects, get to know them enough so you can decide if you want to do business with them but also so you can recommend them to others."

I pray for the strength to fight discouragement.

Today we observe

Paperback Book Day
National Whistleblower Day
National Support Public Education Day

On this day in history

Notable events

In 1956, President Dwight D. Eisenhower signed a law officially declaring "In God We Trust" to be the nation's official motto.

In 1965, President Lyndon B. Johnson signed Medicare into law.

In 2003, the last classic VW Beetle rolled off an assembly line in Puebla, Mexico.

Births

Henry Ford, American industrialist and business magnate, founder of Ford Motor Company and chief developer of the assembly line technique of mass production, was born in Springwells Township, Michigan, 1863

Blanche Knopf, publisher, cofounder and president of Alfred A. Knopf, Inc., 1894

Henry W. Bloch, American businessman and philanthropist, cofounder of the tax-preparation company H&R Block, 1922

Deaths

Jacob Perkins, American inventor, mechanical engineer, and physicist, known as the father of the refrigerator, 1849

Sam Phillips, American record producer, founder of Sun Records and Sun Studio, 2003

Thought for the day

"Organizational health is often neglected because it involves facing realities of human behavior that even the most committed executive is tempted to avoid."

Patrick Lencioni

Read:
Proverbs, Chapter 30

July 31

> ❝ My prayer is not for them alone. I pray also for those who will believe in me through their message, that all of them may be one, Father, just as you are in me and I am in you. May they also be in us so that the world may believe that you have sent me. I have given them the glory that you gave me, that they may be one as we are one—I in them and you in me—so that they may be brought to complete unity. Then the world will know that you sent me and have loved them even as you have loved me. *(John 17:20-23, NIV)*

You'll always have more questions than answers

When it comes to life in general and God in particular, most of us have a lot of questions. Often getting answers only generates more questions. Accept that you will probably always have more questions than answers. This acceptance will give you peace that will lead to joy.

Our world is full of mysteries. Though we are meant to solve some, we are not meant to solve them all. God wants us to trust him, to have faith that he is in control even when we don't understand what is happening or why.

There's an old saying that when the student is ready, the teacher will appear. When we truly need the answers, God will provide them. And if we are not meant to have the answer, we need to accept that.

This is not an excuse for laziness. Of course, we should seek and study. We're not supposed to stay deliberately ignorant. But when we've given something our best effort and we still don't have the answer, accept it and don't stress over it.

Thought for the day

"Well-being is not found in isolation, possessions, or power itself; it usually appears while serving others."

Manuel Arango

Read:
Proverbs, Chapter 31

Today we observe
National Heatstroke Awareness Day

On this day in history

Notable events
- In 1790, the first U.S. patent was granted to Samuel Hopkins for a process of making potash, an ingredient used in fertilizer.
- In 1975, labor leader Jimmy Hoffa was reported missing.
- In 1988, the last Playboy Club, located in Lansing, Michigan, closed.

Births
- John Ericsson, Swedish-American inventor (screw propeller, rotating turret), 1803
- Lydia Moss Bradley, American bank president, philanthropist, and college founder, 1816
- Ahmet Ertegun, Turkish-American businessman, songwriter, record executive, and philanthropist, cofounder of Atlantic Records, 1923
- Mark Cuban, American businessman, investor, film producer, television personality, and owner of the Dallas Mavericks, 1958

Deaths
- Andrew Johnson, 17th U.S. President, 1875
- Francis Edgar Stanley, American inventor, entrepreneur, photographer, cofounder of the Stanley Motor Carriage Company which built steam-powered automobiles, 1918
- Charles E. Hires, American pharmacist, early promoter of commercially prepared root beer, founder of Charles E. Hires Co., which manufactured and distributed Hires Root Beer, 1937
- Mo Ostin, American record executive, 2022

I am thankful for the opportunities to enjoy meals with people I care about.

Christian Business Almanac

August

August was originally named Sextilis, which means the sixth month. It was renamed August to honor Augustus Caesar, the first Roman emperor.

Originally, August had 30 days while July, which was named after Julius Caesar, had 31 days. Augustus did not want his month to have fewer days than Julius' month, so he added a day to make it 31 days long.

August birthstone
Peridot, sardonyx

August flower
Gladiolus, poppy

August is ...
- American Adventures Month
- Black Business Month
- Boomers Making a Difference Month
- Bystander Awareness Month
- Get Ready for Kindergarten Month
- MedicAlert Awareness Month
- National Back to School Month
- National Civility Month
- National Family Fun Month
- National Golf Month
- National Peach Month
- Summer Sun Safety Month
- What Will Be Your Legacy Month

Mark your calendar for these August holidays and observances

First Tuesday in August	National Night Out
First Wednesday in August	National Professional Engineers Day
First Saturday in August	Taxpayer Appreciation Day
First Saturday in August	National Play Outside Day
First Sunday in August	International Forgiveness Day
First Sunday in August	National Kids Day
First Sunday in August	American Family Day
First Monday in August	Exchange Day
Second Saturday in August	Garage Sale Day
Second Sunday in August	National Spirit of '45 Day
Third Sunday in August	World Helicopter Day
Third Sunday in August	God's Preeminence Day
Third Monday in August	Stay at Home with Your Kids Day
Last Sunday in August	Pony Express Day
Last Monday in August	Motorist Consideration Monday
Last Wednesday in August	Willing to Lend a Hand Wednesday

Fun Facts about August

No other month has the same starting day that August does.
August is the busiest month for tourism.
The first week of August is Simplify Your Life Week.
The word August means *inspiring reverence or admiration*.

August 1

The acts of the flesh are obvious: sexual immorality, impurity and debauchery; idolatry and witchcraft; hatred, discord, jealousy, fits of rage, selfish ambition, dissensions, factions and envy; drunkenness, orgies, and the like. I warn you, as I did before, that those who live like this will not inherit the kingdom of God. *(Galatians 5:19-21, NIV)*

Is the Bible's list of sins complete?

If the Bible doesn't specifically forbid something, is it okay to do?

When you're trying to live a life as free from sin as possible, following the Bible is the best place to start. But keep this in mind:

An action isn't a sin because the Bible says it is. The Bible says it's a sin because it *is* a sin.

We are created in God's image as thinking, intelligent beings. We are not meant to blindly obey; we are meant to question and understand so we can live a life that is pleasing to God.

For example, the Bible specifically tells us to not commit murder (Exodus 20:13). But if that verse had somehow gotten left out of the Bible, would murder be okay?

No. It would still be a sin.

It's the same thing for stealing, adultery, lying, lust, greed, gluttony, and so on. These things are not sins because the Bible says they are. The Bible says they are sins because they are sins.

And this is why we can't wiggle around sinful conduct because something we want to do isn't specifically mentioned in the Bible. The Bible mentions hundreds of sins and scholars over the years have tried to list them, even as sinners have tried to figure out a way to excuse them.

Don't get bogged down in the human interpretation of what the Bible says we should and shouldn't do. If we feel like we need to justify our conduct by pointing out that the Bible doesn't specifically forbid it, we're probably doing—or wanting to do—something we shouldn't.

Today we observe

World Wide Web Day

National Planner Day

On this day in history

Notable events

In 1961, Six Flags Over Texas, the first park in the Six Flags chain, had its soft opening (grand opening was on August 5).

In 1981, MTV: Music Television went on the air for the first time with the words "Ladies and gentlemen, rock and roll."

Births

William B. Ziff, Sr., American publisher and author, cofounder of Ziff Davis Inc., 1898

Doug Burgum, American businessman (Great Plains Software, Microsoft Business Solutions Group), investor, philanthropist, and politician (Governor of North Dakota, candidate for U.S. President), 1956

Deaths

Arthur D. Little, American chemist, chemical engineer, inventor, and management consultant who pioneered the concept of contracted professional services, 1935

Thought for the day

"An entrepreneur tends to bite off a little more than he can chew hoping he'll quickly learn how to chew it."

Roy Ash

I am thankful for the opportunity to be an example for future generations.

Read:
Proverbs, Chapter 1

August 2

Instead, be kind to each other, tenderhearted, forgiving one another, just as God through Christ has forgiven you. *(Ephesians 4:32, NLT)*

Manage your to-do list

Effective management of your to-do list helps you prioritize your tasks, stay organized, and meet deadlines. Some tips:

Divide your list into sections. Group like items together in a way that works for you, such as calls, meetings, research, writing, etc.

Know your priorities. Rank your tasks based on urgency and importance. Resist the urge to do the smaller, easier tasks first just because you can get them done and checked off.

Have different lists for tasks, projects, and goals. Break those larger projects down into smaller tasks. Check your task list against your goal list for alignment.

Keep track of completed items. Remind yourself of how productive you've been.

Add fun things to your list. Don't make your to-do list a collection of tedious tasks; add a few things you enjoy.

Don't over-list. As you prioritize your list, only include what you can reasonably expect to do in a day and put the remainder on a list for later scheduling.

At the end of each day, set your most urgent priorities for the following day. When you begin work in the morning, your task list will be ready and you can jump in instead of having to take the time to get organized.

Thought for the day

"A rock pile ceases to be a rock pile the moment a single man contemplates it, bearing within him the image of a cathedral."
Antoine de Saint-Exupery

Read:
Proverbs, Chapter 2

Today we observe

National Coloring Book Day

Take a Penny, Leave a Penny Day

On this day in history

Notable events

In 1865, after 1,062 miles of transatlantic telegraph cable was laid by the SS Great Eastern, the cable snapped near the stern of the ship and the end was lost.

In 1892, George A. Wheeler patented ideas for the first practical moving staircase (escalator), but it was never built.

Births

Elisha Gray, American electrical engineer (developed a telephone prototype) and cofounder of Western Electric Manufacturing Company, 1835

Deaths

Horace Mann, American education reformer, abolitionist, and politician, 1859

Alexander Graham Bell, Scottish-born British-American inventor, scientist, and engineer; cofounder of the American Telephone and Telegraph Company, 1922

Warren G. Harding, 29th U.S. President, 1923

High achievers share these ten characteristics. They:
- are confident and secure,
- enjoy peace of mind,
- have good health and energy,
- enjoy strong relationships,
- are committed to worthy goals and ideals,
- have strong faith,
- welcome change,
- are creative problem-solvers,
- are good listeners, and
- help others.

I pray for endurance.

August 3

The Son radiates God's own glory and expresses the very character of God, and he sustains everything by the mighty power of his command. When he had cleansed us from our sins, he sat down in the place of honor at the right hand of the majestic God in heaven.
(Hebrews 1:3, NLT)

Intentional networking

Networking is not about growing your contact list, it's about building meaningful relationships.

Your hundreds or even thousands of LinkedIn contacts are not your network. Your network is made up of the people you have access to.

Creating a network doesn't happen by magic. You have to be intentional about it.

Begin by identifying the people you want in your network—the people who could have a positive impact on your life, career, and business. Keep this list short so you have time to invest in it.

Before you ask for help, give something of value. Don't make it an immediate quid pro quo. Build the relationship by giving for six months or even a year before you ask for anything.

Think about how you respond to people who connect and immediately try to sell you something, or people who expect you to promptly return an unasked-for favor. Don't be that person.

The most valuable tool for building and maintaining a productive network is a servant's heart. When you focus on how you can help others, they will naturally reciprocate.

Thought for the day

"The first rule of management is delegation. Don't try and do everything yourself because you can't."

Anthea Turner

Read:
Proverbs, Chapter 3

Today we observe

National Sales & Marketing Collaboration Day

On this day in history

Notable events

In 1900, Firestone Tire and Rubber Company was founded.

In 1955, Automobile Association of America ended its support of auto racing, citing the Le Mans disaster and driver Bill Vukovich's death as contributing factors.

In 1977, Radio Shack introduced the TRS-80, one of the first personal computers available to consumer markets.

Births

Elisha Otis, American industrialist, founder of the Otis Elevator Company, 1811

Martha Stewart, American businesswoman, television personality, publisher, and author, founder of Martha Stewart Living Omnimedia, 1941

Deaths

William Butler Ogden, American real estate investor, railroad executive, politician (first mayor of Chicago), and philanthropist, 1877

William Fargo, a pioneer American expressman who helped found the modern-day financial firms of American Express company and Wells Fargo, 1881

Benjamin Franklin Goodrich, American industrialist in the rubber industry and founder of B.F. Goodrich Company, 1888

Ellen Browning Scripps, American journalist, philanthropist, and cofounder of the E. W. Scripps Company, founder of the Scripps Research Institute and Scripps College, 1932

I am thankful for the times when being rejected was the best thing for me.

August 4

> He chose to give us birth through the word of truth, that we might be a kind of firstfruits of all he created. *(James 1:18, NIV)*

We must forgive

Jesus is abundantly clear. When someone hurts us, we must forgive them.

Forgiveness is one of the key tenets of our Christian faith. God forgives us and we are supposed to forgive one another. But it's not always easy. Even so, we should try to do for others as God does for us and as God has commanded us to do: Show mercy and forgive sinners.

Take a successful walk on the path to forgiveness with these steps:

Pray. Use prayer to help you block out all the negative emotions so you can begin the process of forgiving.

Take an honest and complete look at what really happened. Take the time to understand the motivation of the person or people who injured you as well as your role in the situation.

Figure out what good can come of the situation. How is God going to work in your life to turn your pain into something positive?

Let go of getting even. God will take care of justice and judgment.

Pray. Pray always, about everything, especially for the person who harmed you.

As you use these steps to move forward on the path to forgiveness, remember one final thing: forgiving doesn't mean forgetting.

We shouldn't forgive and forget.
What we should do is forgive and learn.
Forgive and grow.
Forgive and let go.
Forgive and be set free.

I am thankful that the Lord is always with me, even when I can't sense his presence.

Today we observe
Assistance Dog Day

On this day in history

Notable events
In 1988, Hertz Corp. was fined $6.85 million and agreed to pay back nearly $16 million for overcharging rental customers and insurance companies for auto repairs.

Births
Warren Avis, American entrepreneur, founder of Avis Car Rentals, 1915
Sheldon Adelson, American business magnate (CEO of Las Vegas Sands casino company), 1933
Barack Obama, 44th U.S. President, 1961

Deaths
J. Howard Marshall, billionaire businessman, academic, and government official, involved with and invested in the petroleum industry, 1995

We are the center of God's attention. He's always there, seeing everything, appreciating that his commands are being followed, grieving when they are not, and ready to step in when one of his children needs help and calls for him.

Thought for the day

"I learned that courage was not the absence of fear, but the triumph over it. The brave man is not he who does not feel afraid, but he who conquers that fear."
Nelson Mandela

Read:
Proverbs, Chapter 4

August 5

O people in Zion, inhabitants of Jerusalem, you shall weep no more. He will surely be gracious to you at the sound of your cry; when he hears it, he will answer you. Though the Lord may give you the bread of adversity and the water of affliction, yet your Teacher will not hide himself any longer, but your eyes shall see your Teacher. And when you turn to the right or when you turn to the left, your ears shall hear a word behind you, saying, "This is the way; walk in it." *(Isaiah 30:19-21, NRSVue)*

Make your time count

How can you reduce the amount of time you spend on activities that don't generate revenue? Take an inventory of how you're spending your time. Then go through your activities list one item at a time with these thoughts in mind:

Be sure the task is essential. Will your business suffer if you aren't doing some of the things you've been doing? If not, stop performing those non-essential tasks and focus on essentials.

Systematize the task. Once you've determined that the task is essential, think through the most efficient way of accomplishing the work. Analyze the procedure and turn it into an identifiable system by creating a step-by-step formula for getting it done.

Delegate. Systematizing makes delegating much easier and more effective. Identify people in your organization who can take over systematized tasks; give them the necessary responsibility and authority for getting the work done.

Outsource. When you don't have the necessary skills for particular tasks within your company, and when hiring an employee with those skills isn't practical, outsource the work. When outsourcing, consider a source that can handle a number of related tasks so you have a single contact for a variety of functions.

I pray for the wisdom to help those who tend to over-complicate things.

Today we observe

Work Like a Dog Day

Blogger Day

On this day in history

Notable events

In 1854, the first telegraph line across the Atlantic Ocean was completed.

In 1914, the world's first electric traffic signal was installed in Cleveland, Ohio.

In 1981, U.S. President Ronald Reagan fired 11,359 air traffic controllers.

Births

Anita Colby, American model, actress, inventor (chair that converts to an inclined bed), author, and business consultant, 1914

Reid Hoffman, American internet entrepreneur, venture capitalist, podcaster, author, and cofounder of LinkedIn, 1967

Deaths

D. W. Brooks, American farmer and businessman, founder of a farm cooperative that became Gold Kist, and founder of several insurance companies that served farming communities, 1999

Oliver W. Hill, American civil rights attorney who helped end the "separate but equal" doctrine, 2007

Thought for the day

"The greatness of a community is most accurately measured by the compassionate actions of its members."

Coretta Scott King

Read:
Proverbs, Chapter 5

August 6

The Lord said to his people: "You are standing at the crossroads. So consider your path. Ask where the old, reliable paths are. Ask where the path is that leads to blessing and follow it. If you do, you will find rest for your souls." But they said, "We will not follow it!" *(Jeremiah 6:16, NET)*

Public-speaking tips

Whether you're making a presentation to a few people on your team or a large group of strangers, use these tips for a powerful performance.

Know your audience. Who are they, how much do they already know about your topic, and what do they need to know?

Smile and make eye contact. Connect with the audience with a natural smile and by making eye contact with individual people.

Don't boast. Bragging is a subtle way of belittling others. Park your ego at the door and share information.

Tell stories. People love stories. Stories help the audience understand and remember the message.

Avoid "death by PowerPoint." Don't overload your slides with too much text, and don't just read what's on the slides.

Use pauses. Give the audience brief moments to absorb what you've said.

Repeat yourself. Your audience can't rewind a live presentation, so repeat the key message or take-home line several times.

Pay attention to audience reactions. Adjust as you go along if you need to.

Have a powerful close. Don't just end your presentation, close it with a strong call to action, a memorable story, or a summary of the most important takeaways.

I pray that I am alert to opportunities to say things that will brighten someone else's day.

Read:
Proverbs, Chapter 6

On this day in history

Notable events
In 1945, the U.S. dropped an atomic bomb on the Japanese city of Hiroshima.
In 1986, Phil Katz released PKARC (Zip file format for data compression) version 1.0 for IBM.

Births
Cecil Howard Green, British-born American geophysicist, electrical engineer, and electronics manufacturing executive; cofounder of Texas Instruments, 1900
E. Michael Burke, American businessman and sports executive, 1916
Jon Postel, American computer scientist who made significant contributions to the development of the internet, particularly with respect to standards, 1943

Deaths
Herbert Schlosser, American television executive, president of NBC (1974-1978), cofounder of A&E, played a key role in the creation of *Saturday Night Live*, 2021

Thought for the day

"A man would do nothing if he waited until he could do it so well that no one would find fault with what he has done."
Cardinal John Henry Newman

August 7

In that day you will no longer ask me anything. Very truly I tell you, my Father will give you whatever you ask in my name. *(John 16:23, NIV)*

Quick decision-making tip

When you need to make a fast decision between two things, flip a coin.

And then listen to your gut.

If your reaction to the coin toss was enthusiasm or relief, you've got your answer.

But if your reaction to the coin toss was disappointment or a strong feeling of "I wish it had gone the other way," then ignore the coin and do what your intuition tells you.

Creating effective strategies

A strategy is a general plan or set of plans intended to achieve something, especially over a long period. Some strategies are more effective than others. To evaluate the effectiveness of a strategy, ask these questions:

Do you have the resources to pursue the strategy? Do you have the money, time, and talent to implement what you want to do?

Can you pursue this strategy more efficiently than your competitors? Will your particular mix of resources let you do it better, faster, and at a lower cost?

Is the strategy sustainable? Once it's implemented, will you be able to maintain the strategy?

Are the internal elements of the strategy aligned? Do the various parts of your strategy fit and mutually reinforce each other?

Is the strategy implementable? Can you actually make it happen?

Thought for the day

"Don't tell me how hard you work. Tell me how much you get done."

James Ling

Today we observe

Lighthouse Day

Professional Speakers Day

On this day in history

Notable events

In 1782, General George Washington, the commander in chief of the Continental Army, created the Badge for Military Merit. The decoration was largely forgotten after the Revolutionary War until it was reinstated as the Order of the Purple Heart on February 22, 1932.

In 1944, IBM dedicated the Harvard Mark I or IBM Automatic Sequence Controlled Calculator (ASCC), one of the earliest general-purpose electromechanical computers used in the war effort during the last part of World War II.

In 1974, French street performer Philippe Petit made the most famous high-wire walk in history, traversing the World Trade Center's Twin Towers at a height of 1,350 feet.

Births

Louis Alan Hazeltine, American engineer, physicist, inventor (Neutrodyne circuit, Hazeltine-Fremodyne Superregenerative circuit), founder of Hazeltine Corporation, 1886

Jimmy Wales, American-British internet entrepreneur, cofounder of Wikipedia, 1966

Deaths

Virginia Apgar, American physician, obstetrical anesthesiologist, medical researcher, and inventor of the Apgar score, a way to quickly assess the health of newborns, 1974

I am thankful for the people and resources that are my support systems.

Read:
Proverbs, Chapter 7

August 8

When the Roman officer who stood facing him saw how he had died, he exclaimed, "This man truly was the Son of God!" *(Mark 15:39, NLT)*

Repurpose your blog content

You're creating great blog content, but is it working as hard for you as it could? Maximize your investment in your blog by using your content in other formats and platforms.

Check out these ides for repurposing your content:
- Combine several blog posts to create an ebook, white paper, special report or user guide.
- Create an infographic based on the content of one or more of your blogs.
- Organize the content into a slide deck and upload to SlideShare.
- Create a video by either converting your slide show into a video and speaking over it, or record yourself speaking about the topic, using your blog as a script.
- Build a presentation around your content and use it to speak to groups.
- Turn one or more of your posts into a podcast.
- Use your content to design a webinar that you can offer live or on-demand.
- Create social media posts by pulling out brief snippets from your blogs and sharing them on the various social platforms your audience uses (be sure to link back to your original article).
- Design an email course using your blogs as individual lessons.
- Compile a "best of" post that links to your most popular five or ten earlier posts.
- Turn a post into a quiz or checklist.
- Use your blog content in your electronic and print newsletters.
- Create a follow-up article that refers to an earlier blog post and adds fresh information, current statistics or perhaps discusses some of the comments made on the original.

Today we observe

National Dollar Day
National Love Your Inmate Day
Global Infinite Possibilities Day
The Date to Create

On this day in history

Notable events

In 1911, the millionth U.S. patent was granted to Francis H. Holton for a tubeless vehicle tire.

In 1988, the Chicago Cubs hosted the first night game in the history of Wrigley Field.

In 2017, Disney announced plans to launch a branded direct-to-consumer streaming service and remove its movies from Netflix.

Births

Robert "Dr. Bob" Smith, American physician and surgeon, cofounder of Alcoholics Anonymous, 1879

Deaths

Arthur Lang, age 115, former boxer, businessman, son of former slaves, 1992

James McLamore, American entrepreneur, founder and first CEO of the Burger King fast food franchise, creator of the Whopper sandwich, 1996

John H. Johnson, African-American publisher (*Negro Digest, Ebony, Jet*), 2005

Thought for the day

"Do not let your happiness depend on something you may lose."

C.S. Lewis

I pray for those who are grieving the loss of a loved one.

Read:
Proverbs, Chapter 8

August 9

Teach me to do your will, for you are my God. May your gracious Spirit lead me forward on a firm footing. *(Psalm 143:10, NLT)*

Decluttering tips

Some people work well in clutter, others don't. But most of us are more productive in a clutter-free space and it reflects more positively on our brand.

Some tips:

Only keep what you need and use. You may find it easier to clear off all your surfaces and slowly add things back as you need them. Or you may be able to survey the room and remove things you haven't touched in months. But get rid of what you don't use—except, of course, for a few personal/sentimental items that we enjoy having nearby.

Organize based on how you use things. Keep the items you use daily within easy reach. The items you need but don't use as often can be further away. If necessary, consider rearranging your space. You may find a different layout will help reduce clutter.

Organize your cables. Label them clearly and get a cable management system to keep them neat and untangled.

Digitize as much as possible. Don't keep paper you don't need. Scan or photograph documents and store them on your computer or phone; they'll will be easier to find than if they're piled on your desk.

Get and use organization tools. Hanging shelves, cabinets, dividers, bins—all of these tools are great if you use them. Get the tools that will work for you.

Clean daily. Make it a habit to put things away and leave your office decluttered at the end of each day.

I pray that I may serve well everyone the Lord places in my path.

Read:
Proverbs, Chapter 9

Today we observe

Book Lovers Day

International Coworking Day

On this day in history

Notable events

In 1945, the U.S. dropped an atomic bomb on Nagasaki, Japan.

In 2010, JetBlue flight attendant Steven Slater quit his job by using the plane's public address system to curse at an abusive passenger then exited the aircraft by sliding down the emergency-escape chute.

Births

Clarence Saunders, American grocer who first developed the modern retail sales model of self service, developer of Piggly Wiggly, Keedoozle, and Foodelectric store concepts, 1881

Ralph Wyckoff, American scientist and pioneer of X-ray crystallography, 1897

Ernest Winston Angley, American Christian evangelist, author, and television station owner, 1921

Marvin Minsky, American cognitive and computer scientist known for research into artificial intelligence, cofounder of MIT's AI laboratory, 1927

Deaths

Bernard Ogilvie Dodge, American botanist and pioneer researcher on heredity in fungi, 1960

Robert Lehman, American banker, head of Lehman Brothers investment bank, racehorse owner, art collector, and philanthropist, 1969

Jay Sebring, American celebrity hairstylist and founder of the hairstyling corporation Sebring International, murdered by members of the Manson Family, 1969

Thought for the day

"The path to wisdom is paved with humility."

Tim Fargo

August 10

Jesus called out to them, "Come, follow me, and I will show you how to fish for people!" *(Matthew 4:19, NLT)*

Ways to boost your creativity

Take care of your health. Get enough sleep, eat a healthful diet, and exercise.

Take a break from technology. Put the devices aways and get out into nature.

Brainstorm. Go for quantity over quality and come up with an abundance of ideas.

Change your routine. Do something different, even if it's only for a day or two.

Learn something new. Take a class in something you've never done before, even if you'll never do it again.

Change the colors in your environment. If you have peaceful colors, add something vibrant. If you have bright, strong colors, tone them down.

Collaborate. Get new ideas by working with and learning from others.

Pick the worst idea. Make a list of terrible ideas and figure out the best features of each one.

Look to the ordinary. Find inspiration in ordinary, everyday things.

Have confidence in your work. Don't be afraid to try new things or experiment.

Thought for the day

"A pessimist, they say, sees a glass of water as being half-empty; an optimist sees the same glass as half-full. But a giving person sees a glass of water and starts looking for someone who might be thirsty."

G. Donald Gale

I am thankful for everyone who has brought their faith into my life.

Read:
Proverbs, Chapter 10

Today we observe

International Vlogging Day

International Update Your Bio Day

On this day in history

Notable events

In 1846, the U.S. Senate passed the act organizing the Smithsonian Institution, which was signed into law by President James K. Polk.

In 1981, the Coca-Cola Company agreed to put $30 million into black-owned businesses and appoint a black person to its board of directors, ended a boycott of the company by a civil rights group.

In 2015, Google announced plans to create a new public holding company, Alphabet Inc., consisting of Google and other companies.

Births

Jay Cooke, American financier, first major investment banker in the U.S., and creator of the first wire house firm, 1821

Edward L. Doheny, American oil tycoon who drilled the first successful oil well in the Los Angeles City Oil Field, 1856

Herbert C. Hoover, 31st U.S. President, 1874

Charles Darrow, American board game designer credited as the inventor of *Monopoly*, 1889

John W. Galbreath, American real estate developer, former owner of the Pittsburgh Pirates, and sportsman, 1897

Leo Fender, American inventor and entrepreneur, founder of Fender Musical Instruments Corporation, 1909

Jimmy Dean, American singer, actor, and businessman, creator of the Jimmy Dean sausage brand, 1928

Kylie Jenner, American media personality and businesswoman, 1997

Deaths

Francis Cabot Lowell, American businessman instrumental in bringing the Industrial Revolution to the U.S. for whom the city of Lowell, Massachusetts is named, 1817

Robert H. Goddard, American engineer, professor, physicist, and inventor, considered the father of modern rocket propulsion, 1945

August 11

He who walks with wise men will be wise, But the companion of fools will suffer harm. *(Proverbs 13:20, NASB1995)*

Grace is not grind

Grace is a word we hear a lot in the Christian community. Often defined as undeserved favor that cannot be earned, people of faith can talk at length about what grace is. Bristan Heaven, Kingdom-driven Leadership Strategist with Kingdom Reach Leadership (Eustis, Florida) and co-president of the Central Florida Christian Chamber of Commerce, tells us what grace is not.

"Grace is not grind," he says. "Grind is me doing it apart from God. Grind is me leaning on my own understanding, doing it on my own strength. That leads to burnout. That leads to exhaustion. That leads to relationships being neglected."

Bringing grace into business means leaning on the power of God for whatever you need, whether it's getting the work done, making connections, or developing successful strategies. It's filtering through the many voices in the marketplace and focusing on God.

"If we're not listening to God, we're listening to someone else," Heaven says, adding that it's not enough to just listen, we have to obey. "It's a matter of keeping in step with the Holy Spirit. Then you experience God's best in your business."

Thought for the day

"We don't always have to reinvent the wheel; sometimes we just need to give the wheel a good push."

Bailey Sparks

I am grateful that I am able to serve others.

Today we observe
National Safe Digging Day / 811 Day
Annual Medical Check Up Day

On this day in history

Notable events
- In 1874, Henry S. Parmelee patented an automatic fire sprinkler head. Parmelee is credited as having the first building in the U.S. equipped with a fire suppression system.
- In 1896, Harvey Hubbell patented a socket for incandescent lamps with a simple on/off switch controlled by a pull chain—a design that remains popular today.
- In 2008, Airbnb officially launched.

Births
- William C. Bartholomay, American business executive and MLB team owner, 1928
- Jerry Falwell, American Baptist pastor, televangelist, and conservative activist, 1933
- Frederick W. Smith, American business magnate and investor, founder of FedEx Corporation, 1944
- Steve Wozniak, American technology entrepreneur, inventor, and philanthropist, cofounder of Apple Computer, 1950
- Joe Rogan, American commentator, podcaster, comedian, actor, 1967

Deaths
- Andrew Carnegie, American industrialist and philanthropist who led the expansion of the American steel industry in the late 19th century, 1919
- Frank Seiberling, American innovator, entrepreneur, founder of Goodyear Tire & Rubber Company, 1955
- Alfred A. Knopf Sr., American publisher, cofounder of Alfred A. Knopf, Inc., 1984
- Sumner Redstone, American billionaire businessman, media magnate, founder and chairman of the second incarnation of Viacom, 2020

Read:
Proverbs, Chapter 11

August 12

> For I am not ashamed of the gospel, because it is the power of God that brings salvation to everyone who believes: first to the Jew, then to the Gentile. *(Romans 1:16, NIV)*

Controlling workplace rumors

The spread of misinformation can be more damaging to a company than any real crisis. This is especially important in smaller organizations where workplace rumors can cause enough concern and insecurity that morale and productivity suffer, and your best employees may decide they'd be better off working elsewhere.

The following tips may stop rumors before they start to fly:

Tell them what's going on before their imaginations take over. What employees are not told, they invent.

Cut the grapevine back with the truth. Honesty acts on a rumor like water acts on a fire.

Keep the workforce informed at every stage of a change. This avoids panic and helps employees feel like an important part of the process.

Avoid closed doors. They're a sure sign that secrets are being told.

Hold clear, direct, face-to-face briefings where questions can be asked and answered. This is the best way to communicate important news. It may be tempting to hide behind memos and emails, but those should be used in addition to face-to-face meetings, not in lieu of them.

Encourage questions and invite ideas. The process of stopping rumors can also identify unforeseen problems and develop innovative solutions.

Thought for the day

"Courage is almost a contradiction in terms. It means a strong desire to live taking the form of readiness to die."

— *G.K. Chesterton*

On this day in history

Notable events

In 1851, Isaac Singer was granted a patent for a commercial sewing machine.

In 1908, the first Model T Ford rolled off the assembly line.

In 1930, Clarence Birdseye was granted a patent for a method for quick freezing food.

In 1981, the IBM PC debuted after a twelve-month development.

Deaths

Eliphalet Remington, American engineer and firearms manufacturer who founded what would become known as Remington Arms, 1861

William Shockley, American inventor, physicist, and eugenicist, Nobel prize winner, known (with Frederick Terman) for being the father of Silicon Valley, 1989

Get all that's available

Are your customers buying things from other suppliers that they could be buying from you? Try these tips to get the maximum amount of business from every customer.

- Tell your existing customers about additional products and services you offer that they may not be aware of.
- Be sure you are talking to everyone at the client company who has the need for your product and the authority to buy it.
- Ask your current contacts for names of others in the organization that you should be talking to.

I pray for the ability to see good in everyone and everything.

Read:
Proverbs, Chapter 12

August 13

Let no one look down on you because you are young, but set an example for the believers in your speech, conduct, love, faithfulness, and purity.
(1 Timothy 4:12, NET)

Why people brag and how to deal with it

Most of us were taught not to brag, but some of us do it anyway. Why? Reasons people brag include:
- Insecurity.
- A desire to be liked.
- Social anxiety.
- Poor social skills.
- Lack of empathy.
- Superiority or inferiority complex.
- Unawareness.
- A need to be the center or attention.

Braggarts can be irritating but we can't always avoid them. Try these tips for dealing with them:
- Remain nonjudgmental and try to understand why they're saying what they're saying.
- Model humility and modesty.
- Disengage by making a brief comment and ending the conversation.
- Consider having a private conversation to address the issue.

This is what the Lord says: "Don't let the wise boast in their wisdom, or the powerful boast in their power, or the rich boast in their riches. But those who wish to boast should boast in this alone: that they truly know me and understand that I am the Lord (Jeremiah 9:23-24, NLT)

Thought for the day

"Pull the string, and it will follow wherever you wish. Push it, and it will go nowhere at all."

Dwight D. Eisenhower

I am thankful for my material blessings.

Today we observe

International Lefthanders Day

World Organ Donation Day

On this day in history

Notable events

In 1889, William Gray received a patent for a coin-operated telephone; his invention popularized the telephone.

Births

Julius Freed, American banker, mechanical engineer, and amateur pigeon racer, notable for his involvement in the creation of the beverage Orange Julius, 1887

Rex Humbard, American television evangelist, author, 1919

Saul Steinberg, American businessman and financier; founder of Leasco, a computer leasing company, which he used in the takeover of Reliance Insurance Company, 1939

Kevin Plank, American businessman and philanthropist, founder of Under Armour, 1972

Deaths

Rufus Porter, American painter, inventor, and founder of Scientific American magazine, 1884

Collis P. Huntington, American industrialist and railroad magnate (Central Pacific Railroad, Southern Pacific Railroad, Chesapeake & Ohio Railway), 1900

J. Willard Marriott, Sr., American entrepreneur, businessman, founder of Marriott Corporation, 1985

Jack Ryan, American designer and businessman who worked at Mattel for 20 years, responsible for the Barbie and Ken dolls, Hot Wheels, Chatty Cathy, and more, 1991

Julia Child, American chef, author, and television personality, 2004

Brooke Astor, American philanthropist, socialite, and writer, 2007

Read:
Proverbs, Chapter 13

August 14

> Just as people are destined to die once, and after that to face judgment, so Christ was sacrificed once to take away the sins of many; and he will appear a second time, not to bear sin, but to bring salvation to those who are waiting for him. *(Hebrews 9:27-28, NIV)*

Retirement preparation

It's important to keep your employees informed about their retirement benefits and help those nearing retirement age prepare for the transition.

Start early. Mention retirement benefits to all new hires, regardless of age. One way to get younger employees to start planning for retirement is to tie the planning into their current priorities. For instance, if your company offers a 401(k) program, promote it as a way to save for later years while also reducing current tax liability.

Keep the communication channels open. If you contribute to a 401(k) or other retirement program, remind employees regularly that you are setting money aside for their future, which rewards them for staying with the organization.

Pre-retirement seminars. While it's important for all employees to be aware of the retirement benefits you offer, it's even more important for older employees to understand exactly what that means for them. Consider offering pre-retirement seminars to help employees prepare well in advance, as much as 15 or 20 years.

Ease the transition. In addition to helping employees prepare for retirement, help them make the transition itself. Consider offering the option of scaling back work schedules as staffers near retirement. You might also ask retirees to return to work as temporaries or to cover during peak periods.

Retirement benefits are valuable, and simply reminding employees of them can ensure that they're perceived that way. Pre-retirement planning shows that your organization really cares about its employees, and workers of any age appreciate that.

Today we observe

National Financial Awareness Day
National Tattoo Removal Day

On this day in history

Notable events

In 1935, President Franklin D. Roosevelt signed the Social Security Act into law.

In 1945, Imperial Japan's surrender in World War II was announced in the U.S. (it was announced on August 15 in Japan due to time zones), bringing the war to an end.

Births

Bion J. Arnold, American electrical engineer and inventor (railroad electrification), 1861

Earvin "Magic" Johnson, American businessman and former professional basketball player, 1959

Tim Tebow, college and professional athlete, sports broadcaster, philanthropist, 1987

Deaths

Charles Crocker, American business tycoon and railroad executive, 1888

William Randolph Hearst, Sr., American businessman, newspaper publisher, and politician, 1951

Thought for the day

"Something I learned early is to not worry about what I can't control... But what I can control is my attitude, my effort, and my focus every single day."

Tim Tebow

I pray for patience and the ability to find joy in waiting.

Read:
Proverbs, Chapter 14

August 15

> "One who is faithful in a very little is also faithful in much, and one who is dishonest in a very little is also dishonest in much. *(Luke 16:10, ESV)*"

Improve your daily Bible reading habit

Want to make daily Bible reading a habit? Use these tips:

Designate a specific time. Make an appointment with yourself to read the Bible at a specific time each day so it becomes part of your routine.

Choose a comfortable place. Read in a location that is quiet and comfortable so you can focus on what you're reading.

Pray before you begin. Pray for guidance and understanding before you start reading.

Use a reading plan. Give your reading structure and direction with a Bible reading plan.

Take notes and journal. Record your thoughts, reflections, and questions as you read. It's okay to write in your Bible!

Use the format you prefer. Choose a print or digital version of the Bible—whichever you like better.

Focus on consistency, not quantity. The key is to read every day, whether it's a single verse, short passage, or longer section.

Join a study group and/or get an accountability partner. Choose someone who will hold you accountable to your Bible reading commitment.

Don't skip and don't quit. Don't give yourself permission to skip a day, but also don't give up if you miss a day. Forgive yourself and begin again.

Today we observe

National Back-to-School Prep Day

National Failures Day

Check The Chip Day

International Apostrophe Day

On this day in history

Notable events

In 1848, the first U.S. patent for a dental chair with adjustable elevation and tilt of the seat and back was issued to M.W. Hanchett.

In 1899, Henry Ford resigned his position as chief engineer at the Edison Illuminating Company's main plant to concentrate on automobile production.

In 1911, Proctor & Gamble introduced Crisco shortening.

Births

Harlow Curtice, American automotive industry executive, president of General Motors (1953-1958), 1893

Julia Child, American chef, author, and television personality, 1912

Melinda French Gates, American philanthropist, former multimedia product developer and manager at Microsoft, author, founder of Pivotal Ventures, 1964

Deaths

Wiley Post, American aviator known for his work in high-altitude flying who helped developed one of the first pressure suits and discovered the jet stream, died in a plane crash with American humorist Will Rogers, 1935

Edward R. Bradley, American businessman, philanthropist, racetrack proprietor, owner and breeder of Thoroughbred racehorses, 1946

Thought for the day

"No one would have crossed the ocean if he could have gotten off the ship in the storm."

Charles Kettering

I am thankful for laughter.

Read:
Proverbs, Chapter 15

August 16

> But he said to me, "My grace is sufficient for you, for my power is made perfect in weakness." Therefore I will boast all the more gladly about my weaknesses, so that Christ's power may rest on me. That is why, for Christ's sake, I delight in weaknesses, in insults, in hardships, in persecutions, in difficulties. For when I am weak, then I am strong. *(2 Corinthians 12:9-10, NIV)*

Increase productivity by task batching

Task batching is a strategy that involves combining similar tasks and working on them simultaneously rather than spreading them out over a day or longer. This provides you with more structure and reduces your overall workload.

Task batching increases focus, reduces stress, improves productivity, saves time, and decreases burnout. Here's how to do it:

- List and prioritize your to-dos.
- Break larger projects down into smaller tasks.
- Categorize tasks according to function, such as what requires communication, what requires research, what requires concentration.
- Organize your schedule and assign tasks to blocks of time.

Give yourself sufficient time to complete each batch of tasks—remember, you're batching them, not stacking them. Schedule the more mentally challenging tasks for the times of day when you're at your peak. When you're focusing on a set of tasks, minimize your distractions by disabling notifications, turning off your phone, and turning on do not disturb mode.

Thought for the day

"Some people regard private enterprise as a predatory tiger to be shot. Others look on it as a cow they can milk. Not enough people see it as a healthy horse, pulling a sturdy wagon."

Winston Churchill

Today we observe

National Tell a Joke Day

Surveillance Day

National Independent Worker Day

On this day in history

Notable events

In 1939, New York City's Hippodrome Theater closed its doors for the last time.

Deaths

John Stith Pemberton, American pharmacist best known as the inventor of Coca-Cola, 1888

Jerry Moss, American recording executive, cofounder of A&M Records, 2023

Expand your mailing list by sharing data

If you're looking to build your mailing list, consider sharing lists with a company that targets the same market you do but isn't a direct competitor. You don't necessarily get a copy of the other company's list or have to give someone else your list. You can create and send a mailing on behalf of the other company and they can do the same for you. Or you can create a joint mailing you both send out. Whatever you do should comply with your privacy and data-sharing policies.

I am grateful that God is always in control, even when I don't understand.

Read: Proverbs, Chapter 16

August 17

"By all these things, I have shown you that by working in this way we must help the weak, and remember the words of the Lord Jesus that he himself said, 'It is more blessed to give than to receive.'" *(Acts 20:35, NET)*

What faith is not

Usually when we talk about faith, we focus on what it is, but to gain a true understanding of Biblical faith, you need to know what it is not.

Faith is not religion. It's not dogma or doctrine, customs, or traditions.

Faith is not mental assent. It's not intellectual agreement or simply knowing in your head that something is true.

Faith is not magic. It's not a way to manipulate God or anyone else into doing what we want when they would not otherwise be willing to do that.

Faith is not an attitude. It's not positive thinking or willing something into being simply because we want it to be so.

Faith is not mere human hope. It's not wishful thinking or desire; it's not just wanting something to be.

Though these things are generally good, they are not the faith God wants us to have in him. God doesn't want us to "hope and pray"—he wants us to pray and know. Hope is defined as a feeling of expectation and desire for a certain thing to happen. Hope is good for the mind and creates a condition that is conducive to faith, but it is not faith. Faith is the means by which the things we hope for are realized. It's evidence of things not seen. It's the confidence in and the assurance of the Word of God.

Have you ever heard someone say "seeing is believing," meaning that they will only believe (or have faith) in something when they can see it? That doesn't make sense. Once something exists in our human world and we can see it, we don't need faith in it. Faith lets you know something in your heart without ever seeing it with your eyes.

Excerpted from *Finding Joy in the Morning: You can make it through the night*

Today we observe

National Nonprofit Day

National I Love My Feet Day

On this day in history

Notable events

In 1891, the first public bathhouse with showers opened in New York City.

In 1903, Joe Pulitzer donated $1 million to Columbia University to begin the Pulitzer Prizes in America.

In 1908, the Bank of Italy (now Bank of America) opened its new headquarters building in San Francisco.

Births

Samuel Goldwyn, Polish-born American film producer and movie mogul, 1879

Hazel Bishop, American chemist, inventor ("No-Smear Lipsticks"), entrepreneur, founder of the cosmetics company Hazel Bishop, Inc., 1906

Larry Ellison, American businessman and entrepreneur, cofounder of Oracle Corporation, 1944

Deaths

John M. Belk, American head of Belk, Inc., 2007

Thought for the day

"Many people die with their music still in them. Why is this so? Too often it is because they are always getting ready to live. Before they know it, time runs out."

Oliver Wendell Holmes, Jr.

I am thankful for plants and flowers.

Read:
Proverbs, Chapter 17

August 18

A**nd I will ask the Father, and he will give you another advocate to help you and be with you forever—the Spirit of truth. The world cannot accept him, because it neither sees him nor knows him. But you know him, for he lives with you and will be in you.** *(John 14:16-17, NIV)*

How to ruin a meeting

Want to guarantee your meeting will be totally unproductive and a complete waste of time? Do these things:

Don't have a clear purpose. Or if you do have a purpose for the meeting, keep it a secret.

Don't prepare. Never do anything in advance that would make the meeting go smoother or be more productive.

Don't have an agenda or, if you do, don't bother to follow it. Let the discussion go down as many rabbit trails as the participants want.

Multi-task during the meeting. Leave your phone on. Browse around social media. Do some online shopping. Read material unrelated to the meeting. Take phone calls that show how important you are.

Spring surprise questions on participants. Don't let them know in advance what they should be ready to report or explain. And if they do have an answer, interrupt them and don't let them finish speaking.

Don't start or end on schedule. Whether you're hosting or simply participating, don't make any effort to be punctual. Punish people who arrived on time by making them wait. Inconvenience people who may have scheduled meetings after yours.

Don't follow up. When the meeting ends, so does your effort. There's nothing left to do until it's time to ruin another meeting.

I pray for our nation and our leaders.

Read:
Proverbs, Chapter 18

Today we observe

Never Give Up Day

On this day in history

Notable events

In 1872, Aaron Montgomery Ward issued the first "catalog" for his mail order business; it was a single sheet listing 163 items and offering credit.

In 2008, the domain name bitcoin.org was registered.

Births

Marshall Field, American entrepreneur and founder of Marshall Field and Company, 1834

Deaths

William Austin Burt, American inventor (typographer, solar compass), legislator, surveyor, and millwright, 1858

Walter Chrysler, American industrial pioneer in the automotive industry, founder of American Chrysler Corporation, 1940

Hiram Fong, American businessman, lawyer, and politician, 2004

Thought for the day

"Do not confuse motion and progress. A rocking horse keeps moving but does not make any progress."

Alfred A. Montapert

August 19

> ❝ You yourselves have seen what I did to Egypt, and how I carried you on eagles' wings and brought you to myself. *(Exodus 19:4, NIV)*

Problem-solving cycle

A systematic approach to solving problems can help you continuously improve your processes and systems.

Identify the problem. To effectively work on a problem, you must know exactly what it is.

Understand the problem. Examine every aspect of the problem so you can come up with a workable solution. Test your understanding by restating the problem in your own words and explaining it to someone else.

Gather, organize, and analyze data. Examine the facts, figures, and details related to the problem. Identify missing information and how to get it.

Brainstorm solutions. Explore alternatives and determine the best course of action.

Implement the solution. Develop a plan and allocate resources.

Monitor and evaluate. Gauge the effectiveness of the solution through appropriate measurement tools.

Prevent recurrence. If the solution solved the problem permanently, develop a standard to prevent organization-wide recurrence.

Thought for the day

"Action is a great restorer and builder of confidence. Inaction is not only the result, but the cause, of fear. Perhaps the action you take will be successful; perhaps different action or adjustments will have to follow. But any action is better than no action at all."

Norman Vincent Peale

I pray for parents and their children.

Today we observe
Aviation Day

On this day in history

Notable events

In 1856, Gail Borden was issued a U.S. patent for his process for making condensed milk.

In 1926, Eastern Airlines was founded as Pitcairn Aviation.

In 1930, Fisher-Price, producer of educational toys for infants, toddlers, and preschoolers, was formed.

In 1964, Syncom 3, the first geostationary communication satellite, launched from Cape Canaveral, Florida.

Births

Charles E. Hires, American pharmacist, early promoter of commercially prepared root beer, founder of Charles E. Hires Co., which manufactured and distributed Hires Root Beer, 1851

Orville Wright, aviation pioneer (Wright Brothers), 1871

Malcom Forbes, American entrepreneur and politician, publisher of *Forbes* magazine, 1919

Edgar F. "Ted" Codd, English computer scientist, inventor of the relational model for database management (while working for IBM), 1923

William J. "Bill" Clinton, 42nd U.S. President, 1946

Deaths

James Geddes, American civil engineer, lawyer, and politician who played a leading role in the construction of the Erie Canal, 1838

Linus Pauling, American chemist, chemical engineer, author, educator, and peace activist, winner of the Nobel Prize in Chemistry and the Nobel Peace Prize, 1994

John Warnock, American computer scientist, inventor, businessman, and philanthropist, cofounder of Adobe Systems, Inc., 2023

Read:
Proverbs, Chapter 19

August 20

Though the fig tree does not bud and there are no grapes on the vines, though the olive crop fails and the fields produce no food, though there are no sheep in the pen and no cattle in the stalls, yet I will rejoice in the Lord, I will be joyful in God my Savior. *(Habakkuk 3:17-18, NIV)*

Types of love

Philia. *Affectionate love.* A love without romantic attraction that occurs between friends and family members, commonly referred to as brotherly love.

Pragma. *Enduring love.* A bonded love that matures over time and requires commitment and dedication.

Storge. *Familiar love.* A love rooted in parents and children (as well as best friends) built upon acceptance and deep emotional connection.

Eros. *Romantic love.* A passionate love displayed through physical affection.

Ludus. *Playful love.* A child-like and flirtatious love commonly found in the beginning stages of a relationship.

Mania. *Obsessive love.* An obsessiveness or madness over a love partner that often leads to jealousy or possessiveness.

Philautia. *Self love.* A healthy form of love where you recognize your self-worth, don't ignore your personal needs, and acknowledge responsibility for your well-being.

Agape. *Selfless love.* The highest level of love to offer, given without any expectations of receiving anything in return.

Thought for the day

"Better to lose count while naming your blessings than to lose your blessings to counting your troubles."

Maltbie D. Babcock

Grow your faith by trusting God in all things.

Today we observe

National Radio Day

On this day in history

Notable events

In 1866, the newly organized National Labor Union unsuccessfully called on the U.S. Congress to mandate an eight-hour workday.

In 1987, the Malcolm Baldrige National Quality Improvement Act became effective, establishing the Malcolm Baldrige National Quality Award to promote improved quality of goods and services in U.S. companies and organizations.

In 1993, toy manufacturing and entertainment company Mattel, Inc. acquired Fisher-Price, Inc.

Births

Thaddeus S. C. Lowe, American aeronaut, scientist, and inventor, father of military aerial reconnaissance in the U.S., 1832

Benjamin Harrison, 23rd U.S. President, 1833

Kingsley Davis, American sociologist and demographer, coined the terms "population explosion" and "zero population growth," 1908

Jerome L. Murray, American inventor of the peristaltic heart pump that made open-heart surgery possible, 1912

Deaths

William Booth, English Methodist preacher who, along with his wife, Catherine, founded the Salvation Army, 1912

Leona Roberts Helmsley, American businesswoman, hotelier, real estate investor, known as the Queen of Mean, 2007

I pray on God's promise symbolized by the rainbow in Genesis 9:12-16.

Read:
Proverbs, Chapter 20

August 21

> When Jesus returned to Capernaum, a Roman officer came and pleaded with him, "Lord, my young servant lies in bed, paralyzed and in terrible pain." Jesus said, "I will come and heal him." *(Matthew 8:5-7, NLT)*

"Don't worry" makes us worry

When you say, "Don't worry," you're telling people they should worry.

This is not about trying to comfort someone who is already worried (although when does simply saying "Don't worry" ever stop someone from worrying?), this is about prefacing a statement with, "Don't worry" and then saying something that might be worrisome.

When you do that, you're planting a negative idea and causing your listener to do exactly what you didn't want them to do—worry.

Here's the communication tip:

Never suggest something you don't want someone to do by telling them they shouldn't do it—especially when they might not have ever thought of it if you hadn't mentioned it.

The classic example of *don't think of a pink elephant* is a perfect illustration. As soon as you read that, you visualized a pink elephant, didn't you?

That's because our brains don't process the "don't" part of a message.

So the employee who requests a meeting with a supervisor and says, "Don't worry, I'm not quitting but I need to talk with you," has likely caused the supervisor some angst.

The preacher who begins with, "Don't worry, I'm not going to give a three-hour sermon," has just caused everyone in the congregation to squirm with dread.

When you say, "Don't worry," the brain of your listener hears, "Worry!!!"

If you really don't want people to worry because of something you're not going to do, just don't do it. Don't say something that will make them think they should be worried.

Today we observe

National Senior Citizens Day

On this day in history

Notable events

- In 1897, Ransom Eli Olds founded Olds Motor Works, which would later become Oldsmobile.
- In 1912, Arthur R. Eldred of Oceanside, New York, became the first person to achieve the rank of Eagle Scout, the highest rank in the Boy Scouts of America.
- In 1888, W. S. Burroughs received a patent for a calculating machine (adding machine).

Births

Kenny Rogers, American singer and entrepreneur, 1938

Sergey Brin, Russian-born American businessman and computer scientist best known for cofounding Google with Larry Page, 1973

Joe Gebbia, American billionaire designer, internet entrepreneur, and philanthropist, cofounder of Airbnb, 1981

Deaths

Robert Moog, American engineer, electronic music pioneer, inventor of the Moog synthesizer, and founder of Moog Music, 2005

Thought for the day

"The human brain is unique in that it is the only container of which it can be said that the more you put into it, the more it will hold."

Glenn Doman

I am thankful for the ability to make a difference in the world.

Read:
Proverbs, Chapter 21

August 22

Then Job answered the Lord: "I know that you can do all things and that no purpose of yours can be thwarted. *(Job 42:2, NRSVue)*

Embracing change

Benjamin Franklin once said, "In this world, nothing is certain except death and taxes." To that, we should add change.

Avoiding change never works. We were created by an unchanging God to be ever-changing people in an ever-changing world.

Instead of resisting change, embrace it with discernment using these ten techniques.

1. **See change as an opportunity for growth and learning.** Develop an open, positive mindset toward change.
2. **When you see change coming, prepare yourself.** Create a plan. Don't try to pretend it isn't going to happen.
3. **Focus on what you value.** How is the change going to impact the people and things that are important to you?
4. **Stay in the present.** Don't regret the past or worry about the future.
5. **Find the positive.** There's always an upside. Look for new opportunities the change brings and take advantage of them.
6. **Practice self-care.** Especially during periods of great change, self-care is critical. Exercise. Eat as healthily as possible. Get sufficient rest. Practice gratitude.
7. **Stay connected to your community, your network.** Regularly communicate with your support group and reach out to people who can help you work through the change.
8. **Remember how you dealt with previous changes.** Use what you learned from those experiences to help you now.
9. **Learn to recognize and reject bad changes.** There are times when you need to reject a bad change to maintain your personal integrity and protect your long-term success.
10. **Pray without ceasing.** When you combine the first nine techniques with prayer and let God take control, you'll have a supernatural ability to embrace change with discernment.

On this day in history

Notable events

In 1902, the Cadillac Automobile Company was founded from the remnants of the Henry Ford Company; it was purchased by General Motors in 1909.

In 1966, the Fillipino Agricultural Workers Organizing Committee (AWOC) and the National Farm Workers Association (NFWA) consolidated to become the United Farm Workers Organizing Committee (UFWOC).

In 1985, House of Hope in Orlando, now the National House of Hope Affiliate Model, opened.

Births

Melville Elijah Stone, American newspaper publisher, founder of the *Chicago Daily News*, 1848

Willis Rodney Whitney, American chemist, founder of the research laboratory of the General Electric Company, known as the father of industrial research, 1868

Deaths

John Fellows Akers, American businessman, president, CEO, and chairman of IBM, 2014

Thought for the day

"We are adopted into God's family through the resurrection of Christ from the dead in which he paid all our obligations to sin, the law, and the devil, in whose family we once lived. Our old status lies in his tomb. A new status is ours through his resurrection."

Sinclair B. Ferguson

I pray for police, firefighters, and other first responders.

Read:
Proverbs, Chapter 22

August 23

Can a woman forget her nursing child or show no compassion for the child of her womb? Even these might forget, yet I will not forget you.
(Isaiah 49:15, NRSVue)

Earning trust

In *Shine: 5 Empowering Principles for a Rewarding Life*, Kris Den Besten talks about earning trust. He writes:

"Trust is the foundation of all successful relationships. It is also the foundation of all successful organizations. Trust is not an entitlement but a virtue that is established over time. Our actions continually are evaluated by those we interact with to determine our level of trustworthiness. As trust grows, opportunity and responsibility also grow with it.

"A primary role of leadership is to develop a high level of trust within the organization. Accordingly, the enduring success of an organization is built on the trustworthiness of its leaders. Likewise, trusted employees are most likely to receive promotions and great opportunity. Customers strongly desire to do business with people they trust.

"I once had a notoriously demanding customer call to discuss his feelings about one of our service managers. He said, 'Nobody makes me angrier than your service manager. He never tells me what I want to hear. He never budges to any of my demands. But he always comes through with what he promises. Most people tell me what I want to hear and then let me down. But not him. I can't say I really like him much, but I certainly respect him. He's earned my trust. That's why I keep coming back for more.'

"A great way to earn trust is: Do what you say. Do it when you say you'll do it. Do it right the first time. Always under-promise and over-deliver."

Read:
Proverbs, Chapter 23

Today we observe
Day for the Remembrance of the Slave Trade & Its Abolition
Hashtag Day

On this day in history

Notable events
In 1869, the first carload of rail freight (boots and shoes) arrived in San Francisco from Boston after a sixteen-day trip.
In 1904, Harry D. Weed received a U.S. patent for automobile tire chains.
In 2007, Chris Messina posted the first hashtag on Twitter (now X).

Births
Kobe Bryant, American professional basketball player, entrepreneur, author, and philanthropist, 1978

Deaths
Alfred S. Bloomingdale, American businessman, heir to the Bloomingdale's department store fortune, "father of the credit card," 1982
David Koch, American businessman (Koch Industries), political activist, philanthropist, and chemical engineer, 2019

Thought for the day

"Thunder is good, thunder is impressive; but it is the lightning that does the work."
Mark Twain

I pray for those who are facing the death of a loved one.

Grow your faith by sharing it with others.
Spread the gospel.

August 24

> **B**ut if you refuse to serve the Lord, then choose today whom you will serve. Would you prefer the gods your ancestors served beyond the Euphrates? Or will it be the gods of the Amorites in whose land you now live? But as for me and my family, we will serve the Lord." *(Joshua 24:15, NLT)*

Why do you ask?

Before you answer a question, find out why it's being asked so you can craft a more effective answer and avoid introducing a negative into the conversation.

The question might indicate a need or it might be just a fleeting, unimportant thought. Consider the question, "Do you have an office in Boise, Idaho?"

If you don't and you simply say no, the conversation stops. But if you say, "That's an interesting question. Why do you ask?"

It may be important to them for you to have a physical presence in Boise, and you may be able to meet that need in another way. Or it might be that their great-aunt lives there and they were just talking with her, so Boise was on their mind.

Finding out the reason behind the question lets you keep the conversation going on a positive note.

You can also use "Why do you ask?" to shut down a conversation.

If someone asks you a personal question you don't want to answer, those four magic words can help you either end an exchange or redirect a conversation to a topic you're more comfortable with. Try politely saying, "Why do you ask?" instead of "None of your business."

Of course, they might have a legitimate reason. Or they might be bold enough to admit they're nosy. And that's when you can either answer them or decline to discuss it. Just because someone asks a question doesn't mean you have to immediately answer it without more information. Make this magic phrase a regular part of your vocabulary and watch how much richer and more productive your conversations become.

On this day in history

Notable events

In 1857, the failure of the New York branch of the Ohio Life Insurance and Trust Company (the entire capital of the Trust's home office had been embezzled and it couldn't pay its investors) triggered the Panic of 1857, one of the most severe economic crises in U.S. history.

In 1869, Cornelius Swartwout was awarded a U.S. patent for a stovetop waffle iron.

In 2011, just six weeks before his death, Apple cofounder Steve Jobs announced his resignation as CEO.

Births

Jerry Zucker, Israeli-born American businessman, investor, and philanthropist, president and CEO of the InterTech Group and the Polymer Group, 1949

Deaths

Henry J. Kaiser, American industrialist known as the father of modern American shipbuilding, 1967

Tom Frost, rock climber, photographer, inventor, climbing equipment manufacturer (Patagonia, Inc.), 2018

Thought for the day

"There are no shortcuts in life when it comes to the big and important things. You cannot skip the hard part and cut right to the good stuff. The hard part is what gives the good stuff its goodness."

Matt Walsh

I am thankful for those who have been lights along my path.

Read:
Proverbs, Chapter 24

August 25

Do not gloat over me, my enemy! Though I have fallen, I will rise. Though I sit in darkness, the Lord will be my light. *(Micah 7:8, NIV)*

Do you live in peace or frustration?

Are you living in the present or living for today? It's a choice between peace and frustration.

The difference is in two small words: *in* and *for*.

In means a period of time or a place. *For* expresses a purpose or reason for something.

To live in the present means to release the past and not worry about the future. It means to keep the lessons you've learned but let go of the regrets. It means to plan and prepare, but not worry about what's going to happen tomorrow.

It does not mean to live as though there is no tomorrow. It does not mean to live solely for personal pleasure and immediate gratification.

When you live in the present, you focus on the now without wasting time or energy on things you can't change (the past) or control (the future). You live in obedience to God and trust him to take care of the future. You're still aware of the future. You still set goals and make plans. But you don't sacrifice the future for your immediate desires.

When you live for today, you have no regard for the consequences of your actions. You become your idol. You do what you want, when you want, because you can, without considering the impact on yourself or others. Living for today might feel good temporarily, but it's a shallow pleasure.

For lasting peace and joy no matter the circumstances, live *in* the present not *for* today.

Read: Proverbs, Chapter 25

Today we observe
National Park Service Founders Day

On this day in history
Notable events
- In 1910, Walden W. Shaw founded the Shaw Livery Company to offer taxi services in Chicago; the company reorganized in 1915 under John D. Hertz as the Yellow Cab Company.
- In 1991, Linus Torvalds announced he was in the process of creating a free operating system; Linux was first released a few weeks later.

Births
- James Lick, American real estate investor, carpenter, piano builder, land baron, and patron of the sciences, 1796
- Joshua Lionel Cowen, American inventor (electric train) and cofounder of Lionel Corporation, a manufacturer of model railroads and toy trains, 1877

Deaths
- John Birch, U.S. Army intelligence officer, Baptist minister and missionary for whom the John Birch Society was named, 1945
- Helen K. Copley, American newspaper publisher and philanthropist, 2004
- Vince Naimoli, American businessman, investor, entrepreneur, and first owner of the MLB team Tampa Bay Devil Rays (now Tampa Bay Rays), 2019

Thought for the day
"In order to be a realist you must believe in miracles."
David Ben Gurion

I am thankful for the roof over my head, the food in my belly, the clothes on my back.

August 26

What exists now is what will be, and what has been done is what will be done; there is nothing truly new on earth. Is there anything about which someone can say, "Look at this! It is new"? It was already done long ago, before our time. *(Ecclesiastes 1:9-10, NET)*

Can you trust God?

In *My Life as a Bush ... and my heart for imitating Jesus*, presidential impersonator John Morgan writes:

"God's plans are audacious, miraculous, and compassionate. His purposes cannot fail. I believe the Lord exists above time itself, so the very concepts of yesterday, today, and tomorrow are meaningless to a God who treats things that haven't happened as if they already had. If God is that confident about our future, then why aren't we?

"Because we resist God's call to live by faith. We don't really trust Him. Instead, we depend on our limited senses, our limited knowledge, and our limited experiences.

"Real life begins, however, when we choose to believe that faith in God is a far better way to interpret reality than science, logic, or emotions. Hebrews 11:1 says, 'Now faith is being sure of what we hope for and certain of what we do not see.' Note the words *sure* and *certain*. These are words of supreme confidence. That is why Paul, who constantly faced severe persecution and hardship, defiantly wrote, 'If God is for us, then who can be against us? ... No, in all these things we are more than conquerors through him who loved us' (Rom. 8:31, 37).

"Paul lived fearlessly, trusting that his life had real meaning and that his mission would not fail. He simply trusted God.

"So can you and I."

Thought for the day

"Never does the human soul appear so strong as when it foregoes revenge and dares to forgive an injury."
— *Edwin Hubbel Chapin*

Today we observe

Women's Equality Day

International Content Creators Day

On this day in history

Notable events

In 1791, John Fitch and James Rumsey, rivals battling over claims to the invention, were each granted a federal patent for the steamboat; they had devised different systems.

In 1843, inventor Charles Thurber received a patent for the first practical typewriter intended for use by "the blind ... and the nervous who cannot execute with a pen."

In 2014, Burger King agreed to purchase Canadian donut chain Tim Hortons for $11.4 billion.

Births

Lee de Forest, American inventor, entrepreneur, and early pioneer in electronics whose inventions helped start the Electronic Age, 1873

Jay Pritzker, American entrepreneur (cofounder of Hyatt Hotels), philanthropist, 1922

Deaths

Andrew W. Mellon, American banker, businessman, industrialist, philanthropist, and politician, 1937

John Willys, American automotive pioneer and diplomat, founder of Willys-Overland Motors, which became the second largest carmaker in the U.S. (after Ford), 1935

Ransom Eli Olds, American automotive industry pioneer after whom the Oldsmobile and REO brands were named, 1950

Charles Lindbergh, American aviator, 1974

I am thankful for everyone I work with in any capacity.

Read:
Proverbs, Chapter 26

August 27

> For his anger lasts only a moment, but his favor lasts a lifetime; weeping may stay for the night, but rejoicing comes in the morning.
> *(Psalm 30:5, NIV)*

When Peace, Like a River (It is Well with my Soul)

Horatio Gates Spafford, 1873

When peace like a river attendeth my way,
when sorrows like sea billows roll;
whatever my lot, thou hast taught me to say,
"It is well, it is well with my soul."

Refrain:
It is well with my soul;
it is well, it is well with my soul.

Though Satan should buffet, though trials should come,
let this blest assurance control:
that Christ has regarded my helpless estate,
and has shed his own blood for my soul.
[Refrain]

My sin oh, the bliss of this glorious thought!
my sin, not in part, but the whole,
is nailed to the cross, and I bear it no more;
praise the Lord, praise the Lord, O my soul! *[Refrain]*

O Lord, haste the day when my faith shall be sight,
the clouds be rolled back as a scroll;
the trump shall resound and the Lord shall descend;
even so, it is well with my soul. *[Refrain]*

I pray for those who are using their special gifts to serve others.

Read:
Proverbs, Chapter 27

Today we observe
World Rock Paper Scissors Day

National Petroleum Day / Oil & Gas Appreciation Day

On this day in history

Notable events

In 1859, the first successful oil well in the United States was drilled near Titusville, Pennsylvania.

In 1900, U.S. Army physician James Carroll allowed an infected mosquito to feed on him in an attempt to isolate the means of transmission of yellow fever, helping his colleague, Army pathologist Walter Reed, prove that mosquitoes transmit this disease.

In 1955, the first Guinness World Records book was published.

Births

Charles Rolls, British automotive and aviation pioneer, cofounder of Rolls-Royce, first Briton to be killed in a plane crash, 1877

Lyndon B. Johnson, 36th U.S. President, 1908

Deaths

William Chapman Ralston, San Francisco businessman and financier, founder of the Bank of California, 1875

W.E.B. Du Bois, American civil rights activist, co-founder of the NAACP, 1963

Douglas Kenney, American comedy writer, producer, performer, and cofounder of *National Lampoon*, 1980

Edwin Louis Cole, American evangelist, pastor, author, and founder of the Christian Men's Network, 2002

Thought for the day

"The first requisite for success is the ability to apply your physical and mental energies to one problem incessantly without growing weary."

Thomas Edison

August 28

You intended to harm me, but God intended it for good to accomplish what is now being done, the saving of many lives. *(Genesis 50:20, NIV)*

God wants our help

In a messy world full of problems, we can become part of the solution when we ask God to show us what to do and then listen to the answer. In *5 Prayers God Loves to Answer*, Larry Selig writes:

"Listening to God for advice is countercultural to the way many leaders, boards, churches, and even individuals go about making decisions. We pray for guidance, share our human wisdom, sometimes consult experts to gain their advice, and then act on the items before us. After the decisions are made, we ask God to bless what we have decided. Driving by our own agendas, and forgetting to see His agenda, we often realize in hindsight that these decisions had flaws which we had not anticipated. And the hoped-for goals were not accomplished."

Prayer is a conversation with God and we should listen as much, or even more, as we speak.

Thought for the day

"Whoever you are, there is some younger person who thinks you are perfect. There is some work that will never be done if you don't do it. There is someone who would miss you if you were gone. There is a place that you alone can fill."

Jacob Braude

I pray for God to work through my weaknesses.

Read:
Proverbs, Chapter 28

Today we observe

I Have a Dream Day
Radio Commercials Day
Clean Your Keyboard Day

On this day in history

Notable events

In 1845, *Scientific American* published its first issue.

In 1907, United Parcel Service was founded in Seattle, Washington as the American Messenger Company by teenagers James E. Casey and Claude Ryan who ran errands and made deliveries on foot or by bicycle.

In 1922, the first radio commercial (a ten-minute ad for a real estate company) aired on WEAF in New York City.

Births

Elizabeth Ann Seton, American Catholic religious sister, founder of the U.S.'s parochial school system, and first person born in what would become the United States to be canonized by the Catholic Church, 1774

Jack Dreyfus, American financial expert and founder of the Dreyfus Funds, 1913

Sheryl Sandberg, American technology executive (COO of Meta Platforms), philanthropist, and writer, 1969

Deaths

Frederick Law Olmsted, American landscape architect (the father of American landscape design) and writer, 1903

Charles Darrow, American board game designer credited as the inventor of *Monopoly*, 1967

Bernard G. Davis, American publisher, cofounder of Ziff Davis Inc., founder of Davis Publications, Inc., 1972

Arthur Jones, American pioneer in the field of physical exercise, inventor (Nautilus exercise machines), and founder of Nautilus, Inc. and MedX, Inc., 2007

Paul MacCready, American aeronautical engineer, inventor (human-powered aircraft), and founder of AeroVironment, 2007

August 29

If any of you is lacking in wisdom, ask God, who gives to all generously and ungrudgingly, and it will be given you. But ask in faith, never doubting, for the one who doubts is like a wave of the sea, driven and tossed by the wind. *(James 1:5-6, NRSVue)*

Say something positive

Every time you think something positive about someone, say it out loud. Don't assume they know or that they'll think you're strange, tell them.

Be generous—but honest!—with compliments. If the best you can do is something superficial, such as to compliment someone on their appearance, that's fine. You can do that with total strangers and you'll make their day.

When you can, go deeper. And be specific. Don't just say, "You're so thoughtful." Instead, cite a particular incident of the other person's thoughtfulness in action, such as, "I've noticed how you always look around the parking lot to see if anyone needs help carrying things." Instead of, "You do a great job," let them know exactly what they did: "Your insight with the research I needed for my project was exactly on point."

Tell people that you appreciate them. It's one of the simplest things you can do and has an incredibly powerful impact on the person you're talking to.

If you're not around someone and their name comes up in a conversation, say something positive about them to others.

The idea is to regularly say things that magnify others' strengths, not their weaknesses. You'll do more than brighten someone's day—you could potentially change their life for the better.

I am thankful for the lessons I have learned from my Biblical ancestors.

Read:
Proverbs, Chapter 29

Today we observe

Individual Rights Day

On this day in history

Notable events

In 1898, the Goodyear Tire & Rubber Company was founded by Frank Seiberling in Akron, Ohio.

In 1997, Netflix was founded by Reed Hastings and Marc Randolph in Scotts Valley, California.

Births

Henry Bergh, American activist, founder of the American Society for the Prevention of Cruelty to Animals (ASPCA) and assisted in founding the New York and Massachusetts Society for the Prevention of Cruelty to Children, 1813

Charles Kettering, American inventor (holder of 186 patents), engineer, founder of Delco, 1876

Brian Chesky, American businessman, industrial designer, and philanthropist, cofounder and CEO of Airbnb, 1981

Deaths

David T. Abercrombie, American topographer and expert in the outdoors, cofounder of Abercrombie & Fitch, 1931

Samuel Irving Newhouse, Sr., American broadcasting businessman, magazine and newspaper publisher, founder of Advance Publications, 1979

Alfred H. Peet, entrepreneur and founder of Peet's Coffee & Tea in Berkeley, California; Peet is credited with starting the specialty coffee revolution in the U.S., 2007

Thought for the day

"The secret of health for both mind and body is not to mourn for the past, nor to worry about the future, but to live the present moment wisely and earnestly."

Siddhartha Gautama

August 30

Guard your heart above all else, for it determines the course of your life.
(Proverbs 4:23, NLT)

When you're in the video, watch it!

These days, more and more of us are appearing on video more often than ever before.

Beyond Zoom meetings, video chats, and even Facebook Live sessions, people who never thought they'd spend time in front of a camera are finding an increasing number of reasons to record and share messages.

These recordings are a great opportunity to improve the way we look and speak—but only if we watch them and learn from them.

If you're uncomfortable watching yourself on video, get over it. It might be uncomfortable, but do it anyway. Ask yourself these questions:

- How's your posture?
- Are you fidgeting in a way that could distract your audience?
- Are you speaking clearly and distinctly without a lot of unnecessary pauses or uhs and ums?
- Is your expression warm and natural?

The key is to view with an eye toward constructive criticism, not to beat yourself up because you made a few mistakes or your appearance isn't celebrity-perfect. At the same time, look for the things you did well and celebrate them—no need to be modest when you nailed it. Critique your performance and you'll see yourself getting better with each presentation.

Thought for the day

"If you can learn from hard knocks, you can also learn from soft touches."

Carolyn Kenmore

On this day in history

Notable events

In 1890, President Benjamin Harrison signed the first law requiring inspection of meat products (salted pork and bacon intended for exportation).

In 1995, CNN launched its website, CNN.com.

Births

Warren Buffett, American business magnate, investor, and philanthropist, 1930

Ernie Ball, American entrepreneur and musician who developed guitar-related products, founder of Ernie Ball, Inc., 1930

Carol E. Reiley, American business executive, computer scientist, model, and pioneer in teleoperated and autonomous robot systems in surgery, space exploration, disaster rescue, and self-driving cars, 1982

Deaths

Max Factor, Sr., Polish-American businessman, beautician, entrepreneur, inventor, and founder of the cosmetics giant Max Factor & Company, 1938

Dorothy Schiff, American businesswoman, owner and publisher of the *New York Post*, 1989

Sometimes people come into your life to help you see things from a different perspective. When they tell you their angle, even though you may disagree and it may make you angry, it's worth considering. You don't have to accept it, but it's good to understand it.

I am thankful for the ability to be friends with and love sinners.

Read:
Proverbs, Chapter 30

August 31

Peace I leave with you; my peace I give you. I do not give to you as the world gives. Do not let your hearts be troubled and do not be afraid. (John 14:27, NIV)

Prayer for the future

Written by Ken Untener for Cardinal Dearden (commonly known as "The Prayer for St. Oscar Romero")

It helps, now and then, to step back and take a long view.

The kingdom is not only beyond our efforts, it is even beyond our vision.

We accomplish in our lifetime only a tiny fraction of the magnificent enterprise that is God's work. Nothing we do is complete, which is a way of saying that the kingdom always lies beyond us. No statement says all that could be said. No prayer fully expresses our faith. No confession brings perfection. No pastoral visit brings wholeness. No program accomplishes the church's mission. No set of goals and objectives includes everything.

This is what we are about. We plant the seeds that one day will grow. We water seeds already planted, knowing that they hold future promise.

We lay foundations that will need further development. We provide yeast that produces far beyond our capabilities.

We cannot do everything, and there is a sense of liberation in realizing that. This enables us to do something, and to do it very well. It may be incomplete, but it is a beginning, a step along the way, an opportunity for the Lord's grace to enter and do the rest.

We may never see the end results, but that is the difference between the master builder and the worker.

We are workers, not master builders; ministers, not messiahs. We are prophets of a future not our own.

Amen.

Read: Proverbs, Chapter 31

Today we observe

World Distance Learning Day
International Blog Day
Love Litigating Lawyers Day

On this day in history

Notable events

In 1842, American blacksmith Micah Rugg received a patent for a machine for trimming the heads of nuts and bolts.

In 1897, Thomas Edison received a patent for the kinetographic camera, the forerunner of the motion picture film projector.

In 2009, The Walt Disney Company announced plans to acquire Marvel Entertainment, Inc. for approximately $4 billion.

Births

Marvin Davis, American industrialist and film mogul, chair of Davis Petroleum, one-time owner of 20th Century Fox, Pebble Beach Corp., Beverly Hills Hotel, and Aspen Skiing Company, 1925

William DeWitt, Jr., American businessman, cofounder of the investment firm Reynolds, DeWitt & Co., and professional sports team owner/investor, 1941

Deaths

J. Erik Jonsson, American businessman, cofounder and early president of Texas Instruments, Inc., mayor of Dallas, philanthropist, 1995

Thought for the day

"Order and simplification are the first steps toward the mastery of a subject."
Thomas Mann

I pray that I will share God's abundant mercy with others.

Christian Business Almanac

September

The name September comes from the Latin *septem* (seven) because September was originally the seventh of ten months in the oldest known Roman calendar. After the calendar reform that added January and February to the beginning of the year, September became the ninth month but its name didn't change. It had 29 days until the Julian reform, which added a day.

September birthstone
Sapphire

September flower
Astor, forget-me-not, morning glory

September is ...
- Childhood Cancer Awareness Month
- Domestic Violence Awareness Month
- International Update Your Resume Month
- National Courtesy Month
- National Food Safety Month
- National Preparedness Month
- National Suicide Prevention Month
- Self Improvement Month
- World Alzheimer's Month

Mark your calendar for these September holidays and observances

First Friday in September	National Food Bank Day
First Friday in September	Bring Your Manners to Work Day
First Monday in September	Labor Day
Day following Labor Day	Telephone Tuesday
Friday after Labor Day	401(k)/403(b) Day
First Sunday after Labor Day	National Grandparents Day
Second Monday in September	National Boss/Employee Exchange Day
Second Thursday in September	National School Picture Day
Third Saturday in September	Software Freedom Day
Third Saturday in September	Locate an Old Friend Day
Third Sunday in September	National Back to Church Sunday
Third Thursday in September	International Day of Listening
Last Sunday in September	Gold Star Families Day
Last Thursday in September	World Maritime Day
Last Saturday in September	Save Your Photos Day

Fun Facts about September

The month of September is associated with the Roman god of fire, possibly because it was a hot summer month back when it was the seventh month of the year.

September and December begin on the same day of the week.

September does not end on the same day of the week as any other month.

There are more pop and classic songs with "September" in the title than any other month (unverified but fun trivia).

September is the most popular month to be born in.

September 1

O Lord, you are my God; I will exalt you; I will praise your name, for you have done wonderful things, plans formed of old, faithful and sure. *(Isaiah 25:1, NRSVue)*

Bible verses are not bumper stickers

The Bible is divided into books, chapters, and numbered verses, which makes it easier to read and refer to sections than if it were one long text. But just because most Scripture verses are short enough to go on a bumper sticker or social media meme doesn't mean we should understand them that way.

To fully understand any given verse we must first put it in context of the Bible's overall message as well as the book in which the verse appears. Who wrote the book and why? When was it written? To whom? What was the author trying to accomplish? What contemporary issues were influencing the author?

Read the entire chapter and then study the verse itself. Is it calling the reader to action? Is it offering a significant contrast? Is it showing us a cause and effect?

You may want to read commentaries by scholars who have an extensive knowledge of the Bible's original languages, historical and cultural settings, and literary features. You may also want to talk with a pastor or discuss it with study partners.

Many verses have wonderful stand-alone messages that we can use in our everyday lives and businesses. But even those are worth studying in greater depth so that we may completely understand what God wants for us.

I pray for the ability to recognize and resist the enemy.

Read:
Proverbs, Chapter 1

Today we observe

World Letter Writing Day

World Day of Prayer for the Care of Creation

Child Identity Theft Awareness Day

Building & Code Staff Appreciation Day

On this day in history

Notable events

- In 1897, the Boston subway opened; it was the first underground rapid transit system in North America and those tunnels are still in use.
- In 1914, the last known passenger pigeon died at the Cincinnati Zoo.
- In 1998, a law passed in 1991 (the Intermodal Surface Transportation Efficiency Act of 1991) went into effect, requiring all vehicles sold in the U.S. to have airbags on both sides of the front seat.

Births

James Gordon Bennett, Sr., Scottish-born American businessman who was the founder, editor, and publisher of the *New York Herald*, 1795

Mark Hopkins, Jr., American business tycoon and railroad executive, 1813

Gary Maddox, American professional baseball player, entrepreneur, and philanthropist, 1949

Deaths

Jimmy Buffett, American singer-songwriter, musician, author, and businessman, 2023

Thought for the day

"Concentrate all your thoughts upon the work at hand. The sun's rays do not burn until brought to a focus."

Alexander Graham Bell

September 2

Blessed is the man who endures trial, for when he has stood the test he will receive the crown of life which God has promised to those who love him. *(James 1:12, RSV)*

Ten things that will make you feel better

Get through tough times and make good times better by doing one or more of these ten things.

Break bread with others. Think about the feasts, banquets, suppers and family meals that are mentioned in the Bible, about how Jesus used meals for teaching. Share a meal with someone—it doesn't have to be elaborate, it just needs to be something you do together.

Turn off the news. Give yourself a break from the pain, misery, and negativity.

Take care of your body. Exercise, get plenty of rest, eat a healthful diet (most of the time). When you feel good physically it's easier to feel better emotionally.

Celebrate. There's always something to celebrate. Do something to observe a good thing, big or small, in your life.

Floss your teeth. Get that debris out.

Pray for yourself. Ask God to protect you, guide you, and help you live out His plan for you.

Take a tech break. For an hour, a day, or longer if you can, put down your phone, get off social media, turn off the television, step away from the computer.

Spend time with your pet(s)—or get one. Take the dog for a walk, cuddle the cat, or play with whatever pet you have. Bask in their innocence and unconditional love.

Read a novel. Lose yourself in a fantasy world of your choosing—romance, suspense, thriller, action, whatever you prefer.

Identify and practice your personal stress-relievers. Be intentional about doing things that relieve stress for you. Figure out what helps you and schedule time to do it.

Today we observe

Franchise Appreciation Day

On this day in history

Notable events

In 1789, the United States Treasury Department was founded.

In 1969, the first automatic teller machine (ATM) in the U.S. debuted, dispensing cash to customers at Chemical Bank in Rockville Centre, New York.

Births

Albert Spalding, American pitcher, manager, and executive in the early years of professional baseball and cofounder of A.G. Spalding sporting goods company, 1850

Andrew Grove, Hungarian-American businessman and engineer, pioneer in the semiconductor industry, served as the third CEO of Intel Corporation, 1936

Peter Ueberroth, American sports and business executive known for his involvement in the Olympics and Major League Baseball, 1937

Deaths

William R. Wilkerson, founder of *The Hollywood Reporter*, Las Vegas real estate developer, and businessman, 1962

Thought for the day

"The most satisfying thing in life is to have been able to give a large part of one's self to others."

Pierre Teilhard de Chardin

I am thankful for all I have learned and experienced.

Read: Proverbs, Chapter 2

September 3

He cuts off every branch in me that bears no fruit, while every branch that does bear fruit he prunes so that it will be even more fruitful. ... When you produce much fruit, you are my true disciples. This brings great glory to my Father. *(John 15:2, 8, NIV)*

Let disappointments strengthen your faith

Disappointments are a part of life and business. Things don't always go as we'd hoped and expected. But they can strengthen our faith.

Instead of mournfully asking God why something happened, ask what (as in: What am I to learn from this? What am I to do next?) and how (as in: How do you want to use me?).

Let the entire process of the disappointment, from the details of what happened to how you felt about it, remind you that God is always at work and he will use this for good. Let it shape and refine you, let it bring you closer to God as you turn to him for comfort and guidance, let it strengthen your faith.

Is this often easier said than done? Yes. But the more you do it, the easier it will be—and the stronger your faith will grow.

On this day in history

Notable events

In 1833, *The Sun* began publication in New York; it was the first successful penny daily newspaper in the U.S. It ceased publication in 1950.

In 1931, the Lackawanna railroad inaugurated electric suburban service from Hoboken to Montclair, New Jersey, in an effort to keep smoke down around New York.

In 1995, AuctionWeb was founded by Pierre Omidyar; the company changed its name to eBay in 1997.

Births

Mark Hopkins, Jr., American businessman and railroad executive (Central Pacific Railroad), 1814

Louis Sullivan, American architect, called a "father of skyscrapers" and "father of modernism," 1856

Edward Filene, American businessman and philanthropist, best known for building the Filene's department store chain and for his role in pioneering credit unions across the U.S., 1860

Adam Curry, American podcaster, internet entrepreneur, and media personality, 1964

Deaths

Robert E. Gross, American businessman, investor, president of Lockheed Aircraft Corporation (1934-1956), 1961

W. Clement Stone, American businessman, philanthropist, self-help book author, 2002

Life is like a rip current in the ocean. When you get caught in a rip current, the best thing to do is stop struggling and fighting where it's taking you. That's how you survive. You may wind up somewhere unexpected, but you'll be fine.

Thought for the day

"The purpose of an education is to replace an empty mind with an open one."
Malcolm Forbes

I am thankful for people who tell me the truth even when it hurts.

Read:
Proverbs, Chapter 3

September 4

> Are not two sparrows sold for a penny? Yet not one of them will fall to the ground outside your Father's care. *(Matthew 10:29, NIV)*

Be in charge of technology

In *Even Silence is Praise: quiet your mind and awaken your soul with Christian meditation*, Rick Hamlin has some guidance on our relationship with technology. He talks about the time he decided to go on a cell phone fast during Lent.

"I wasn't going to give the phone up for forty days—I had to be realistic. (Don't ever give yourself spiritual challenges that are impossible to meet.) I'd give it up for several hours a day. That's all. I'd put it in a drawer or a secret pocket of my briefcase where I wouldn't respond to it. Couldn't look at it or look for it for, say, four or five hours.

"I failed. Miserably."

And then he realized that what he had to do was not get rid of his phone, but get rid of it controlling him. After sharing the story of Jesus killing the fig tree that wasn't producing fruit, he writes:

"We're meant to get rid of what doesn't produce fruit in ourselves. Don't coddle our failures of goodness and generosity and abundance; don't make excuses for them; don't work around them. Confront them. Weed out the adversaries. Kill the fig-less tree. I had to do that with my phone. I had to make it my ally in faith, not my enemy. … Why have something in your life that doesn't produce fruit?"

I pray for my business colleagues.

Grow your faith by scheduling and prioritizing your prayer time.

On this day in history

Notable events

In 1888, George Eastman received a patent for the shutter on a roll-film hand camera and a trademark for the Kodak name.

In 1951, President Harry S. Truman's speech at a conference in San Francisco was broadcast across the nation, the first time a television program was broadcast coast to coast.

In 1998, Google was formally incorporated by Larry Page and Sergey Brin.

Births

William E. Dodge, American businessman, politician, and activist, cofounder of Phelps Dodge Corporation (one of America's largest mining companies), founding member of YMCA of the U.S., 1805

Lewis Howard Latimer, American inventor (evaporative air conditioner, improved process for manufacturing carbon filaments for light bulbs, improved toilet system for railroad cars), patent consultant, author, 1848

Henry Ford II, American automobile executive, president of Ford Motor Company (1945-1960), 1917

Dennis Murphy, sports entrepreneur, founder of World Team Tennis and Roller Hockey International, cofounder of World Hockey Association and American Basketball Association, 1926

John McCarthy, American computer scientist, cognitive scientist, one of the founders of the discipline of artificial intelligence, 1927

Thought for the day

"If I only had three words of advice, they would be, Tell the Truth. If I got three more words, I'd add, All the Time."

Randy Pausch

Read:
Proverbs, Chapter 4

September 5

Whoever loves a quarrel loves sin; whoever builds a high gate invites destruction. *(Proverbs 17:19, NIV)*

Managing self-doubt

You've probably heard of the imposter syndrome, which is when successful, high achieving people believe that they are really frauds and that sooner or later, they're going to be found out.

Whether you actually suffer from the imposter syndrome or just the occasional bout of self-doubt, here are a few ways to deal with it:

Recognize that perfection is impossible. Things won't always go smoothly, and you will make mistakes and even fail. Stop judging yourself and instead leverage those mistakes and failures to your advantage.

Identify and change negative self-talk. When that voice in your head starts telling you all about your weaknesses and shortcomings, turn it around to focus on your strengths and accomplishments. Keep a running score of your wins in your head and refer to it often.

Recognize your achievements. Don't underestimate or ignore what you've accomplished. Give yourself credit for what you've done.

Share your knowledge. Let the process of telling others about your experiences give you a sense of progress and meaning as it builds the support and appreciation you'll receive from your team.

Set realistic goals. If your goals are unattainable, failure is inevitable. Your goals should be ambitious but achievable. Remember to make them SMART (specific, measurable, achievable, relevant, and time-bound).

I pray for those who are restless.

Read:
Proverbs, Chapter 5

Today we observe
National GIF Day

On this day in history

Notable events
In 1882, an estimated 10,000 workers assembled in New York City to participate in America's first Labor Day parade.
In 1885, Sylvanus Bowser, inventor of the first U.S. gas pump, made his initial sale to Jake Gumper, owner of a service station in Fort Wayne, Indiana.

Births
Arthur Nielsen, American businessman, electrical engineer, and market research analyst, founder of the A.C. Nielsen Company, 1897
Carly Fiorina, American businesswoman, politician, and financier, CEO of Hewlett-Packard (1999-2005), 1954

Deaths
D. James Kennedy, American pastor, evangelist, Christian broadcaster, and author, 2007

Thought for the day

"I have always found that my view of success has been iconoclastic: success to me is not about money or status or fame, it's about finding a livelihood that brings me joy and self-sufficiency and a sense of contributing to the world."

Anita Roddick

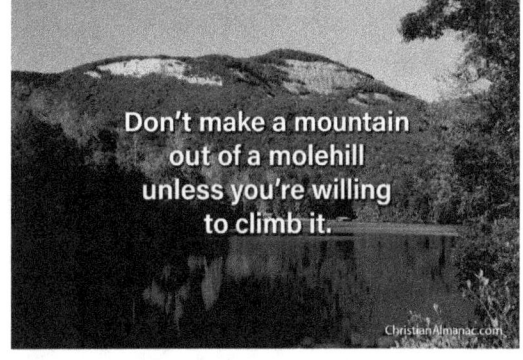

September 6

A**nd let us consider how to stir up one another to love and good works, not neglecting to meet together, as is the habit of some, but encouraging one another, and all the more as you see the Day drawing near.** *(Hebrews 10:24-25, ESV)*

Dealing with indirect fallout

When something bad happens in your industry, but not directly to your company, your first response may be one of relief. Even so, you're likely to be in the path of some negative fallout, and you need to address it.

For example, when a plane crashes, all airlines are concerned about reassuring the traveling public. When a lithium-ion battery catches fire, makers of products powered by them put out warnings.

Your business may not be subject to so dramatic a risk, but unless you have a monopoly, another company's misfortune could affect you.

You can approach this on three levels: national, local, and as an individual. If you have a national association, look to it for guidance and an action plan. Associations know how to mobilize immediately. They have the media contacts and information-distribution processes already in place.

Your local association or professional organization may also be a resource. Or you may choose to handle the situation on your own. Whatever you do, take an educational approach.

Educating the public is a big part of the recovery process for an industry that's been injured. Offer tips to help people avoid a repeat of whatever happened, or to make them feel more comfortable and to reestablish trust.

If people have suffered, express sympathy and offer support—even to the point of holding a fundraiser for victims. The key is to take action quickly, using a strategy that is tasteful and appropriate for the circumstances and will put your company in a positive position.

Today we observe

Read a Book Day

Fight Procrastination Day

On this day in history

Notable events

In 1905, Atlanta Life Insurance Company was founded as Atlanta Mutual.

In 1916, the U.S.'s first supermarket, Piggly Wiggly, opened in Memphis.

Births

Jane Addams, American social activist and reformer, social worker, author, women's suffrage leader, cofounder of the American Civil Liberties Union, first American woman to be awarded the Nobel Peace Prize, 1860

Joseph P. Kennedy Sr., American businessman, investor, philanthropist, and politician, 1888

J. Erik Jonsson, American businessman, cofounder and early president of Texas Instruments, Inc., mayor of Dallas, philanthropist, 1901

Deaths

Art Modell, American businessman, entrepreneur, and NFL team owner, 2012

Richard DeVos, American businessman, cofounder of Amway, 2018

Thought for the day

"When opportunity knocks, open the door even if you're in your bathrobe."

Heather Zschock

I am thankful for all the people in my life who make me happy.

Read:
Proverbs, Chapter 6

September 7

Seek the Lord and the strength he gives. Seek his presence continually.
(Psalm 105:4, NET)

How to judge Christianity

Have you ever wondered how someone could claim to be a Christian and still do something evil or sinful? It's simple: Like people of all faiths and even no faith, Christians are fallible humans. They're not perfect, they make mistakes, and sometimes they give in to temptation and frustration.

Jesus is quite clear in his teachings about what we should believe and how we should behave. And one of the most important things he taught was not to judge but to forgive others when they fall short of perfection. Because even when they try their best, most people will at times miss the mark.

There are Christians who lie, cheat, and steal. There are Christians who gossip, indulge in gluttony, and betray people who trusted them. There are even Christians who commit murder.

When Christians sin, they don't stop being Christians. If they believe that Jesus Christ is their Lord and Savior, no matter what they do, they're still Christians. If they repent, they're forgiven—but they will still face the consequences of their sin.

When people make the choice to follow Jesus, they are not automatically imbued with all the knowledge and wisdom of the Son of God. They are works in progress.

Judging Christianity by the behavior of sinful, imperfect people will blind you to the amazing peace and joy that comes with following Christ.

The way to judge Christianity is to know what it is, and you do that by learning it. As in all things, begin with the source: the Bible.

Instead of looking at what people do, look at what Jesus did, said, and taught.

That's the only way to judge Christianity.

Today we observe

National Buy a Book Day

On this day in history

Notable events

In 1850, a *Scientific American* article on iron railroad bridges reported that the New York and Erie Railroad would erect no more iron bridges and would replace the existing ones as soon as wooden bridges could be built.

In 1915, John Gruelle received a patent for his Raggedy Ann doll.

Births

Edward Asahel Birge, American professor and administrator at the University of Wisconsin-Madison, pioneer in the study of limnology, 1851

David Packard, American electrical engineer and cofounder of Hewlett-Packard, 1912

Deaths

Matthias W. Baldwin, American inventor and machinery manufacturer, founder of Baldwin Locomotive Works, builder of Old Ironsides, the most famous of early locomotives, 1866

Walter A. Brown, American sports executive, founder and original owner of the Boston Celtics, which he funded with a mortgage on his home, 1964

Thought for the day

"People think that at the top there isn't much room. They tend to think of it as an Everest. My message is that there is tons of room at the top."

Margaret Thatcher

I am thankful for technology.

Read:
Proverbs, Chapter 7

September 8

There are also bodies in the heavens and bodies on the earth. The glory of the heavenly bodies is different from the glory of the earthly bodies. The sun has one kind of glory, while the moon and stars each have another kind. And even the stars differ from each other in their glory. *(1 Corinthians 15:40-41, NLT)*

You can't manage time

Time management is a misnomer. You cannot manage time; time simply is. Yet we often say high achievers are good at time management. What they're actually good at is managing themselves. They:

Set clear, specific, measurable goals. This can't be emphasized enough. High achievers know what they want to accomplish and when they expect to do it.

Develop detailed plans. High achievers know exactly what they have to do to accomplish their goals; they leave nothing to chance.

Make and prioritize daily task lists. High achievers know exactly what tasks they need to perform each day and which tasks are most important; they refuse to be distracted by anything that is not on their list. Because they are more organized, they get more done.

Concentrate on one thing at a time. High achievers do not multi-task; they focus on one thing at a time until it's completed, then move on to the next task.

Develop a sense of urgency. High achievers do not procrastinate; when something needs to be done, they do it.

Do what the most valuable use of their time is. Anything else is a waste of time—and high achievers don't waste time.

Today we observe

Standard Gravity Day

On this day in history

Notable events

In 1930, Scotch tape was developed by Richard G. Drew at 3M in St Paul, Minnesota.

Births

Lex Wexner, American billionaire businessman, philanthropist, and founder of Bath & Body Works, Inc., 1937

Ken Hendricks, American businessman and entrepreneur, who, along with his wife and business partner Diane Hendricks, grew a shingle supply company into a $2.6 billion fortune, 1941

Lachlan Murdoch, British-American businessman and mass media heir (Nova Entertainment, News Corp., Fox Corporation), 1971

Deaths

Edward L. Doheny, American oil tycoon who drilled the first successful oil well in the Los Angeles City Oil Field, 1935

Joshua Lionel Cowen, American inventor (electric train) and cofounder of Lionel Corporation, a manufacturer of model railroads and toy trains, 1965

Percy Spencer, American physicist and inventor known for inventing the microwave oven, 1970

S. Truett Cathy, American businessman, investor, author, and philanthropist, founder of Chick-fil-A, 2014

I pray for those who are trying to figure out their way forward.

Read:
Proverbs, Chapter 8

Thought for the day

"It takes a great deal of courage to stand up to your enemies, but even more to stand up to your friends."

J.K. Rowling

September 9

> When a crime is not punished quickly, people feel it is safe to do wrong.
> *(Ecclesiastes 8:11, NLT)*

Are you condescending?

Condescension is defined as an attitude of patronizing superiority. It's often coupled with arrogance, and it never leaves people feeling good.

Sometimes people are intentionally condescending; sometimes they don't realize how offensive they're being. Here are some behaviors most people find condescending—if you're doing them, you might want to stop.

Saying "You know better than that." It's a belittling rebuke that is better left unsaid.

Name-dropping. Unless there's a valid reason to mention the names of important people you know, don't.

Calling people by demeaning nicknames. *Honey, sweetie, chief,* and even *boss* (if that person is not your boss) are irritating and often offensive. Take the time to learn people's real names and use them.

The old sandwich method for criticism. The feedback formula of praise, criticism, and praise is seen as a way to soften the blow of criticism, but most people recognize it and the praise often comes across as forced. Be kind and direct in your critiques and give affirmation when it's deserved.

Interrupting people to correct them. Not only will you embarrass the speaker, you'll look like a know-it-all jerk. Unless it's absolutely critical to make the correction immediately, wait until there's a discrete opportunity to do it and be tactful.

I pray on the Great Commandment that applies to everyone: Matthew 22:34-40.

Read:
Proverbs, Chapter 9

Today we observe
Tester's Day

On this day in history

Notable events

In 1926, the National Broadcasting Company (NBC) was created by the Radio Corporation of America (RCA) shortly after the acquisition of the radio network operations of AT&T, which had decided to withdraw from radio.

In 1947, the first computer bug was recorded by computer scientist Grace Hopper who found a moth trapped in a computer.

Births

Colonel Harland Sanders, American businessman and founder of Kentucky Fried Chicken restaurant chain, 1890

Richard B. Sellars, American business executive (chairman and CEO of Johnson & Johnson), philanthropist, 1915

Farrah Gray, American businessman, investor, author, and motivational speaker, 1984

Deaths

E. H. Harriman, American financier and railroad executive, 1909

Albert Spalding, American pitcher, manager, and executive in the early years of professional baseball and cofounder of A.G. Spalding sporting goods company, 1915

Ernie Ball, American entrepreneur and musician who developed guitar-related products, founder of Ernie Ball, Inc., 2004

William B. Ziff, Jr., American publishing executive and author, CEO of Ziff Davis Inc., 2006

Thought for the day

"The battles that count aren't the ones for gold medals. The struggles within yourself—the invisible, inevitable battles inside all of us—that's where it's at."

Jesse Owens

September 10

> ❝ O Israel, can I not do to you as this potter has done to his clay? As the clay is in the potter's hand, so are you in my hand. *(Jeremiah 18:6, NLT)*

The beauty of sacrificial love

In *Who You Are When No One's Looking*, Bill Hybels writes this about sacrificial love:

"Sacrificial love is the foundation of every key relationship in life. It revolutionizes marriage. It intensifies and fortifies friendship. In the business world, it can change the way we treat our colleagues, employees and customers. In our communities it allows us to reach out to many people and make their lives better. ... [T]oday's world desperately needs more of it.

"So, if sacrificial love is so great, why is it so tough to pull off? Commit yourself to practicing sacrificial love, and a few days—or hours, if you're like me—into your experiment, you'll discover you're utterly wiped out. After a certain amount of giving and serving and expending, you may begin to feel numb, as if you have nothing left to give. And in fact, you *don't* have anything left to give. You, my friend, are running on empty.

"Even if you've run completely out of love, it's still possible to refill the tank. It's possible to love people not only sacrificially but also steadfastly, which is precisely what God calls us to do—not to run the hundred-yard dash in loving people but to run the marathon. We have to learn how to refuel ourselves when we run out of love."

Thought for the day

"I believe in Christianity as I believe that the sun has risen: not only because I see it, but because by it I see everything else."
— C.S. Lewis

I am thankful for answered prayers.

Today we observe

World Suicide Prevention Day

Swap Ideas Day

On this day in history

Notable events

In 1846, Elias Howe received a patent for his hand-cranked sewing machine.

Births

Isaac K. Funk, American Lutheran minister, editor, publisher, cofounder of Funk & Wagnalls Company, 1839

Edwin Louis Cole, American evangelist, pastor, author, and founder of the Christian Men's Network, 1922

Walter Ralston Martin, American Baptist minister, author, founder of the Christian Research Institute, 1928

Deaths

Ted Stepien, American businessman (founder of Nationwide Advertising Service), entrepreneur, and NBA team owner, 2007

Gratitude changes everything

Instead of saying "I have to" with dread, try enthusiastically embracing what you are fortunate enough to get to do.

"I get to serve through my work and earn money for my efforts."

"I get to tell someone I love them."

"I get to exercise and care for my body."

"I get to overcome new challenges and solve problems."

"I get to make someone's day better."

"I get to spend time with friends and family."

"I get to care for my home by cleaning and maintaining it."

"I get to live out God's plan for my life."

It's all a matter of perspective.

Read:
Proverbs, Chapter 10

September 11

> ❝ But to you who are listening I say: Love your enemies, do good to those who hate you, bless those who curse you, pray for those who mistreat you. *(Luke 6:27-28, NIV)*

This is my Father's World

Maltbie Davenport Babcock, 1901

This is my Father's world,
And to my listening ears
All nature sings, and round me rings
The music of the spheres.
This is my Father's world:
I rest me in the thought
Of rocks and trees, of skies and seas--
His hand the wonders wrought.

This is my Father's world:
The birds their carols raise,
The morning light, the lily white,
Declare their Maker's praise.
This is my Father's world:
He shines in all that's fair;
In the rustling grass I hear Him pass,
He speaks to me everywhere.

This is my Father's world:
O let me ne'er forget
That though the wrong seems oft so strong,
God is the Ruler yet.
This is my Father's world:
Why should my heart be sad?
The Lord is King: let the heavens ring!
God reigns; let earth be glad!

Thought for the day

"Nothing is more noble, nothing more venerable than fidelity. Faithfulness and truth are the most sacred excellences and endowments of the human mind."

Cicero

I am thankful for the people who have invested in my spiritual journey.

Today we observe

Patriot Day

National Emergency Responders Day

"I Want to Start My Own Business" Day

On this day in history

Notable events

In 1941, construction began on the Pentagon, the headquarters building of the U.S. Department of Defense, in Arlington, Virginia.

In 1977, the Atari 2600 home video game console was introduced.

In 2001, four coordinated suicide terrorist attacks against the U.S. were carried out by al-Qaeda, an Islamist extremist group, killing 2996 people and injuring thousands.

Births

D. W. Brooks, American farmer and businessman, founder of a farm cooperative that became Gold Kist, and founder of several insurance companies that served farming communities, 1901

Charles M. Geschke, American businessman, computer scientist, cofounder of Adobe, Inc., 1939

Robert Palmer, American businessman, final chairman and CEO of Digital Equipment Corp., 1940

David Tepper, American billionaire hedge fund manager, professional sports team owner, 1957

Deaths

Ralph C. Smedley, founder of Toastmasters International, 1965

Collett E. Woolman, American airline entrepreneur, founder of Delta Air Lines, 1966

T. Boone Pickens, American business magnate and financier, author, chaired the hedge fund BP Capital Management, 2019

Read:
Proverbs, Chapter 11

September 12

For you are all children of God through faith in Christ Jesus. And all who have been united with Christ in baptism have put on Christ, like putting on new clothes. There is no longer Jew or Gentile, slave or free, male and female. For you are all one in Christ Jesus. *(Galatians 3:26-28, NLT)*

Those who came before us made certain that this country rode the first waves of the industrial revolutions, the first waves of modern invention, and the first wave of nuclear power, and this generation does not intend to founder in the backwash of the coming age of space. We mean to be a part of it—we mean to lead it.

We set sail on this new sea because there is new knowledge to be gained, and new rights to be won, and they must be won and used for the progress of all people.

We choose to go to the moon. We choose to go to the moon in this decade and do the other things, not because they are easy, but because they are hard, because that goal will serve to organize and measure the best of our energies and skills, because that challenge is one that we are willing to accept, one we are unwilling to postpone, and one which we intend to win, and the others, too.

Many years ago the great British explorer George Mallory, who was to die on Mount Everest, was asked why did he want to climb it. He said, "Because it is there."

Well, space is there, and we're going to climb it, and the moon and the planets are there, and new hopes for knowledge and peace are there. And, therefore, as we set sail we ask God's blessing on the most hazardous and dangerous and greatest adventure on which man has ever embarked.

Excerpted from President John F. Kennedy's address at Rice University, Houston

I pray for those who honor human life in their professions.

Read:
Proverbs, Chapter 12

Today we observe
National Day of Encouragement

On this day in history
Notable events
In 1962, President John F. Kennedy delivered his famous speech about going to the moon within the decade.

Births
Richard March Hoe, American inventor and industrialist known for designing a rotary printing press that used a continuous roll of paper and revolutionized newspaper publishing, 1812

Richard Jordan Gatling, American inventor (Gatling gun, first hand-cranked machine gun), 1818

Morris Michtom, Russian-born American businessman and inventor, created the teddy bear, cofounder of the Ideal Novelty and Toy Company, 1869

Alfred A. Knopf Sr., American publisher, cofounder of Alfred A. Knopf, Inc., 1892

Deaths
Edward A. Calahan, American inventor credited with inventing ticker tape, gold and stock tickers, and a multiplex telegraph system, 1912

Marjorie Merriweather Post, American socialite, businesswoman, and philanthropist, 1973

Ray Dolby, American engineer, sound expert, and inventor, 2013

Thought for the day
"The mark of the immature man is that he wants to die nobly for a cause, while the mark of the mature man is that he wants to live humbly for one."

J.D. Salinger

September 13

> ❝ A new command I give you: Love one another. As I have loved you, so you must love one another. *(John 13:34, NIV)*

Earn your team's respect

Whether you're a seasoned leader or new to the role, here's how to earn the respect of your team.

Give respect. Treat everyone, regardless of their position, with respect.

Lead by example. Walk your talk. Model the behavior you want to see from your team. Be authentic and consistent.

Listen. Give others adequate time to express themselves and share what they know. Ask questions. Be willing to learn.

Propose, don't dictate. Even when what you're saying isn't open for debate, don't make it sound like an order.

Don't micromanage. Trust your employees to get the job done. Let them know you're available if they need you, but get out of their way and let them do their jobs.

Be approachable. Let your team know they can come to you without fear.

Get to know your team on a personal level. Take a genuine interest in who they are as individuals both on and off the job.

Be humble. Admit when you don't know something or have made a mistake.

Give credit and accept responsibility. When things go well, give credit where it's due in a public way. Take responsibility when things don't go well.

Recognize successes. Find out how your team likes to be recognized, whether it's public praise or a private congratulations, and reward them for their accomplishments.

Forgive mistakes and failures. Create an environment where failure is seen as an opportunity to learn and grow. Coach and mentor others. Share your wisdom and help them grow.

Stick to your word. If you say something, honor it, and if you make a commitment, keep it—unless it's wrong, and then you need to correct it as soon as possible.

Today we observe

Positive Thinking Day

National Hug Your Boss Day

On this day in history

Notable events

In 1947, the first Billy Graham evangelistic campaign began in the Civic Auditorium in Grand Rapids, Michigan, and was attended by 6,000 people.

In 1963, Mary Kay Ash launched her namesake cosmetic company with $5,000 in life savings.

Births

Milton S. Hershey, American chocolatier, businessman, and philanthropist, 1857

Ed Roberts, American engineer, entrepreneur, and medical doctor who invented the first commercially successful personal computer, known as the father of the personal computer, 1941

John W. Henry, American businessman, commodities trader, MLB franchise owner, 1949

Thought for the day

"The critical ingredient is getting off your butt and doing something. It's as simple as that. A lot of people have ideas, but there are few who decide to do something about them now. Not tomorrow. Not next week. But today. The true entrepreneur is a doer, not a dreamer."

Nolan Bushnell

I pray for those who are suffering because of someone else's sins.

Read:
Proverbs, Chapter 13

September 14

> Thousands upon thousands are waiting in the valley of decision. There the day of the Lord will soon arrive. *(Joel 3:14, NLT)*

What to say instead of "I don't know"

There's absolutely nothing wrong with admitting you don't know something, but there are times when you might want to avoid saying those exact words.

When you don't have an answer but you don't want to shut down the conversation, try these phrases:

"I'm not sure, but I can find out."

"That's a good question. Let's research it together."

"I've wondered the same thing."

"It depends on [the variable], but the estimate [or range] is …"

"It depends. I need to get more information before I can give you an answer."

"I need to think about it. I'll get back to you."

"That's a good question. Why do you ask?"

"I wish I had an answer."

When you don't know the answer, don't lie or try to pass the buck. If you lie, you'll probably get caught. If you say something like, "That's someone else's job," it reflects poorly on you.

Improvements aren't always visible

Ongoing improvement is a laudable goal. We want to get better as individuals, as teams, as organizations. Sometimes our forward steps are huge—and sometimes they're so small as to be barely noticeable.

Even when you can't see immediate improvement, if you're doing the right things, keep going. We must appreciate those small changes, those tiny steps, those fractions on the measurement scale because they will eventually add up to major results over time.

Today we observe
National Coloring Day

Commercial Motor Vehicle Driver Appreciation Day

On this day in history

Notable events

In 1638, 31-year-old clergyman John Harvard died, leaving his library and half of his estate to a local college; in honor of its first benefactor, the school adopted the name Harvard College.

In 1886, the first U.S. patent for a typewriter ribbon was issued to George Kerr Anderson.

Births

Lawrence Klein, American economist known for his work in creating computer models to forecast economic trends, 1920

John Gutfreund, American banker, business, investor, CEO of Salomon Brothers, Inc., 1929

Deaths

William Seward Burroughs, American inventor of the first workable adding machine, 1898

William McKinley, 25th U.S. President (third President to be assassinated), 1901

Fred DeLuca, American businessman, cofounder of the Subway restaurant chain, 2015

Thought for the day

"The greatest good you can do for another is not just to share your riches but to reveal to him his own."

Benjamin Disraeli

I am thankful for good conversation.

Read:
Proverbs, Chapter 14

September 15

Trust in the Lord and do good. Then you will live safely in the land and prosper. Take delight in the Lord, and he will give you your heart's desires. Commit everything you do to the Lord. Trust him, and he will help you. *(Psalm 37:3-5, NLT)*

Acting like a Christian doesn't make you one

But it's a good first step.

We've all heard people say that it isn't enough to act like a Christian, if you haven't accepted Jesus as your savior when you die, you won't make it to Heaven.

At the most basic level, according to Scripture, that's true. But does that mean that non-Christians shouldn't act like Christians?

The definition of a Christian is simple: It's someone who believes in Jesus Christ and accepts him as their savior. It's only natural that someone who is a Christian would follow what Jesus taught.

But there are people who look at what Jesus taught and think it's a good way to live, yet don't accept Jesus as the Son of God. They aren't Christians but they try to act like one because it's a lifestyle that just makes sense: be kind, serve, forgive, care, respect, honor.

There's nothing wrong with acting like a Christian even if you're not one.

This is not about the "fake it till you make it" career advice that used to be so popular. This isn't about claiming to believe something you don't. It's about following the teachings of Jesus because that's a simple way to make the world a better place.

Here's the thing about being a Christian: it's a journey. It's a process through which we grow and evolve. We're not born as believers. We become believers after we learn about Jesus.

It's okay for people to act like Christians when they're not—because sometimes, in the process of acting like a Christian, a person's heart will open and they'll become one.

Today we observe

National Online Learning Day

On this day in history

Notable events

In 1885, a U.S. patent was issued for saccharine, the artificial sweetener discovered by Constantin Fahlberg.

In 1917, Forbes magazine was founded by B. C. Forbes.

In 1997, the domain google.com was registered.

In 2008, Wall Street brokerage firm Lehman Brothers sought Chapter 11 bankruptcy protection.

Births

William H. Taft, 27th U.S. President and 10th Chief Justice of the U.S. Supreme Court, the only person to have served in both offices, 1857

Max Factor, Sr., Polish-American businessman, beautician, entrepreneur, inventor, and founder of the cosmetics giant Max Factor & Company, 1877

Jim Kimsey, American businessman and philanthropist, cofounder of America Online (AOL), 1939

Deaths

Garner Ted Armstrong, American evangelist, minister, author, educator, radio and television commentator, 2003

Thought for the day

"In Religion the Creature is apt to forget its Creator; ... it is otherwise in political affairs."

Gouverneur Morris

I am thankful for the ability to let go of what's not important.

Read:
Proverbs, Chapter 15

September 16

"O our God, won't you stop them? We are powerless against this mighty army that is about to attack us. We do not know what to do, but we are looking to you for help." *(2 Chronicles 20:12, NLT)*

Eliminate negative self-talk

Don't put yourself down. That's no way to talk about God's creation.

God made us in his image. When we say negative things about ourselves, we are saying negative things about God. God can handle it, but it's not good for us.

Negative self-talk—those unpleasant and destructive thoughts that run through our minds and sometimes make their way to our lips—can be insidious because we often don't realize we're doing it. But it can sap the joy out of our days.

There are plenty of ways to eliminate negative self-talk—an online search on "how to eliminate negative self-talk" will produce millions of results with all kinds of advice and techniques for turning off those nasty little voices in your head. What it all comes down to is this: If you wouldn't say it to someone you love, don't say it to yourself.

Thought for the day

"When people insult you, don't take offense, don't take it personally, but do listen to their words. They are telling you how they see the world, and they are telling you the exact negative qualities that they possess. The Law of Mirrors states that one can only see what's in them, regardless if it is what is actually present in reality or not. Release the need to defend or try to explain to them that you're not being whatever-nasty-insult-they've-thrown-at-you, but evaluate instead all of these insults, and realize that this is who they are. Then, decide if a person with those qualities is one who you'd like in your life or not."

Doe Zantamata

Today we observe
Working Parents Day

On this day in history

Notable events

In 1893, the largest land run in history began with more than 100,000 people pouring into the Cherokee Strip of Oklahoma to stake their claims to the best acres.

In 1908, Buick Motor Company head William C. Durant spent $2,000 to incorporate General Motors in New Jersey.

In 1920, a horse-drawn wagon exploded on Wall Street, New York, killing 40 people and injuring hundreds; the bombing remains unsolved.

In 2018, Marc and Lynne Benioff announced the purchase of *Time* magazine for $190 million.

Births

Charles Crocker, American business tycoon and railroad executive, 1822

James Cash Penney, American department store founder (JCPenney), 1875

Robert Schuller, American televangelist, pastor, and author best known for his weekly Hour of Power television program, 1926

Vince Naimoli, American businessman, investor, entrepreneur, and first owner of MLB team the Tampa Bay Devil Rays (now Tampa Bay Rays), 1937

Deaths

Irene Hayes, a Ziegfeld girl and businesswoman, owner of a leading Manhattan florist and Gallagher's Steak House, 1975

I pray that those who need the Lord's attention will recognize it when they receive it.

Read:
Proverbs, Chapter 16

September 17

Study this Book of Instruction continually. Meditate on it day and night so you will be sure to obey everything written in it. Only then will you prosper and succeed in all you do. *(Joshua 1:8, NLT)*

How some major brands got their names

Google is not only a noun, but has become a verb, as in "Google that." The name is derived from the word googol, which stands for one followed by one hundred zeros.

Sony comes from a mix of a Latin word *sonus*, which means sound, and American slang Sonny, used to describe a young, proactive, stylish person.

The legend that Adidas means "all day I dream about sports" isn't true. The company got its name from its founder, Adolf Dassler, whose nickname was Adi.

Adobe was named for the creek that ran behind founder John Warnock's house in Los Altos, California.

IBM began as the Computing, Tabulating & Recording Company. According to legend, Thomas J. Watson, IBM's CEO from 1914 to 1956, was a former employee of National Cash Register and he wanted to build something bigger than the company he had worked for. He thought something international was obviously larger than national.

Intel is a blend of the words integrated and electronics.

Reebok is Afrikaans for the grey rhebok, a type of African antelope.

Arby's doesn't stand for roast beef, it stands for the initials of its founders, the Raffel Brothers.

Audi was taken from the Latin for *Horch*, which means listen. Founder August Horch's name was already being used by his previous auto manufacturing company.

Today we observe
Constitution Day

On this day in history

Notable events

In 1991, the Linux open-source Unix-like operating system was first released by Linus Torvalds.

In 2007, AOL announced the relocation of one of its corporate headquarters from Dulles, Virginia to New York City, and the combination of its advertising units into a new subsidiary called Platform A.

Births

James Lick, American real estate investor, carpenter, piano builder, land baron, and patron of the sciences, 1796

Joshua Lionel Cowen, American inventor (electric train) and cofounder of Lionel Corporation, a manufacturer of model railroads and toy trains, 1877

J. Willard Marriott, Sr., American entrepreneur, businessman, founder of Marriott Corporation, 1900

Jim Rohn, American entrepreneur, author, and motivational speaker, 1930

Deaths

Charles Alfred Pillsbury, American businessman, flour industrialist, and politician, cofounder of the Pillsbury Company, 1899

Charles H. Percy, American businessman (president of Bell & Howell Corporation, 1949-1964) and politician, 2011

Thought for the day

"As I walked out the door toward the gate that would lead to my freedom, I knew if I didn't leave my bitterness and hatred behind, I'd still be in prison."

Nelson Mandela

I pray to always be gracious in victory.

Read:
Proverbs, Chapter 17

September 18

> He went on a little farther and bowed with his face to the ground, praying, "My Father! If it is possible, let this cup of suffering be taken away from me. Yet I want your will to be done, not mine." *(Mathew 26:39, NLT)*

Why Christians should start businesses

Why do people start businesses? The list of reasons is long—they want to be in control, make money, pursue their passion, have flexibility in how they work, and more. Andrew Crapuchettes, founder and CEO of RedBalloon.work, believes Christians approach entrepreneurship from a different perspective.

"It's very difficult to start a business. It's a lot of work," Crapuchettes says. "But as Christians, we have the best *why* of why we are starting a business. We're starting a business to bless our community, to bless our customers, to bless our employees. And when you have started a business and you're successful, you're given a very interesting voice in your community. I have a voice that I would not have if I was not striving to grow my business. Your business is way bigger than just making money."

Christian business owners have a unique opportunity to spread the gospel by the way they operate their companies and provide goods and services. Crapuchettes says, "When you live out your faith in the way that you're running your business, it has a profound impact on people and you don't have to hand out pamphlets or jam [Christianity] down their throat."

Crapuchettes says perhaps the most important reason for Christians starting businesses is that we are made in God's image. "We are mini creators following the great Creator," he says. "We love God. And whether you're a Christian or not, you realize that you were created and therefore you want to be a creator. I think that's why a lot of Christians realize they should start businesses."

Today we observe

National Day of Civic Hacking

Read An Ebook Day

Global Company Culture Day

On this day in history

Notable events

In 1837, Charles Lewis Tiffany and John B. Young founded Tiffany, Young and Ellis, a "stationery and fancy goods emporium," which was renamed Tiffany & Company in 1853.

In 1927, Columbia Phonograph Broadcasting System went on the air with 47 radio stations.

In 1958, in what became known as the "Fresno Drop," Bank of America mailed 60,000 residents unsolicited BankAmericards (the credit card would later become Visa).

In 1997, Ted Turner announced he would donate $1 billion over the next decade to United Nations programs.

Deaths

James G. Batterson, American designer, builder, and a founder of Travelers Insurance Company, 1901

William S. Harley, American mechanical engineer and businessman, cofounder of the Harley-Davidson Motor Company, 1943

Marshall Field IV, publisher, businessman, owner of the *Chicago Daily News*, 1965

Thought for the day

"Personality can open doors, but only character can keep them open."

Elmer G. Letterman

I am thankful for the seasons of life.

Read:
Proverbs, Chapter 18

September 19

The mind governed by the flesh is death, but the mind governed by the Spirit is life and peace. *(Romans 8:6, NIV)*

Don't become insulated

Regardless of its size, running a business is demanding. As your company grows, the nature of those demands changes and you may find yourself losing touch with your customers and employees.

Simple awareness of the risk of becoming insulated goes a long way toward preventing the problem. Be proactive and look for ways to eliminate barriers that may arise between you and your employees and customers.

You may have regular meetings with your senior managers, but there's no substitute for listening and interacting with customers and employees at all levels. The bigger your company gets, the harder it is to stay close to the people you depend on for your company's success.

A good technique is to view your company as an inverted pyramid with yourself at the bottom, customers at the top, and workers and suppliers in the middle. Your job is to support those workers and suppliers so you can all serve the customers.

Thought for the day

"I've seen extreme bravery from the least likely of people. Life is about the moments when it's all gone wrong. That's when we define ourselves."

Bear Grylls

I am thankful for those who are with me as we struggle through life's challenges together.

On this day in history

Notable events

In 1876, American inventor Melville Bissell received a U.S. patent for the carpet sweeper, which he invented because the dust from packing materials at his crockery shop was affecting his wife Anna's health.

Deaths

James A. Garfield, 20th U.S. President (second President to die by assassination; first left-handed U.S. President), 1881

Condé Nast, American publisher, entrepreneur, and business magnate, founder of the mass media company Condé Nast, 1942

Chester Carlson, American physicist, inventor, and patent attorney known for inventing electrophotography (xerography, the dry photocopying process), 1968

Orville Redenbacher, American food scientist and businessman, 1995

Ellis Marsalis Sr., American businessman, poultry farmer turned hotelier, Esso franchise owner, and civil rights activist, 2004

Make a list of the people whose opinions you care about—*really* care about. It should be short.

Don't concern yourself with the opinions of anyone who is not on that list. The thoughts and expectations of people who don't really know you and don't really matter is a heavy load you don't need to carry.

People will judge you by your actions, not your intentions.
You may have a heart of gold—but so does a hard-boiled egg.

Read:
Proverbs, Chapter 19

September 20

For I am the Lord your God who takes hold of your right hand and says to you, Do not fear; I will help you. *(Isaiah 41:13, NIV)*

How to ask good questions

When you're having trouble getting the answers you need, it might be because you aren't asking good questions. Good questions are clear, concise, and usually open-ended to allow the respondent flexibility in their reply.

Some tips for asking good questions:

Do your homework. Research the topic ahead of time so the respondent doesn't have to spend time providing you with basic information.

Be specific. There are times when general questions are appropriate, but if you need a specific answer, you must ask a specific question.

Avoid leading questions. If you're looking for honest information, don't ask questions that seem to target a predetermined response.

Ask questions that encourage discussion. Make it a conversation, not an inquisition.

Use an appropriate tone. Consider the topic and situation, and speak in a way that's appropriate.

Watch for nonverbal cues. In addition to hearing the words, you need to "hear" what isn't said.

Allow the person to answer. Don't rush the respondent; allow plenty of time for them to answer.

Ask follow-up questions. If you need additional information, ask for it.

Listen to the answers. After you ask a question, pay attention to what the respondent is saying.

Grow your faith by identifying and removing any obstacles to peace in your life.

Today we observe
International NFT Day

On this day in history

Notable events

In 1853, Elisha Graves Otis sold his first "hoist machines" (elevators) featuring an automatic safety brake that he had recently patented.

In 1954, the first successful test compilation and execution of a computer program using what became FORTRAN was run by Harlan Herrick at IBM.

In 2013, Take-Two Interactive Software, Inc. said their Grand Theft Auto V game reached $1 billion in worldwide sales after just three days on the market.

Births

Bruce Pasternack, American businessman, president and CEO of Special Olympics International (2005-2007), 1947

Lloyd Blankfein, American investment banker, senior chairman of Goldman Sachs, 1954

Deaths

Walter Haas, Jr., American businessman (Levi Strauss & Co.) and sports team owner, 1995

Thought for the day

"The success of economic freedom in increasing human prosperity, extending our life spans and improving the quality of our lives in countless ways is the most extraordinary global story of the past 200 years."
John Mackey

I pray for employees who receive unsatisfactory reviews.

Read:
Proverbs, Chapter 20

September 21

You did not choose me, but I chose you and appointed you so that you might go and bear fruit—fruit that will last—and so that whatever you ask in my name the Father will give you. *(John 15:16, NIV)*

Leading as a servant

Truly great leaders are great servants. In her book, *The Ins-N-Outs of In-N-Out Burger*, Lynsi Snyder (president and owner of the iconic burger chain), writes about her leadership style.

"Looking back over my young adult years, I see that my personal challenges and my growth through meeting and overcoming them has made me stronger. I've been humbled more than once, that's for sure. But I've seen that leading with humility can be a good thing. In my job today, I find that I spend a lot of time learning. I try to continually put myself in the shoes of others. And I see myself, even in the position of president, as a servant. It's my job to serve others and help anyone I can.

"When people ask me what kind of leader I am today, I explain that I practice servant leadership. (I say "practice" because I don't always get it right.) Servant leadership means I treat others the way I want to be treated, with dignity and respect. I long to protect others the way I wish I had someone to protect me when I was choosing my way of destruction. Servant leadership means recognizing and engaging the whole person. I don't merely look at a person's work performance or provide a paycheck to them. I see each individual as a person. At In-N-Out Burger, we talk a lot about teamwork and how we care for one another. My goal is for each associate to succeed both in this company and in life. We are united, knowing we have each other's backs."

I pray that everything I say and do will honor Christ.

Today we observe

Pause the World Day

On this day in history

Notable events

- In 1784, the *Pennsylvania Packet and Daily Advertiser* began publishing daily editions, becoming the first daily newspaper in the U.S.
- In 1895, the Duryea Motor Wagon Company became the first American auto manufacturer to open for business.
- In 1897, the *New York Sun* published the famous "Yes, Virginia, there is a Santa Claus" editorial.

Births

- Preston Tucker, American automobile and aviation entrepreneur who developed the innovative Tucker 48 sedan, 1903
- Henry Beachell, American plant breeder whose research led to the development of hybrid rice cultivars, known as the most important person in rice improvement in the world, 1906

Deaths

- Henry E. Warren, American entrepreneur, inventor (synchronous electric clock and 134 other inventions), founder of Warren Telechron Company, 1957
- Earle Dickson, American inventor best known for inventing the Band-Aid brand adhesive bandage, 1961
- Rex Humbard, American television evangelist, author, 2007

Thought for the day

"Truth is like the sun. You can shut it out for a time, but it ain't goin' away."
Elvis Presley

Read:
Proverbs, Chapter 21

September 22

Therefore, as God's chosen people, holy and dearly loved, clothe yourselves with compassion, kindness, humility, gentleness and patience. Bear with each other and forgive one another if any of you has a grievance against someone. Forgive as the Lord forgave you. And over all these virtues put on love, which binds them all together in perfect unity. *(Colossians 3:12-14, NIV)*

The opposite of good blog content

In addition to publishing good blog content, you want to avoid bad. Bad blog content is content that fits any of these descriptions:

Misleading headlines. Your titles and headlines should be catchy and intriguing, but accurate. Don't use annoying bait-and-switch headlines or promise more than you deliver.

Content copied from other sites with or without permission. Search engines will penalize your site for duplicate content, and material copied without permission is a violation of intellectual property rights. Be sure you have the rights to use everything that is on your site.

Plagiarized material. Don't claim to be the author of something you didn't write—it's theft, and it can get you in all kinds of legal trouble as well as damage your reputation. And it's just plain wrong.

Sloppy content. This includes material that is poorly written with typos and spelling, grammar and syntax errors as well as information that is incorrect. Proofread and fact-check thoroughly.

Headlines and content stuffed with keywords and written primarily for search engines. Search engines can recognize keyword-stuffing and will penalize you for it. If you write in a natural style for human readers and give them a reason to share your content, the search engines will rank your site higher.

Links to or from dubious sites. Your links are a reflection of the company you keep. Only allow links that reflect positively on you.

Today we observe

American Business Women's Day
National Eat Local Day
Remote Employee Appreciation Day

On this day in history

Notable events

In 1862, President Abraham Lincoln issued a preliminary Emancipation Proclamation, which set a date for freedom of more than 3 million enslaved people in the U.S.

Births

Roger S. Nichols, American recording engineer, producer, and inventor (rubidium nuclear clock), 1944

Deaths

Othmar Ammann, Swiss-American civil engineer whose bridge designs include the George Washington Bridge, Verrazzano-Narrows Bridge, Bayonne Bridge and others; he also directed the planning and construction of the Lincoln Tunnel, 1965

Thought for the day

"Anyone who stops learning is old, whether at twenty or eighty. Anyone who keeps learning stays young. The greatest thing in life is to keep your mind young."
Henry Ford

I am thankful that I am sometimes allowed to be part of saving a soul.

Read:
Proverbs, Chapter 22

September 23

Teach me your ways, O Lord, that I may live according to your truth! Grant me purity of heart, so that I may honor you. (Psalm 86:11, NLT)

You deserve to be heard

Do you sometimes feel that people don't listen to you? It could be because you aren't speaking clearly. Whether you're talking one-on-one or to a group, try these techniques to improve your communication skills.

Relax and be confident. Don't let tension tighten up your throat and hinder your delivery.

Breathe from your diaphragm. Using your diaphragm correctly will slow your breathing rate, decrease oxygen demand, and make it less likely that you'll run out of breath before you finish your sentence.

Use pauses. Give your audience some time to process what they've heard. Pauses can be powerful.

Replace filler words with silence. Eliminate filler words (ah, uh, um) and simply be quiet.

Be concise. Don't use more words than you need to. Don't over-explain.

Articulate your words. Pronounce each syllable clearly.

Slow down. You don't have to sound like the person giving the disclaimer at the end of an ad. Don't put your audience to sleep, but speak slowly enough so they can understand and absorb what you're saying.

Avoid buzzwords, jargon, and acronyms. Speak in plain language your audience will understand.

Thought for the day

"Don't put off for tomorrow what you can do today because if you enjoy it today, you can do it again tomorrow."

James A. Michener

Read:
Proverbs, Chapter 23

Today we observe

International Day of Sign Languages

On this day in history

Notable events

In 1953, WD-40 was invented and recorded for the first time in the Rocket Chemical Company's logbook; the name WD-40 was its original test designation.

Births

Mary Church Terrell, American educator, political activist, and first president of the National Association of Colored Women, 1863

Deaths

William Marsh Rice, American businessman and investor who bequeathed his fortune to found Rice University in Houston, Texas, 1900

Don't put new employees on probation

The word "probation" carries a very negative implication—most of the time, a person on probation has done something wrong and is being watched to see if it's going to happen again. That's not a very welcoming attitude to extend to a new employee.

Instead, call the initial trial period an "employment introductory" period. Define it as the time when your company and a new employee are being introduced to each other to determine whether or not you want to make your relationship permanent. Reserve "probation" for employees with performance problems.

I am thankful for the services of my suppliers.

September 24

> ❝What do you mean, 'If I can'?" Jesus asked. "Anything is possible if a person believes." *(Mark 9:23, NLT)*

How to stop worrying

We know we shouldn't worry, but that's one of those "easier said than done" things for many people. Try these tips to reduce how much time you spend on the destructive process of worrying.

Write down what you're worried about. The process of writing down your worries clarifies them and helps you evaluate them.

Analyze your worries. What's the likelihood of this actually happening? If it does happen, how can you deal with it?

Determine if you can control what you're worried about. If you can, put together an action plan for dealing with it. If you can't, accept the uncertainty.

Practice mindfulness and meditation. Take your focus away from negative thoughts and enjoy a state of calm. Practice deep breathing exercises and other relaxation techniques.

Step outside your worries. Look at your worries as though a friend was feeling them. What would you say to that person?

Learn your worry triggers. What situations or people make you worry or increase your anxiety? Can you avoid those triggers?

Talk about your worries. Sometimes a face-to-face conversation with a trusted friend or family member is the most effective way to put your worries in perspective and calm yourself.

We are commanded to love one another—and that includes people who aren't good for us for a wide range of reasons. It's okay to love those people from a distance.

Today we observe

Punctuation Day

On this day in history

Notable events

In 1902, pioneering cookbook author Fannie Farmer, who changed the way Americans prepare food by advocating the use of standardized measurements in recipes, opened Miss Farmer's School of Cookery in Boston.

In 1929, Jimmy Doolittle flew the first aircraft to be flown only on instruments (blind flying).

In 1952, Kentucky Fried Chicken opened its first franchise in Salt Lake City, Utah.

Births

Jim Henson, American puppeteer, animator, cartoonist, actor, inventor, and filmmaker, creator of the Muppets, 1936

Deaths

Carl Laemmle, German-American film producer and cofounder of Universal Pictures, 1939

Marvin Davis, American industrialist and film mogul, chair of Davis Petroleum, one-time owner of 20th Century Fox, Pebble Beach Corp., Beverly Hills Hotel, and Aspen Skiing Company, 2004

Keith Hufnagel, American skateboarder, entrepreneur, and fashion designer, founder of the streetwear brand HUF, 2020

Thought for the day

"Don't spend your precious time asking 'Why isn't the world a better place?' It will only be time wasted. The question to ask is 'How can I make it better?' To that there is an answer."

Leo Buscaglia

--- ---

I pray for my personal relationships.

Read:
Proverbs, Chapter 24

September 25

Jesus replied, "What is impossible with man is possible with God." *(Luke 18:27, NIV)*

We have a moral obligation to be happy

Being happy is good for us and the people in our lives. Even when we're not actually feeling happy, we should act as if we are.

"Whether or not you're happy, and most importantly, whether or not you act happy is about altruism, not selfishness, because it is about how we affect others' lives," says Dennis Prager, American talk show host and founder of Prager University.

When we're not happy and we show it, we have a negative impact on the people around us—spouses, children, other family members, friends, and colleagues. Why do that to them?

"No matter how unhappy you may feel at any given moment, you can—and have to—make a decision on how to act," Prager says. "We may not be free to control whether we feel sad or happy, but we are free to control whether or not we present a happy countenance to others. We all have the capacity to control how we express ourselves, no matter how we feel."

And how we act will affect how we feel. When we *act* happy, we will begin to *feel* happy. "We think that our actions are determined by our feelings. But we have the power to achieve the opposite—to shape our feelings by our actions," Prager says. "How we act influences our feelings more than our feelings should ever be allowed to influence our behavior. Being happier is good for us and it is what we owe everybody who is in our lives."

Being happy is one of the easiest ways we can serve others.

Read: Proverbs, Chapter 25

Today we observe

National "If You See Something, Say Something" Awareness Day

National Day of Remembrance for Murder Victims

On this day in history

Notable events

In 2018, Instagram cofounders Kevin Systrom and Mike Krieger resigned from Instagram and parent company Facebook.

Births

Alfred Vail, American inventor and early telegraph pioneer, 1807

Melville Reuben Bissell, American entrepreneur and inventor of the carpet sweeper, 1843

Olive Ann Beech, American aerospace businesswoman, cofounder of the Beech Aircraft Corporation, known as the first lady of aviation, 1903

Paul MacCready, American aeronautical engineer, inventor (human-powered aircraft), founder of AeroVironment, 1925

Marc Benioff, American internet entrepreneur, billionaire, and philanthropist, cofounder of Salesforce, owner of *Time* magazine, 1964

Deaths

Jacob Schiff, German-born American banker, businessman, and philanthropist who helped finance the expansion of American railroads, 1920

Thought for the day

"We must quit bending the Word to suit our situation. It is we who must be bent to that Word, our necks that must bow under the yoke."

Elisabeth Elliot

I pray for the strength to make the sacrifices I must.

September 26

And do not get drunk with wine, which is debauchery but be filled by the Spirit, speaking to one another in psalms, hymns, and spiritual songs, singing and making music in your hearts to the Lord, always giving thanks to God the Father for all things in the name of our Lord Jesus Christ, and submitting to one another out of reverence for Christ. *(Ephesians 5:18-21, NET)*

Our journey home

Life is about coming home.

In our life on this Earth, we go out, we travel, we do interesting, exciting things—and sometimes boring, unexciting things—and then we come home.

It is in our nature to look forward to coming home. Home is (or should be) our refuge, the place we share with our loved ones, a comfortable place where we rest and recharge for our next adventure.

This desire for being home, this comfort we take in that place wherever it may be, is God's way of helping us understand what it's going to be like to be with him in heaven for eternity.

It's built into our language—when people die, we say they've gone home to be with the Lord or that God has called them home. And though we will miss our loved ones, we rejoice in the knowledge that they have completed their journey and are indeed home forever.

Think about this the next time you're on your way home and eager to get there. The pleasure we feel when we arrive at our earthly home is nothing compared to the joy our final journey home will bring.

Thought for the day

"Think of fear like alcohol. It impairs judgment. You shouldn't make any decisions while under its influence."

Gregory Berns

Read:
Proverbs, Chapter 26

Today we observe

National Situational Awareness Day

National Day of Praise and Worship

Johnny Appleseed Day (also on March 11)

On this day in history

Notable events

In 1914, the FTC was created when President Woodrow Wilson signed the Federal Trade Commission Act into law.

In 1928, work began at Chicago's new Galvin Manufacturing Corporation which had been incorporated the day before; in 1930, Galvin introduced the Motorola radio, the first mass-produced commercial car radio.

Births

Johnny Appleseed (John Chapman), American pioneer nurseryman and missionary, 1774

Bill France, Sr., American businessman, racing driver, NASCAR founder, 1909

Jack LaLanne, American fitness and nutrition guru, motivational speaker, known as the godfather of fitness, 1914

Deaths

Levi Strauss, German-born American clothing designer who founded the first company to manufacture blue jeans (Levi Strauss & Co.), 1902

Edward Filene, American businessman and philanthropist, best known for building the Filene's department store chain and for his role in pioneering credit unions across the U.S., 1937

William Strunk, Jr., American professor of English and author of *The Elements of Style*, 1946

Paul Newman, American actor, entrepreneur, and philanthropist, 2008

I am thankful to have Jesus as my example of perfect leadership.

September 27

Confess your sins to each other and pray for each other so that you may be healed. The earnest prayer of a righteous person has great power and produces wonderful results. *(James 5:16, NLT)*

Are you feeling overwhelmed?

No matter what business you're in or what role you play, it's easy to feel overwhelmed at times. Author and editor Terry Whalin has advice for writers that anyone in business can also use. He writes:

"At times the work is daunting and the results are often unpredictable and outside of anything I can control. Also while I accomplish and complete individual tasks, the work is never done and there is always more to be done.

"When you have these feelings (and everyone does), what do you do? Before I give you some active suggestions, let's talk about what not to do. First, don't quit. Then don't procrastinate and do nothing. Each of us spin our wheels from time to time but snap out of it and get going."

How do we get going and keep going? Whalin says to make time to plan and organize how we will move forward. Understand the working environment you need and create it. He also recommends that we keep learning, experimenting, growing, moving, and caring for ourselves. "There is value and reduction of stress through taking simple actions to care for yourself."

Thought for the day

"If you have time to whine and complain about something then you have the time to do something about it."
Anthony J. D'Angelo

I pray for the invisible people.

Read:
Proverbs, Chapter 27

Today we observe
Ancestor Appreciation Day

On this day in history

Notable events
- In 1908, the first production Ford Model T left the factory (it was built on August 12).
- In 1922, scientists at the Naval Aircraft Radio Laboratory near Washington, DC, demonstrated that a ship could be detected if it passed through a radio wave being broadcast between two stations—the essentials of radar.

Births
- Ezra Fitch, American real estate developer and hobbyist outdoorsman who bought into and later fully owned the company that became Abercrombie & Fitch, 1865
- Charles H. Percy, American businessman (president of Bell & Howell Corporation, 1949-1964) and politician, 1919
- Alan Shugart, American engineer, entrepreneur, and business executive, founder of Shugart Associates and Seagate Technology, 1930
- Gwyneth Paltrow, American actress, businesswoman, and philanthropist, 1972

Be generous with your attention

One of the most valuable gifts you can give is your attention. Yet we all have more demands on our time than we can possibly meet, so how can we be generous with our attention? It's possible to do it concisely and efficiently.

When we are engaging with someone, be totally present. Eliminate distractions and give them your undivided attention. Listen to what they have to say and let them know they've been heard. Two or three minutes of genuine attention is worth far more than twenty minutes of distracted interaction.

September 28

We destroy arguments and every proud obstacle to the knowledge of God, and take every thought captive to obey Christ, *(2 Corinthians 10:5, RSV)*

Don't try to be liked by everyone

Jesus tells us to love one another, to be kind, to serve, and to care for one another. But we don't have to like everyone, and it's okay if everyone doesn't like us.

Do you like everyone you know? Probably not. And it makes sense that not everyone who knows you likes you. As uncomfortable as that might make you feel, it's okay.

Be pleasant and courteous to everyone, but don't try to be liked by everyone—especially if it means putting on a front about who you really are. Just be yourself and you will attract the people you need in your life.

Watch for the green flags

We often talk about red flags that serve as warnings. What about the green flags? Here are some green flags that signal someone is worth knowing:
- They are supportive of you and your goals.
- They celebrate your wins.
- They remember small things about you.
- They respect your boundaries.
- They truly listen to you.
- They allow you to be yourself.
- They make you feel safe.
- You feel energized after spending time with them.
- You can be honest with them.

I am thankful for my faith journey.

Read:
Proverbs, Chapter 28

Today we observe
National Good Neighbor Day
Read a Child a Book You Like Day

On this day in history

Notable events
- In 1901, King C. Gillette founded the American Safety Razor Company to sell his safety razor with the first disposable blade that worked; the following year, he changed the company's name to Gillette Safety Razor Company.
- In 2008, SpaceX launched the Falcon 1, the first ever private spacecraft, into orbit.

Births
- William S. Paley, American businessman who began his career in the family cigar business and is best known for building the Columbia Broadcasting System into one of the foremost radio and television network operations in the U.S., 1901
- Ed Sullivan, American television host and broadcasting pioneer, 1901
- Seymour Cray, American electrical engineer, supercomputer architect, founder of Cray Research, called the father of supercomputing, 1925

Deaths
- Daniel Guggenheim, American mining magnate and philanthropist, 1930
- Charles Duryea, American engineer of the first-ever working American gasoline-powered car and cofounder of Duryea Motor Wagon Company, 1938
- William E. Boeing, American aviation pioneer, founder of the Pacific Airplane Company, which was renamed Boeing and is one of the largest aerospace manufacturers in the world, 1956

Thought for the day

"Rank does not confer privilege or give power. It imposes responsibility."

Peter Drucker

September 29

F or surely I know the plans I have for you, says the Lord, plans for your welfare and not for harm, to give you a future with hope. *(Jeremiah 29:11, NRSVue)*

Help someone every day

Make it a point to do something helpful every day. Do it for someone you know or a stranger. Do it for a family member or a work colleague. It doesn't matter who you do it for—just be of service.

You don't have to make a big, time-consuming effort (although great if you can). It could be as simple as carrying a package for someone, picking up something someone dropped, or letting someone go ahead of you in the checkout line so they can get out of the store quickly.

If you're going out to lunch, offer to bring something back for a coworker. If you're going shopping, ask your neighbor if they need anything. If you make a big pot of soup, share part of it with someone who could use a break from cooking. When you bring your trash can in, bring your neighbor's in, too.

When you actively look for ways to be helpful, you'll find that you attract the same behavior from others.

When you make it a point to help someone in some way every day, you'll be blessed by the joy of serving *and* the joy of building rich, rewarding relationships.

Leave the past in the past.
Don't spend time regretting.
If you look back at all, only do it long enough to see how far you've come.

I pray that I will find the Lord's presence in everything that confronts me.

Read:
Proverbs, Chapter 29

Today we observe
Michaelmas

On this day in history

Notable events

In 1916, American oil tycoon John D. Rockefeller became the world's first billionaire.

In 1982, flight attendant Paula Prince bought a bottle of cyanide-laced Tylenol and was found dead on October 1, becoming the final of seven victims of a product-tampering mass murder that led to copycat crimes and new tamper-proof medicine containers.

Births

William R. Wilkerson, founder of *The Hollywood Reporter*, Las Vegas real estate developer, and businessman, 1890

Robert Lehman, American banker, head of Lehman Brothers investment bank, racehorse owner, art collector, and philanthropist, 1891

Gene Autry, American actor, singer, businessman, radio and television station owner, and MLB team owner, 1907

Vincent DeDomenico, American entrepreneur, inventor of Rice-A-Roni, founder of Napa Valley Wine Train, 1915

Deaths

Henry Ford II, American automobile executive, president of Ford Motor Company (1945-1960), 1987

August Anheuser "Gussie" Busch, Jr., American brewing magnate, 1989

Thought for the day

"A grateful heart is a beginning of greatness. It is an expression of humility. It is a foundation for the development of such virtues as prayer, faith, courage, contentment, happiness, love, and well-being."

James E. Faust

September 30

> "I have told you these things, so that in me you may have peace. In this world you will have trouble. But take heart! I have overcome the world." *(John 16:33, NIV)*

Appreciate your competition

Operating with excellence and working with integrity is as important in our competitor relationships as it is anywhere else in our businesses. But too often we view competitors as the enemy.

In *Work as Worship: How Your Labor Becomes Your Legacy*, Mark Goldstein says we need to remember that the rising tide raises all ships.

"If we're doing what God has called us to do, we should not be afraid of competition," Goldstein says. "Competition is healthy. It can make us better. At the same time, you want to see your competitors doing well because it makes your industry do well."

Know enough about your competitors to work with them if the situation calls for it. "I call it coopetition," Goldstein says. "For example, you may call on somebody, and they need something, but it's not really in your sweet spot. Or it might be one of those things that cause more work than it's worth. But you may have a competitor that is ideal for this customer. What does it say about you when you call a competitor and tell them, 'I've got this prospect and they need this. I could do it, but I don't really want to because the project isn't right for us. Is this something you'd be comfortable doing? If so, I'll make the introduction.'

"It says you want to do the right thing by your customers, your employees, and your company. It says you operate with integrity. And it will come back to you. There will come a day when that competitor has a prospect that isn't in their wheelhouse, and they're going to call you."

Even if you don't gain specific business from the referral, you've shown both the customer and the competitor how things ought to be done.

Today we observe
International Podcast Day

On this day in history
Notable events
In 1882, the first centrally located electric lighting plant began operation on the Fox River in Appleton, Wisconsin.
In 1980, the first Ethernet standard was published by Digital Equipment Corporation, Intel, and Xerox.
In 1998, the Internet Corporation for Assigned Names and Numbers (ICANN), an American nonprofit organization responsible for coordinating the maintenance and procedures of several databases related to the namespaces and numerical spaces of the internet, was incorporated in California.
In 2005, Michael Eisner resigned as CEO of The Walt Disney Company.

Births
Thomas W. Lamont, American banker and philanthropist, 1890
Irving B. Kahn, American media proprietor, inventor (teleprompter), founder of TelePrompTer Corporation, early cable television developer, 1917

Deaths
Frances Lear, American activist, author, magazine publisher, 1996

Thought for the day

"You begin saving the world by saving one man at a time; all else is grandiose romanticism or politics."

Charles Bukowski

I am thankful for the people who believe in me and encourage me.

Read:
Proverbs, Chapter 30

Christian Business Almanac

October

October means "the eighth month" in Latin—and it was in the ancient Roman calendar. When two months were added to the beginning of the calendar, October became the tenth month.

The Anglo-Saxons called October Winterfylleth, the name containing the words for winter and full moon, because winter was said to begin from the first full moon of the month.

October birthstone
Tourmaline and opal

October flower
Marigold and cosmos

October is ...
- Breast Cancer Awareness Month
- Bullying Prevention Awareness Month
- Children's Health Month
- Church Safety and Security Month
- Clergy Appreciation Month
- Crime Prevention Month
- Cybersecurity Awareness Month
- Domestic Violence Awareness Month
- Financial Planning Month
- Mental Illness Awareness Month
- National Fire Prevention Month
- National Women's Business Month

Mark your calendar for these October holidays and observances

First Saturday in October	National Healthcare Entrepreneurs Day
First Sunday in October	Day of Prayer for the Peace of Jerusalem
First Thursday in October	National Women-Owned Business Day
First Tuesday in October	National Fruit at Work Day
Second Monday in October	Columbus Day
Second Sunday in October	Clergy Appreciation Day
Second Tuesday in October	International Face Your Fears Day
Second Wednesday in October	National Stop Bullying Day
Third Monday in October	Clean Your Virtual Desktop Day
Third Monday in October	International Adjust Your Chair Day
Third Thursday in October	Conflict Resolution Day
Third Thursday in October	Get to Know Your Customers Day
Third Wednesday in October	National Teach Business Day
Third Wednesday in October	Support Your Local Chamber of Commerce Day

Fun Facts about October

October is the sixth of seven months of the year with 31 days.

In the northern hemisphere, the Draconid meteor shower can be seen in October. The Orionid meteor shower is visible in both hemispheres.

The last two to three weeks in October and occasionally the first week of November are normally the only time of the year during which all of the big four major professional sports leagues (basketball, hockey, football, and baseball) in the U.S. and Canada schedule games.

October 1

"Come to me, all who labor and are heavy laden, and I will give you rest. Take my yoke upon you, and learn from me, for I am gentle and lowly in heart, and you will find rest for your souls. For my yoke is easy, and my burden is light." *(Matthew 11:28-30, ESV)*

The joy is in the journey

When you're running a race, whether actual or metaphorical, crossing the finish line is important. After all, it's the goal. But all the things that happened along the way are even more important.

That's how life is. Our dreams are important, but living every day is what matters.

So I recommend having fun, because there is nothing better for people in this world than to eat, drink, and enjoy life. That way they will experience some happiness along with all the hard work God gives them under the sun. (Ecclesiastes 8:15, NLT)

We need goals. We need a destination. But we should never lose sight of the fact that God wants us to enjoy the journey, to revel in the daily things we are doing to live out his purpose for our lives.

They worshiped together at the Temple each day, met in homes for the Lord's Supper, and shared their meals with great joy and generosity—all the while praising God and enjoying the goodwill of all the people. And each day the Lord added to their fellowship those who were being saved. (Acts 2:46-47, NLT)

When our worldly dreams come true, we'll celebrate—but what we're going to treasure are the memories of getting there and the blessings we received along the way.

Thought for the day

"Should you find a wise critic to point out your faults, follow him as you would a guide to hidden treasure."

Dhammapada

On this day in history

Notable events

In 1880, the Edison Lamp Works, the first incandescent lamp factory in the U.S., opened in Menlo Park, New Jersey.

In 1920, *Scientific American* magazine reported that the rapidly developing medium of radio would soon be used to broadcast music.

In 1926, aviator Wiley Post was injured in an oil rig accident when a piece of metal pierced his left eye; he used the settlement money to buy his first aircraft.

In 1971, Walt Disney World opened for visitors.

In 2003, enforcement of the U.S. National Do Not Call Registry began.

Births

William E. Boeing, American aviation pioneer, founder of the Pacific Airplane Company, which was renamed Boeing and is one of the largest aerospace manufacturers in the world, 1881

James "Jimmy" Carter, 39th U.S. President, 1924

Deaths

James Lick, American real estate investor, carpenter, piano builder, land baron, and patron of the sciences, 1876

Jerome H. Lemelson, American engineer, inventor, and holder of more than 600 patents, 1997

Walter Annenberg, American businessman, investor, philanthropist, and diplomat who owned and operated Triangle Publications, 2002

Samuel Irving Newhouse Jr., American publisher, heir to a substantial magazine and media business, Advance Publications, 2017

I am thankful for precious memories.

Read: Proverbs, Chapter 1

October 2

We can make our plans, but the Lord determines our steps.
(Proverbs 16:9, NLT)

Why join a Christian chamber of commerce?

Most businesspeople are aware of the benefits of joining a local chamber of commerce. You can network with other members, develop resources in the community, gain exposure for your business, find new customers, take advantage of educational opportunities, get involved in political and legislative action, and more.

Many areas have an abundance of chambers, including community, city, regional, state, and national chambers. Chambers may also define themselves in other ways, such as faith, ethnicity, market niches, and even lifestyle.

With all those choices, it can be a challenge to decide which chambers are worth your time and money and will benefit you and your company. Why choose a Christian chamber of commerce?

For all the reasons you'd join any chamber, plus the bonus of being part of a community of fellow believers who don't leave their faith at the door when they go to work.

"We are doing business in a divisive, dark, and broken world. We need people around us to lift us up, pray for us, encourage us," says Krystal Parker, president of the U.S. Christian Chamber of Commerce.

"A Christian chamber is relevant, necessary, and non-negotiable for Christian business leaders," Parker says. "We have some of the best businesses, products, services, and thought leaders in their respective industries in our member chambers. We pray for each other and infuse the Holy Spirit into our conversations. We are lifting and supporting one another in our businesses, and as we do that, we are creating Kingdom commerce."

Today we observe
National Custodial Workers Day

On this day in history
Notable events
- In 1965, a team of scientists in a University of Florida lab invented the sports drink Gatorade.
- In 1984, Papa John's restaurant (Papa John's International, Inc.) was founded when "Papa" John Schnatter installed an oven in a broom closet in the back of his father's tavern.
- In 2015, Alphabet Inc., an American multinational technology conglomerate holding company was created through a restructuring of Google, formed.

Births
Charles Stark "Doc" Draper, American scientist and engineer, known as the father of inertial navigation, 1901
Huda Kattan, American makeup artist, beauty blogger, and entrepreneur; founder of the cosmetics line Huda Beauty, 1983

Deaths
Freelan Oscar Stanley, American inventor, entrepreneur, hotelier, and architect, best remembered as the cofounder of the Stanley Motor Carriage Company which built steam-powered automobiles, 1940
Gene Autry, American actor, singer, businessman, radio and television station owner, and MLB team owner, 1998

Thought for the day
"Approach life knowing there will be plenty to go around. Be generous."
Frank McKinney

I pray for my children.

Read:
Proverbs, Chapter 2

October 3

I know the Lord is always with me. I will not be shaken, for he is right beside me. *(Psalm 16:8, NLT)*

Tips for building customer loyalty

Find out what your customers want and provide it. Don't guess; ask them through surveys, focus groups, and at other contact opportunities.

Dazzle them with service they'll want to tell their friends about. Be so remarkable they can't help talking about you.

Be responsive. Don't make your customers wait for service. Take care of their needs immediately.

Make customers feel welcome. Greet people enthusiastically when they walk through the door. When they call, make it obvious that you're delighted to hear from them.

Set yourself apart. Differentiate your company through the quality of your products and services.

Always tell the truth. Never, ever attempt to deceive your customers in any way—they'll find out, they'll leave, and they'll never come back.

Keep your facility sparkling. How well you care for your store, office, or plant is a sign of how well you care about your customers.

If it's wrong, make it right. When a mistake is made, apologize and correct it right away—whether it's your fault or not.

Ask for feedback. Give your customers a chance to tell you what they like and don't like about your operation and your products, then use that input to improve.

Guarantee your products and services. Put your guarantee in writing and honor it.

Be patient. Building loyalty takes time. You've got to be in it for the long term.

Read:
Proverbs, Chapter 3

On this day in history

Notable events

In 1952, the first U.S. video recording on magnetic tape giving credible results of off-air black and white recordings was made by John T. Mullin at the electronics division of Bing Crosby Enterprises, Inc.

Births

John B. Gorrie, Nevisian-born American physician and scientist, credited as the inventor of mechanical refrigeration, 1803

George Brayton, American mechanical engineer and inventor, known for introducing the constant pressure engine that is the basis for the gas turbine, 1830

Timothy Thomas Fortune, American orator, civil rights leader, writer, editor, and publisher, 1856

Fred DeLuca, American businessman, cofounder of the Subway restaurant chain, 1947

Deaths

Elias Howe, Jr., American engineer and inventor best known for the creation of the modern lockstitch sewing machine, 1867

Thought for the day

"God proved His love on the Cross. When Christ hung, and bled, and died, it was God saying to the world, 'I love you.'"

Billy Graham

I pray for those who are desperate.

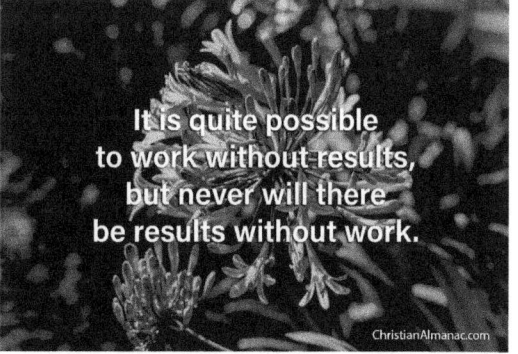

October 4

So we are always confident, knowing that while we are at home in the body we are absent from the Lord. For we walk by faith, not by sight. (2 Corinthians 5:6-7, NKJV)

Make time for a nap

Naps are good for you.

The National Sleep Foundation says that humans are hardwired to feel a little tired in the middle of the afternoon. According to a Pew Research Center poll, one-third of adults in the United States take naps. What's more, naps are biblical.

Consider:

Late one afternoon, after his midday rest, David got out of bed and was walking on the roof of the palace. As he looked out over the city, he noticed a woman of unusual beauty taking a bath. (2 Samuel 11:2, NLT)

We shouldn't follow David's example of what he did after his nap—just pointing out that he took naps.

As they sailed across, Jesus settled down for a nap. (Luke 8:23, NLT)

Jesus knew the importance of rest.

It is useless for you to work so hard from early morning until late at night, anxiously working for food to eat; for God gives rest to his loved ones. (Psalm 127:2 NLT)

According to the National Sleep Foundation, naps can restore alertness, enhance performance, and reduce mistakes and accidents. A study at NASA on sleepy military pilots and astronauts found that a 40-minute nap improved performance by 34 percent and alertness 100 percent.

Famous people who took naps include Winston Churchill, Albert Einstein, John F. Kennedy, Ronald Reagan, Leonardo Da Vinci, Thomas Edison, and Margaret Thatcher.

Churchill said, "Don't think you will be doing less work because you sleep during the day. That's a foolish notion held by people who have no imaginations. You will be able to accomplish more." So take naps. You're in good company.

Today we observe

Improve Your Office Day

On this day in history

Notable events

In 1985, the Free Software Foundation was founded in Massachusetts by Richard Stallman to support the free software movement.

Births

Rutherford B. Hayes, 19th U.S. President, 1822

Malcolm Baldrige, Jr., American businessman and U.S. Secretary of Commerce (1981-1987), quality proponent for whom the Malcolm Baldrige National Quality Award was named, 1922

Russell Simmons, American entrepreneur, writer, and record executive, 1957

Deaths

Joan Whitney Payson, American heiress, businesswoman, MLB team owner, and philanthropist, 1975

Edward Lowe, American businessman and entrepreneur, noted for the invention of cat litter, 1995

Loretta Lynn, American country singer-songwriter, author, and businesswoman, 2022

Thought for the day

"Success is to be measured not so much by the position that one has reached in life as by the obstacles which he has overcome while trying to succeed."

Booker T. Washington

I am thankful for the people who care for me when I am ill.

Read:
Proverbs, Chapter 4

October 5

The Lord turned to him and said, "Go in the strength you have and save Israel out of Midian's hand. Am I not sending you?" "Pardon me, my lord," Gideon replied, "but how can I save Israel? My clan is the weakest in Manasseh, and I am the least in my family." The Lord answered, "I will be with you, and you will strike down all the Midianites, leaving none alive." *(Judges 6:14-16, NIV)*

What a Friend we Have in Jesus

Joseph Medlicott Scriven, 1855

What a friend we have in Jesus,
all our sins and griefs to bear!
What a privilege to carry
everything to God in prayer!
O what peace we often forfeit,
O what needless pain we bear,
all because we do not carry
everything to God in prayer!

Have we trials and temptations?
Is there trouble anywhere?
We should never be discouraged;
take it to the Lord in prayer!
Can we find a friend so faithful
who will all our sorrows share?
Jesus knows our every weakness;
take it to the Lord in prayer!

Are we weak and heavy laden,
cumbered with a load of care?
Precious Savior, still our refuge--
take it to the Lord in prayer!
Do your friends despise, forsake you?
Take it to the Lord in prayer!
In his arms he'll take and shield you;
you will find a solace there.

Thought for the day

"Never give up. Realise that when you face problems, you are almost there. 'No' is negotiable. Ninety percent of people give up when they are ten percent from achieving their goals. The word that stops them is 'no'."

Barry Bull

Today we observe

National Do Something Nice Day

On this day in history

Notable events

In 1943, a public service patent for a "Dispensing Apparatus," the first aerosol can used in a commercial application, was granted to Lyle D. Goodhue and William N. Sullivan.

Births

Jonathan Edwards, American revivalist preacher, philosopher, and Congregationalist theologian, 1703

Chester A. Arthur, 21st U.S. President, 1829

Robert H. Goddard, American engineer, professor, physicist, and inventor, considered the father of modern rocket propulsion, 1882

Ray Kroc, American fast-food entrepreneur (McDonald's) and owner of San Diego Padres baseball team, 1902

Deaths

Earl Tupper, American businessman and inventor, founder of Tupperware Corporation, 1983

Seymour Cray, American electrical engineer, supercomputer architect, founder of Cray Research, called the father of supercomputing, 1996

Steve Jobs, American computer entrepreneur and cofounder of Apple, 2011

Ruth Benerito, American chemist and inventor in the textile industry, known for the development of wash-and-wear cotton fabrics, 2013

I pray for those who pray for me.

Read:
Proverbs, Chapter 5

October 6

And even when you ask, you don't get it because your motives are all wrong—you want only what will give you pleasure. *(James 4:3, NLT)*

Ten ways to find joy

1. Limit your consumption of hard news and political commentary. Stay informed, but don't overload.

2. Restrict your consumption of social media. Use it to keep up with your friends and for necessary business purposes, but shut out the negativity.

3. Make your discussions actual discussions. Don't argue with people who don't want to hear your point of view, who just want to browbeat you into accepting theirs.

4. Consume plenty of helpful information. Keep your brain busy. Read, watch, and listen to plenty of how-to material. Take a class. Learn a new skill. Take advantage of the abundance of on-demand learning resources we have at our disposal.

5. Read and watch positive fiction. Read good novels. Watch quality television shows and movies. Exercise your imagination by allowing writers and filmmakers to show you times and places that you'll never see in the real world.

6. Read the Bible. Read a few chapters (or even just a few verses) every day and take comfort in its amazing message.

7. Form or join discussion groups that focus on the positive. Meet online or in-person on a regular schedule for positive, constructive conversation.

8. Go to God in prayer every day. Turn your worries and fears over to him and ask for his guidance.

9. Actively worship every day. When we worship, we show reverence and adoration for God. Make everything you do—work, play, relaxation—a form of worship.

10. Trust God. God's got you. Trust him.

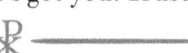

I pray that I can hold someone up while they face and fight their battle.

Today we observe

National Coaches Day

Inbox Zero Day

On this day in history

Notable events

In 1908, Henry Simon Winzeler founded the Ohio Art Company, a manufacturer of metal picture frames and other novelty items; 52 years later, the company launched its first toy, Etch-A-Sketch.

In 2010, Kevin Systrom launched Instagram; the photo-sharing app racked up 25,000 users in one day.

Births

George Westinghouse, American entrepreneur and engineer, founder of the original Westinghouse Electric Corp., 1846

Frank Seiberling, American innovator, entrepreneur, founder of Goodyear Tire & Rubber Company, 1859

Reginald Fessenden, Canadian-American inventor who received hundreds of patents, with the most notable related to radio and sonar, 1866

John Warnock, American computer scientist, inventor, businessman, and philanthropist, cofounder of Adobe Systems, Inc., 1940

Deaths

William Keith Kellogg, American industrialist in food manufacturing, founder of the Kellogg Company, 1951

Charles E. Merrill, American investment banker, stockbroker, philanthropist, and cofounder of Merrill Lynch, 1956

Thought for the day

"Have a heart that never hardens, and a temper that never tires, and a touch that never hurts."

Charles Dickens

Read: Proverbs, Chapter 6

October 7

Again Jesus spoke to them, saying, "I am the light of the world. Whoever follows me will never walk in darkness but will have the light of life." *(John 8:12, NRSVue)*

Tips for successful networking at an online conference

Attending online conferences allows you to access the information from the conference without the hassle and expense of attending in person, but it also limits your opportunities to make connections and build relationships.

Use these tips for a successful virtual conference experience:

Set your intentions in advance. Decide ahead of time what you'll share about yourself, what you have to offer others, and what you need help with.

Prepare your introduction. Develop and practice your introduction so you can tell people about yourself clearly and concisely.

Put your name on your online image. Meeting platforms like Zoom allow you to customize what shows up on the screen. Make sure it has your name and either a title, company name, or website.

Make yourself memorable in a positive way. Be sure your appearance and background are appropriate for the event and give others something to remember.

Write out some chat contributions in advance. Many online conferences invite participants to put info in the chat about who you are and how to connect with you. Write this out ahead of time and keep the document open so you can quickly and accurately copy and paste it.

Take a screenshot of the meeting. This will help you to remember the names and faces of the people you were with.

When a conversation ends, repeat your name. Most people have trouble remembering names, especially in situations when they're meeting a lot of new people at once, so reinforce your name.

Today we observe
National Forgiveness & Happiness Day

On this day in history

Notable events

In 1856, Cyrus Chambers, Jr., of Pennsylvania received a U.S. patent for the first practical folding machine to fold book and newspaper sheets.

In 1913, for the first time, Henry Ford's entire Highland Park, Michigan automobile factory was run on a continuously moving assembly line, increasing the affordability and production volume of the Model T.

Births

William Still, African American businessman, writer, historian, abolitionist, conductor of the Underground Railroad, 1821

Martha Berry, American educator and founder of Berry College, 1865

Deaths

Willis Carrier, American engineer best known for inventing modern air conditioning, founder of Carrier Corporation, 1950

Clarence Birdseye, American inventor, entrepreneur, and naturalist, considered the founder of the modern frozen food industry, founder of the frozen food company Birds Eye, 1956

Thought for the day

"I have seen what a laugh can do. It can transform almost unbearable tears into something bearable, even hopeful."

Bob Hope

I am thankful for the lessons I have learned from pain.

Read:
Proverbs, Chapter 7

October 8

God has given each of you a gift from his great variety of spiritual gifts. Use them well to serve one another. *(1 Peter 4:10, NLT)*

When is "as soon as possible"?

When someone asks you for something "as soon as possible," do you know when the deadline is?

When you ask for something "as soon as possible," when do you expect to get it?

Many people think this phrase conveys urgency while being courteous—but neither is true.

In most cases, it's not clear (and unclear communication is frustrating and time-wasting) and the person on the receiving end of the message likely has no idea when the deadline really is. Does it mean you should drop what you're doing and get to work on this request? Or does it mean you should finish your current project and put this next in line?

Instead of asking for something as soon as possible, be specific: "I need the information by Wednesday at noon." Or if you have some flexibility, explain it: "I'd like to have it by Thursday, but if you need until Friday, I can work with that."

When you're on the receiving end of an "as soon as possible" request, ask for a specific deadline: "Exactly when do you need it?" Or offer a deadline: "I can get that for you by two o'clock on Tuesday. Does that work for you?"

You can be polite and professional and still express your needs and expectation specifically, so stop saying, "as soon as possible."

Today we observe
Alvin C. York Day

On this day in history

Notable events

In 1871, the Great Chicago Fire began, destroying an estimated 3.3 square miles of the city and more than 17,000 structures, and killing approximately 300 people.

In 1945, Percy Spencer and Raytheon filed for a patent for their microwave oven; the patent was awarded in 1950.

Births

Collett E. Woolman, American airline entrepreneur, founder of Delta Air Lines, 1889

John T. Walton, American businessman and philanthropist, son of Walmart founder Sam Walton, 1946

Reed Hastings, American businessman, cofounder and executive chairman of Netflix, Inc., 1960

Deaths

Franklin Pierce, 14th U.S. President, 1869

George W. Mason, American industrialist, served as chairman and CEO of the Kelvinator Corporation, the Nash-Kelvinator Corporation, and American Motors Corporation, known for introducing several compact car lines, 1954

John D. Hertz, American businessman, racehorse owner/breeder, philanthropist; founder of the Yellow Cab Company and related businesses, 1961

Brown Meggs, American writer, music executive, and publisher know for signing the Beatles to their first distribution contract in the U.S., 1997

Al Davis, American football coach, executive, NFL team owner, 2011

I am thankful for unexpected downtime.

Thought for the day

"You will never change your life until you change something you do daily. The secret of your success is found in your daily routine."

John C. Maxwell

Read:
Proverbs, Chapter 8

October 9

Anyone who has been stealing must steal no longer, but must work, doing something useful with their own hands, that they may have something to share with those in need. *(Ephesians 4:28, NIV)*

If all you can do is pray, pray

It's a common scenario: There's a need, but you don't have the resources (time, money, whatever) to assist. So you say, "I'm sorry, all I can do is pray."

That's doing a lot.

Confess your sins to each other and pray for each other so that you may be healed. The earnest prayer of a righteous person has great power and produces wonderful results. (James 5:16, NLT)

James doesn't say, give medicine or visit. He says pray for each other because prayer is powerful and effective.

Pray in the Spirit at all times and on every occasion. Stay alert and be persistent in your prayers for all believers everywhere. And pray for me, too. Ask God to give me the right words so I can boldly explain God's mysterious plan that the Good News is for Jews and Gentiles alike. (Ephesians 6:18-19, NLT)

Paul isn't asking people to do things for him. He's not asking people to bring him food or take him someplace. He's asking for prayer. That tells us how important prayer is.

Afterward, when Jesus was alone in the house with his disciples, they asked him, "Why couldn't we cast out that evil spirit?" Jesus replied "This kind can be cast out only by prayer." (Mark 9:28-29, NLT)

Jesus was talking about demons in a child. But he was also talking about the power of prayer. There was nothing else that would work in this situation but prayer.

When you feel like there's nothing you can do but pray, remember that prayer is the best and most important thing you can do.

I pray for those who are quiet and don't share their needs.

Today we observe

World Post Day

International Subscription Day

On this day in history

Notable events

- In 1917, Clarence Saunders, founder of Piggly Wiggly, patented the concept of the "self-serving store."
- In 1936, the Hoover Dam began sending electricity over transmission lines spanning 266 miles of mountains and deserts to provide power to Los Angeles.

Births

- Mary Ann Shadd Cary, African American activist, journalist, publisher, teacher, and lawyer, 1823
- Charles Rudolph Walgreen, American businessman, founder of Walgreens, 1873
- Brian Lamb, American journalist, founder of C-SPAN, 1941
- James Robison, American pastor, televangelist, theologian, and author; founder of the Christian relief organization Life Outreach International, 1943

Deaths

- Joseph Glidden, American businessman, farmer, philanthropist, inventor of modern barbed wire, 1906
- Ray Noorda, American electrical engineer, businessman, CEO of Novell, Inc., known as the father of computer networking, 2006

Thought for the day

"Always err on the side of doing right. You and only you are responsible for your ethics."

Griffin Bell

Read:
Proverbs, Chapter 9

October 10

He says, "Be still, and know that I am God; I will be exalted among the nations, I will be exalted in the earth." *(Psalm 46:10, NIV)*

The art of apologizing

In the comic strip "For Better or For Worse," a wise teacher told the pre-teen Elizabeth, "An apology is the superglue of life! It can repair just about anything!"

For an apology to be effective, it must be offered willingly and sincerely. And if you're apologizing for something more serious than casually bumping someone in the checkout line, you need to give it some thought. Here's how to develop the art of apologizing:

Say you're sorry. Begin with the word sorry. Don't say you regret what happened or use other language that avoids what you need to say, which is that you're sorry.

Take responsibility. Acknowledge the offense and admit that your behavior was unacceptable. Don't minimize your conduct. Be specific—clearly articulate what you're apologizing for.

Don't cast blame. Don't blame anyone else for what you did, whether it's the person you're apologizing to or a third party.

Explain but don't excuse. This can be a challenge. You want to explain why something happened but don't make excuses for it. You might actually say that there is no excuse for what you did.

Express remorse. Share your feelings of regret or shame for the suffering you caused.

Offer to make amends. If it's possible to repair physical damage, arrange to do that. If the situation involves hurt feelings, acknowledge that and explain what you'll do to prevent it from happening again. If appropriate, ask what you can do to make amends.

I am thankful for new scientific discoveries.

Today we observe
National SHIFT10 Day

On this day in history

Notable events
- In 1850, the Chesapeake & Ohio Canal was completed and opened for business along its entire 184.5-mile length from Washington, DC to Cumberland, Maryland.
- In 1865, John Wesley Hyatt patented a billiard ball made of a composition material resembling ivory.
- In 1933, a U.S. patent was issued to Waldo L. Semon for a method of making plasticized PVC, now known simply as vinyl.

Births
- Earle Dickson, American inventor best known for inventing the Band-Aid brand adhesive bandage, 1892
- Jay Sebring, American celebrity hairstylist and founder of the hairstyling corporation Sebring International, murdered by members of the Manson Family, 1933

Deaths
- Adolphus Busch, German-born cofounder of Anheuser-Busch (with his father-in-law, Eberhard Anheuser), philanthropist, 1913
- James Buchanan Duke, American tobacco and electric power industrialist, founder of the American Tobacco Company, 1925
- Elijah McCoy, Canadian-American engineer and inventor (lubrication systems for steam engines); the popular expression "the real McCoy" has been attributed to his oil-drip cup invention, 1929

Thought for the day

"We can't solve problems by using the same kind of thinking we used when we created them."

Albert Einstein

Read:
Proverbs, Chapter 10

October 11

All scripture is inspired by God and is useful for teaching, for reproof, for correction, and for training in righteousness, so that the person of God may be proficient, equipped for every good work. *(2 Timothy 3:16-17, NRSVue)*

How to implement quiet time in your workplace

Quiet time or quiet hours refers to scheduling work time when you turn off your phone, close your email, don't attend meetings, and shut your door for a certain number of hours so you can concentrate on a specific task or project. Quiet time policies have proven to be effective at increasing productivity and general workplace benefits.

Here's how to implement quiet time in your organization:

Set the rules. People need to know what's expected. Decide on the number of hours and the particular days that will be considered quiet. Articulate what people can and can't do during quiet time. What else does the team need to know for a successful adoption of the new system?

Test it. Your initial set of rules may or may not be effective, so do a test launch and evaluate the results. Make any adjustments that may be necessary for the full implementation.

Track long-term performance. Check the company's milestones every week or month for changes. Conduct surveys among workers to identify where improvements in the program could be made.

Understand that sometimes you'll need to violate the rules. If there is an emergency during designated quiet hours, people need to know they must handle it properly.

I pray to earn the trust of those I serve.

Read:
Proverbs, Chapter 11

Today we observe
Take Your Parents to Lunch Day

Spread Joy Day

On this day in history

Notable events

In 1929, JCPenney opened a location in Milford, Delaware, making the mid-range department store present in all 48 contiguous states.

In 1968, *Apollo 7*, the first manned *Apollo* mission, launched with astronauts Walter M. Schirra Jr., Donn F. Eisele, and Walter Cunningham to conduct an eleven-day orbit of Earth and transmit the first live television broadcasts from orbit.

In 1983, the last hand-cranked (magneto) telephones went out of service as 440 telephone customers in Bryant Pond, Maine, were switched to direct-dial service.

Births

Henry John Heinz, American entrepreneur, founder of H. J. Heinz Company, known for creating tomato ketchup, 1844

Fred Trump, Sr., American real estate developer and businessman, father of Donald Trump, 1905

Peter Thiel, German-American entrepreneur, venture capitalist, and political activist; cofounder of PayPal, Palantir Technologies, and Founders Fund; first outside investor in Facebook, 1967

Deaths

James Franklin Hyde, American inventor who created silica, 1999

Thought for the day

"Letting go of the old self and the negative things associated with who you were is critical to becoming the person you want to be."

Lee Murray

October 12

> ❝ The human heart is the most deceitful of all things, and desperately wicked. Who really knows how bad it is? *(Jeremiah 17:9, NLT)*

Do you read About pages?

When you're visiting websites for advice and information, how do you know if the advice is good and the information is accurate? One way is to read the About page.

In his AsktheBuilder.com newsletter, home improvement expert Tim Carter discussed AI-generated content about home building and repairs, and the chances such content could give you advice that might not work and might even create bigger problems for you. He wrote:

"When you end up on a home improvement website page and are reading a column that interests you, do you STOP and click the About Us page? Do you go find out WHO wrote the column and WHAT is the DEPTH of the author's experience?"

Some additional ways to verify the quality and accuracy of information on a website include:
- Check multiple sources, including offline sources if possible, to see if they agree with the information on the site.
- Consider the professionalism of the site, including overall design, navigation, and quality and accuracy of writing (an abundance of typos and poor grammar is a huge red flag).
- Check the contact page for phone, email, and physical address.
- If the site contains advertising, consider the quantity and content of those ads.
- Look to see if the information is clearly sourced and the articles include an author's name and bio. It's also a good sign if other authorities are cited.

But start with the About page. If it doesn't inspire confidence in the source, look elsewhere.

If you have a website, check your About page. Would it give a reader confidence that you're qualified to do what you do?

Today we observe
National Savings Day

On this day in history
Notable events
In 1920, construction of the Holland Tunnel began.
In 1999, the United Nations projected the six billionth baby was born somewhere in the world.

Births
Elmer Ambrose Sperry, American entrepreneur and inventor, founder of Sperry Gyroscope company, known as the father of modern navigation technology, 1860
Jean Nidetch, American businesswoman, entrepreneur, founder of Weight Watchers, 1923

Deaths
Margaret E. Knight, American businesswoman and inventor, notably of a machine to produce flat-bottomed paper bags, called the most famous 19th-century woman inventor, founder of Eastern Paper Bag Company, 1914

Thought for the day
"Far and away the best prize that life offers is the chance to work hard at work worth doing."
Theodore Roosevelt

I pray for the courage to ask the hard questions.

> Grow your faith by setting aside time to listen to God.

Read:
Proverbs, Chapter 12

October 13

> But God remembered Noah and all the beasts and all the livestock that were with him in the ark. And God made a wind blow over the earth, and the waters subsided. *(Genesis 8:1, ESV)*

Ten ways to make a difference

Have you ever had a stranger do something that brightened your day? It might have been a small but thoughtful gesture the other person quickly forgot but you remembered.

It doesn't take much to boost someone's spirits, to make them smile, to give them something good to pass along, even if it's someone you don't know and are likely to never see again. Think about how much better the world would be if we were intentional about making a positive difference in the lives of others.

Try one or more of these ten easy ways to make a priceless difference.

1. When you're thinking something nice, say it out loud.
2. Hold the door or elevator, even if you have to wait a minute.
3. Offer to get something off a high shelf for a short person or assist someone in a wheelchair or who is otherwise physically limited.
4. Let someone with just a few items go ahead of you in the checkout line.
5. Praise a child.
6. Pay a stranger a compliment.
7. Say please and thank you.
8. Apologize immediately if you're at fault.
9. Smile and speak when passing people in public.
10. Read someone's t-shirt and say something positive about it.

Are these things small? Yes. Will they matter? Maybe. Would anyone notice if you didn't do them? Probably not.

But if you do them, and if they matter, and if the people you impact decide to pass it along, you've made an incalculable difference in the world.

Today we observe

National Train Your Brain Day

International Plain Language Day

International Day for Failure

On this day in history

Notable events

In 1792, the cornerstone of the White House was laid.

In 1792, the first edition of *The Old Farmer's Almanac* was published by editor Robert B. Thomas.

In 2023, Microsoft completed its $69 billion takeover of Call of Duty maker Activision Blizzard.

Births

Leon Leonwood Bean, American inventor, author, founder of L.L. Bean, a retailer specializing in clothing and outdoor recreation equipment, 1872

Dorothy Lee Bolden, domestic worker, founder of the National Domestic Workers Union of America, 1923

Jerry Jones, American businessman and entrepreneur, NFL team owner, 1942

Deaths

Milton S. Hershey, American chocolatier, businessman, and philanthropist, 1945

Ed Sullivan, American television host and broadcasting pioneer, 1974

Walter Houser Brattain, American physicist and Nobel laureate for his work on transistors, 1987

Thought for the day

"Time is like money. The less we have of it the further we make it go."

Josh Billings

I am thankful for my achievements.

Read:
Proverbs, Chapter 13

October 14

But the fruit of the Spirit is love, joy, peace, forbearance, kindness, goodness, faithfulness, gentleness and self-control. Against such things there is no law. *(Galatians 5:22-23, NIV)*

Churches in the marketplace

The marketplace is a massive mission field. Craig Hohnberger, cofounder and senior partner with Buji ActionCoach (Columbus, Ohio), points out that 100 percent of the lost are in the marketplace. Regardless of their beliefs, people are buying goods and services for themselves, their families, and their businesses.

"The marketplace is the frontline of Kingdom building," Hohnberger says. "As Christians, we are priests (1 Peter 2:9) and our businesses are churches in the marketplace."

As churches in the marketplace, he says, business leaders need to disciple people to be more like Christ and we need to witness to people who do not yet know Christ. We can do that by building well-run, profitable companies that serve a purpose that is greater than the business' product or service.

Business leaders at all levels are influencers—they influence their employees, colleagues, customers, and suppliers. Not only is this is a tremendous responsibility that can't be taken lightly, it's an opportunity to share the Gospel to those who might not otherwise hear it.

Thought for the day

"The function of wisdom is to discriminate between good and evil."

Marcus Tullius Cicero

I am thankful for the challenges that strengthen me.

Read:
Proverbs, Chapter 14

Today we observe

International E-waste Day

World Standards Day

On this day in history

Notable events

In 1922, the first automated telephones, the Pennsylvania exchange in New York City, became operational.

Births

Elwood Haynes, American inventor, metallurgist, entrepreneur, and industrialist; designer of one of the earliest automobiles made in the U.S., 1857

Dwight D. Eisenhower, 34th U.S. President, 1890

W. Edwards Deming, American business theorist, industrial engineer, statistician, management consultant, and writer known as the father of the quality movement, 1900

George Harold Brown, American research engineer, speaker, and prolific inventor (held more than 80 patents) who led RCA's efforts to develop a color television system still in use today, 1908

Frank E. Resnik, American businessman, CEO and chairman of Philip Morris USA, 1928

Ralph Lauren, American fashion designer, philanthropist, and businessman best known for the Ralph Lauren Corporation, 1939

Deaths

Clarence Saunders, American grocer who first developed the modern retail sales model of self service, developer of Piggly Wiggly, Keedoozle, and Foodelectric store concepts, 1953

> Grow your faith by keeping a daily prayer journal. List what you prayed for, then go back and record what happened.

October 15

Then Jesus declared, "I am the bread of life. Whoever comes to me will never go hungry, and whoever believes in me will never be thirsty. *(John 6:35, NIV)*

What can we learn from others in different industries?

What do a medical office and a trucking company have in common? Or an independent restaurant and a large manufacturing plant?

They're all trying to sell quality products or services at a reasonable or even premium price.

You may think you're dealing with issues that no one outside your industry could possibly understand or be able to help with. You're not. The strategies for running an efficient, profitable business transcend industries.

When you find yourself stuck as you're looking for a solution to a problem or trying to come up with that great idea that will take your company to the next level, look at other fields for inspiration. Look for patterns, principles, and strategies that are working in one sector that can be applied in another.

Mastermind groups or business roundtables are great resources for leaders who recognize what different industries have in common and who want to help each other by sharing ideas and experiences. If you've been operating in a silo, it's time to step out and go wide. The opportunities and benefits are limitless.

I pray on the qualifications for leadership in 2 Samuel 23:2-4 & 6-7.

Your fears and anxieties are lying to you. Don't believe them.

Today we observe
National Grouch Day

Global Handwashing Day

On this day in history

Notable events

In 1950, Telanserphone (later Aircall) of New York City, the first American radio paging service, sent its first page to a doctor who was on a golf course 25 miles away.

In 2004, the National Highway Traffic Safety Administration ruled that hearse manufacturers no longer had to install anchors for child-safety seats in their vehicles.

In 2007, the Fox Business Network (FBN) was launched.

Births

Hiram Fong, American businessman, lawyer, and politician, 1906

Lee Iacocca, American automobile executive and author, 1924

John Coleman, American journalist, cofounder of The Weather Channel, and broadcaster, 1934

Deaths

Herbert Henry Dow, American industrialist (Dow Chemical) and inventor, 1930

Edie Adams, American comedian, actress, singer, and businesswoman, 2008

Paul Allen, American businessman, investor, and philanthropist, cofounder of Microsoft, 2018

Suzanne Somers, American actress, author, and businesswoman, 2023

Thought for the day

"Never ruin an apology with an excuse."
Benjamin Franklin

Read:
Proverbs, Chapter 15

October 16

> ❝God does all these things to a person—twice, even three times—to turn them back from the pit, that the light of life may shine on them. *(Job 33:29–30, NIV)*

Retirement is not biblical

Are you looking forward to the time when you can stop working and just relax all day? Michelle Ogden, founder and CEO of Ogden Wealth, LLC (Maitland, Florida), suggests you might want to rethink that.

"We were created to work. It's part of God's plan for us," she says. "When God created Adam and put him in the Garden of Eden, he told him to work it and take care of it. Period. Not work until he was 65. Not work until he had saved enough money to retire. God just said to work."

Ogden says it's not biblical to assume we'll reach a time when we no longer work. "The Bible doesn't address our modern-day concept of retirement, but it still offers plenty of guidance for how to approach this season," she says. "The Bible praises work and condemns laziness. To define retirement as a time when you can stop working and cease being productive is completely unbiblical—and not very enjoyable."

Because much of our identity and community comes from the work we do, she says, "It's essential that we don't simply retire *from* something—we need to retire *to* something. Transition into something different that you're going to love as much or more."

When you reject the traditional concept of retirement, you're in good company. "Think about some of the best-known servants of God in the Bible. Even at very advanced ages, they never stopped working for the Lord," Ogden says. "Think about the people you know who are in their senior years. When you look at the ones who live each day in deep joy, what do they have in common? They all do some sort of work."

Her advice: "It's okay to leave our jobs, but what are we leaving them for? Make it about reassignment, not retirement."

Today we observe

Dictionary Day
National Department Store Day

On this day in history

Notable events
In 1923, brothers Walt and Roy Disney launched the Disney Brothers Cartoon Studio, now called The Walt Disney Company.

Births
Noah Webster, Jr., American lexicographer, textbook pioneer, English-language spelling reformer, editor, and author, 1758
Suzanne Somers, American actress, author, and businesswoman, 1946

Deaths
Jon Postel, American computer scientist who made significant contributions to the development of the internet, particularly with respect to standards, 1998

Thought for the day

"There is no way to understand the real options involved in the future unless you become involved in creating them."
Robert Theobald

I am thankful for the amazing generosity of others.

Pray even when you think you don't have time or you don't feel like it. That's when you need prayer the most.

Read:
Proverbs, Chapter 16

October 17

Anyone who does not provide for their relatives, and especially for their own household, has denied the faith and is worse than an unbeliever. (1 Timothy 5:8, NIV)

Never ask anyone to do something you wouldn't do

There are so many lessons to be gained from the story of Jesus washing the disciples' feet. One important one is to never ask anyone to do something you wouldn't do.

This doesn't mean that a senior manager must also clean a few dirty toilets, it means that the senior manager must be willing to clean those toilets if necessary and treat the person who does with respect.

There's more to this important life and business guideline than doing the dirty, low-level jobs. For example:

Don't ask someone to do something unethical that you wouldn't do but would benefit from.

Don't ask an employee or service provider to make personal sacrifices to get the work done that you're not willing to make yourself (and even if you are, think carefully about making that request).

Don't ask customers to do things you don't like to do in order to do business with you, such as providing unnecessary personal information or having to navigate a challenging website.

Don't ask employees or suppliers to cut corners that would reduce the quality of your product to the point that you wouldn't use it yourself.

If you're not willing to do it, why should anyone else be?

Thought for the day

"Sin may be personal but it is never private. It always affects those around you."
Rick Warren

Read:
Proverbs, Chapter 17

Today we observe
Mulligan Day

On this day in history

Notable events

In 1904, the Bank of Italy (later Bank of America) opened in San Francisco.

In 1919, the Radio Corporation of American (RCA) was formed as a patent trust owned by General Electric (GE), Westinghouse, AT&T Corporation and United Fruit Company.

Births

Doug McMillon, American businessman, president and CEO of Walmart, Inc., who joined the company as a summer associate in high school, 1966

Deaths

Carl Linder Jr., American businessman and philanthropist, founder of American Financial Group, 2011

Stanford R. Ovshinsky, American engineer, scientist, businessman, and inventor (over 400 patents), best known for nickel-metal hydride battery and phase-change memory, 2012

Why we require God

"I have also shown people why, on purely rational grounds, without the God of the Bible, there is no objective good and evil, since without the biblical God, 'good' and 'evil' are purely subjective personal or societal opinions," says Dennis Prager, American talk show host and writer. "And I have shown that without the God of the Bible, our lives and all human life have no ultimate significance, that our lives have no more ultimate meaning than some rock on some planet."

I pray for the people who wish me ill.

October 18

> ❝ Your eye is like a lamp that provides light for your body. When your eye is healthy, your whole body is filled with light. But when your eye is unhealthy, your whole body is filled with darkness. And if the light you think you have is actually darkness, how deep that darkness is! *(Matthew 6:22-23, NLT)*

Friends in low places

In *Live a Life that Matters for God*, Jack Alan Levine writes this about who we associate with:

"God says in Romans 12:16, 'Don't be proud, but be willing to associate with people of low position. Do not be conceited.'

"How comfortable are you associating with people of low position? It's not about job title; it's not about bank account. It's about heart.

"There's no difference between us and people who are homeless or otherwise underprivileged. We might have a nicer address and a nicer house and probably a nicer bank account than they do; compared to them, we're probably the richest people in the world. But you know what? That could be me. That could be you. We could get sick tomorrow, or lose our job and then our house. It could all happen to any of us. It's just the cards that God dealt us.

"God is the potter. We are the clay. Who are we to say to the potter, 'Look what you've done?' God is using us for his purposes. We're to be grateful for that, but we're to make sure that we never look down on someone else based on their position, their color, their bank account, their job, where they live, how they talk, or what they look like."

Thought for the day

"Do not pray for tasks equal to your powers. Pray for powers equal to your tasks."

Phillips Brooks

Read:
Proverbs, Chapter 18

On this day in history

Notable events
In 1954, Texas Instruments demonstrated its all-transistor AM radio.

Births
Ellen Browning Scripps, American journalist, philanthropist, and cofounder of the E. W. Scripps Company, founder of the Scripps Research Institute and Scripps College, 1836

Harvey W. Wiley, American chemist who advocated for the passage of the Pure Food and Drug Act of 1906, 1844

Charles Scribner II, American publisher, president of Charles Scribner's Sons, founding member of the American Publishers Association, 1854

Deaths
Thomas Edison, American inventor and businessman, 1931

Charles Strite, American inventor (automatic pop-up toaster), 1956

Elizabeth Arden, Canadian-American businesswoman, founder of the cosmetics empire now known as Elizabeth Arden, Inc., 1966

Vincent DeDomenico, American entrepreneur, inventor of Rice-A-Roni, founder of Napa Valley Wine Train, 2007

I pray to know when to speak and when to be silent.

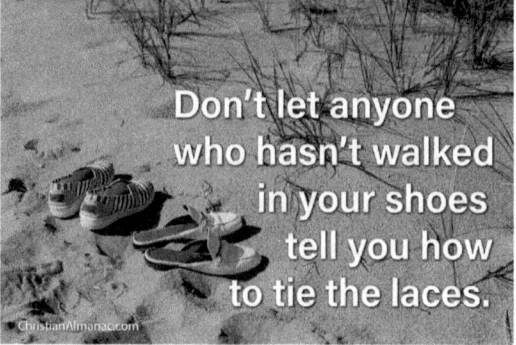

October 19

"You are blessed because you believed that the Lord would do what he said." *(Luke 1:45, NLT)*

How to reduce burnout risk

Workplace burnout is a real problem and much of it can be rightfully blamed on the organization. But if we're feeling burned out, we may share some of the responsibility.

These tips will help you reduce the risk of burnout, even when the corporate culture is working against you.

Prioritize self-care. Don't sacrifice your physical, emotional, and mental wellbeing for the sake of your job. Eat well, get plenty of rest, take breaks, and engage in activities that will help you relax and recharge.

Think positively. Be intentionally optimistic. Certainly you need to be realistic, but focusing on the positive will reduce stress, which leads to burnout.

Set boundaries. Create clear lines between your professional and personal lives. Also, set realistic expectations for your work performance.

Don't over commit. Be honest and transparent about your workload and availability. Know what you can and can't do, and say no when it's appropriate.

Don't try to multitask. Our brains can only do one thing at a time. Trying to juggle multiple tasks or projects simultaneously will leave you overwhelmed and unable to be effective at anything. Focus on one task at a time. Use time-blocking techniques and delegate when possible.

Ask for help when you need it. Even in a small organization, you don't have to handle everything by yourself. It's better to ask for assistance than to miss a deadline or do poor quality work.

Hone your time management skills. Learn to manage your time effectively using techniques such as breaking tasks down into smaller chunks, creating to-do lists, using technology, and realistic goal setting.

On this day in history

Notable events

In 1973, the OAPEC oil embargo began, leading to the U.S. automotive market switching to smaller, more fuel-efficient cars.

In 1976, the first major revision to U.S. copyright law since 1909 became effective with the Copyright Act of 1976.

In 1987, the first Blockbuster video rental store opened in Dallas, Texas, with 8,000 tapes displayed on shelves around the store and a computerized checkout process.

In 1987, on what has become known as Black Monday, the stock market crashed 22.6 percent in one day, the largest-ever one-day percentage decline in the Dow Jones Industrial Average.

Births

Cassius Marcellus Clay, American planter, politician, military officer, and abolitionist, 1810

Charles E. Merrill, American investment banker, stockbroker, philanthropist, and cofounder of Merrill Lynch, 1885

Deaths

George Pullman, American industrialist and inventor (railway sleeping car), 1897

Philip Drinker, American industrial hygienist, inventor of the first widely used iron lung, 1972

Lewis Urry, Canadian-American chemical engineer and inventor; invented both the alkaline battery and lithium battery while working for Eveready Battery, 2004

Thought for the day

"Integrity is the essence of everything successful."

Richard Buckminster Fuller

I am thankful for the hands that raised me.

Read:
Proverbs, Chapter 19

October 20

> ❝ Father, I want those you have given me to be with me where I am, and to see my glory, the glory you have given me because you loved me before the creation of the world. *(John 17:24, NIV)*

Do all to the glory of God

He who surrenders himself without reservation to the temporal claims of a nation, or a party, or a class is rendering to Caesar that which, of all things, most emphatically belongs to God: himself.

It is for a very different reason that religion cannot occupy the whole of life in the sense of excluding all our natural activities. For, of course, in some sense, it must occupy the whole of life. There is no question of a compromise between the claims of God and the claims of culture, or politics, or anything else. God's claim is infinite and inexorable. You can refuse it or you can begin to try to grant it. There is no middle way.

Yet in spite of this it is clear that Christianity does not exclude any of the ordinary human activities. St. Paul tells people to get on with their jobs. He even assumes that Christians may go to dinner parties, and, what is more, dinner parties given by pagans. Our Lord attends a wedding and provides miraculous wine. Under the aegis of his Church, and in the most Christian ages, learning and the arts flourish. The solution of this paradox is, of course, well known to you. "Whether ye eat or drink or whatsoever ye do, do all to the glory of God."

All our merely natural activities will be accepted, if they are offered to God, even the humblest, and all of them, even the noblest, will be sinful if they are not. Christianity does not simply replace our natural life and substitute a new one; it is rather a new organization which exploits, to its own supernatural ends, these natural materials.

Excerpted from "Learning in War Time," a sermon by C.S. Lewis, 1939

Today we observe

Information Overload Day
National Day on Writing
Community Media Day

On this day in history

Notable events

In 1928, Wien Alaska Airways was incorporated; it was the first airline in Alaska and one of the first in the U.S. It ceased operations in 1984.

Births

Alfred Gwynne Vanderbilt, American businessman and member of the Vanderbilt family, died in the sinking of the RMS *Lusitania*, 1877

Tracy Hall, American physical chemist and early pioneer in the research of synthetic diamonds, 1919

Brown Meggs, American writer, music executive, and publisher know for signing the Beatles to their first distribution contract in the U.S., 1930

Deaths

Lawrence Dale Bell, American industrialist and founder of Bell Aircraft Corporation, 1956

Herbert C. Hoover, 31st U.S. President, 1964

Lawrence Klein, American economist known for his work in creating computer models to forecast economic trends, 2013

Thought for the day

"Nothing is impossible; the word itself says I'm possible!"

Audrey Hepburn

I am thankful that God's Word never changes.

Read:
Proverbs, Chapter 20

October 21

"Have I not commanded you? Be strong and courageous. Do not be afraid; do not be discouraged, for the Lord your God will be with you wherever you go." *(Joshua 1:9, NIV)*

Are you looking in the right direction?

One of the first things a driving instructor teaches is that you will likely steer your vehicle in the direction you're looking. Former car racing champion and driving instructor Gary Magwood puts it simply: "You steer where you stare."

That's fine if you're on an open road without obstacles. It could be trouble on a congested street or if there's a wreck ahead.

In driving and in life, your hands follow your vision. What you do will move you in the direction you're looking.

If you spend a lot of time looking at (or for) the negative, that's the direction your life will take. If you continually look back in regret, anger, or frustration, that's what the future will likely hold for you.

When a situation is going the way you want, stop and consider where you're looking. Are you looking at the problems or the solutions? Are you looking at the failures or the successes? Are you looking at the world or at the kingdom of God? Discipline yourself to look where you truly want to go.

Thought for the day

"The best way to show that a stick is crooked is not to argue about it or to spend time denouncing it, but to lay a straight stick alongside it."

Dwight L. Moody

I pray to see those who need my strength and faith.

Read: Proverbs, Chapter 21

Today we observe
National Check Your Meds Day

On this day in history
Notable events
In 1989, Peter Bynoe and Betram Lee purchased the Denver Nuggets for $65 million.

Births
William A. Mitchell, American food chemist and inventor (received over 70 patents) who was the key inventor behind Pop Rocks, Tang, Cool Whip, and powdered egg whites, 1911

Samuel W. Alderson, American inventor best known for developing the crash test dummy, 1914

Martin Gardner, American author and popular science and mathematics writer, and magician, authored the "Mathematical Games" column in *Scientific American* for twenty-five years, 1914

Kim Kardashian, media personality, businesswoman, activist, 1980

Ask a friend to check out your website

Is your website user-friendly and effective? One way to check is to ask a friend or family member to test it. Find someone outside of your organization who isn't already familiar with the site. Give them a specific task, such as finding a certain piece of information, subscribing to your email list, or making a (refundable) purchase.

Ask them for honest feedback on the process. Was the purpose of your site clear to them? Was accomplishing the task easy or difficult? If they didn't know you, would they have completed the task or abandoned it? What suggestions do they have for improvement?

Use their input to make positive changes on your site.

October 22

> Every good and perfect gift is from above, coming down from the Father of the heavenly lights, who does not change like shifting shadows. *(James 1:17, NIV)*

Essential critical thinking skills

The ability to analyze facts objectively and form a judgment is a type of emotional intelligence we call critical thinking. Critical thinking skills help you see beyond the obvious, think clearly and rationally, and be more effective at problem-solving and decision-making. Important critical thinking skills include:

The ability to identify biases. Recognizing the biases of others and yourself will help you reduce the influence bias has on your judgment.

The ability to draw conclusions based on available information. Use the facts you have plus what you know about other situations to determine a course of action.

The ability to do effective research. When you don't have all the necessary information, you need to be able to discover the facts and figures you need to form an opinion or course of action.

The ability to identify a problem and what's influencing it. Recognizing the problem is important, but equally so is to find causes so you can reach a solution.

The ability to practice intellectual curiosity. Critical thinkers aren't afraid to question anything and everything with an open mind.

The ability to judge relevance. Not all information is equal; know what to give more weight to as you're doing an evaluation.

Improve your critical thinking skills by:
- Questioning your assumptions.
- Questioning other people's opinions before adopting them.
- Weighing the consequences of various choices before taking action.
- Playing games that require critical thinking skills.
- Seeking out diversity of thought.

Today we observe
Smart is Cool Day

On this day in history

Notable events

In 1906, Henry Ford became president of Ford Motor Company (the company's first president was investor John S. Gray and Ford was the vice president and chief engineer).

In 2016, AT&T announced it would acquire Time Warner for $85.4 billion.

Births

Stephen Moulton Babcock, American agricultural chemist, best known for the Babcock test, used to determine butterfat content in milk and cheese processing, 1843

Collis P. Huntington, American industrialist and railroad magnate (Central Pacific Railroad, Southern Pacific Railroad, Chesapeake & Ohio Railway), 1821

William Higinbotham, American physicist, member of team that developed the first nuclear bomb, inventor of *Tennis for Two*, the first interactive analog computer game, 1910

Deaths

John G. Shedd, American businessman and philanthropist, second president and board chair of Marshall Field & Company, 1926

Thought for the day

"If we learn to open our hearts, anyone, including the people who drive us crazy, can be our teacher."

Pema Chedron

I pray for my clients and customers.

Read:
Proverbs, Chapter 22

October 23

I know how to live on almost nothing or with everything. I have learned the secret of living in every situation, whether it is with a full stomach or empty, with plenty or little. For I can do everything through Christ, who gives me strength. *(Philippians 4:12-13, NLT)*

Helping employees through financial emergencies

One of the many ways Children's Discovery Center (Toledo, Ohio) demonstrates the faith of its founder and leaders is by paying above-market wages and providing generous benefits. But sometimes life happens, and employees are faced with an unexpected expense they can't cover.

"We recognized the need to establish a benevolent account to assist with emergency situations," says Lois Rosenberry, the company's founder, president, and CEO.

To request assistance, employees complete an application that explains the situation and how much is needed. The request is reviewed and, if approved, funds are dispersed in the form of a grant that does not have to be repaid.

Rosenberry says, "In many instances, we have been able to keep good employees who otherwise may have resigned."

Thought for the day

"Achievement seems to be connected with action. Successful men and women keep moving. They make mistakes, but they don't quit."

Conrad Hilton

I am thankful for the promise of God as my protection.

Read:
Proverbs, Chapter 23

On this day in history

Notable events
In 2001, Apple unveiled the first iPod, which could hold and play about 1,000 songs.

Births
Samuel Morey, American inventor (early internal combustion engines) and steamship pioneer, 1762
Henry John Heinz, III, American businessman and politician, 1938

Deaths
Luther George Simjian, Armenian-American inventor and entrepreneur who held more than 200 patents (most significant were a pioneering flight simulator, the first ATM, and improvement to the teleprompter), 1997
Jack Chick, American cartoonist and publisher (Chick Publications), best known for cartoon gospel tracts, 2016

Strengthen your presentations

Present to share and teach, not to impress. Find out what your audience needs to know and present that in a way they'll understand.

Don't repeat what others have said. If someone else has said it already, you don't need to say it again.

Be concise and to the point. Details and supporting data can be provided outside your presentation to those who want and need it.

When you don't know something, be transparent and honest. If you get a question you can't answer, say that you'll find out and get back to the individual or group with the information.

Respect the schedule. Stay within the allotted time or, better yet, finish sooner.

October 24

If you refrain from trampling the Sabbath, from pursuing your own interests on my holy day; if you call the Sabbath a delight and the holy day of the Lord honorable; if you honor it, not going your own ways, serving your own interests or pursuing your own affairs; then you shall take delight in the Lord, and I will make you ride upon the heights of the earth; I will feed you with the heritage of your ancestor Jacob, for the mouth of the Lord has spoken. *(Isaiah 58:13–14, NRSVue)*

Do less, but do it better

If you're feeling frustrated because you're not getting enough done, it might be time to change your strategy to doing less. Often, productivity is reduced because we're trying to do too much. We spread ourselves too thin and consequently nothing gets done, or what does get done doesn't get done well.

Instead of trying to accomplish a long list of tasks, pick one or two of them, and do them exceptionally well.

Of course, if you're going to take the do less but better approach, you need to prioritize what you actually do. Those tasks need to be the most important items on your to-do list. And when they're done, you can move to the next most important items—and do them better.

Before you criticize

Often what irritates us most about other people are the same characteristics we have that we don't like about ourselves. When we're getting ready to find fault with someone, we should instead ask ourselves what it is about us that most closely resembles what we're getting ready to criticize. If we're objective and honest—as painful as it might be—we might discover a transformational self-improvement opportunity.

Rather than spending time expressing negative emotions directed either outwardly or inwardly, focus on the positive changes we can make in ourselves.

I pray that I will always seek God first.

Today we observe
Take Back Your Time Day

On this day in history
Notable events
- In 1861, Western Union completed the first transcontinental telegraph line and the first transcontinental telegraph message was sent by Justice Stephen J. Field of California to President Abraham Lincoln.
- In 1929, "Black Thursday" marked the beginning of the Wall Street Crash of 1929.
- In 1939, nylon stockings went on sale in the U.S. for the first time to employees at DuPont's Wilmington, Delaware nylon factory. Nationwide sales began on May 15, 1940.

Births
- Nathaniel C. Wyeth, American mechanical engineer and inventor best known for the plastic soda bottle, 1911
- Frank Piasecki, American engineer and helicopter aviation pioneer, 1919

Deaths
- S. B. Fuller, American entrepreneur, publisher, founder of the Fuller Products Company, 1988
- John McCarthy, American computer scientist, cognitive scientist, one of the founders of the discipline of artificial intelligence, 2011

Thought for the day

"I would rather earn one percent off 100 people's efforts than 100 percent of my own efforts."

John D. Rockefeller

Read:
Proverbs, Chapter 24

October 25

> And it is impossible to please God without faith. Anyone who wants to come to him must believe that God exists and that he rewards those who sincerely seek him. *(Hebrews 11:6, NLT)*

Respond to online reviews

Reviews are an integral part of the purchase process for most consumers. As important as it is to ask for reviews, it's equally—if not more—important to respond to them, whether they're negative or positive.

Monitor the sites where reviews are posted and respond personally to every one, using the reviewer's name if possible. Thank the reviewer for taking the time to leave their input. Include language in your comment that makes it clear you actually read the review and are not using boilerplate responses.

If the reviewer asks a question, answer it. If they write something inaccurate, politely correct it.

For positive reviews, let them know you're glad to hear they had a good experience.

When the review is negative, don't get defensive. Be conversational and professional. Apologize, empathize, and take ownership of the situation. Offer a practical resolution to the issue, but don't ask the reviewer to change their review.

Each online review platform has its own flagging or appeals process. It's a good idea to research that in advance so you can take swift action when necessary. If a review violates the platform's terms of service or you suspect a review is fake, report it to the platform immediately.

Dealing with online reviews takes time and effort, but it's an essential element in preserving your brand reputation and strengthening your customer relationships.

On this day in history

Notable events

In 2001, Microsoft released Windows XP for retail sale.

Births

John Francis Dodge, American automobile pioneer (cofounder of Dodge Brothers Company), 1864

John Willys, American automotive pioneer and diplomat, founder of Willys-Overland Motors, which became the second largest carmaker in the U.S. (after Ford), 1873

Deaths

Frank J. Sprague, American inventor who contributed to the development of the electric motor, electric railways, and electric elevators, 1934

Peter L. Jensen, Danish-American engineer, inventor, and entrepreneur, founder of Magnavox and Jensen Radio Manufacturing Company, 1961

Why are you doing that?

Do everything for a reason. Not just because that's the way it's always been done or because that's the policy, but for a reason.

Always know why you're doing what you're doing and be sure it's for the best reason.

Thought for the day

"We must not allow the clock and the calendar to blind us to the fact that each moment of life is a miracle and mystery."
— *H. G. Wells*

 *Read:* Proverbs, Chapter 25

I am thankful when I am able to check things off my to-do list.

October 26

I consider that our present sufferings are not worth comparing with the glory that will be revealed in us. *(Romans 8:18, NIV)*

Dealing with distracting thoughts

One of the challenges many of us have in prayer is focusing on praying and not being distracted by noise, whether it's in our minds or our environment. In *Even Silence is Praise: quiet your mind and awaken your soul with Christian meditation*, Rick Hamlin writes:

"I don't want to think about that is a sure recipe for thinking about anything. That which you pretend to bury grows into a little gremlin. That which you doggedly ignore will speak up—loudly.

"Catch-and-release is a technique I've heard recommended. It makes a lot of sense: catch the thought or interruption, and release it. Better yet, put it into a prayer. *That song reminds me of my mom.* Pray for her. *That radiator needs to be fixed.* Pray for those who live on the streets without heat. *Can't that woman come up with a better ringtone for her phone?* becomes *Lord, help me let go of all my judgmental attitudes.* Make your prayers short. Brevity is the soul of wit. The point is, you can catch and release any of it, and all of it, to God."

Thought for the day

"Business opportunities are like buses, there's always another one coming."
— Richard Branson

I pray to be a gracious loser when I don't win.

Read:
Proverbs, Chapter 26

Today we observe
National Day of the Deployed

On this day in history

Notable events
- In 1861, the Pony Express mail service between Missouri and California using relays of horse-mounted riders ceased operations.
- In 1881, the Earp brothers faced off against the Clanton-McLaury gang in the legendary shootout at the O.K. Corral in Tombstone, Arizona.
- In 2010, with cassette tapes being nearly obsolete, Sony took the Walkman cassette player off the market.

Births
- C. W. Post, American innovator, breakfast and cereal foods manufacturer, and pioneer in the prepared-food industry, founder of what is now Post Consumer Brands, 1854
- Benjamin Guggenheim, American businessman, member of the Guggenheim family, died in the sinking of the *Titanic*, 1865
- Napoleon Hill, controversial American self-help author best known for his book, *Think and Grow Rich*, 1883
- Charles Bedaux, French-American efficiency engineer who developed the Bedaux plan for measuring and compensating industrial labor, 1886
- John S. Knight, American newspaper publisher and editor, cofounder of Knight Ridder newspapers, 1894

Deaths
- Harry Payne Whitney, American businessman and thoroughbred horse breeder, 1930
- Igor Sikorsky, Russian-American aviation pioneer in helicopters and fixed-wing aircraft, 1972
- William S. Paley, American businessman who began his career in the family cigar business and is best known for building the Columbia Broadcasting System into one of the foremost radio and television network operations in the U.S., 1990

October 27

W e are careful to be honorable before the Lord, but we also want everyone else to see that we are honorable. *(2 Corinthians 8:21, NLT)*

Honor the Sabbath

On February 9, 1945, as World War II still raged, government officials placed an emergency call to Correct Craft (Orlando, Florida), one of several suppliers building boats for the military. General Dwight D. Eisenhower needed hundreds of boats to cross the Rhine River on March 10. The company's owner, Walter C. Meloon, prayed and told the Army Correct Craft would produce 300 boats—*six times* the normal production schedule for February.

The plant geared up for the seemingly impossible task by adding workers and retooling the facility. Government expeditors provided assistance and support, and asked Correct Craft to run a seven-day-a-week operation during the emergency.

Meloon refused, saying, "We intend to do the work to the glory of God. It's not his plan to work seven days a week. God built this world in six days and rested on the seventh. That's what we're going to do, and we're going to trust him for the results."

The initial order was completed four days ahead of schedule, and then Correct Craft built another 100 boats that other manufacturers who were operating seven days a week were unable to produce. In all, Correct Craft delivered 406 boats in less than a month, and General Eisenhower's plan was a success.

"It's called a miracle in boatbuilding," Meloon said. "To us, it was simply an indication that the Lord honors the obedience of his children."

I am thankful for the ability to feel and express my emotions.

Read:
Proverbs, Chapter 27

Today we observe
International Religious Freedom Day
National Mentoring Day
National Civics Day

On this day in history

Notable events
In 1904, the New York City subway opened.
In 1997, Intel and Digital Equipment announced a settlement in a patent litigation lawsuit filed by Digital that included the sale of Digital's semiconductor manufacturing operations to Intel for about $700 million.
In 2006, Chick-fil-A founder Truett Cathy became the owner of the last Ford Taurus to roll off the assembly line in Hapeville, Georgia.
In 2022, Elon Musk took ownership and control of Twitter and immediately fired four executives.

Births
Isaac Singer, American inventor, actor, and businessman, founder of what became one of the first American multinational businesses, the Singer Sewing Machine Company, 1811
Theodore Roosevelt, 26th U.S. President, 1858
John M. Mack, American inventor (Mack "Bulldog" truck engine) and manufacturer, cofounder of the Mack Brothers Company which became Mack Trucks Inc., 1864
Owen D. Young, American industrialist, businessman, lawyer, diplomat, known for the plan to settle Germany's World War I reparations and for the creation of Radio Corporation of America (RCA), 1874

Thought for the day

"Respect your efforts, respect yourself. Self-respect leads to self-discipline. When you have both firmly under your belt, that's real power."

Clint Eastwood

October 28

A nyone who resolves to do the will of God will know whether the teaching is from God or whether I am speaking on my own. *(John 7:17, NRSVue)*

Integrate a life of faith in business

"A 'Christian company' or 'kingdom businessperson' without faith in God and his Word and without the presence and leading of the Holy Spirit is nothing more than a human effort wearing religious clothing," says international lawyer and cofounder of the International Christian Chamber of Commerce James Lockett.

He offers these five principles for integrating a life of faith in business:

1. Listen and obey. Be radically obedient. We can go no further in the natural realm than we have already gone in the Spirit. We receive by faith through the Holy Spirit. Live a life of integrity, loving God and your neighbors.

2. Let God be God. Don't limit what God might do. Our ways are not his ways, so get out of God's way.

3. Surrender to God's guidance. What often makes no sense at the time can lead to great success. If we do business with faith, we please God. He is a rewarder.

4. Expect miracles. In John 14:12, Jesus says, "Anyone who believes in me will do the same works I have done, and even greater works." Greater works should be normative in our walk and include many other miracles and deeds that Jesus never did.

5. Walk in your calling. God will not be a tool in your hand, but he will bless the tool in your hand. Answer when he tells you to cast your net on the other side of the boat.

I pray for those who encourage me as I grow in my faith.

Read:
Proverbs, Chapter 28

Today we observe
National First Responders Day

On this day in history

Notable events

In 2010, the Federal Communications Commission ordered Verizon to pay $25 million to the U.S. Treasury and a minimum of $52.8 million to approximately 15 million customers who were erroneously charged "mystery" data fees.

In 2021, Facebook CEO Mark Zuckerberg announced the company's new name: Meta.

Births

Eliphalet Remington, American engineer and firearms manufacturer who founded what would become known as Remington Arms, 1793

Jonas Salk, American medical researcher and virologist who created the polio vaccine, 1914

Bill Gates, American business magnate, investor, philanthropist, and writer, cofounder of Microsoft, 1955

Indra Nooyi, Indian-American businesswoman, former chairman and CEO of PepsiCo, 1955

Jawed Karim, American software engineer and internet entrepreneur, cofounder of YouTube, 1979

Deaths

Cleveland Abbe, American meteorologist, inventor, advocate of time zones, known as the father of the U.S. Weather Bureau, 1916

Doris Duke, American billionaire tobacco heiress, philanthropist, and socialite, 1993

Thought for the day

"Always be a first-rate version of yourself, instead of a second-rate version of somebody else."

Judy Garland

October 29

It is you who light my lamp; the Lord, my God, lights up my darkness. *(Psalm 18:28, NRSVue)*

Dating in the workplace

More than three-quarters of Americans have at least considered dating someone they worked with, and more than half of them actually did. The problem is, not every dating couple has a successful ending—and even when they do, personal relationships can create problems in the workplace.

Your company doesn't necessarily need to ban coworkers dating, but you should have a policy on personal relationships at work. Consider including:

- A clear definition of a personal relationship.
- A statement that provides common sense practices, such as discouraging or prohibiting relationships between supervisors and their direct reports.
- A requirement to report a personal relationship that has developed and a confidential mechanism so that employees can inform their supervisors or HR.
- Guidelines for conduct at work, such as prohibiting employees from engaging in inappropriate physical conduct during working time and in working areas.
- Documentation procedures, such as having individuals involved in a romantic relationship sign a consensual relationship agreement.
- Guidelines for how problems that may arise from a personal relationship, either while it exists or after it has ended, will be resolved.

I pray for the causes I believe in and support.

Read:
Proverbs, Chapter 29

Today we observe

National Internet Day

World Online Networking Day

On this day in history

Notable events

In 1945, ballpoint pens went on sale in the U.S. for the first time at Gimbels in New York City for $12.50 each; thousands of pens were sold in the first week.

In 1996, AOL changed its hourly fee to a flat monthly rate.

In 2008, in an attempt to keep costs down and their planes flying, Delta Air Lines and Northwest Airlines merged, creating the world's largest airline.

Deaths

Joseph Pulitzer, Hungarian-American newspaper publisher and politician, established the Pulitzer Prize, 1911

Moorfield Storey, American lawyer, activist, and civil rights leader; first president of the NAACP, 1929

Louis B. Mayer, Canadian-American film producer, cofounder of Metro-Goldwyn-Mayer (MGM), 1957

Thought for the day

"You cannot live a perfect day without doing something for someone who will never be able to repay you."

John Wooden

October 30

When you search for me, you will find me; if you seek me with all your heart, *(Jeremiah 29:13, NRSVue)*

What to do when you're the source of your problems

We all have problems, but blaming others for them is a waste of time. A more effective approach is to look inward, figure out what you could do differently, and what you can change. Jordan B. Peterson, Canadian psychologist and author, says that while it's easier to blame someone else for your misery, you can't change other people. But with courage and discipline, you can change yourself.

"There are people who seem to be consigned to a terrible fate. But most of us aren't," Peterson says. "Most of us have a chance to make our lives better."

Peterson's advice is to start small.

"As yourself a few questions: Have you taken full advantage of the opportunities offered to you? Are you working to your fullest capacity at school or at work? Have you set your own house in order? If the answer is no, try this: stop doing what you know to be wrong. Stop today."

Don't worry about the why of what you're doing, Peterson says. "Don't waste time asking how you know that what you're doing is wrong. You can know something is right or wrong without knowing why. It's not a matter of accepting some externally imposed morality. It's a dialogue with your own conscience. What are you doing that's wrong, from your own perspective? What could you put right, right now?"

You might not see immediate results, but over time, Peterson says, "You'll stop getting in your own way."

No one person can fix the world, but we can fix ourselves and, in doing so, make the world a better place.

Read:
Proverbs, Chapter 30

Today we observe
Checklist Day

Speak Up For Service Day

On this day in history

Notable events
In 1938, Orson Welles' broadcast of "The War of the Worlds" caused a national panic.

Births
John Adams, 2nd U.S. President (served as the first Vice President under George Washington), 1735

Albert Rice Leventhal, American publisher (Little Golden Books), 1907

Verne Winchell, American businessman, founder of Winchell's Donuts, served as chairman, president, and CEO of the Denny's restaurant chain, 1915

Ivanka Trump, American businesswoman and entrepreneur, 1981

Deaths
William H. Webb, American shipbuilder and philanthropist, called America's first true naval architect, 1899

Thought for the day

"A conscience that is bound by the Word of God is a force that no nation, system, or age can withstand."

R. Bruce Bickel

I pray that I always look to God for answers.

> Grow your faith by exercising self-control so you will not be susceptible to temptation.

October 31

But someone may ask, "How will the dead be raised? What kind of bodies will they have?" What a foolish question! When you put a seed into the ground, it doesn't grow into a plant unless it dies first. And what you put in the ground is not the plant that will grow, but only a bare seed of wheat or whatever you are planting. Then God gives it the new body he wants it to have. A different plant grows from each kind of seed. Similarly there are different kinds of flesh—one kind for humans, another for animals, another for birds, and another for fish. *(1 Corinthians 15:35–39, NLT)*

Time off is not a reward, it's a requirement

Do you think of time off (weekends and vacations) as something you've *earned* or as something you *need*?

If you think of rest as something you've earned, you've bought into a self-destructive work ethic that will ultimately do you more harm than good. We need rest and relaxation to perform at our best at work or whatever endeavor we choose.

In agriculture, crops are rotated, and land is deliberately not used for one or more vegetative cycles. This allows the soil to recover its production potential and reduces the pest population. These fallow periods are not the land's rewards for the previous season's production; they are preparation for the next season. Without them, the fields wouldn't produce as much as they do with them.

When Jesus went off by himself to rest, it was not only because he was weary, it was because he knew that's what he needed to prepare himself for whatever he had to do next.

We are made to work and rest. But rest is not a reward for work, it's part of the necessary preparation for carrying out God's call. Respect the human need for rest for yourself and others and enjoy its energizing effect.

Today we observe

All Saints' Eve
Halloween
National Evangelism Day
Reformation Day

On this day in history

Notable events
In 1954, color television sets were made available to the public.

Births
Juliette Gordon Low, American activist and founder of the Girl Scouts of America, 1860
Eugene Meyer, American banker, businessman, financier, and newspaper publisher (*The Washington Post*), 1875
Donald Pritzker, American entrepreneur, businessman, president of Hyatt, 1932
Hobart "Hobie" Alter, American surf and sailing entrepreneur and pioneer, creator of the Hobie Cat catamarans, 1933

Deaths
Éleuthère Irénée du Pont, French-American chemist and industrialist, founded the gunpowder manufacturer E. I. du Pont de Nemours and Company (the original DuPont company), 1834

Thought for the day

"Have the clarity and courage to not enter every door and to not accept every invitation. Protect your peace."

Thema Davis

I pray that I love God's children more every day.

Read:
Proverbs, Chapter 31

Christian Business Almanac

November

November gets its name from the Latin *novem* meaning nine because it was the ninth month of the ancient Roman calendar.

The Anglo-Saxons called November by two names: Wind Monath (Wind Month), for the icy winds in the northern hemisphere at this time of year, and Blod Monath (Blood Month), describing the time of year when cows were killed to provide sustenance for the long winter.

November birthstone
Topaz and citrine

November flower
Chrysanthemum

November is ...
Alzheimer's Disease Awareness Month
Child Safety and Protection Month
COPD Awareness Month
Diabetes Awareness Month
International Creativity Month
Lung Cancer Awareness Month
National Adoption Month
National Family Caregivers Month
National Homeless Youth Awareness Month
National Novel Writing Month (NaNoWriMo)
Native American Heritage Month
Pancreatic Cancer Awareness Month
World Communication Month

Mark your calendar for these November holidays and observances

Third Tuesday in November	National Entrepreneur's Day
First Wednesday in November	International Stress Awareness Day
First Thursday in November	World Digital Preservation Day
First Thursday in November	International Project Management Day
First Monday in November	Job Action Day
Third Thursday in November	Great American Smokeout
Fourth Thursday in November	Thanksgiving
Friday after Thanksgiving	Black Friday
Saturday after Thanksgiving	Small Business Saturday
Monday after Thanksgiving	Cyber Monday, National Email Unsubscribe Day
Tuesday after Thanksgiving	Giving Tuesday

Fun Facts about November

November is the last of four months to have a length of 30 days and the fifth and last of five months to have a length of fewer than 31 days.

November marks the beginning of the winter holiday season for most people.

William Shakespeare wrote a total of 37 plays and 154 sonnets in the English language, and did not make any mention of the month of November in any of his writings.

November is the month when the highest number of memes are posted and shared on the internet (unverified).

November 1

It is the same way with the resurrection of the dead. Our earthly bodies are planted in the ground when we die, but they will be raised to live forever. Our bodies are buried in brokenness, but they will be raised in glory. They are buried in weakness, but they will be raised in strength. They are buried as natural human bodies, but they will be raised as spiritual bodies. For just as there are natural bodies, there are also spiritual bodies. *(1 Corinthians 15:42-44, NLT)*

Don't get too comfortable

Comfortable is defined as "providing physical ease and relaxation" and "as large as is needed or wanted."

It's okay to be comfortable, to have a cozy chair to relax in, to enjoy air conditioning in the summer and heat in the winter, to make enough money to meet your needs and have a few luxuries.

But don't get too comfortable for too long. Being comfortable invites complacency. It inhibits ambition. It creates dependency. And eventually, it stops us from fully living and realizing our potential.

What would the world look like if George Washington had chosen the comfort of Mount Vernon over leading the Army through the Revolutionary War and serving as the first President of the United States? What if Cornelius Vanderbilt had been comfortable working in his father's ferry business and never built the financial empire that changed the landscape of America with shipping, railroads, and more? What if Abraham Lincoln had opted for the comfortable life of a lawyer in Illinois instead of leading the United States through the Civil War?

Does this mean you shouldn't wear those comfy slippers? Of course not—just don't wear them all the time.

When you set goals, cross "comfortable" off your list. Be uncomfortable so you can seek ways to be meaningful, to have a positive impact, to make the world better.

Read:
Proverbs, Chapter 1

Today we observe
All Saints' Day
Give Up Your Shoulds Day
Kidpreneur Day
National Family Literacy Day

On this day in history

Notable events
In 1951, *Jet* magazine was launched.
In 1982, Honda because the first foreign-owned company to make cars in the U.S.
In 1985, Microsoft launched Microsoft Windows for the first time; it would be followed by several improved versions.

Births
George Parker, American inventor and industrialist, founder of Parker Pen Company, 1863
Charles Koch, American billionaire businessman, philanthropist, and author, co-owner of Koch Industries, 1935
Tim Cook, American business executive, CEO of Apple Inc., 1960

Deaths
Victor Mills, American chemical engineer for Procter & Gamble credited for the creation of modern disposable diapers and the Pampers brand, and the production concept for Pringles, 1997

Thought for the day

"As I grow older, I pay less attention to what men say. I just watch what they do."
Andrew Carnegie

I pray that I may not seek or need the approval of others.

November 2

> But blessed are those who trust in the Lord and have made the Lord their hope and confidence. They are like trees planted along a riverbank, with roots that reach deep into the water. Such trees are not bothered by the heat or worried by long months of drought. Their leaves stay green, and they never stop producing fruit. *(Jeremiah 17:7-8, NLT)*

Today we observe
All Souls' Day
Plan Your Epitaph Day

The choice of heaven or hell

In *Deep Waters: Lift Your Gaze*, Kim M. Clark writes:

"The stakes of unbelief in Jesus as our personal Savior is beyond huge—it's eternal. It is much bigger than our life here on this earth. We have a choice: eternity in heaven with our Creator or in the eternal unquenchable fires of hell.

"Walk gingerly, my friend. Heed the counsel of God incarnate, Jesus Christ. Listen to and obey the gentle tugging at your heart by the Holy Spirit, who urges all of us to reconcile with our Creator. We were created to worship God alone. Without doing what we were created for, we are continually looking for something to fill that God-sized hole in our hearts. The only thing that will fill the emptiness is the Spirit of God through our faith in his Son, Jesus Christ."

Thought for the day

"Do not spoil what you have by desiring what you have not; but remember that what you now have was once among the things you only hoped for."

Epicurus

I pray for the everyday, unsung heroes.

Read:
Proverbs, Chapter 2

On this day in history

Notable events

In 1907, banker and industrialist J. P. Morgan locked 40-50 bankers in his library to force them to find a solution to the pending banking crisis known as the Panic of 1907.

In 1988, the first computer worm spread across the internet, launched by Cornell University student Robert Tappan Morris. Morris was prosecuted and became the first person convicted under the then-new Computer Fraud and Abuse Act.

Births

James K. Polk, 11th U.S. President, 1795

Warren G. Harding, 29th U.S. President, 1865

Amar Bose, American entrepreneur, electrical and sound engineer, founder of Bose Corporation, 1929

Pat Croce, American entrepreneur, sports team executive and owner, author, and TV personality, 1954

Lee "Q" O'Denat, American internet entrepreneur (WorldStarHipHop.com), 1973

Deaths

Isaac Rice, German-American businessman (founder of General Dynamics Electric Boat, Electric Vehicle Company), investor, and author, 1915

Simon Guggenheim, American businessman, politician, and philanthropist, 1941

Thomas Midgley, Jr., American mechanical and chemical engineer who played a major role in developing leaded gasoline and some of the first chlorofluorocarbons (CFCs), both products that were later banned; his legacy is one of negative environmental impact and his death was publicly reported as an accident but privately declared a suicide, 1944

William C. Coleman, American businessman and politician, founder of the Coleman Company, a maker of camping equipment, 1957

November 3

You will keep in perfect peace those whose minds are steadfast, because they trust in you. Trust in the Lord forever, for the Lord, the Lord himself, is the Rock eternal. *(Isaiah 26:3-4, NIV)*

How to show gratitude

As Thanksgiving approaches (in the U.S.), there's a lot of extra conversation about gratitude. And no matter how crazy things get, we have a lot to be thankful for.

For this moment, let's focus on being thankful for what other people do—either for the world in general or for us specifically.

What's the best way to express our gratitude—besides (or in addition to) gifts of flowers, candy, jewelry, or money? Be specific.

"Thanks for all you do" is not especially meaningful. It's better than nothing, but not by much. Instead, be specific.

At work:

"Thanks for helping me put together that presentation."

"Thanks for fixing my computer."

"Thanks for your bright smile and cheery greeting every morning."

At home:

"Thanks for emptying the dishwasher."

"Thanks for taking out the garbage."

"Thanks for planning the menus, keeping track of the food we have on hand, and doing the grocery shopping."

In other situations:

"Thanks for serving on that committee and taking on that special project."

"Thanks for helping me get my packages to my car."

"Thanks for loaning me your umbrella."

That extra effort to be specific lets the person receiving your message know that you genuinely noticed and appreciate what they did and you're not just mouthing automatic, meaningless words out of habit.

Read:
Proverbs, Chapter 3

On this day in history

Notable events

In 1911, Louis Chevrolet and Billy Durant founded the Chevrolet Motor Car Company.

In 1952, Clarence Birdseye first began marketing frozen peas in Chester, New York.

In 2009, Warren Buffet announced he would purchase Burlington Northern and Santa Fe Railway; the deal was valued at over $44 billion and completed by February 12, 2010.

Births

D. James Kennedy, American pastor, evangelist, Christian broadcaster, and author, 1930

Phil Katz, American computer programmer best known as the co-creator of the Zip file format for data compression, 1962

Gabe Newell, American businessman and cofounder of the video game company Valve, 1962

Deaths

Solomon R. Guggenheim, American businessman, art collector, and philanthropist, 1949

Ralph Wyckoff, American scientist and pioneer of X-ray crystallography, 1951

Harlow Curtice, American automotive industry executive, president of General Motors (1953-1958), 1962

E. Cuyler Hammond, American biologist and epidemiologist, one of the first researchers to establish a link between smoking and lung cancer, 1986

Thought for the day

"May I not be remembered for what I did in this generation, but may the results of my labor be seen for eternity."

Mark Goldstein

I pray that I will not only believe in God, I will also believe God.

November 4

> "Do not let your hearts be troubled. You believe in God; believe also in me. My Father's house has many rooms; if that were not so, would I have told you that I am going there to prepare a place for you? And if I go and prepare a place for you, I will come back and take you to be with me that you also may be where I am. *(John 14:1-3, NIV)*

It's okay to be afraid

The Bible tells us to not be afraid.

Don't be afraid, for I am with you. Don't be discouraged, for I am your God. I will strengthen you and help you. I will hold you up with my victorious right hand. (Isaiah 41:10, NLT)

God doesn't want us to be fearful.

For God has not given us a spirit of fear and timidity, but of power, love, and self-discipline. (2 Timothy 1:7, NLT)

But there are times when it's okay to be afraid because fear can be your mind's way of alerting you to danger. It can even be God working to remove you from a situation he doesn't want you to be in.

Learn to do a quick assessment when you feel afraid. Is there an actual threat (either immediate or potential) that you should protect yourself from? If so, take appropriate action to protect yourself, your family, and your business—and don't be embarrassed about it

If not, consider ways to deal with your emotions, including counseling, prayer, and reading Scripture.

We shouldn't live in fear, but we should recognize the value of this God-given emotion.

Thought for the day

"The measure of a man's real character is what he would do if he knew he would never be found out."

Thomas Babington Macaulay

Read:
Proverbs, Chapter 4

Today we observe

Use Your Common Sense Day

Check Your Blood Pressure Day

On this day in history

Notable events

In 1879, James and John Ritty of Dayton, Ohio patented the first cash register, known as Ritty's Incorruptible Cashier.

In 1939, Packard unveiled the first automobile in the world with air conditioning.

In 1984, Michael Dell created PCs Limited while he was a student at the University of Texas at Austin; he later changed the company's name to Dell.

Births

Benjamin Franklin Goodrich, American industrialist in the rubber industry and founder of B.F. Goodrich Company, 1841

Ruth Handler, American businesswoman and inventor (Barbie doll); cofounder of toy manufacturer Mattel, founder of Ruthton Corp., which designed and manufactured prosthetic breasts for women who had undergone mastectomies, 1916

Trevor Blackwell, Canadian-American computer programmer, engineer, and entrepreneur, founder of Anybots (an American robotics company) and partner at Y Combinator, 1969

Deaths

George Peabody, American financier and philanthropist, considered the father of modern philanthropy, 1869

Daisy Bates, American civil rights activist, publisher, journalist, and lecturer, 1999

I am thankful that when I am confused and unsure, I can place it all with the Lord.

November 5

> ❝ Do not judge others, and you will not be judged. For you will be treated as you treat others. The standard you use in judging is the standard by which you will be judged. *(Matthew 7:1, NLT)*

Business gift-giving

Whether it's for Christmas, birthdays, anniversaries, or other occasions, choosing gifts for key clients and business associates can be a challenge. How do you select a gift that is useful, ethical, politically correct, reasonably priced, has no potential for liability, and won't offend anyone?

First, decide who will be on your gift list. Then determine the recipients' policies on accepting gifts and get a feel for the individual's attitude about gifts beyond the formal policies. Next, set your budget and select the gifts. Some ideas to consider:

Plants. Plants are a neutral gift with an environmental flavor. Be sure to include a tag with care instructions.

Memorabilia. If you have a news clipping of your client being mentioned in a positive way, or if you have a photograph of your client at a happy event, have it framed. It will likely be hanging on the wall and be a reminder of your thoughtfulness for years to come.

Books. Books are always a good choice in business or personal gift-giving. Be sure the bookstore has a liberal return policy, avoid controversial subjects that might offend, and don't buy anything dated that may be hard to exchange.

Charitable donations. Either give a specific donation in a particular customer's name to a charity you know they support, or give a single large donation to a charity of your choice and send out a letter to everyone saying that's what you've done in lieu of individual gifts.

No gift at all. This is a perfectly acceptable alternative to the gift-giving dilemma. If you decide not to give gifts, don't make a big deal about it. Chances are no one will notice.

Today we observe

International Volunteer Managers Day

On this day in history

Notable events

- In 1895, George Selden was granted the first U.S. patent for an automobile (his internal combustion engine along with a carriage it was meant to power).
- In 1935, Parker Brothers launched the board game *Monopoly*.

Births

- Raymond Loewy, French-born American industrial designer known as the father of streamlining and the father of industrial design, 1893
- Kris Jenner, American businesswoman, entrepreneur, and media personality, 1955

Deaths

- Otis Tufts, American machinist and inventor, who built printing machines, steam engines, firefighting equipment, and invented the steam pile driver, 1869
- Paul Galvin, American businessman and cofounder of Motorola, 1959
- Victor Grinich, American pioneer in the semiconductor industry, member of the "traitorous eight" that founded Silicon Valley, cofounder of Fairchild Semiconductor, 2000

Thought for the day

"There are two things a person should never be angry at, what they can help, and what they cannot."

Plato

I pray for the legacy I will leave.

Read:
Proverbs, Chapter 5

November 6

Instead, "If your enemies are hungry, feed them. If they are thirsty, give them something to drink. In doing this, you will heap burning coals of shame on their heads." Don't let evil conquer you, but conquer evil by doing good. *(Romans 12:21. NLT)*

Customers are your best prospects

Without qualified prospects, your business would come to a grinding halt, so it makes sense to invest in the process of developing new business. But don't look exclusively outward for that new business—you may find a substantial portion of it can come from existing accounts.

Closing your first sale with a new customer is just the beginning of your relationship. You know the customer has a need for your product; now it's time to develop and expand on that need. Find out what uses the customer might have for your product beyond the initial purchase. Take the time to understand why they bought from you in the first place. Was it quality? Price? Delivery time? Your charming personality? Or because you just happened to be there when they needed something? Once you understand the reason, you can appeal to that decision-making process to sell additional products.

"Service after the sale" should be more than a slogan. It's absolutely crucial to the development of repeat business. After every order, send a confirmation and express your appreciation. Follow up to see that the order is shipped and received on time. Most important, make sure the customer is using the product properly and to its fullest extent.

Regular contact with your customers says you are interested in them as people, not just as commission checks. Keep track of customers' birthdays, anniversaries, hobbies, and other personal information. Sending a card or a small gift once in a while helps turn customers into friends—and people like to buy from their friends.

Today we observe
World Paper Free Day

On this day in history
Notable events
In 1975, Hewlett-Packard Company went public.

Births
Charles Henry Dow, American journalist and cofounder of Dow Jones & Company and *The Wall Street Journal*, 1851

James D. Norris, American businessman, investor, commodities dealer, sports team owner, racehorse owner/breeder, 1906

Mark McCormack, American lawyer, sports agent, writer, founder of International Management Group, now IMG, 1930

Laurene Powell Jobs, American billionaire businesswoman, executive, and philanthropist, founder of Emerson Collective and XQ Institute, widow of Steve Jobs, 1963

Jerry Yang, Taiwanese-American billionaire computer programmer, internet entrepreneur, and venture capitalist, cofounder and former CEO of Yahoo! Inc., 1968

Deaths
Billy Sunday, American baseball player and Christian evangelist, 1862

Thought for the day

"When we try to pick out anything by itself, we find it hitched to everything else in the universe."

John Muir

I pray for those who feel unwelcome.

Read:
Proverbs, Chapter 6

November 7

And the Lord said to Satan, "Have you considered my servant Job, that there is none like him on the earth, a blameless and upright man, who fears God and turns away from evil? He still holds fast his integrity, although you incited me against him to destroy him without reason." *(Job 2:3, ESV)*

Who told you it couldn't be done?

And why are you listening to that person?

When someone tells you your goals are impossible, the first question you should ask is:

Why is that person qualified to set your limitations?

Those who are quickest to tell you why something won't work are usually the ones least qualified to do so. They're the ones leading mediocre lives. They're the ones who don't take chances. And they have a short list of achievements.

Maybe they've tried once and failed, so they never try again. Whatever the reason, they're usually pessimists who delight in seeing others fail and who are quick to say "I told you so" when something doesn't work out for you.

The people we need to listen to are the ones who are least likely to be telling us how to live our lives because they're busy living—and loving—their own. They're busy being successful. And they don't listen to people who want to see them fail.

Of course, we all need advice. We all can benefit from someone else's experience and perspective. But listen to the people who want to help you succeed, not the ones who are trying to hold you back.

I pray for persecuted people around the world.

Read:
Proverbs, Chapter 7

Today we observe
National Day for Victims of Communism

On this day in history
Notable events
In 1876, a patent for the first U.S. cigarette manufacturing machine was issued to Albert Hook.
In 1965, the Pillsbury Doughboy debuted in TV commercials for the first time.
In 1994, WXYC, the student radio station at the University of North Carolina at Chapel Hill, provided the first ever internet radio broadcast.

Births
Billy Graham, American Baptist evangelist, 1918

Deaths
Charles Thurber, American inventor and firearms maker who made important innovations in the early development of the typewriter, 1886

Thought for the day

"The difference between an obstacle and an opportunity is our attitude towards it. Every opportunity has a difficulty, and every difficulty has an opportunity."
J. Sidlo Baxter

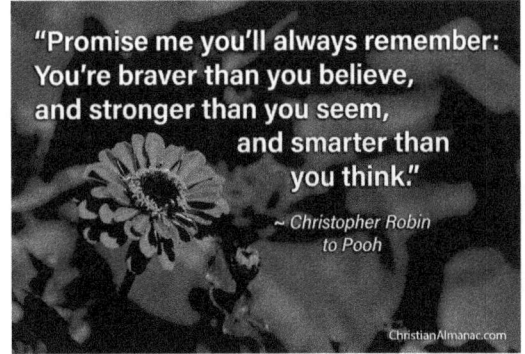

November 8

We may throw the dice, but the Lord determines how they fall.
(Proverbs 16:33, NLT)

What breakrooms and restrooms have in common

How often do you take an objective look at your company's employee breakrooms, restrooms, and locker rooms?

"I've walked the halls and had conversations with hundreds of companies across Central Florida, and I've found that toxic employers never invest in these two places that don't earn them money," says Dawn Sipley, president of the human resources services firm Sipley the Best (Sanford, Florida). "Another sign of poor management is decorations—are you using the same weird, musky, partially crushed, crinkled, dated decorations year after year?"

The quality of your employees' space sends a loud and clear message about how much you value and care for them. Just because it's an area customers don't see doesn't mean you shouldn't keep it pleasant, clean, and comfortable. And just because you only use those holiday decorations once a year (whether or not customers see them) doesn't mean you shouldn't regularly freshen them up.

Your employee spaces may not generate revenue directly, but they make a substantial contribution to your bottom line in the form of happier, more engaged employees and reduced turnover.

Thought for the day

"Next to trying and winning, the best thing is trying and failing."
— *Lucy Maud Montgomery*

I pray to embrace everything it truly means to be a Christian.

Today we observe
National STEM/STEAM Day
National Parents as Teachers Day

On this day in history

Notable events

In 1933, Franklin D. Roosevelt introduced the Civil Works Administration as part of the New Deal. The program created about 4 million American jobs and ended on March 31, 1934.

Births

George H. Bissell, American entrepreneur and industrialist; founder of Pennsylvania Rock Oil, the first petroleum company in America; considered the father of the American oil industry, 1821

Milton Bradley, American business magnate, game pioneer and publisher, credited with launching the board game industry, 1836

Frank L. Gillespie, American businessman, founder of Supreme Life Insurance Company, 1876

Jack Kilby, American electrical engineer, inventor, Nobel Prize winner, co-inventor of the handheld calculator and thermal printer, 1923

Samuel Irving Newhouse Jr., American publisher, heir to a substantial magazine and media business, Advance Publications, 1927

Robert Tappan Morris, American computer scientist and entrepreneur, creator of the Morris worm, cofounder of the online store Viaweb and venture capital funding firm Y Combinator, 1965

Deaths

Otto Frederick Rohwedder, American engineer, jeweler, and inventor (first automatic bread-slicing machine for commercial use), 1960

Napoleon Hill, controversial American self-help author best known for his book, *Think and Grow Rich*, 1970

Read:
Proverbs, Chapter 8

November 9

For no matter how many promises God has made, they are "Yes" in Christ. And so through him the "Amen" is spoken by us to the glory of God. *(2 Corinthians 1:20, NLT)*

The strength of integrity

In *Shine: 5 Empowering Principles for a Rewarding Life*, Kris Den Besten discusses integrity, writing:

"When your works glorify God as you serve with all of your heart, soul, mind, and strength—and Christ shines in you—others will notice. Many will be impressed. But don't get me wrong. Often people who notice will not be singing your praises. Some will call you closed-minded, irrational, or just plain stupid. Some will be angry that you won't compromise your values to benefit them. Do not be surprised by this kind of hostility. Scripture anticipates the negative reaction that may come from your choices to honor Christs: 'Blessed are you when men hate you, when they exclude you and insult you and reject your name as evil, because of the Son of Man' (Luke 6:22).

"If integrity was easy and always had instant positive results, more people and businesses would practice it. However, practicing integrity is not about achieving success or praise among people. It is about obeying the commands of God, recognizing His goodness, and walking in step with Him. When we focus our energy on serving others, honoring God, and improving continually, a great amount of momentum is generated. Momentum enhances performance and increases opportunities. It can make a whole company feel unstoppable. If left unguided, however, momentum can quickly take a person or company down the wrong path. Navigation by values helps channel momentum in the right direction. Values provide a guardrail, keeping momentum on the right track: the track of integrity."

Read:
Proverbs, Chapter 9

Today we observe
World Social Media Kindness Day

On this day in history

Notable events

In 1960, 37 American brokerage firms were ordered to pay $1.03 billion to cheated NASDAQ investors.

In 1962, the famous Ford Rotunda in Dearborn, Michigan (originally built for the 1933 Century of Progress exposition in Chicago) was destroyed by a fire that began while workmen were preparing the Rotunda for its Christmas display.

In 1967, *Rolling Stone* magazine launched its debut issue in newspaper format.

Births

Gail Borden Jr., American businessman, land surveyor, newspaper publisher, and inventor known for creating a process to make sweetened condensed milk, 1801

Hedy Lamarr, Austrian-American actress and inventor (radio guidance system for Allied torpedoes), 1914

Yvon Chouinard, American rock climber, environmentalist, philanthropist, and outdoor industry businessman (Patagonia), 1938

Deaths

Edwin Drake, American businessman and first American to successfully drill for oil, 1880

Thought for the day

"The best way to learn to be an honest, responsible adult is to live with adults who act honestly and responsibly."

Claudia Jewett

I am thankful for random compliments from strangers.

November 10

When he comes, he will prove the world to be in the wrong about sin and righteousness and judgment: *(John 16:8, NIV)*

The power of prayer: healing plastic bags

J. Gunnar Olson, founder of the International Christian Chamber of Commerce, tells how God performed a miracle in his business. His company, Alfapac, manufactures high-tech plastic films.

They were getting ready to ship more than a thousand pallets of huge plastic bags that were used to cover bales of hay in farmlands across Europe when they discovered that every bag had sealed shut. The bags were impossible to open and useless.

It was a catastrophe that would seriously damage the customers and put the company out of business. Olson's response was to gather his family together and pray. He said, "Lord, you have heard what we have heard. What do you say?"

Olson's wife said, "When we prayed, I felt the Lord was saying, 'If I can change water into wine, what is plastics?'"

On Sunday night, as a family, they drove to the factory and Olson saw the bags for the first time. He prayed, "Listen, Heaven, and listen, Earth, who is the Lord over Alfapac? His name is Jesus. And in the name of Jesus we now command all the molecules to migrate back."

Then Olson and his family laid hands on all the pallets. It took them three hours. And then they went home.

When Olson returned to the factory on Monday morning, he said, "Everyone employed in the company was out there, opening thousands of boxes. I say to the glory of the Lord, there was not one sealed bag. God healed everything."

On this day in history

Notable events

In 1903, Mary Anderson was granted a patent for an automatic windshield wiper but she never made any money from her invention.

In 1969, *Sesame Street* debuted on television.

In 1911, Andrew Carnegie formed Carnegie Corporation, a philanthropic foundation "to promote the advancement and diffusion of knowledge and understanding."

In 1987, Microsoft was the first to offer a bundle of applications at a discounted price, competing with other companies that sold applications separately.

Births

Henry Eyster Jacobs, American religious educator, Biblical commentator, and Lutheran theologian, 1844

Jack Northrup, American aircraft industrialist and designer, founder of the Northrop Corporation, 1895

Deaths

Harry Ford Sinclair, American industrialist, founder of Sinclair Oil, 1956

William Higinbotham, American physicist, member of team that developed the first nuclear bomb, inventor of *Tennis for Two*, the first interactive analog computer game, 1994

Gene Amdahl, American computer architect and high-tech entrepreneur known for his work on mainframe computers at IBM and at his own companies, founder of Amdahl Corporation, 2015

Thought for the day

"Regret for the things we did can be tempered by time; it is regret for the things we did not do that is inconsolable."

Sydney J Harris

I pray to stay focused on the reason for our celebrations as the holiday season begins.

Read:
Proverbs, Chapter 10

November 11

> Some nations boast of their chariots and horses, but we boast in the name of the Lord our God. *(Psalm 20:7, NLT)*

Lead as Socrates taught

The ancient Greek philosopher Socrates is known for his method of teaching by asking questions. The Socratic method—a dialog between teacher and students—is widely used in law and medical schools today, and it also works well in business.

The idea is to ask questions, challenge assumptions, and provoke creative thinking and learning. The leader begins by asking difficult questions and then encourages dialog among the entire team. This is not an inquisition, it's a conversation where information is exchanged, new ideas are developed, and people are comfortable thinking out loud.

The Socratic method for problem-solving takes longer than simply telling your team what to do, so it isn't practical to use all the time. But it can be empowering, productive, and beneficial for your organization.

Do you have a leadership aura?

People who project a leadership aura, often referred to as leadership presence, have developed these characteristics:

They look like leaders. They are well-groomed, appropriately dressed, and present themselves professionally.

They use positive body language. They maintain an open body posture, listen actively, and speak clearly.

They are confident. Their movements, gestures, voice, and ability to maintain eye contact all reflect their internal sureness.

They speak well. Their tone and cadence are controlled. They speak with clarity and accuracy.

They are consistent. Their conduct is aligned with their values all the time.

Today we observe
Veterans Day

On this day in history

Notable events

In 1918, World War I ended.

In 1926, Route 66 came into official existence as a highway and was one of the original highways in the U.S. Numbered Highway System.

In 1972, the Dow Jones Index passed the 1,000 mark for the first time.

Births

Daisy Bates, American civil rights activist, publisher, journalist, and lecturer, 1914

Deaths

Charles Scribner IV, American publisher, head of Charles Scriber's Sons publishing company, 1995

Peter Drucker, Austrian-American management consultant, educator, and author; invented the concept known as management by objectives; known as the founder of modern management, 2005

Thought for the day

"What's money? A man is a success if he gets up in the morning and goes to bed at night and in between does what he wants to do."

Bob Dylan

I am thankful for things I often take for granted.

Read:
Proverbs, Chapter 11

November 12

In everything set them an example by doing what is good. In your teaching show integrity, seriousness and soundness of speech that cannot be condemned, so that those who oppose you may be ashamed because they have nothing bad to say about us. *(Titus 2:7-8, NIV)*

Say your name

How often have you forgotten the name of someone you've met only a few times before—or even someone you know well? It's frustrating and embarrassing.

When you're in a situation and it's either obvious or likely that the person you're speaking with has forgotten your name, extend the grace you'd like to receive. Find a way to say your name and remind them of how they know you. Some suggestions:

"It's been a while. I'm Joe Smith."

"We met at the conference. I'm Mary Adams."

"I haven't seen you since we worked with the radio station. I'm Shannon Brown."

If you're wearing a name tag, make sure it's visible, but don't assume everyone can read it. Better to say your name to someone who knows it than to leave a potentially important contact trying to remember who you are.

On this day in history

Notable events

In 1927, the Holland Tunnel officially opened, creating the first road crossing between New York and New Jersey.

In 2019, Disney launched its film and television streaming service, Disney+.

Births

DeWitt Wallace, American magazine publisher, cofounder of Reader's Digest, 1889

Jack Ryan, American designer and businessman who worked at Mattel for 20 years, responsible for the Barbie and Ken dolls, Hot Wheels, Chatty Cathy, and more, 1926

Ronald Burkle, American billionaire businessman, investor, cofounder and managing partner of The Yucaipa Companies, LLC, 1952

Steve Huffman, American web developer and entrepreneur, cofounder and CEO of Reddit, 1983

Deaths

Stan Lee, American comic book writer, editor, publisher, and producer, 2018

What we produce is not for ourselves. The tree produces fruit, but the fruit doesn't nourish the tree, it nourishes those who consume it. The fruit you produce is not for you, it's for others.

I pray for those who are faithful in the workplace.

Read:
Proverbs, Chapter 12

Thought for the day

"Older and wiser voices can always help you find the right path, if you are only willing to listen."

Jimmy Buffett

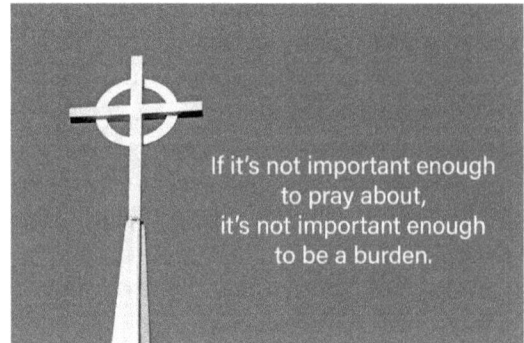

If it's not important enough to pray about, it's not important enough to be a burden.

November 13

I know, my God, that you examine our hearts and rejoice when you find integrity there. You know I have done all this with good motives, and I have watched your people offer their gifts willingly and joyously.
(1 Chronicles 29:17, NLT)

Why read the Bible every day?

We're all busy, but when you don't have enough hours in the day, what falls by the wayside? Don't let it be your daily Scripture reading. Here's why we need to read the Bible every day:

To receive daily guidance. The enemy is attacking us daily, pulling us in the wrong direction. Scripture gives us the daily spiritual nourishment we need to resist the enemy and stay on the path God has planned for us.

To grow our faith. Reading the Bible every day gives us the knowledge we need to keep growing in faith.

To equip us for good work. The Bible is a manual for missionaries, whether your mission field is in some far off place or your own backyard—or even your workplace.

To protect us from temptation. God's Word was what made Jesus able to resist Satan's temptations. Daily Bible study is a strong guard against the appeals of the world.

To develop our ability to witness. Non-believers need believers to help bring them to Christ. Reading the Bible daily gives us the knowledge we need to be an effective witness for the Lord.

To learn how to forgive. Forgiving is not easy. Daily Scripture reading will help you rid yourself of anger, bitterness, and malice.

To remind us of what God has done. Keeping the stories in the Bible fresh in our minds and hearts gives us strength and security for the future.

To learn, remember, and trust God's promises. The Bible tells us over and over what God has promised, and those promises help us resist anxiety and fear.

On this day in history

Notable events
In 1940, Willys-Overland submitted the Jeep prototype to the U.S. Army; by 1945, more than 600,000 Jeeps had been manufactured.

Births
Scott McNealy, American businessman, cofounder of the computer technology company Sun Microsystems, founder of Curriki, an online open education service, 1954

Paul Graham, British-American computer scientist, entrepreneur, investor, and author, cofounder of the online store Viaweb and venture capital funding firm Y Combinator, 1964

Deaths
Helen H. Malsed, American toy inventor of more than two dozen toys and games; notable toys include the Slinky Dog and Slinky Train, 1998

Thought for the day

"If you treat an individual as if he were what he ought to be and could be, he will become what he ought to be and could be."
Johann Wolfgang von Goethe

When thinking about a confrontation, consider if any real good will come from it.

I pray that I will not only be thankful, but that I will show my gratitude to others.

Read:
Proverbs, Chapter 13

November 14

Husbands, love your wives, just as Christ loved the church and gave himself up for her to make her holy, cleansing her by the washing with water through the word, and to present her to himself as a radiant church, without stain or wrinkle or any other blemish, but holy and blameless. *(Ephesians 5:25-27, NIV)*

The value of skill stacking

Just as there is value in specialization, there is value in having a wide range of skills and talents, especially when those skills support each other and, through that support, create a unique set of skills. Combining similar and complementary skills as a single portfolio is known as skill stacking (or talent stacking).

For example, a marketing professional who is also proficient in data analytics can develop creative marketing strategies and then analyze data to refine and optimize those strategies to improve the results. A graphic artist who acquires social media skills can create the artwork and then manage the social media campaigns. An attorney with a gift for public speaking and an understanding of recording technology can create a podcast that could generate revenue by attracting new clients or serving as an advertising platform for other companies.

Skill stacking can provide a more rewarding and diverse work experience, make work more interesting and challenging, and offer new opportunities while increasing the value of employees who practice it. Make skill stacking a part of your company culture by encouraging employees to explore and expand their skill sets to enhance their careers as they help grow the organization.

When we listen, God speaks.

When we obey, God acts.

Today we observe
National Seatbelt Day

On this day in history
Notable events
In 2006, Texas state officials closed the last two of the famed Pig Stand restaurants, the only remaining pieces of the nation's first drive-in restaurant empire, because the owners were bankrupt and owed unpaid sales taxes; in 2007, one Pig Stand was able to reopen.

Births
Robert Fulton, American inventor and engineer (first commercial steamboat), 1765

Malcolm McLean, American businessman, inventor of the modern intermodal shipping container, founder of McLean Trucking Company, Sea-Land Service, Inc., and Trailer Bridge, Inc., 1913

Peter Norton, American programmer, software publisher, author, and philanthropist, best known for the computer programs and books that bear his name and portrait, 1943

Deaths
Booker T. Washington, American educator, author, orator, and adviser to several U.S. presidents, died in Tuskegee, Alabama, 1915

Thought for the day

"Life's challenges are not supposed to paralyze you; they're supposed to help you discover who you are."

Bernice Johnson Reagon

I pray that I will be kind in every interaction.

Read:
Proverbs, Chapter 14

November 15

> ❝ You shall not have in your bag two kinds of weights, a large and a small. You shall not have in your house two kinds of measures, a large and a small. A full and fair weight you shall have, a full and fair measure you shall have, that your days may be long in the land that the Lord your God is giving you. For all who do such things, all who act dishonestly, are an abomination to the Lord your God. *(Deuteronomy 25:13-16, ESV)*

Don't give back

When kind, generous, service-minded people do charitable work, they often say that they want to "give back."

Why not simply *give*?

Giving back means returning something. It means you have something that was loaned or given to you and you're giving it back. But how many of the organizations that you support with money and time have given you anything except the privilege of helping them?

To give back is to pay a debt. You may not be in debt to the non-profit agency that helps families in crisis, but you want to help it accomplish its mission. You may not be in debt to a friend who is recovering from surgery, but you want to take them a meal or help in some other way.

You're not giving back, you're just giving.

Even if you've been on the receiving end of kindness and generosity from friends and strangers who didn't owe you a thing, it probably wasn't an "I'm going to help you and now you owe me" transaction. It was an "I care about you, and I want to do this for you" situation. It was an unconditional gift.

Give because you want to make a difference, give because it makes you feel good, and, most important, give because God tells you to give—not to *give back*, but to *give*. Christian giving is an act of worship.

If we only give back, if we don't simply give, are we giving much at all?

Today we observe

America Recycles Day

On this day in history

Notable events

In 1867, the first stock ticker was unveiled in New York City, making up-to-the-minute prices available to investors around the country.

In 1969, Dave Thomas opened his first Wendy's restaurant in Columbus, Ohio.

In 1971, Intel released its 4004 microprocessor, the first chip to house a complete CPU and the first commercially available microprocessor.

In 2001, Microsoft released the Xbox gaming console.

Births

Elijah Craig, American Baptist preacher and entrepreneur, credited with the invention of bourbon whiskey, 1738

Deaths

Elmer McCollum, American biochemist known for his work on the influence of diet on health, discovered vitamins A, B, and D, devised the vitamin naming system, 1967

Preston Robert Tisch, American businessman, chairman and part owner of Loews Corporation, NFL team owner, 2005

Thought for the day

"The greatest failure in life is being successful in the wrong assignment."

Myles Munroe

Read: Proverbs, Chapter 15

I pray that I am able to see the blessings in rejection.

November 16

> ❝ Don't store up treasures here on earth, where moths eat them and rust destroys them, and where thieves break in and steal. Store your treasures in heaven, where moths and rust cannot destroy, and thieves do not break in and steal. Wherever your treasure is, there the desires of your heart will also be. *(Matthew 6:19-21, NLT)*

Surround yourself with people who complement you

The adage that we buy from people we know, like, and trust extends beyond sales. It's human nature to like people who are like we are.

When we're in a leadership role, it's natural to gravitate toward people that we know, like, and trust—and therefore who are like we are—when we assemble our teams.

It might feel good and safe, but it's a big mistake.

A better strategy is to surround yourself with people with different skills and abilities, people whose strengths are your weaknesses.

This begins with an honest self-assessment. What is the team's goal? What core skills are required to reach that goal? What do you bring to the table and where are you lacking?

This exercise allows you to identify the needed complementary skills that will enable the members of the team to be more creative and effective.

Foster a culture of trust and collaboration that maximizes the benefits of diversity in thought and skills. Especially when you're the leader, encourage your team to challenge assumptions and present dissenting opinions—and treat the people who offer them with courtesy and respect. Building complementary teams is a key way to create an organization that is greater than the sum of its parts.

Read:
Proverbs, Chapter 16

On this day in history

Notable events

In 1889, the Oahu Railway and Land Company (OR&L) began operating on Hawaii's third largest island, Oahu, making it possible to move agricultural products from inland to port.

In 1914, the U.S. Federal Reserve Bank opened.

Births

Gene Amdahl, American computer architect and high-tech entrepreneur known for his work on mainframe computers at IBM and at his own companies, founder of Amdahl Corporation, 1922

Deaths

Harold Alfond, American businessman who founded the Dexter Shoe Company and established the first factory outlet store, 2007

Robert "Dr. Bob" Smith, American physician and surgeon, cofounder of Alcoholics Anonymous, 1950

Thought for the day

"Certain thoughts are prayers. There are moments when, whatever be the attitude of the body, the soul is on its knees."

Victor Hugo

I pray that I see everyone's individual special genius.

> Grow your faith by intentionally seeking opportunities to brighten someone else's day.

November 17

We reject all shameful deeds and underhanded methods. We don't try to trick anyone or distort the word of God. We tell the truth before God, and all who are honest know this. *(2 Corinthians 4:2, NLT)*

The power of second-order thinking

The simplest definition of second-order thinking is the practice of thinking things through—that is, going past the initial impulse or action and considering the long-term consequences of our decisions. Second-order thinking can help you avoid problems, solve the problems you have, and take better actions for any purpose.

First-order thinking is quick, simple, and common. Are you hungry? Eat a donut, some chips, or something else that's immediately available. It's a solution that almost anyone can do.

Second-order thinking is more deliberate and complex. It takes first-order thinking and asks, "And then what?"

When you practice second-order thinking, you consider the consequences of your decisions beyond the moment. You slow down your decision-making process and think about the short-, medium-, and long-term outcomes of your actions on yourself and others.

Apply second-order thinking in all aspects of your personal and business life. You can do it in your head or write it down. With discipline, you'll learn to see what others don't. It's a tool that will allow you to outperform others routinely.

Thought for the day

"When a thing is done, it's done. Don't look back. Look forward to your next objective."

George C. Marshall

Read:
Proverbs, Chapter 17

On this day in history

Notable events

In 1970, Douglas Engelbart received a patent for his invention of an "X-Y Position Indicator for a Display System" (the first computer mouse).

Births

William Arnold Anthony, American physicist, educator, and researcher; introduced and taught Cornell University's electrical engineering course, one of the first in the U.S., 1835

Deaths

Herman Hollerith, American businessman and inventor (first electric tabulating machine), founder of a company that was combined with several other companies in 1911 to form what would eventually become IBM, 1929

Prayer

Make my body healthy and agile,
my mind sharp and clear,
my heart joyful and contented,
my soul faithful and loving.
Above all let me live in your presence, for with you all fear is banished and there is only harmony and peace.
Let every day combine the beauty of spring, the brightness of summer,
the abundance of autumn,
and the repose of winter.
And at the end of my life on earth,
grant that I may come to see and know you in the fullness of your glory.

~ St. Thomas Aquinas

I pray for those who are worried and fearful.

November 18

> But select from all the people some capable, honest men who fear God and hate bribes. Appoint them as leaders over groups of one thousand, one hundred, fifty, and ten. *(Exodus 18:21, NLT)*

Why should people do business with you?

Have you thought about why people should do business with you? Maybe it's because you're honest. Maybe it's because the value of what you offer is more than it costs. Maybe it's because you know your purpose and mission and are committed to them.

Make a list of why people should do business with you. Write down everything you can think of from the small, minor things to the big, monumental things. Don't be modest. If you're really good at what you do (and of course you are!), write that down. If you're a good listener and know how to help your customers solve problems, write that down. If you have great connections and can refer customers to other sources they might need, write that down.

You don't have to share the list with anyone—although you should. After all, you're working hard to provide a superior product or service. Why not tell people why it's in their best interest to spend their money with you instead of someone else?

Thought for the day

"One of the secrets of life is that all that is really worth the doing is what we do for others."

Lewis Carroll

I am thankful that you, Lord, are my help and deliverer.

Read:
Proverbs, Chapter 18

Today we observe
National Injury Prevention Day

On this day in history

Notable events
- In 1883, U.S. and Canadian railroad operators instituted four standard continental time zones to end the confusion of dealing with thousands of local times.
- In 1963, the first push-button telephone was introduced and Touch-Tone dialing was offered to Bell Telephone customers.

Births
George Gallup, American pioneer of survey sampling techniques and inventor of the Gallup poll, 1901

Deaths
Chester A. Arthur, 21st U.S. President, 1886
Joseph P. Kennedy Sr., American businessman, investor, philanthropist, and politician, 1969
Peter Buck, American physicist, restaurateur, and philanthropist, cofounder of the Subway restaurant chain, 2021

Let us Break Bread Together

African-American Spiritual

Let us break bread together on our knees.
Let us break bread together on our knees.

Refrain:
When I fall on my knees with my face to the rising sun,
O Lord have mercy on me.

Let us drink wine together on our knees.
Let us drink wine together on our knees.
[Refrain]

Let us praise God together on our knees.
Let us praise God together on our knees.
[Refrain]

November 19

> Jesus Christ is the same yesterday and today and forever.
> *(Hebrews 13:8, NIV)*

Success can be a product of environment

Environment impacts performance. Desert creatures thrive in the heat and shrivel in the cold. Arctic animals flourish in sub-zero temperatures but can't survive in extreme heat.

It's the same with people. A person who excels in one environment might fail in another.

Whether you're hiring for your company or considering another position for yourself, be sure to consider the workplace conditions. A superstar in one organization might be a dismal failure in another due to the environment, and vice versa. Someone who works best alone isn't likely to do well in an open workspace with a lot of people. Someone who feeds on the energy of others won't perform well in solitary setting.

If you have people on your team who you believe aren't performing to their full potential, take a look at their working conditions. It's possible an environmental adjustment could help both their production and their job satisfaction.

Thought for the day

"Sometimes, you get what you want. Other times, you get a lesson in patience, timing, alignment, empathy, compassion, faith, perseverance, resilience, humility, trust, meaning, awareness, resistance, purpose, clarity, grief, beauty, and life. Either way, you win."

Brianna Wiest

I pray for my business relationships.

Today we observe
International Men's Day

On this day in history

Notable events

In 1959, about two years after it was introduced, Ford announced it was discontinuing the Edsel.

In 2007, Amazon announced the launch of the portable e-reader Kindle.

Births

James A. Garfield, 20th U.S. President (second President to die by assassination; first left-handed U.S. President), 1831

Billy Sunday, American baseball player and Christian evangelist, 1862

Peter Drucker, Austrian-American management consultant, educator, and author; invented the concept known as management by objectives; known as the founder of modern management, 1909

Peter Ruckman, American pastor, author, and founder of the Pensacola Bible Institute, 1921

Jack Welch, American businessman and CEO of General Electric, 1935

Ted Turner, American entrepreneur, television producer, media proprietor (founder of CNN and Turner Broadcasting System), and philanthropist, 1938

Calvin Klein, American fashion designer and entrepreneur, founder of Calvin Klein Inc., 1942

Jack Dorsey, American internet entrepreneur, philanthropist, programmer, cofounder and former CEO of Twitter (now X), principal executive officer of Block, Inc., 1976

Deaths

George H. Bissell, American entrepreneur and industrialist; founder of Pennsylvania Rock Oil, the first petroleum company in America; considered the father of the American oil industry, 1884

Read:
Proverbs, Chapter 19

November 20

When I am afraid, I put my trust in you. In God, whose word I praise—in God I trust and am not afraid. What can mere mortals do to me?
(Psalm 56:3-4, NIV)

Become intentionally innovative

In business, without a great product, nothing else matters, and it takes innovation to keep your products great and in demand. In *Education of a CEO: Lessons for Leaders*, Correct Craft CEO Bill Yeargin writes, "Innovation can happen through luck or intention. Since we cannot count on being lucky, we need to be intentional about innovation. Plus, being intentional is a great way to also improve our luck!"

Companies that are not innovating won't survive. Yeargin writes, "Innovation is more than technology; it is developing new and creative ways to do everything."

To build an intentionally innovative organization, Yeargin recommends:

Create the right mindset. You need a growth mindset to be intentionally creative. Great leaders create tremendous clarity around the importance of innovation to their organization.

Create the right environment. Invest, allow failure, and celebrate innovation.

Stop swirling. Yeargin says swirling is talking around an issue without acting on it. Successful innovators don't swirl, they move toward a problem or opportunity, and act.

Make sure you are fulfilling a need. No matter how innovative you think your idea is, you can't monetize it if people are not willing to pay for it.

Be willing to fail. Being highly risk averse makes innovation difficult. Take a chance on things that might not work.

Read:
Proverbs, Chapter 20

Today we observe
Give Your Computer a Name Day
Future Teachers of America Day

On this day in history

Notable events
In 1958, Jim and Jane Henson founded Muppets, Inc., now known as The Jim Henson Company.
In 1974, the U.S. Department of Justice filed an antitrust suit against AT&T, resulting in the breakup of AT&T and its Bell System.
In 1985, Microsoft released Windows 1.0.

Births
William Painter, American mechanical engineer, inventor (the crown cork bottle cap and bottle opener), and founder of Crown Holdings, Inc., 1838
Joseph R. Biden, 46th U.S. President, 1942

Deaths
Clyde Cessna, American aircraft designer, aviator, and early aviation entrepreneur, best known as the principal founder of the Cessna Aircraft Corporation, 1954
Eugene Kleiner, Austrian-American engineer and venture capitalist, pioneer of Silicon Valley, one of the original founders of Fairchild Semiconductor, 2003
Jake Burton Carpenter, American snowboarder and inventor, founder of Burton Snowboards, 2019

Thought for the day

"Courage is what it takes to stand up and speak. Courage is also what it takes to sit down and listen."
Sir Winston Churchill

I pray for the volunteers who are essential for our churches, schools, and nonprofits to function.

November 21

The Lord has filled Bezalel with the Spirit of God, giving him great wisdom, ability, and expertise in all kinds of crafts. He is a master craftsman, expert in working with gold, silver, and bronze. He is skilled in engraving and mounting gemstones and in carving wood. He is a master at every craft. And the Lord has given both him and Oholiab son of Ahisamach, of the tribe of Dan, the ability to teach their skills to others. The Lord has given them special skills as engravers, designers, embroiderers in blue, purple, and scarlet thread on fine linen cloth, and weavers. They excel as craftsmen and as designers. *(Exodus 35:31-35, NLT)*

Choose to forgive

Forgiving is an essential element of our Christian faith, and it's one of the hardest things God asks us to do. In *5 Prayers God Loves to Answer*, Larry Selig explains that forgiveness is a choice, not a feeling. He writes:

"Often, we struggle with forgiving others who have hurt either us or someone we love. The hurt may feel too deep, the other person may seem undeserving, or withholding forgiveness may be an attempt to get even. But between the hurt and our response, there is a critical choice to make: choose to forgive and receive God's forgiveness for our sins against Him and others, or withhold our forgiveness and give permission to others, including the devil, to control our thoughts and emotions. But even worse, when we withhold forgiveness, we are asking God to withhold His forgiveness toward us. A critical choice indeed.

"Forgiveness is a decision of our will, not an emotional feeling. We may not feel like forgiving. But if we realize the higher cost of not forgiving, choosing to forgive becomes increasingly necessary. And this often means asking God for help. His answer is always, 'I will help you forgive, if you are willing. That is why I sent My Son to die for you, to set you and others free from the burden and consequences of sin.'"

> Grow your faith by spending time with like-minded believers.

On this day in history

Notable events

In 1989, President George H. W. Bush signed a law banning smoking on most domestic airline flights.

In 1995, the Dow Jones closed above the 5,000 mark for the first time.

Births

William Beaumont, U.S. Army surgeon who became known as the father of gastric physiology for his research on human digestion on Alexis St. Martin, 1785

Hetty Green, American businesswoman and financier known as the richest woman in America during the Gilded Age and often unfairly referred to as the Witch of Wall Street, 1834

Georgia Frontiere, American businesswoman, entertainer, and philanthropist, NFL team owner, 1927

George Zimmer, American businessman, founder of Men's Wearhouse, Generation Tux, and zTailors, 1948

Thought for the day

"Organizing is what you do before you do something so that when you do it, it is not all mixed up."

A.A. Milne

I am thankful that I have the ability to resist evil through prayer.

Read:
Proverbs, Chapter 21

November 22

Religion that is pure and undefiled before God and the Father is this: to visit orphans and widows in their affliction, and to keep oneself unstained from the world. *(James 1:27, RSV)*

How to be a good audience

Whether it's a small meeting or large conference, the audience can have a significant impact on the performance of the speaker. These tips will help you be a better audience:

Make eye contact with and smile at the speaker. This is easier in a smaller group, but even when the speaker is up on a stage, make eye contact if you can and offer a welcoming smile.

Show that you're listening. Let your facial expressions make it clear that you're listening.

Take notes. Jot down key points and your own reactions to what you hear.

Turn off your phone and put it away. You may want to use your phone to take pictures of the speaker's slides, but don't check email or respond to messages during the presentation.

Be totally present. The speaker will appreciate it and you'll get more out of the event.

Express your appreciation. If circumstances permit, thank the speaker and let them know one or two key points that stood out to you. Follow up with a note or even a social media connection request.

Thought for the day

"It is foolish and wrong to mourn the men who died. Rather we should thank God such men lived."

George S. Patton

I pray for understanding in confusing times.

On this day in history

Notable events

In 1909, brothers Orville and Wilbur Wright founded the Wright Company, a commercial aviation business, with the intention of capitalizing on their invention of the practice airplane.

In 1932, a U.S. patent for a motorized pump that metered and displayed the exact gallons of gasoline or other liquid and also accurately computed and showed the price in dollars and cents when delivery was made was issued to inventors Robert J. Jauch, Ivan R. Farnham, and Ross H. Arnold.

In 1983, the last wringer-washer made in the U.S. was built by the Maytag Company, the last U.S. company to make hand-operated washers.

In 2005, Microsoft released the Xbox 360.

Births

Edward Bernays, a pioneer in the field of public relations and propaganda, known as "the father of public relations," 1891

Wiley Post, American aviator known for his work in high-altitude flying who helped developed one of the first pressure suits and discovered the jet stream, 1898

Doris Duke, American billionaire tobacco heiress, philanthropist, and socialite, 1912

Eugene Stoner, American machinist and firearms designer most associated with the development of the ArmaLite AR-15, 1922

Arthur Jones, American pioneer in the field of physical exercise, inventor (Nautilus exercise machines), and founder of Nautilus, Inc. and MedX, Inc., 1926

Deaths

George Washington Gale Ferris, Jr., American engineer and inventor (Ferris Wheel), 1896

John F. Kennedy, 35th U.S. President (fourth President to be assassinated), 1963

Mary Kay Ash, American businesswoman and founder of Mary Kay Cosmetics, Inc., 2001

Read:
Proverbs, Chapter 22

November 23

The Lord God took the man and put him in the Garden of Eden to work it and take care of it. *(Genesis 2:15, NIV)*

Will it really work for you?

Not all time-saving technology actually saves time. Not all productivity-enhancing technology will actually make you more productive.

Before you invest in technology—whether it's an app, a device, or a piece of equipment—be sure it will do what it promises for *you*.

Consider the cost of the tool itself, the time it will take to learn to use it, and the results it will produce. What's the return on investment and how long will it take? Will you and your team embrace or resist the change involved?

There's nothing wrong with being old school or a little behind the technology curve, especially if what you're already doing works better than the latest gadgets.

How to be great

The most successful people, the people who have established themselves as great in their field, know they don't know everything and they can't do it alone.

Whatever you want to become great at, whether it's business or something else, learn from people who are at least five to ten steps ahead of you. Seek out people who have done what you want to do and who know what you need to know to counsel and coach you. Accept their wisdom and be coachable.

I am thankful for the skills that allow me to serve the marketplace.

Read:
Proverbs, Chapter 23

On this day in history

Notable events

In 1889, the first jukebox went into operation in San Francisco; it would become a national phenomenon in diners and restaurants.

In 1897, a U.S. patent was issued to Andrew Jackson Beard for his invention of the "Jenny coupler," which does the dangerous job of hooking railroad cars together by simply allowing them to bump into each other. It has probably saved countless lives and limbs, and remains in use today.

In 1936, the first issue of *Life* magazine was published.

Births

Franklin Pierce, 14th U.S. President, 1804

Hal Lindsey, American evangelical writer and television host, 1929

John Hampton "Papa John" Schnatter, American entrepreneur and philanthropist, founder of the Papa John's pizza restaurant chain, 1961

Gwynne Shotwell, American businesswoman and engineer, president and COO of SpaceX, 1963

Thought for the day

"In the workplace, employees will spend roughly half their waking hours working and living in the environment you create as the leader. There is a lot at stake and people are counting on you. The role of the leader is a very high calling."

James C. Hunter

November 24

You fools! You know how to interpret the weather signs of the earth and sky, but you don't know how to interpret the present times.
(Luke 12:56, NLT)

Speakers: Don't start with a bored audience

The person who introduces guest speakers sets the stage for the presentation. They can either get the audience excited or have them dozing before you take the microphone.

If you do guest speaking at any level, know these two things:

One, your corporate bio is not your speaker introduction. Two, a boring introduction is a hurdle that's easy to avoid.

Most organizations will have already shared your bio in their promotional materials, so the audience already knows your formal credentials. Your introduction should be something livelier, something that will capture the audience's attention and provide a strong lead-in to your talk.

Don't expect your host to come up with that alone. Write the introduction you want and provide it ahead of time. Bring a paper copy with you in case the host doesn't transfer it to their phone or print it out.

All you need to say is, "Here's my introduction." No other explanation is necessary.

Most of the time, the host will read what you provided verbatim—and be glad to have it.

Tips for writing a good introduction:
- Include a greeting.
- Tell the audience what the subject is and why it's important to them.
- Establish why the presenter is qualified to speak on the topic.
- Keep it brief., upbeat, and positive.
- Avoid clichés.
- End with a "please help me welcome" line that will encourage applause.

You've worked hard to create a dazzling presentation, so give yourself the edge of a great introduction.

On this day in history

Notable events
In 1903, Clyde J. Coleman was issued a patent for an electric automobile starter.

In 2020, the Dow Jones Industrial Average closed above 30,000 points for the first time.

Births
Zachary Taylor, 12th U.S. President, 1784

John Froelich, American inventor, invented the first gasoline-powered tractor that would go in forward and reverse, 1849

Stanford R. Ovshinsky, American engineer, scientist, businessman, and inventor (over 400 patents), best known for nickel-metal hydride battery and phase-change memory, 1922

Deaths
Hiram Stevens Maxim, an American-British prolific inventor (automatic fire sprinkler, curling iron, steam inhaler, more) known as the creator of the first automatic machine gun, 1916

Roger Putnam, businessman, politician, and trustee of the Lowell Observatory who facilitated the search for Pluto, 1972

Phyllis Fraser (also known as Phyllis Cerf Wagner), American socialite, writer, publisher, and actress, cofounder of Beginner Books, 2006

Thought for the day

"It is wise to remember that you are one of those who can be fooled some of the time."

— Laurence J. Peter

I pray that I may not desire being honored or praised.

Read:
Proverbs, Chapter 24

November 25

For I am the Lord your God, the one who takes hold of your right hand, who says to you, 'Don't be afraid, I am helping you.' *(Isaiah 43:2, NET)*

Benefits of reading for pleasure

Why do you read? It might be to maintain your professional skills, keep up with the latest news and trends, as part of a course of study, or for simple pleasure. If you think you don't have time to read for pleasure, think again. There are a number of benefits of reading purely for fun.

Pleasure reading reduces stress by allowing you to take a break from your usual environment so you can relax and refocus. It increases your vocabulary and exercises your imagination. You can learn something, even if you're reading fiction. Reading is a mental exercise, which means it improves brain function. Reading can also help make you a better writer. Finally, it's convenient. It's easy to take books or other reading material with you, and reading doesn't disturb anyone around you.

Ways to be more productive

- Limit distractions by identifying and eliminating what's keeping you from focusing on the task at hand.
- Do the most important or challenging things first.
- Get up and get to work early.
- Break large tasks into smaller chunks.
- Make efficient processes more efficient.
- Find repeatable shortcuts and automate as much as possible.
- Don't multitask.
- Eliminate (or substantially reduce) inefficient communication.
- Take breaks and relax.
- Say no.

Read:
Proverbs, Chapter 25

On this day in history

Notable events

In 1975, Robert S. Ledley was granted a U.S. patent for a whole-body CT diagnostic X-ray scanner, which set the basic design for modern CT scanners.

Births

Andrew Carnegie, American industrialist and philanthropist who led the expansion of the American steel industry in the late 19th century, 1835

John F. Kennedy, Jr., American attorney and magazine publisher, 1960

Deaths

Harriet Hubbard Ayer, American cosmetics entrepreneur and journalist, 1903

Charles Kettering, American inventor (holder of 186 patents), engineer, founder of Delco, 1958

Konrad Wachsmann, German-American modernist architect known for his contribution to the mass production of building components, 1980

Thought for the day

"You look at any giant corporation, and I mean the biggies, and they all started with a guy with an idea, doing it well."

Irvine Robbins

I pray that I may see God working among us.

> Grow your faith by taking an inventory of how you spend your time and evaluating what you've done for the Lord.

November 26

It was by faith that Noah built a large boat to save his family from the flood. He obeyed God, who warned him about things that had never happened before. By his faith Noah condemned the rest of the world, and he received the righteousness that comes by faith. *(Hebrews 11:7, NLT)*

Give thanks for the small blessings

How often do you take conscious note of the small things that bless you, the simple moments of delight that bring you joy?

It could be the sound of a child's laughter, the feel of a gentle spring breeze, the fragrance of cookies baking, or the sight of a hummingbird darting through a garden. These ordinary things are evidence of God's extraordinary grace.

Every good and perfect gift is from above, coming down from the Father of the heavenly lights, who does not change like shifting shadows. (James 1:17, NIV)

As you go through your day, pay attention to these small ways in which God reveals himself and let them bring you gladness.

The right outcome is more important than being right

It's nice to be right, but no one is right all the time. Instead of trying for personal perfection, try to be less wrong and focus on better outcomes for everyone, no matter whose idea it is or who gets credit.

Be human and vulnerable. Set your ego aside and focus on creating the best possible result. Learn how to recover from mistakes and view them as an opportunity to learn and grow. Sometimes being wrong is the best thing for you.

Read:
Proverbs, Chapter 26

On this day in history

Notable events

In 1867, the first U.S. patent for a refrigerated railroad car was issued to J.B. Sutherland.

In 1948, the first Polaroid Land Camera model 95 sold for $89.75 at the Jordan Marsh department store in Boston.

Births

Ellen G. White, American author and cofounder of the Seventh-day Adventist Church, 1827

Willis Carrier, American engineer best known for inventing modern air conditioning, founder of Carrier Corporation, 1876

Maurice McDonald, American entrepreneur, cofounder (with his brother Richard McDonald) of McDonald's fast food restaurants, 1902

Victor Grinich, American pioneer in the semiconductor industry, member of the "traitorous eight" that founded Silicon Valley, cofounder of Fairchild Semiconductor, 1924

Deaths

Sojourner Truth, preacher, abolitionist, and women's rights advocate, 1883

Washington Atlee Burpee, American horticulturist and founder of Burpee Seeds, 1915

John Browning, American firearm designer, founder of Browning Arms Company, 1926

Verne Winchell, American businessman, founder of Winchell's Donuts, served as chairman, president, and CEO of the Denny's restaurant chain, 2002

Thought for the day

"We are supposed to forgive everyone; everyone includes ourselves."

Denis Waitley

I pray to remember that even when I am surprised, I am living God's plan.

November 27

> "At that time I will put you on trial. I am eager to witness against all sorcerers and adulterers and liars. I will speak against those who cheat employees of their wages, who oppress widows and orphans, or who deprive the foreigners living among you of justice, for these people do not fear me," says the Lord of Heaven's Armies. *(Malachi 3:5, NLT)*

Sending direct mail? How to choose a service provider

Direct mail continues to be a powerful marketing tool. Consider these issues when choosing a direct mail firm.

Degree of automation. Some mail houses are highly automated, but only serve high-volume mailers. Others are less automated, do more manual work, and serve smaller mailers. Find a match between your volume and how much automation you want and need.

Capacity and infrastructure. Does the mail house have the equipment and staffing to handle your specific mail pieces?

Customer service. How flexible is the mail house? Can they work with you if you have a delay on your end (which could cost more), or do you have to fit into their production schedule (which is how they keep their prices down)?

Effective direct mail marketing requires choosing a mail house that offers the right mix of hands-on people and equipment to do your specific job.

Thought for the day

"The beginning of anxiety is the end of faith, and the beginning of true faith is the end of anxiety."

George Mueller

I pray to release the grudges I've been carrying.

Read:
Proverbs, Chapter 27

On this day in history

Notable events

In 1924, the first Macy's department store held its first ever parade on Thanksgiving Day (originally known as Macy's Christmas Parade).

In 1948, Honda Motors opened a location in the U.S. for the first time.

Births

Forrest C. Shaklee, American chiropractor, philosopher, and entrepreneur, founder of the Shaklee Corporation, credited with creating the first vitamin in the U.S., 1894

William E. Simon, American businessman, philanthropist, U.S. Secretary of the Treasury (1974-1977), president of the U.S. Olympic Committee (1981-1985), 1927

Deaths

Clement Studebaker, American wagon and carriage manufacturer, cofounder of the H&C Studebaker Company, precursor of the Studebaker Corporation, 1901

The best question to ask yourself

When you feel like you're spinning your wheels or you're overwhelmed with too much to do, stop and ask yourself this question:

Am I working on the right things?

The question is not about how much you can do, but whether you're doing the right things. Are you spending time doing tasks that could—and should—be delegated to someone else? Are you spending time on things that might not even need to be done?

To reduce stress and improve your productivity, take a step back, look at the big picture, and be sure you're working on the right things.

November 28

> For we are his workmanship, created in Christ Jesus for good works, which God prepared beforehand, that we should walk in them.
> *(Ephesians 2:10, ESV)*

If the customer is wrong, listen

You've probably heard the traditional business adage:

Rule 1: The customer is always right.

Rule 2: If the customer is ever wrong, see rule 1.

The reality is that customers are not always right—but they are always the customer. And when they're wrong, you can learn from them.

Customers who are demanding, unreasonable, and even just confused can be a wealth of information you can use to improve and grow your company. Listening closely to customers who are wrong can help you identify unmet needs, build alignment, avoid future mistakes, and increase customer trust and loyalty. Here's how:

Ask open-ended questions. Get customers talking freely—they may provide you with some unexpected and game-changing insights.

Ask follow-up questions. Don't expect customers to tell you everything you need to know with their first answer. Ask for clarifications and more details.

Focus on the problem. It's tempting to want to talk about what you did right, but the purpose of your conversation is to resolve the problem and learn how you can improve in the future, so stay focused on the negatives.

Accept the customers' emotions. If they need to blow off steam, let them. If they start going down a rabbit hole, don't stop them—it's possible that side trip will reveal some valuable insights.

Welcome silence. Give your customers time to think. If you ask a question they don't answer immediately, be patient and wait. You don't have to fill the silence with noise.

On this day in history

Notable events

In 1914, the New York Stock Exchange reopened for bond trading after shutting its doors on July 31 due to the outbreak of World War I; stock trading resumed on December 12, 1914.

In 1922, the first use of skywriting in advertising was demonstrated over Times Square in New York City. The message "Hello USA. Call Vanderbilt 7200" generated 47,000 phone calls to the Vanderbilt Hotel in the next three hours.

Births

John Wesley Hyatt, American entrepreneur (founder of Hyatt Roller Bearing company), inventor (mainly known for simplifying the production of celluloid), holder of more than 200 patents, 1837

Helen K. Copley, American newspaper publisher and philanthropist, 1922

Berry Gordy, American record executive, songwriter, and producer, founder of the Motown record label, 1929

Thought for the day

"A simple strategy that will save you so many headaches: Don't care about winning trivial arguments. Someone says something you don't agree with? Smile, nod, and move on to more important things. Life is short. Not caring about having the last word will save you so much time."

— *James Clear*

I pray that I may see God in everything, even—and especially—in the things that don't seem Godly.

Read:
Proverbs, Chapter 28

November 29

Through him all things were made; without him nothing was made that has been made. In him was life, and that life was the light of all mankind. The light shines in the darkness, and the darkness has not overcome it. *(John 1:3-5, NIV)*

How to be happy

Life is precious and too short to be unhappy. Gad Saad, professor at Concordia University and author of *The Saad Truth About Happiness*, offers these ways to maximize your happiness:

1. Find the right spouse. Choose a spouse you like as well as love, someone with whom you share values and who is your best friend. Approach your marriage with humility.

2. Work your way to the right profession. Choose a job you find fulfilling and meaningful.

3. Seek the sweet spot. Use the inverted U curve to find the optimum amount of whatever you're considering.

4. Stay playful. Life is serious business and without play it can be overwhelming. Don't lose your play instinct.

5. Pursue many interests. An enriching way to live is to pursue knowledge across multiple disciplines.

6. Be persistent and resilient. Don't get discouraged when things aren't going as planned. Push forward and stay in the game. And don't be afraid to fail.

7. Minimize regret. Don't let yourself get mired in regrets and misery. "Be happy," Saad says. "It's a better way to live."

On this day in history

Notable events
In 1972, Atari released Pong, the first commercially successful video game.
In 2021, Twitter announced that Jack Dorsey was stepping down as CEO and would be replaced by Parag Agrawal.

Births
Philip L. Carret, American investor and founder of Pioneer Fund, one of the first mutual funds in the U.S., 1896
Robert A. Swanson, American venture capitalist, cofounder of the biotechnology giant Genentech, 1947 (unconfirmed)

Deaths
Horacy Greeley, founder and editor of the *New York Tribune*, 1872

Small daily habits can lead to big results

Whatever your goals, creating and sticking to daily habits will help you reach them. Try these:

Establish a routine. Some people swear by early rising, others by exercise, others by a meal schedule. Figure out what works for you and do it every day. Be sure to include a commitment to daily prayer and time with God.

Learn something new. Do something every day that will allow you to expand your knowledge and sharpen your skills.

Manage your spending of both money and time. Be sure you're getting a positive return on your investment and eliminate what you don't need.

Thought for the day

"Children will not remember you for the material things you provided but for the feeling that you cherished them."
Richard L. Evans

Read:
Proverbs, Chapter 29

I pray on what Jesus commands of his disciples in John 13:34.

November 30

> "And when you stand praying, if you hold anything against anyone, forgive them, so that your Father in heaven may forgive you your sins." *(Mark 11:25, NIV)*

Create a business blue zone

Blue zones are regions in the world that enjoy exceptional longevity, so named because the scientists who conducted the original survey used a blue pen on a map to mark villages with long-lived populations. But blue zones don't have to be geographic regions. You can create a business blue zone in your company by creating a culture that values a healthy workforce.

Support healthful eating. If you provide meals and/or snacks, avoid highly processed junk food and offer healthier options.

Promote intergenerational connections. It's likely that your workforce consists of multiple generations. Find ways for all ages to connect with and learn from one another.

Encourage movement. An inactive lifestyle is a cause of many chronic diseases. Look for ways to incorporate movement into your environment, even if it's just walking through the office or taking the stairs rather than the elevator.

Provide resources for physical and mental health. Offer workplace wellness programs and health benefits. Foster a culture that encourages work-life balance.

Bring your faith to work. Live out your faith by demonstrating integrity, compassion, and service in all you do.

Creating a business blue zone will not only mean healthier employees, it will mean an overall healthier company.

The most arrogant person in the room is the most insecure.
The most judgmental person has the biggest hidden story.
Keeping this in mind makes it easier to love and serve these people.

Today we observe

International Computer Security Day

Atlantic hurricane season ends

On this day in history

Notable events

In 1858, John Landis Mason received a U.S. patent for his invention, the Mason jar. Patent No 22186 is likely the most commonly seen patent number in glass manufacturing history because it was embossed on millions, or even billions, of fruit jars.

In 1886, George Westinghouse's first successful U.S. alternating current (AC) power plant opened in Buffalo, New York.

Births

Cyrus West Field, American businessman and financier, cofounder of the Atlantic Telegraph Company, credited with getting the first telegraph line across the Atlantic Ocean completed, 1819

Mark Twain (Samuel Langhorne Clemens), American author, entrepreneur, publisher, and lecturer, 1835

Joan Ganz Cooney, American television writer and producer, a founder of Sesame Workshop, co-creator of *Sesame Street*, 1929

Deaths

Paul Crouch, American television evangelist and cofounder with his wife Jan of the Trinity Broadcasting Network, 2013

George H.W. Bush, 41st U.S. President, 2018

Thought for the day

"When you clench your fist, no one can put anything in your hand."

Alex Haley

I pray to serve the Lord by serving others.

Read:
Proverbs, Chapter 30

Christian Business Almanac

December

December was originally the tenth month of the year and got its name from the Latin word *decem* (ten). It's the final month of the year, and the last of seven months to have 31 days.

The Anglo-Saxons called December Winter Monath (Winter Month) and Yule Monath, which refers to the custom of burning a Yule log during this month as part of pagan Yule celebrations. After many Anglo-Saxons converted to Christianity, they called December Heligh Monath (Holy Month).

December birthstone
Turquoise, zircon, tanzanite

December flower
Narcissus, holly

December is ...
- HIV/AIDS Awareness Month
- International Sharps Injury Prevention Awareness Month
- Learn a Foreign Language Month
- National Car Donation Month
- National Fruit Cake Month
- National Write a Business Plan Month
- Seasonal Affective Disorder Awareness Month
- Universal Human Rights Month

Mark your calendar for these December holidays and observances

Second Friday in December	National Salesperson Day
Third Thursday in December	National Regifting Day
Third Friday in December	National Ugly Christmas Sweater Day
The Saturday before Christmas	Super Saturday or Panic Saturday

Fun Facts about December

December originally had 30 days. When January and February were added to the calendar, December was shortened to 29 days. In the subsequent Julian calendar, two days were added, making December 31 days long.

In the Northern Hemisphere, December contains the winter solstice, the day with the fewest daylight hours, and the summer solstice in the Southern Hemisphere, the day with the most daylight hours.

December 1

For God is not unjust so as to forget your work and the love you have demonstrated for his name, in having served and continuing to serve the saints. *(Hebrews 6:10, NET)*

Do an annual website audit

Have you ever landed on a website and found information that's out of date or inconsistent, links that don't work, or images that don't display? Could there be pages like that on your website?

Most business websites these days reflect the rapidly-changing environment in which we operate. New content gets added and old material doesn't always get updated. That's understandable—even small companies can easily have hundreds or thousands of pages on their websites.

The solution? An annual website audit.

Go through every page on your website, making sure the information is accurate, all the links work, and images and text display properly. You don't have to do it all at once; schedule several times throughout the year when you'll check groups of pages so it's not an overwhelming chore.

It's tedious and time-consuming, but it's a worthwhile investment. Compare it to those special annual freshening-up things you do for your brick-and-mortar location, like shampooing the carpets, painting, or deep-cleaning.

Create a spreadsheet that lists all the pages and blog posts on your site. Once you have the spreadsheet built, keep it current by adding new pages when they're posted. Check each page once a year and log the details on your spreadsheet.

Review the page title, description, content, keywords, internal links, and external links. Identify your most-viewed pages; figure out what it is about the content on those pages that makes them popular and how you can duplicate that for other pages. Also look for content gaps and make corrections when you find areas where your content is thin or missing altogether.

Today we observe
National Christmas Book Day

On this day in history

Notable events

In 1913, Henry Ford implemented a new type of manufacturing process: the moving assembly line. This innovation shortened the time it took to build a car from more than twelve hours to one hour and 33 minutes.

In 1913, Gulf Refining Co. opened the first drive-in gas station in Pittsburgh, Pennsylvania. The station also offered tube and tire installation, free water and air, crankcase services, and commercial road maps.

In 1998, Exxon and Mobil merged; the $80 billion deal created ExxonMobil Corporation.

In 2001, Trans World Airlines (TWA) ceased operations.

Births

Peter Kalikow, real estate developer and past owner/publisher of the *New York Post*, 1942

Nicholas Negroponte, academic, computer scientist, and author, founder of MIT's Media Lab, founder of One Laptop per Child Association, 1943

Deaths

Norman Abramson, American engineer and computer scientist known for developing the ALOHAnet system, which formed the basis of the protocols essential in the ethernet now in wide use, 2020

Thought for the day

"The darker the night, the brighter the stars. The deeper the grief, the closer is God!"

Fyodor Dostoevsky

I pray to lead with love.

Read:
Proverbs, Chapter 1

December 2

You know the generous grace of our Lord Jesus Christ. Though he was rich, yet for your sakes he became poor, so that by his poverty he could make you rich. *(2 Corinthians 8:9, NLT)*

Formatting tips your readers will appreciate

Whether you're writing emails, short articles or long reports, be kind to your readers. Make it easy for them to understand and absorb your content. These formatting tips will help:

Organize your information. Don't share your first draft with anyone. Do your "brain dump"—get everything down that needs to be included, then get it organized. Put the most important information first, then provide more details. End with a close that wraps everything up or provides a call to action.

Use short sentences and paragraphs. Don't publish a gray wall of text. White space makes your material easier on the eyes and brain. Have just one idea in each sentence and paragraph. Limit sentences to twenty-five words or fewer and paragraphs to two or three sentences.

Create lists. When you have a series of items, use numbered or bulleted lists to present them.

Cut, cut, cut. Remember that less is more. Delete unnecessary adjectives and adverbs. Rewrite complex phrases in simpler language using fewer words. Focus on what your readers want and need to know, then cut the rest.

Give to God what is not from God and let him take care of it.
Don't hold on to anything that is not from God.

Read:
Proverbs, Chapter 2

Today we observe
World Nuclear Energy Day

On this day in history
Notable events
In 2001, Enron Corporation filed for Chapter 11 bankruptcy protection, sparking one of the largest corporate scandals in U.S. history.

Births
William Cooper, American merchant, land speculator and developer, founder of Cooperstown, New York, 1754

S. Joseph Begun, German-American engineer and inventor known for his contributions to magnetic recording, underwater acoustics, and telecommunications, 1905

Peter Goldmark, Hungarian-American engineer instrumental in developing the long-playing $33^{1}/_{3}$ rpm phonograph disc, 1906

Randolph Apperson Hearst, American newspaper publisher, son of William Randolph Hearst, father of Patty Hearst, 1915

Deaths
Henry Clay Frick, American industrialist, financier, and art patron, founder of H.C. Frick & Company coke manufacturing company, chairman of Carnegie Steel Company, known for strikebreaking and being a member of the South Fork Fishing and Hunting Club (blamed for causing the Johnstown flood), 1919

Thought for the day
"What you do makes a difference, and you have to decide what kind of difference you want to make."
Jane Goodall

I am thankful for the weather and the changing of the seasons.

December 3

And you will say in that day: "Give thanks to the Lord, call upon his name, make known his deeds among the peoples, proclaim that his name is exalted. *(Isaiah 12:4, ESV)*

Count the steps

Do you have stairs in or around your home or workplace? For your safety, know the number of steps in each set of stairs.

According to the American Journal of Emergency Medicine, more than one million people per year are treated in emergency departments for stair-related injuries.

You'll be safer on stairs when you know how many steps you have to take to reach the top or bottom of the staircase.

This is especially important if you are in the dark, carrying something (such as a child, pet, laundry basket, large box, etc.), or for any other reason can't see your feet or the steps.

It's great that so many people are counting steps for fitness these days. Go one step further—count and remember the steps on your stairways to reduce your risk of falling.

Thought for the day

"Do not wish to be anything but what you are, and try to be that perfectly."
St. Francis de Sales

I pray that I can be a vehicle for the Christmas spirit to fill the hearts and lives of others.

> Grow your faith by identifying your spiritual gifts, aligning them with your purpose, and serving others through them.

Today we observe
3D Printing Day

On this day in history

Notable events
- In 1979, the last Pacer rolled off the assembly line at the American Motors Corporation (AMC) factory in Kenosha, Wisconsin.
- In 1992, the first SMS text message was sent; engineer Neil Papworth used a personal computer to send the message "Merry Christmas" to the phone of a colleague.
- In 2019, Google cofounders Larry Page and Sergey Brin stepped down from their respective roles as CEO and president of parent company Alphabet; Sundar Pichai became head of both.

Births
- Cleveland Abbe, American meteorologist, inventor, advocate of time zones, known as the father of the U.S. Weather Bureau, 1838
- Charles Alfred Pillsbury, American businessman, flour industrialist, and politician, cofounder of the Pillsbury Company, 1842
- Helen Robson Walton, American philanthropist, wife of Wal-Mart Stores, Inc., founder Sam Walton, 1919
- Peter C. Schultz, American businessman and co-inventor of the fiber optics used for telecommunications, 1942
- Sean Parker, American entrepreneur and philanthropist, cofounder of the file-sharing service Napster, first president of Facebook, 1979

Deaths
- John Bartlett, American writer and publisher (*Bartlett's Familiar Quotations*), 1905
- Mary Baker Eddy, American religious leader, author, and publisher, founder of The Church of Christ, Scientist and *The Christian Science Monitor* plus three religious magazines, 1910

Read:
Proverbs, Chapter 3

December 4

> "My food," said Jesus, "is to do the will of him who sent me and to finish his work. *(John 4:34, NIV)*

Sparking innovation

Innovation is a cornerstone of successful businesses. It's an essential part of companies that stay ahead of the market, that turn customers into raving fans, that thrive no matter the circumstances and challenges.

There's no standing still; you're either moving forward (and growing) or backward (and declining). The challenge of being an organization that's moving forward and growing is that growth often leads to complexity.

"Complexity crushes innovation," says Krystal Parker, president of the U.S. Christian Chamber of Commerce. "The more money you make, the more people you hire—it leads to more policies, rules, processes, and layers of management. That slows down the machine."

The solution is simplicity. Parker offers six ways to simplify your business.

1. Be sure every process and rule you have in place, every decision you make, aligns with your company's purpose and mission.
2. Make it easy to do business with you.
3. Eliminate redundancy.
4. Eliminate unnecessary meetings and bureaucracy.
5. Look at every position, ask tough questions, and restructure as necessary.
6. Assess how you as the leader are spending your time.

"No organization, no business, naturally drifts toward simplicity as it grows," Parker says. "It will get more complex. What we have to do as leaders is examine what we're doing in the organization, understand the why, and simplify everywhere we can. That's what will keep us innovating and growing."

Today we observe

Extraordinary Work Team Recognition Day

On this day in history

Notable events

In 1881, the *Los Angeles Times* was published for the first time.

Births

Chester Greenwood, American engineer, inventor (earmuffs), and manufacturer, 1858

Deaths

Charles Henry Dow, American journalist and cofounder of Dow Jones & Company and *The Wall Street Journal*, 1902

Alfred Fuller, Canadian-American businessman, entrepreneur, and philanthropist (Fuller Brush Company), 1973

Thought for the day

"God doesn't want something from us. He simply wants us."

C.S. Lewis

I pray for the ability to release anger.

 Read: Proverbs, Chapter 4

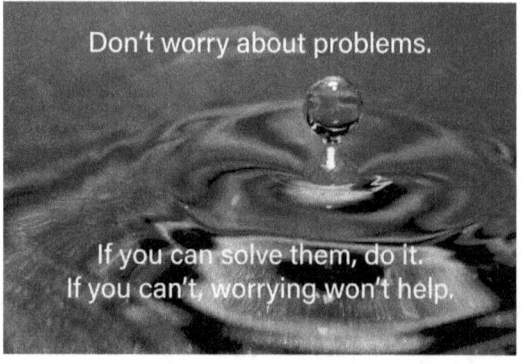

Don't worry about problems. If you can solve them, do it. If you can't, worrying won't help.

December 5

G uide me into your truth and teach me. For you are the God who delivers me; on you I rely all day long. *(Psalm 25:5, NET)*

Plan your charitable giving for next year

Maximize your charitable giving by setting it up a year in advance.

"I recommend planning your charitable giving once a year," says Michelle Ogden, founder and CEO of Ogden Wealth, LLC (Maitland, Florida). "Set aside time in December to do your research and put together a list of the organizations you're going to support the following year. Choose organizations that produce visible results and back up your decision with resources like Charity Navigator. Do this even for those that you've checked out before because things can change."

Once you've selected the charities and determined the amount you'll give, Ogden says, "Set up the donation schedule for the year and you're done. Of course, if you find a new organization you want to give to, you can—or you can put it on your list for the following year."

Put all of next year's tax deadlines on your calendar so you don't miss any important filings or payments.

Thought for the day

"If you yourself are at peace, then there is at least some peace in the world."
Thomas Merton

I am thankful for the opportunity to be kind to others.

Read:
Proverbs, Chapter 5

Today we observe
National Blue Jeans Day

On this day in history

Notable events
In 1876, Daniel Stillson was granted a U.S. patent for the first practical pipe wrench.
In 1933, Utah ratified the 21st Amendment, repealing the 18th Amendment and officially ending Prohibition in the U.S.
In 1955, the American Federation of Labor and Congress of Industrial Organizations (AFL-CIO) was formed.
In 2022, rental car company Hertz announced it would pay $168 million to settle customers' claims related to the company falsely reporting that customers stole vehicles.

Births
Martin Van Buren, 8th U.S. President (first President to be born as a U.S. citizen), 1782
Clyde Cessna, American aircraft designer, aviator, and early aviation entrepreneur, best known as the principal founder of the Cessna Aircraft Corporation, 1879
Philip K. Wrigley, American chewing gum manufacturer and MLB executive, son of William Wrigley Jr., 1894
Walt Disney, American animator, film producer, and entrepreneur, 1901

Deaths
Glenn L. Martin, American aviation pioneer and entrepreneur, founder of an aircraft company that eventually became Lockheed Martin, 1955
Walter Dorwin Teague, American industrial designer, architect, illustrator, writer, and entrepreneur who pioneered the establishment of industrial design as a profession in the U.S., often referred to as the dean of industrial design, 1960
Hazel Bishop, American chemist, inventor ("No-Smear Lipsticks"), entrepreneur, founder of the cosmetics company Hazel Bishop, Inc., 1998
Jim Rohn, American entrepreneur, author, and motivational speaker, 2009

December 6

> **B**ut love your enemies, do good to them, and lend to them without expecting to get anything back. Then your reward will be great, and you will be children of the Most High, because he is kind to the ungrateful and wicked. Be merciful, just as your Father is merciful. *(Luke 6:35-36, NIV)*

Recognizing servant leaders

What does a servant leader look like? Here are key characteristics of servant leaders:

They have strong communication skills. They know how to accurately convey information to a variety of groups. They listen more than they talk and can learn from anyone.

They are empathetic. They can understand and share the feelings of others.

They stand behind their team. They support and defend their teams as necessary. They never throw anyone under the bus.

They celebrate the success of others. They are not envious.

They're persuasive rather than authoritative. They convince rather than coerce, and they're effective at building consensus within groups.

They have foresight. They can predict what will happen or be needed in the future.

They accept and value others as they are, where they are. They do not, however, accept negative behaviors or poor performance. They know the difference between who people are and what they do.

They are aware. They know what's going on in the world and in their own organization.

They lead by example. They know, share, and live their values.

They empower others. They promote and encourage personal and professional growth in the people they lead.

They add value to those around them. They intentionally build others up and make others feel valued and appreciated.

They build community. They know how to bring people together and create a sense of belonging.

On this day in history

Notable events

In 1865, the 13th Amendment to the U.S. Constitution was ratified, officially ending the institution of slavery.

In 1877, the *Washington Post* published its first edition.

In 2022, production of the Boeing 747 ended as the final 747 rolled out of the company's factory.

Births

Fred Duesenberg, German-American automobile and engine designer, manufacturer, and racer, credited with introducing an eight-cylinder engine and four-wheel hydraulic brakes, cofounder of the Duesenberg Motor Company, 1876

Irv Robbins, Canadian-born American businessman, cofounder of the Baskin-Robbins ice cream parlor chain, 1917

Craig Newmark, American internet entrepreneur and philanthropist, best known as the founder of the classifieds website Craigslist, 1952

Deaths

Robert A. Swanson, American venture capitalist, cofounder of the biotechnology giant Genentech, 1999

Thought for the day

"If you want to stand out, don't be different. Be outstanding."

Meredith West

I am thankful to be able to study and learn new things.

Read:
Proverbs, Chapter 6

December 7

A voice of one calling: "In the wilderness prepare the way for the Lord; make straight in the desert a highway for our God. (Isaiah 40:3, NIV)

Achieving work-life balance

Even when you're working in a Kingdom business, and especially when you're not, you need balance between the time you spend working and doing other things. Finding equilibrium between your professional and personal lives will improve your overall well-being, enhance your relationships, and make you more productive. Try these tips for achieving work-life balance:

Do an evaluation. Reflect on your situation so you can understand what's working and what needs adjusting.

Identify your priorities. What matters to you and are you doing enough of it? Can you integrate responsibilities to honor more than one priority at a time? Be sure self-care is one of your top priorities.

Set boundaries. Define what you will and won't do, set boundaries, and enforce them.

Create beneficial routines. Routines will help you complete tasks more efficiently.

Disconnect from work during non-work hours. Take time to truly relax and reset.

Go on vacation. You need time away for rest and restoration.

Commit to family and friends. Honor the time you commit to spending with family and friends, whether you're just relaxing with them or on some exciting adventure. Nurture those relationships.

Take up a hobby. Do something outside of work that will help you relax and engage a different part of your brain.

Review and adjust. Your business responsibilities will evolve, and your personal circumstances will shift. Regularly review your work-life balance and make adjustments to stay optimized.

I pray that when God calls, I never hesitate to say, "Send me."

Today we observe

National Pearl Harbor Remembrance Day
International Civil Aviation Day
National Letter Writing Day

On this day in history

Notable events

In 1941, Japan launched a surprise attack on the U.S. Naval base at Pearl Harbor, drawing the U.S. into World War II.

Births

Benjamin Eisenstadt, American businessman, inventor, and philanthropist, designer of the modern sugar packet, developer of Sweet'N Low, and founder of Cumberland Packing Corporation, 1906

Victor Kiam, American entrepreneur, owner and spokesman for Remington Products, owner of the New England Patriots football team, 1926

Deaths

Rube Goldberg, American cartoonist, sculptor, author, engineer, and inventor, best known for cartoons depicting complicated gadgets performing simple tasks in indirect, convoluted ways, 1970

Peter Goldmark, Hungarian-American engineer instrumental in developing the long-playing 33 1/3 rpm phonograph disc, 1977

Jay Van Andel, American businessman, cofounder of the Amway Corporation, 2004

Saul Steinberg, American businessman and financier; founder of Leasco, a computer leasing company, which he used in the takeover of Reliance Insurance Company, 2012

Thought for the day

"Good people can't stand the sight of deliberate evil; the wicked can't stand the sight of well-chosen goodness."

Eugene H. Petersen

Read:
Proverbs, Chapter 7

December 8

"For even the Son of Man did not come to be served, but to serve, and to give his life as a ransom for many." *(Mark 10:45, NIV)*

When a client is a bully

Sadly, bullies are everywhere and it's important to recognize them. In business, common bullying behaviors include aggressive communication, verbal threats or intimidation, and unreasonable demands or expectations. How should you handle a client who is a bully?

There are always risks when confronting a bully, but if you accept their negative behavior, it won't get better and could get worse. Stand your ground and insist on being treated with respect. Be professional and stay calm. Don't give a bully the power to control your emotions.

Always set boundaries and expectations upfront and in writing, and consistently enforce them. If you get resistance, refer to your written agreement.

In a conversation with a bully, focus on the real dispute. If you can, identify issues that are not in dispute and confirm your agreement on them. After you get the bully to clearly say what he wants, restate it and ask if that's all you need to resolve. Make notes and follow up with a "this will confirm our conversation" email to document what was said.

Because bullies need to feel like they've won, you may want to make some small concessions, but balance that against the risk of setting a precedent that will only lead to a repeat of the bullying.

Sometimes standing up to a bully works and you can move forward with a mutually beneficial relationship. Sometimes the only way to handle a bully is to walk away. No amount of business is worth your self-respect and peace of mind.

Read:
Proverbs, Chapter 8

Today we observe
National Blue Collar Day

On this day in history

Notable events

In 2010, SpaceX became the first privately held company to launch, orbit, and recover a spacecraft.

Births

Eli Whitney, American inventor, best known for inventing the cotton gin, 1765

William C. Durant, American automobile industry pioneer, cofounder of General Motors and Chevrolet, founder of Frigidaire, 1861

Deaths

William Henry Vanderbilt, American railroad magnate and philanthropist who nearly doubled the Vanderbilt family fortune bequeathed to him by his father, Cornelius, 1885

Evelyn Berezin, American computer designer of the first computer-driven word processor, 2018

Thought for the day

"Character is what God and the angels know of us; reputation is what men and women think of us."

Horace Mann

I pray for those who find Christmas season a time of pain and grief.

> Grow your faith by intentionally putting on the armor of God every day.

December 9

> "Therefore I tell you, do not worry about your life, what you will eat or drink; or about your body, what you will wear. Is not life more than food, and the body more than clothes? *(Matthew 6:25, NIV)*

Understand and avoid projection bias

Projection bias is when individuals overestimate the extent to which others share their opinions and/or assume that their tastes or preferences will remain the same over time. Essentially, it's projecting your biases onto others and into the future.

A simple example of projection bias is assuming that everyone else enjoys the same type of food that you do and that your tastes won't change. In business, it's assuming that your customers make their buying decisions based on the same reasoning you use or that everyone has the same access to technology.

Projection bias is a cognitive shortcoming that causes us to make short-sighted decisions that might not hold up in the long run. Understanding projection bias is a good first step to avoiding its negative impact.

Tips for dealing with projection bias:

Assume nothing and explain the obvious. It might be common sense to you, but it isn't to everyone. The process of explaining will clarify your thoughts, generate new ideas, and give other team members a chance to offer their alternatives.

Know your audience. Develop a deep understanding of the people who are buying from you as well as the people you want to convert to customers. Don't assume you know them without doing research.

Foster diverse perspectives. Diversity of thought will help you counter biases you would otherwise miss.

Build checks and balances into all your processes to look for projection bias. Establish a review team that can serve as fresh eyes.

On this day in history

Notable events

In 1968, Doug Engelbart and a small team of researchers from the Stanford Research Institute stunned the computing world with a demonstration at a San Francisco computer conference of the computer mouse, graphical user interface, display editing and integrated text and graphics, hyper-documents, and two-way video-conferencing with shared workspaces.

Births

William C. Durant, American automobile industry pioneer, cofounder of General Motors and Chevrolet, 1861

Clarence Birdseye, American inventor, entrepreneur, and naturalist, considered the founder of the modern frozen food industry, founder of the frozen food company Birds Eye, 1886

Dick Van Patten, American actor, comedian, businessman, animal welfare advocate, 1928

Deaths

Ezra Cornell, American businessman and philanthropist (founder of Western Union Telegraph and Cornell University), 1874

You can't hear God speak if you've already decided what you want him to say.

Thought for the day

"We awaken in others the same attitude of mind we hold toward them."
— *Elbert Hubbard*

I pray on the gift of peace in John 14:27.

Read:
Proverbs, Chapter 9

December 10

Exult in his holy name; rejoice, you who worship the Lord. Search for the Lord and for his strength; continually seek him. Remember the wonders he has performed, his miracles, and the rulings he has given, you children of his servant Israel, you descendants of Jacob, his chosen ones. *(1 Chronicles 16:10-13, NLT)*

Ask for feedback

To grow personally and professionally, we need to know what we do well, where we can improve, and how we are perceived. One of the most efficient ways to do that is to get feedback.

Feedback can be tough to handle, especially when it's critical, but the ability to receive it gracefully and then act on it allows us to focus our efforts, make corrections, and ultimately achieve our goals.

Before you ask for feedback, think about what you hope to gain. If you're looking for validation or an ego-boost, consider another way. Your goal should be actionable takeaways that you can implement.

Ask the right people for feedback. Choose people you interact with regularly, who have a relevant perspective, and whom you trust.

Prepare questions that will give you the answers you need. A combination of open-ended and yes/no questions will guide the feedback session. Also be prepared to ask follow-up questions that will give you greater insight into the perspective of the person giving you feedback.

During the feedback session, keep your defenses down, don't take perceived criticisms personally, and maintain a positive attitude. Show respect for the input you're getting by making notes.

Finally, express your appreciation. Let people know how their feedback has affected you by sharing your follow-up plan and progress.

On this day in history

Notable events

In 1915, the one millionth Ford car rolled off the assembly in at the River Rouge plant in Detroit—a milestone that didn't get much attention and even the company didn't notice it at the time.

Births

Matthias W. Baldwin, American inventor and machinery manufacturer, founder of Baldwin Locomotive Works, builder of Old Ironsides, the most famous of early locomotives, 1795

William G. McGowan, American entrepreneur and founder and chairman of MCI Communications, 1927

Douglas Kenney, American comedy writer, producer, performer, and cofounder of *National Lampoon*, 1946

Deaths

Henry Wells, American businessman whose companies were predecessors of American Express and Wells Fargo, 1878

Horace Elgin Dodge, Sr., American automobile manufacturing pioneer, cofounder of Dodge Brothers Company, 1920

Frank Conrad, American electrical engineer and inventor (holder of more than 200 patents), best known for radio development, including his work as a pioneer broadcaster, 1941

Armand Hammer, American business magnate most closely associated with Occidental Petroleum, 1990

Thought for the day

"Don't rule out working with your hands. It does not preclude using your head."

Andy Rooney

I am thankful for the respect and appreciation of others.

Read: Proverbs, Chapter 10

December 11

And I will lead the blind in a way that they do not know, in paths that they have not known I will guide them. I will turn the darkness before them into light, the rough places into level ground. These are the things I do, and I do not forsake them. *(Isaiah 42:16, ESV)*

Be an approachable leader

Effective leaders, the ones that are able to build great teams of high performers, draw people to them. Executive coach Joel Garfinkle offers these tips to be more approachable:

Greet everyone. Speak to everyone warmly, every day. Learn people's names. Make eye contact and practice open body language.

Show you care. Regularly check in with your team. Give your full, undivided attention, ask follow-up questions, and reflect and recap what you've heard.

Offer help. The simple question "How can I help?" signals that you are listening and willing to aid in the solution.

Ask for help. Provide the opportunity for others to shine while you make sure you get the best solution and right person doing the job.

Have a sense of humor. Be willing to laugh at a situation and use a little humor to break the tension.

Be optimistic. Acknowledge when there are troubles, but express confidence in the team's abilities. Believe in a better future and help make it happen.

Make time to chat. Get to know people and connect on a personal level. Follow up from previous conversations and show that you're invested in what they say.

Loosen up. Don't be rigid. While there will always be some separation between leaders and the people who work for them, think of your role as a facilitator, not dictator.

I pray to always recognize the truth.

Today we observe
Holiday Food Drive for Needy Animals Day

On this day in history

Notable events

In 2008, financier Bernard Madoff was arrested and charged with masterminding a long-running Ponzi scheme, one of the biggest investment frauds in Wall Street history.

Births

James L. Kraft, Canadian-American entrepreneur and inventor (pasteurization process for cheese), founder of Kraft Foods, Inc., 1874

Bernard G. Davis, American publisher, cofounder of Ziff Davis Inc., founder of Davis Publications, Inc., 1906

Deaths

Lewis Howard Latimer, American inventor (evaporative air conditioner, improved process for manufacturing carbon filaments for light bulbs, improved toilet system for railroad cars), patent consultant, author, 1928

Charles Rudolph Walgreen, American businessman, founder of Walgreens, 1939

Maurice McDonald, American entrepreneur, cofounder (with his brother Richard McDonald) of McDonald's fast food restaurants, 1971

George Harold Brown, American research engineer, speaker, and prolific inventor (held more than 80 patents) who led RCA's efforts to develop a color television system still in use today, 1987

Thought for the day

"Better to do something imperfectly than to do nothing flawlessly."

Robert H. Schuller

Read:
Proverbs, Chapter 11

December 12

Do not be yoked together with unbelievers. For what do righteousness and wickedness have in common? Or what fellowship can light have with darkness? *(2 Corinthians 6:14, NIV)*

Find opportunity in disaster

Catastrophes happen. In business, it could be the perfect marketing plan failed. Or the trusted employee betrayed you. Or a major customer abandoned you. Or anything that makes you wonder how you're going to survive.

Before you indulge in a downward spiral of self-pity, visualize yourself in the future, thanking God for putting you in circumstances even better than you were in prior to the catastrophe. Then deal with the situation at hand, pray, and trust God to provide the path you need to take.

Sometimes it takes a disaster to find the opportunity God wants for us.

Tell God that you trust him

Yes, he knows it, but tell him—and do it every day. Say, "I trust you, God. I know that you will guide me, protect me, comfort me, and give me the strength I need to live out your will for my life."

It's a commitment you're making as much to yourself as you are to him.

It's fine to *say* that we trust in God. It's far more powerful to personally tell God specifically that you trust him. Do it every day—and follow through on your commitment.

Thought for the day

"Of all the liars in the world, sometimes the worst are our own fears."
Rudyard Kipling

I pray to release the gifts God has given me into the world.

On this day in history

Notable events

In 1980, Apple went public at $22 per share, generating more capital than any IPO since Ford went public in 1956 and later becoming the first U.S. company valued at over $1 trillion.

Births

Henry Wells, American businessman whose companies were predecessors of American Express and Wells Fargo, 1805

William Kissam Vanderbilt I, American businessman, philanthropist, and horse breeder; born into the Vanderbilt family, he managed the family's railroad investments, 1849

Edward R. Bradley, American businessman, philanthropist, racetrack proprietor, owner and breeder of Thoroughbred racehorses, 1859

Philip Drinker, American industrial hygienist, inventor of the first widely used iron lung, 1894

Robert Noyce, American physicist and entrepreneur, cofounder of Fairchild Semiconductor and Intel Corporation, 1927

Deaths

John Wanamaker, American merchant (operated on the then-revolutionary principle of "one price and goods returnable"), philanthropist, and religious, civic, and political figure, 1922

David Sarnoff, Russian-American businessman who headed a conglomerate of telecommunications and media companies (including RCA and NBC), credited with Sarnoff's Law, which states that the value of a broadcast network is proportional to the number of viewers, 1971

Alan Shugart, American engineer, entrepreneur, and business executive, founder of Shugart Associates and Seagate Technology, 2006

Read:
Proverbs, Chapter 12

December 13

No discipline is enjoyable while it is happening—it's painful! But afterward there will be a peaceful harvest of right living for those who are trained in this way. *(Hebrews 12:11, NLT)*

Build a strong culture

Culture plays an essential part in the success or failure of a business. Every company has a culture—it's the personality of the organization, the shared set of workplace values, beliefs, and behaviors. Benefits of a strong culture include higher engagement, productivity, and morale; reduced turnover; greater creativity and innovation; increased revenue and profits; and more.

Andrew Crapuchettes, founder and CEO of RedBalloon.work, offers these tips for building a great culture:

1. Kill gossip in your workplace. Do not allow anyone to talk about others behind their backs. If someone comes to you complaining about someone else, invite the other person into the conversation to reach a resolution.

2. Align authority and responsibility. Every individual must have the authority to appropriately manage their responsibilities.

3. Hire wisely and fire fast. Take the time necessary to make good hiring decisions, but when you realize you've made a mistake, let the person go. Don't get so over-invested in new hires (or even longer-term employees) that you keep them longer than you should. When someone isn't a fit with your culture, the smartest and kindest thing to do for yourself and them is let them move on to a place where they'll be happier.

On this day in history

Notable events

In 2018, Apple announced a major expansion of its operations in Austin, Texas, including a new $1 billion campus in North Austin, plus new sites and expansions in other cities.

Births

John Henry Patterson, American industrialist and founder of National Cash Register Company (NCR), known for pioneering business practices such as constructing the first "daylight factory" buildings with floor-to-ceiling windows that let in light and fresh air, 1844

Jack Tramiel, American businessman, Holocaust survivor, founder of Commodore International, 1928

Gavin Andresen, software developer, founder of the Bitcoin Foundation, 1966

Taylor Swift, American singer-songwriter, producer, director, businesswoman, 1989

Deaths

Thomas A. Watson, American telephone pioneer, shipbuilder, assistant to Alexander Graham Bell, one of the original organizers of the Bell Telephone Company, 1934

Cornelius Vanderbilt Whitney, American businessman, film producer, government official, writer, and philanthropist, 1992

Allen K. Breed, American inventor, entrepreneur, and pioneer in the automotive industry's acceptance of airbags, 1999

Henry Beachell, American plant breeder whose research led to the development of hybrid rice cultivars, known as the most important person in rice improvement in the world, 2006

I am thankful for the time I spend away from business.

Read:
Proverbs, Chapter 13

Thought for the day

"The enemy wants to define you by your scars. Jesus wants to define you by His scars."

Louie Giglio

December 14

> "I will surely bless you and make your descendants as numerous as the stars in the sky and as the sand on the seashore. Your descendants will take possession of the cities of their enemies, and through your offspring all nations on earth will be blessed, because you have obeyed me." *(Genesis 22:17-18, NIV)*

How to get new business from old accounts

Looking for new business among current clients is often more interesting and satisfying than making traditional cold calls. More important, it's usually easier and more rewarding. Try these techniques:

Your service calls should also be sales calls. You won't get an order with every customer contact, but you want to make sure the opportunity is there.

Completely penetrate the account. Be sure you are talking to everyone at the client company who has the need for your product and the authority to buy it. Ask your current contacts for names of others you should be talking to.

Help someone be a hero. Watch for opportunities to create a new need. When you see a problem that your products can solve, share the information with your customer. Help the buyer be a star within the organization because he or she was smart enough to recognize—and then purchase a product to solve—the problem.

Let people help you. Referrals are great prospects for new business. Let your satisfied customers do you a favor by giving you the names of their friends and associates.

Strike a balance. Manage your time so that you nurture and grow your existing accounts but also continue to prospect for new ones.

I pray that I live, and not just live for.

Read:
Proverbs, Chapter 14

On this day in history

Notable events
In 2017, The Walt Disney Company announced it would acquire 21st Century Fox in a $52.4 billion deal.

Births
Erastus Corning, American businessman, investor, politician, and founder of Erastus Corning & Co., 1794
Michael Ovitz, American businessman, investor, and philanthropist, cofounder of Creative Artists Agency, president of The Walt Disney Company (Oct. 1995-Jan. 1997), 1946

Deaths
George Washington, American Founding Father, Commander-in-Chief of the Continental Army during the War for Independence, and first President of the United States, 1799
John Harvey Kellogg, American businessman, inventor, and physician, director of the Battle Creek Sanitarium, developer of a variety of bland vegetarian foods including granola and flaked breakfast cereal, 1943
Richard Gurley Drew, American inventor who invented masking tape and cellophane tape, 1980
Ahmet Ertegun, Turkish-American businessman, songwriter, record executive, and philanthropist, cofounder of Atlantic Records, 2006
Lillian Menasche, founder and CEO of the Lillian Vernon Corporation (first company traded on the American Stock Exchange founded by a woman), 2015

Thought for the day

"Joy does not simply happen to us. We have to choose joy and keep choosing it every day."

Henri J.M. Nouwen

December 15

But the Lord said, "Go, for Saul is my chosen instrument to take my message to the Gentiles and to kings, as well as to the people of Israel. And I will show him how much he must suffer for my name's sake." *(Acts 9:15-16, NLT)*

Reject FOMO—there's joy in missing out

Sometimes the fear of missing out (FOMO) can cause us to miss out on things that are more precious than what we're chasing. If you're packing every waking minute with activity, you might want to learn the joy of missing out (JOMO).

Rest allows your creativity and focus to flourish. Taking time for yourself by disengaging from work and related stressors can nurture and strengthen your personal relationships. And when you practice this type of self-care, you set a positive example for your team.

The result is greater creativity and productivity; stronger, more engaged teams; and reduced or even eliminated burnout.

When you make the decision to miss out on some things, you give yourself the time to focus on what really matters. Embrace that joy.

Thought for the day

"Entrepreneurs have two basic assets: their creativity and their relationships."
Mark Victor Hansen

Read:
Proverbs, Chapter 15

> Grow your faith by expressing honest appreciation to the people you encounter who make your life better.

Today we observe
Bill of Rights Day

On this day in history

Notable events
- In 1836, the U.S. Patent Office located in Blodget's Hotel in Washington, D.C. was destroyed by fire. As a result of the loss of decades of patent documents and files, the Patent Office changed the way it handled record keeping, assigning numbers to patents and requiring multiple copies of supporting documentation.
- In 1925, New York's Madison Square Garden opened and became one of the world's most famous sporting venues.

Births
- Charles Duryea, American engineer of the first-ever working American gasoline-powered car and cofounder of Duryea Motor Wagon Company, 1861
- Arthur D. Little, American chemist, chemical engineer, inventor, and management consultant who pioneered the concept of contracted professional services, 1863
- J. Paul Getty, Sr., American-born British petroleum industrialist, founder of Getty Oil Company, 1892

Deaths
- Maggie L. Walker, African-American businesswoman, teacher, bank founder, and publisher, 1934
- Walt Disney, American animator, film producer, and entrepreneur, 1966
- Forrest C. Shaklee, American chiropractor, philosopher, and entrepreneur, founder of the Shaklee Corporation, credited with creating the first vitamin in the U.S., 1985

I pray that I will find joy in my trials and struggles.

December 16

> "Give, and you will receive. Your gift will return to you in full—pressed down, shaken together to make room for more, running over, and poured into your lap. The amount you give will determine the amount you get back." *(Luke 6:38, NLT)*

Create a culture of curiosity

In our rapidly changing world, a culture that values curiosity, experimentation, and continuous learning is essential for innovation and growth. Curiosity is a natural human instinct that serves as a powerful bridge to endless opportunities and creativity. Seeking to expand our knowledge trains our brains to spot new ideas and discoveries.

Albert Einstein said, "I have no special talents. I am only passionately curious." Curious leaders and employees ask relevant questions, discover new solutions, and explore new possibilities.

Curiosity drives motivation and sparks creativity. It's also an important element in building relationships. Having a genuine interest in others is the foundation of strong relationships.

To cultivate curiosity in the workplace:
- Make asking questions and challenging norms acceptable.
- Welcome new ideas.
- Encourage all employees, whatever their position, to contribute ideas and participate in innovation and evolution.
- Embrace diversity of thought and let fresh ideas collide.
- Have curiosity-driving events, such as book clubs or "Why?" and "What if…?" days.
- Reward asking, effort, and learning in addition to success.

I am thankful for traditions at home and in the workplace.

Read:
Proverbs, Chapter 16

Today we observe
Wright Brothers Day
National Device Appreciation Day

On this day in history
Notable events
In 1773, in a protest of the British Parliament's Tea Act of 1773 that became known as the Boston Tea Party, a group of Massachusetts colonists disguised as Mohawk Indians boarded three British tea ships and dumped 342 chests of tea into the harbor.

In 1905, *Variety*, covering all phases of show business, was first published.

In 1954, the first U.S.-made synthetic diamonds were created by H. Tracy Hall at G.E. Research Laboratories; they were as small as sand grains, which was the size needed as industrial abrasives.

Births
Cy Leslie, American businessman, founder of Voco Records, Pickwick Records, and MGM/UA Home Entertainment Group, 1922

Deaths
Colonel Harland Sanders, American businessman and founder of Kentucky Fried Chicken restaurant chain, 1980

Roy E. Disney, American businessman, senior executive for The Walt Disney Company, nephew of Walt Disney, son of Roy O. Disney, 2009

Robert G. Wilmers, American billionaire banker, chairman and CEO of M&T Bank, 2017

Colin Kroll, American entrepreneur, cofounder of the video hosting service Vine and trivia game app HQ Trivia, 2018

Thought for the day

"Be less curious about people and more curious about ideas."

Marie Curie

December 17

People from many nations will come and say, "Come, let us go up to the mountain of the Lord, to the house of Jacob's God. There he will teach us his ways, and we will walk in his paths." For the Lord's teaching will go out from Zion; his word will go out from Jerusalem. *(Isaiah 2:3, NLT)*

Key elements of goal-setting

Use these key elements of goal-setting as your guide for developing and achieving your goals.

Desire. To be motivated to achieve your goal, it must be something you strongly desire for yourself.

Belief. To actually achieve your goal, you must believe that you have the ability to do so, which is why your goals must be realistic.

Write. Write the goal down in complete detail.

Benefit. Make a list of the specific benefits you will enjoy when you accomplish your goal.

Analysis. Analyze your current status so you have a clear starting point.

Deadline. Set a deadline for when you will accomplish your goal.

Obstacles. Identify and list the obstacles you will have to overcome to attain your goal.

Knowledge. Identify the additional knowledge will you need to acquire to reach your goal.

Assistance. List the individuals and organizations whose support and help you will need to achieve your goal. Include what you can provide for them in exchange.

Plan. Formulate a detailed plan with all the actions you need to take to reach your goal.

Visualize. Develop a clear mental picture of your goal as it will be when attained and "look" at that picture every chance you get.

Implement. Put your plan into action with determination and persistence.

Read:
Proverbs, Chapter 17

On this day in history

Notable events

In 1880, the Edison Illuminating company was established by Thomas Edison to construct electrical generating stations in New York City.

In 1903, Orville and Wilbur Wright made the first successful flight of a self-propelled, heavier-than-air aircraft; the biplane stayed aloft for 12 seconds and covered 120 feet on its inaugural flight.

In 1976, Ted Turner's WTCG TV station (later WTBS) completed its satellite uplink, making it possible to carry its eclectic mix of programming to almost every TV in the nation.

Births

Joseph Henry, American scientist, first secretary of the Smithsonian Institution, known for electromagnetic induction, inventor of a precursor to the electric doorbell and electric relay, 1797

Deaths

George Brayton, American mechanical engineer and inventor, known for introducing the constant pressure engine that is the basis for the gas turbine, 1892

Harvey Hubbell II, American inventor, entrepreneur, and industrialist best known for inventing the electrical plug and pull-chain light socket, 1927

Thought for the day

"If you're trying to persuade people to do something, or buy something, it seems to me you should speak their language."

David Ogilvy

I pray for those who are seeking forgiveness.

December 18

For it is with your heart that you believe and are justified, and it is with your mouth that you profess your faith and are saved. As Scripture says, "Anyone who believes in him will never be put to shame." For there is no difference between Jew and Gentile—the same Lord is Lord of all and richly blesses all who call on him, for, "Everyone who calls on the name of the Lord will be saved." *(Romans 10:10-13, NIV)*

Pay peanuts and you get monkeys

Before you look at the cost of a product or service, consider the value of the benefits it will provide. Be willing to pay a fair price for quality and results.

British advertising tycoon David Ogilvy put it this way:

"Clients who haggle over their agency's compensation are looking through the wrong end of the telescope. Instead of trying to shave a few measly cents off the agency's fifteen percent, they should concentrate on getting more sales results from the eighty-five percent they spend on time and space. That is where the leverage is. No manufacturer ever got rich by underpaying his agency. Pay peanuts and you get monkeys."

This applies to all aspects of business. Will it earn or save more than it costs? Is the price fair? Certainly you want to negotiate a mutually-beneficial deal, but once you've reached that, stop haggling. Put yourself in the shoes of your supplier—how does it make you feel when a customer tries to drive your price down to an unreasonable level? Look through the right end of the telescope.

Thought for the day

"Happiness is a perfume you cannot pour on others without getting a few drops on yourself."

Ralph Waldo Emerson

Read:
Proverbs, Chapter 18

On this day in history

Notable events

- In 1958, the first American communications satellite was launched; it operated for 35 days.
- In 1991, General Motors announced plans to close twenty-one factories and eliminate about 74,000 jobs by 1995.
- In 2002, fashion designer Calvin Klein announced he was selling his company to shirt-maker Phillips-Van Heusen for $430 million.

Births

- Washington Duke, an American tobacco industrialist who began his career as a subsistence farmer, namesake of Duke University, founder of W. Duke, Sons & Co., a tobacco manufacturer that would later be merged with other companies to form American Tobacco Company, 1820
- Walter Dorwin Teague, American industrial designer, architect, illustrator, writer, and entrepreneur who pioneered the establishment of industrial design as a profession in the U.S., often referred to as the dean of industrial design, 1883
- Edwin Howard Armstrong, American electrical engineer and inventor who developed FM radio and the superheterodyne receiver system, 1890

Deaths

- Randolph Apperson Hearst, American newspaper publisher, son of William Randolph Hearst, father of Patty Hearst, 2000
- Joseph Barbera, American animator and cofounder of Hanna-Barbera, 2006

I pray for those who are overwhelmed by the Christmas season.

December 19

T he Lord detests lying lips, but he delights in those who tell the truth. *(Proverbs 12:22, NLT)*

Before you shut down for the holidays

We all look forward to taking time off over Christmas and New Year's. If your business is one that usually shuts down for the holidays, be sure someone will be monitoring your website and social media accounts while you're closed.

Hackers don't take Christmas off, and they can do a lot of damage in a minimal amount of time. Keep an eye on your online presence and be prepared to take immediate action if something is amiss.

Elon Musk's employee test

Elon Musk has a simple, three-pronged test for every employee. The person must be excellent, necessary, and trustworthy.

Excellent is defined as "extremely good; outstanding." In the business world, it means knowing the industry, having the necessary skills (and maintaining them) to do the job, taking responsibility, and, above all, being willing and able to do the work.

Necessary is defined as "absolutely needed, required." If a person or position isn't necessary, they shouldn't be part of the company.

Trustworthy is defined as "worthy of confidence, dependable." Certainly trustworthy is a part of excellence, but it's more. It's an essential virtue.

Elon Musk's standards are easy to apply and good for any organization.

> Grow your faith by turning an anxious thought into a positive prayer.

On this day in history

Notable events

In 1843, *A Christmas Carol* by Charles Dickens was first published in London; the first edition sold out by Christmas Eve and by the end of 1844 thirteen editions had been released.

In 1974, the Altair 8800 microcomputer went on sale in the U.S. as a do-it-yourself computer kit for $397.

Births

Henry Clay Frick, American industrialist, financier, and art patron, founder of H.C. Frick & Company coke manufacturing company, chairman of Carnegie Steel Company, known for strikebreaking and being a member of the South Fork Fishing and Hunting Club (blamed for causing the Johnstown flood), 1849

Roger Putnam, businessman, politician, and trustee of the Lowell Observatory who facilitated the search for Pluto, 1893

Peter Buck, American physicist, restaurateur, and philanthropist, cofounder of the Subway restaurant chain, 1930

Abigail Johnson, American billionaire businesswoman, president and CEO of Fidelity Investments, 1961

Deaths

Frederick Terman, American professor and academic administrator at Stanford University, credited with William Shockley as being the father of Silicon Valley, 1982

Thought for the day

"The best way to destroy an enemy is to make him a friend."

Abraham Lincoln

I pray for those who need healing.

Read: Proverbs, Chapter 19

December 20

If you need wisdom, ask our generous God, and he will give it to you. He will not rebuke you for asking. *(James 1:5, NLT)*

Types of toxic people to avoid

Gossips. People who routinely engage in idle talk or rumor, especially about the personal affairs of others, have a negative effect in workplaces and communities. Gossips often have reputations for being lazy and troublemakers. Make it a policy to avoid participating in gossip and disengage from people who do. Find things to talk about besides other people. Remember, people who gossip *with* you will gossip *about* you.

Liars. Lying is a complex social behavior with myriad motivations. The two types of lies are pro-social (well-meaning "white lies" designed to protect someone's feelings) and anti-social lies (an attempt to manipulate a situation in the liar's favor). If someone lies to you once, you may want to consider the circumstances and give them an opportunity to rebuild trust. If they lie regularly and often, avoid them or at least move them to a role that doesn't require you to rely on them for the truth.

Dream killers. These are the people who don't enjoy seeing others reach their goals and would rather sling arrows at yours than be supportive. They focus on the negatives, trying to drag you down. Replace dream killers with people who believe in and support you.

Energy vampires. These are the people who drain you and leave you feeling exhausted. It's okay to want to understand and help them, but it's more important to protect yourself by setting boundaries or avoiding them.

While we are commanded to love one another, it's okay to love some people from a distance.

Today we observe
Go Caroling Day

On this day in history

Notable events
In 1790, the first U.S. cotton mill (a mill with water-powered machinery for spinning, roving, and carding cotton) began operating on the banks of the Blackstone River in Pawtucket, Rhode Island.

In 2020, 3M announced it would stop making and using so-called "forever chemicals" (common materials linked to a range of health problems including cancer).

Births
Harvey S. Firestone, American manufacturer and founder of Firestone Tire and Rubber Company. 1868

Harvey Hubbell II, American inventor, entrepreneur, and industrialist best known for inventing the electrical plug and pull-chain light socket, 1857

Gordon Getty, American businessman and classical music composer, fourth child of oil tycoon J. Paul Getty, 1933

Deaths
William B. Ziff, Sr., American publisher and author, cofounder of Ziff Davis Inc., 1953

Roy O. Disney, American businessman and cofounder of The Walt Disney Company, 1971

W. Edwards Deming, American business theorist, industrial engineer, statistician, management consultant, and writer known as the father of the quality movement, 1993

Thought for the day

"When we strive to become better than we are, everything around us becomes better too."

Paulo Coelho

I pray for those who are mature in their faith.

Read:
Proverbs, Chapter 20

December 21

"See, I have set you this day over nations and over kingdoms, to pluck up and to break down, to destroy and to overthrow, to build and to plant."
(Jeremiah 1:10, ESV)

Cancel that sales meeting

Instead of holding sales meetings, hold sales training classes conducted by your salespeople.

Successful salespeople learn their craft and sharpen their skills through education. Letting individual members of your sales team participate as trainers allows them to share their knowledge at the same time that they're further developing their skills.

Some topics to cover in peer-to-peer sales training:
- Presentation skills.
- Prospecting techniques.
- Account penetration.
- Overcoming objections.
- Dealing with unusual situations.
- New product information.
- Pricing and estimating.
- Project management.
- Proper documentation and reporting according to company requirements.
- Goal setting and analysis.
- Using selling skills in non-selling situations.
- Time management and planning.

Keep the content positive—make it, "Here's what you can do," not "Don't do this." Be encouraging and supportive, and don't let any negativity creep into the process.

Be sure everyone has an equal chance to participate. One way is to put the dates of upcoming sessions on slips of paper in a container and let each salesperson draw a date to be the teacher. Or schedule alphabetically or by seniority—any way you prefer as long as it's fair, equitable, and doesn't show favoritism. Provide guidance on choosing a topic but let team members make the final decision on what they present.

On this day in history

Notable events

In 2012, the music video for "Gangnam Style," a song by the Korean rapper Psy, became the first YouTube video to reach one billion views.

Births

George W. Fuller, American sanitary engineer responsible for important innovations in water and wastewater treatment, 1868

Paul Winchell, American ventriloquist, comedian, actor, humanitarian, and inventor (artificial heart), 1922

Alex d'Arbeloff, Georgian-American entrepreneur, cofounder of Teradyne (manufacturer of automatic test equipment), 1927

Deaths

Barry Gray, American radio personality known as the father of talk radio, 1996

Ken Hendricks, American businessman and entrepreneur, who, along with his wife and business partner Diane Hendricks, grew a shingle supply company into a $2.6 billion fortune, 2007

Edgar Bronfman, Sr., Canadian-American businessman (president, treasurer and CEO of Seagram) and philanthropist, 2013

Thought for the day

"If you can't sleep, then get up and do something instead of lying there worrying. It's the worry that gets you, not the lack of sleep."

— Dale Carnegie

I pray for those who doubt their true worth.

Read:
Proverbs, Chapter 21

December 22

He will cover you with his feathers. He will shelter you with his wings. His faithful promises are your armor and protection. *(Psalm 91:4, NLT)*

Qualities that command respect

Respect isn't automatic; it must be earned. Think about the people you respect—they likely share these qualities:

They're polite and courteous to everyone—family members, coworkers, bosses and subordinates, people who serve them in various capacities, and strangers.

They show respect to others.

They're active listeners.

They're helpful and always looking for opportunities to lend a hand, whether it's something small like carrying a package for someone or large like jumping into a big project.

They don't make excuses; they own their actions and take responsibility for their mistakes.

They forgive; they don't hold onto anger or grudges.

They're humble and never arrogant.

They're loyal to people, organizations, and their values.

They're always growing as a person, willing to change and learn new things.

They're resilient and able to persist and bounce back in the face of adversity.

They're honest.

They're compassionate and able to recognize others' struggles.

They operate with integrity, always doing the right thing because it's the right thing.

They're kind and generous, sharing their time and resources with others even when there's no direct benefit to them.

They are grateful for the blessings they've enjoyed in life.

Read:
Proverbs, Chapter 22

Today we observe
Cookie Exchange Day
International Don't Text & Drive Day

On this day in history

Notable events

In 1882, the first string of electric lights decorating a Christmas tree was created by Edward H. Johnson, an associate of Thomas Edison.

In 1968, the first U.S. live telecast from a manned spacecraft in outer space was transmitted from *Apollo 8*.

Births

Connie Mack, American Baseball Hall of Fame catcher, manager, and team owner, 1862

Deaths

William Cooper, American merchant, land speculator and developer, founder of Cooperstown, New York, 1754

Wherever you go, leave a heart print.

Thought for the day

"You should never be surprised when someone treats you with respect, you should expect it."

Sarah Dessen

I pray for those who are afraid.

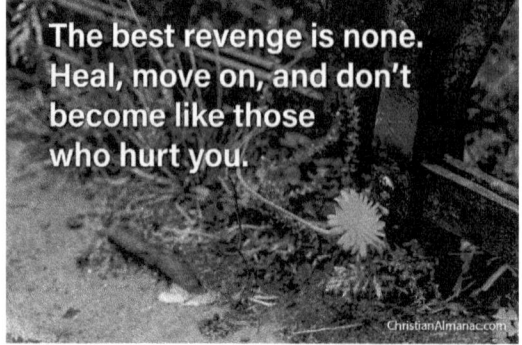

December 23

"The grass withers and the flowers fall, but the word of our God endures forever." *(Isaiah 40:8, NIV)*

The power of Christmas

Christmas is such a unique idea that most non-Christians accept it, and I think sometimes envy it. If Christmas is the anniversary of the appearance of the Lord of the Universe in the form of a helpless baby, it's quite a day. It's a startling idea, and the theologians, who sometimes love logic more than they love God, find it uncomfortable. But if God did do it, He had a tremendous insight.

People are afraid of God and standing in His very bright light. But everyone has seen babies and almost everyone likes them. So if God wanted to be loved as well as feared, He moved correctly here. And if He wanted to know people, as well as rule them, He moved correctly, because a baby growing up learns all there is to know about people.

If God wanted to be intimately a part of Man, He moved correctly. For the experience of birth and familyhood is our most intimate and precious experience.

So it comes beyond logic. It's what a bishop I used to know called a kind of divine insanity. It is either all falsehood or it is the truest thing in the world. It is the story of the great innocence of God the baby. God in the power of Man. And it is such a dramatic shot toward the heart, that if it is not true, for Christians nothing is true.

So even if you did not get your shopping all done, and you were swamped with the commercialism and frenzy, be at peace. And even if you are the deacon having to arrange the extra seating for all the Christmas Christians that you won't see until Easter, be at peace. The story stands.

It's all right that so many Christians are touched only once a year by this incomparable story. Because some final quiet Christmas morning, the touch will take.

The text of Harry Reasoner's Christmas Eve 1973 message on ABC News

On this day in history

Notable events

In 1913, President Woodrow Wilson signed the Owen-Glass Act, creating the Federal Reserve System.

In 1970, the North Tower of the World Trade Center opened; it was the tallest building in the world at the time.

Births

James Buchanan Duke, American tobacco and electric power industrialist, founder of the American Tobacco Company, 1856

Madam C. J. Walker, African-American entrepreneur, philanthropist, and activist, founder of Madam C. J. Walker Manufacturing Company, recorded as the first female self-made millionaire in America in the *Guinness Book of World Records*, 1867

Susan Lucci, American actress, television host, author, and entrepreneur, 1946

Following Jesus keeps life simple. Sometimes it's easy, sometimes it's hard, but it's always clear. Jesus focused on what mattered most—his ministry, praying, relationships, teaching, healing, serving, and resting—and taught his followers to do the same.

Thought for the day

"Act as if what you do makes a difference. It does."

William James

I pray for those pursuing a life well-lived.

Read:
Proverbs, Chapter 23

December 24

And because Joseph was a descendant of King David, he had to go to Bethlehem in Judea, David's ancient home. He traveled there from the village of Nazareth in Galilee. He took with him Mary, to whom he was engaged, who was now expecting a child. And while they were there, the time came for her baby to be born. She gave birth to her firstborn son. She wrapped him snugly in strips of cloth and laid him in a manger, because there was no lodging available for them. *(Luke 2:4-7, NLT)*

Joy to the World

Isaac Watts, 1719

Joy to the world, the Lord is come!
Let earth receive her King!
Let every heart prepare Him room,
and heav'n and nature sing,
and heav'n and nature sing,
and heav'n, and heav'n and nature sing.

Joy to the world, the Savior reigns!
Let men their songs employ,
while fields and floods, rocks, hills, and
  plains
repeat the sounding joy,
repeat the sounding joy,
repeat, repeat the sounding joy.

No more let sins and sorrows grow,
nor thorns infest the ground;
He comes to make His blessings flow
far as the curse is found,
far as the curse is found,
far as, far as the curse is found.

He rules the world with truth and grace,
and makes the nations prove
the glories of His righteousness
and wonders of His love,
and wonders of His love,
and wonders, wonders of His love.

I pray for parents and grandparents.

Grow your faith through giving generously.

Today we observe

Christmas Eve

On this day in history

Notable events

In 1851, a devastating fire at the Library of Congress in Washington, D.C. destroyed about two-thirds of its 55,000 volumes.

In 1893, Henry Ford completed his first successful gas motor; he and his wife tested the small one-cylinder engine in their kitchen.

Births

Joseph M. Juran, Romanian-born American engineer, management consultant, and author, advocate for quality and quality management, 1904

Howard Hughes, American business magnate, record-setting pilot, engineer, film producer, and philanthropist, 1905

Deaths

Johns Hopkins, American merchant, investor, and philanthropist, 1873

Norman Vincent Peale, American Protestant clergyman, author of *The Power of Positive Thinking*, 1993

Bill Bowerman, American track and field coach, co-founder of Nike, 1999

Roy Neuberger, American financier (cofounder of investment firm Neuberger Berman) and art patron, 2010

Thought for the day

"Riches do not consist in the possession of treasures, but in the use made of them."
Napoleon Bonaparte

Read:
Proverbs, Chapter 24

December 25

For to us a child is born, to us a son is given; and the government will be upon his shoulder, and his name will be called "Wonderful Counselor, Mighty God, Everlasting Father, Prince of Peace." *(Isaiah 9:6, RSV)*

Oh Come all Ye Faithful

John Fransic Wade c. 1740-1841
Trans. Frederick Oakeley, 1841

O come, all ye faithful, joyful and triumphant,
O come ye, O come ye to Bethlehem!
Come, and behold Him, born the King of angels!

Refrain:
O come, let us adore Him;
O come, let us adore Him;
O come, let us adore Him, Christ, the Lord!

God of God, Light of Light,
lo, He abhors not the virgin's womb;
very God, begotten not created; *[Refrain]*

Sing, choirs of angels; sing in exultation;
sing, all ye citizens of heav'n above!
Glory to God, all glory in the highest! *[Refrain]*

Yea, Lord, we greet Thee, born this happy morning;
Jesus, to Thee be all glory giv'n!
Word of the Father, now in flesh appearing! *[Refrain]*

Today we observe
Christmas

On this day in history

Notable events
In 1830, the Best Friend of Charleston became the first regularly scheduled steam locomotive passenger train in the U.S.
In 1968, the *Apollo 8* crew broadcast while orbiting the moon and read passages from the Bible to celebrate Christmas.
In 1990, the first successful trial run of the World Wide Web was completed.

Births
Clara Barton, American nurse, founder of the American Red Cross, 1821
Louis Chevrolet, Swiss-American race car driver, mechanic, inventor, and entrepreneur, cofounder of the Chevrolet Motor Car Company, 1878
Glenn McCarthy, American oil tycoon, prospector, and entrepreneur who owned many businesses in various sectors of the economy, 1907
Jimmy Buffett, American singer-songwriter, musician, author, and businessman, 1946

Deaths
Linus Yale, Jr., American mechanical engineer, manufacturer, and inventor (cofounder of Yale Lock Company), 1868

Trust God more than yourself

Do you find yourself saying, "As soon as I can do this [in the world], I'll be able to do that [in ministry]"?

What you're really saying is that you're not going to trust God until after you've achieved something based on your own ability. That's not faith.

God wants us to trust him, to take that first step even when we can't see beyond it. Have faith!

Thought for the day

"To forgive is to set a prisoner free and discover that the prisoner was you."
            Lewis B. Smedes

I am thankful for the birth of Jesus.

Read:
Proverbs, Chapter 25

December 26

For God so loved the world that he gave his one and only Son, that whoever believes in him shall not perish but have eternal life. For God did not send his Son into the world to condemn the world, but to save the world through him. *(John 3:16-17, NIV)*

It was in the Bible first

These common phrases and sayings have their origins in the Bible:

The blind leading the blind

When referring to people who don't know what they're doing and who are in charge of others who don't know what they're doing, we often say it's a case of the blind leading the blind, implying the potential for disastrous results. Jesus said of the Pharisees:

"Leave them; they are blind guides. If the blind lead the blind, both will fall into a pit." (Matthew 15:14, NIV)

Bite the dust

To say someone or something bites the dust is an irreverent way to say he or it has died or are in some other way finished. We often use the phrase with a degree of lightheartedness, but Solomon was serious when he wrote:

May the desert tribes bow before him and his enemies lick the dust. (Psalm 72:9, NIV)

By the skin of your teeth

The phrase "by the skin of your teeth" is usually used to describe a narrow escape from danger ("I missed being hit by the car by the skin of my teeth") or a barely achieved success ("I passed the exam by the skin of my teeth"). Job said it when he was enumerating his tribulations:

"...I have escaped only by the skin of my teeth." (Job 19:20, NIV)

Rise and shine

This popular way of telling someone to wake up and get out of bed has its roots in the Old Testament.

Arise, shine; for thy light is come, and the glory of the Lord is risen upon thee. (Isaiah 60:1. KJV)

Today we observe

Boxing Day

Kwanzaa

National Candy Cane Day

National Thank-You Note Day

Second Day of Christmas

On this day in history

Notable events

- In 1878, Wanamaker's in Philadelphia became the first U.S. department store to install electric lights.
- In 1967, a U.S. patent was granted to E. E. Headrick for a "flying saucer" that would be manufactured by Wham-O Manufacturing and called Frisbee.

Deaths

Harry S. Truman, 33rd U.S. President, 1972

Preston Tucker, American automobile and aviation entrepreneur who developed the innovative Tucker 48 sedan, 1956

Glenn McCarthy, American oil tycoon, prospector, and entrepreneur who owned many businesses in various sectors of the economy, 1988

Gerald R. Ford, 38th U.S. President, 2006

Thought for the day

"Ideas are like rabbits. You get a couple and learn how to handle them, and pretty soon you have a dozen."

John Steinbeck

I pray that I am always honest with God.

Read:
Proverbs, Chapter 26

December 27

He replied, "You of little faith, why are you so afraid?" Then he got up and rebuked the winds and the waves, and it was completely calm. *(Matthew 8:26, NIV)*

More common phrases and sayings that originated in the Bible:

Wash your hands of the matter

Don't want to have anything else to do with a situation? You might say you're washing your hands of the matter, as Pontius Pilate did.

When Pilate saw that he was getting nowhere, but that instead an uproar was starting, he took water and washed his hands in front of the crowd. "I am innocent of this man's blood," he said. "It is your responsibility!" (Matthew 27:24, NIV)

Drop in a bucket

Referring to something as a drop in a bucket means that it's insignificant, which is how Isaiah compared nations to God's greatness:

To the Lord, all nations are merely a drop in a bucket or dust on balance scales; all of the islands are but a handful of sand. (Isaiah 40:15, CEV)

Fly in the ointment

The fly in the ointment is a single thing or person that is a source of annoyance or that is spoiling an otherwise positive or enjoyable situation—a phrase that dates back to the Old Testament.

Dead flies make the perfumer's ointment give off a stench; so a little folly outweighs wisdom and honor. (Ecclesiastes 10:1, ESV)

Put words in one's mouth

When you tell someone what to say, or when you say that someone meant one thing when that person meant something else, you might be accused of putting words in that person's mouth. We've been doing that since Biblical days, as shown when Joab gave the wise woman these instructions:

"… Go to the king and speak to him as follows." And Joab put the words into her mouth. (2 Samuel 14:3, NRSV)

Today we observe

National Fruitcake Day

Third Day of Christmas

On this day in history

Notable events

In 1932, Radio City Music Hall opened in New York City.

Births

Cyrus S. Eaton, Canadian-American investment banker, businessman, and philanthropist, known for his occasionally ruthless financial manipulations and his passion for world peace, 1883

Deaths

Ewart Abner, American record company executive, part owner and general manager of Vee-Jay Records, president of Motown Records (1973-1975), 1997

Thought for the day

"Wishes cost nothing unless you want them to come true."

Frank Tyger

I pray that I will know Jesus better every day.

Read: Proverbs, Chapter 27

A house divided against itself cannot stand

Abraham Lincoln used this phrase in his nomination acceptance speech of 1858, but Jesus said it first.

Jesus knew their thoughts and said to them, "Every kingdom divided against itself will be ruined, and every city or household divided against itself will not stand." (Matthew 12:25, NIV)

December 28

And don't forget to do good and to share with those in need. These are the sacrifices that please God. *(Hebrews 13:16, NLT)*

Public speaking tips

Whether you're speaking to a small group of colleagues or at a major industry conference, these tips will help you make an effective presentation that will accomplish your purpose as it boosts your career and business.

Know the audience. Research the people you'll be speaking to so you can tailor your content and approach appropriately.

Start strong. Grab the audience's attention early. Ask a question, give a surprising statistic, tell a short but interesting story—do something that will get people listening and wanting to hear more.

Use effective pacing. Don't rush through your presentation. Give the audience time to think about what you've said. Well-placed pauses can be powerful.

Speak in familiar terms. Use language your audience will understand. Avoid using technical terms or jargon that might be unfamiliar to listeners.

Be yourself. Relax and be authentic. Let the audience get to know the real you.

Keep the audience involved. Get them to actively participate. Ask for a show of hands to questions, for people to shout out answers, or even to have an audience member join you on stage.

Expect the unexpected. Some presentations will go perfectly; others won't. Be prepared for your slide show file to corrupt, the internet connection to fail, or even to lose your train of thought. Stay calm, maintain a sense of humor, and adapt.

I pray for the members of our military and their families.

Read:
Proverbs, Chapter 28

Today we observe

National Chocolate Candy Day

Fourth Day of Christmas

On this day in history

Notable events

In 1732, Benjamin Franklin began publishing *Poor Richard's Almanack.*

In 1869, the Knights of Labor, a labor union of tailors in Philadelphia, held the first Labor Day ceremonies in American history.

In 1912, the first municipally owned streetcars became operational in San Francisco.

Births

Woodrow Wilson, 28th U.S. President, 1856

John von Neumann, Hungarian-American mathematician, physicist, computer scientist, engineer, and polymath, known for mathematical formulation of quantum mechanics, game theory, spectral theory, ergodic theory, and more, 1903

Stan Lee, American comic book writer, editor, publisher, and producer, 1922

John Fellows Akers, American businessman, president, CEO, and chairman of IBM, 1934

Philip Anschutz, American billionaire businessman and philanthropist who owns or controls companies in a variety of industries, 1939

Linus Torvalds, Finnish-American software engineer, creator and lead developer of the Linux kernel, 1969

Deaths

Florence Lawrence, Canadian-American stage performer, film actress, and inventor; she designed the first auto signaling arm, a predecessor of the modern turn signal, and the first mechanical brake signal, 1938

Thought for the day

"If you are really thankful, what do you do? You share."

W. Clement Stone

December 29

And Jesus grew in wisdom and stature, and in favor with God and man. *(Luke 2:52, NIV)*

If it worked before, can it work again?

We're always on the lookout for the latest concept, a different way of doing something, or a new approach to an old issue. While "because that's the way we've always done it" is a justifiably maligned phrase in management, sometimes the past is a great source of ideas for the future.

Study the history of your industry, your company, and your competitors. What worked spectacularly well in product development, marketing, or management? What are the legends from decades ago that people are still talking about? How can you use that as the foundation for something new today?

Don't just rinse and repeat. Give the idea a fresh twist. Update it to make it appropriate for today's audience and technology.

Just because something has already been done doesn't mean you can't do it again—but bigger and better this time.

When you pray for cake and God gives you flour, sugar, eggs, oil, a pan, and an oven, be willing to mix up the ingredients and bake it. God is generous and faithful, but you must do your part.

I pray to remember that God is always with me.

Read:
Proverbs, Chapter 29

Today we observe
Fifth Day of Christmas

On this day in history

Notable events

In 1851, the first U.S. YMCA opened in Boston, Massachusetts.

In 1952, the first hearing aid to use the newly-developed transistor (the Sonotone 1010 hybrid transistor hearing aid by Sonotone Corporation, Elmsford, New York) went on sale.

In 1997, Intel cut the price on its Pentium II processor from $401 to $268 to spur Pentium II PC sales.

Births

Charles Goodyear, American self-taught chemist and manufacturing engineer who developed vulcanized rubber (the Goodyear Tire and Rubber Company was named after but not founded by him), 1800

Asa Packer, American businessman, railroad construction pioneer, founder of Lehigh University, 1805

Andrew Johnson, 17th U.S. President, 1808

William S. Harley, American mechanical engineer and businessman, cofounder of the Harley-Davidson Motor Company, 1880

Robert C. Baker, American inventor of the chicken nugget and other poultry-related inventions, 1921

Wayne Huizenga, American businessman and sports team owner, 1937

Deaths

Sidney R. Garfield, American medical doctor and pioneer of health maintenance organizations; cofounder of Kaiser Permanente healthcare system, 1984

Andy Granatelli, American motorsports entrepreneur, author, CEO of STP, 2013

Thought for the day

"Change might not be fast and it isn't always easy. But with time and effort, almost any habit can be reshaped."

Charles Duhigg

December 30

Put on the full armor of God, so that you can take your stand against the devil's schemes. *(Ephesians 6:11, NIV)*

Boost your creative juices

Creativity is not something you either have or you don't. We are all creative beings. How creative we are (or aren't) depends on how purposeful we are in cultivating this skill. Try the following tips:

Repurpose. Find new uses for existing things. Try a new perspective.

Pay attention to trends. Let the creativity of others inspire you. When something resonates, see what you can do with it.

Look for multiple answers. Most problems have more than one solution. Come up with several before you decide what to do.

Play. Have some fun and see what you come up with when you're not being serious.

Dump traditions and habits that block creativity. Question the rules that inhibit individuality.

Establish habits that spark creativity. Come up with some new inspirational rituals that will condition your brain to be creative.

Identify and overcome limited resources. Don't have what you need? Think about what you have that will work.

Seek new experiences. Deliberately put yourself in new situations.

Keep learning. Creativity requires knowledge. Make time to study, explore and expand your information base.

Rest. Relax and let yourself have sufficient downtime; you'll often get great ideas when you're least expecting them.

Use the negativity of others as your motivation. If negative comments can lead to improvement, great. If not, don't let criticism discourage you.

Support the creativity of others. Encourage your friends and colleagues.

Welcome failure. Not every new idea is going to work. It takes courage to try, fail, and try again. Have courage!

Today we observe
Sixth Day of Christmas

On this day in history

Notable events

In 1854, the first U.S. oil company, the Pennsylvania Rock Oil Company, was incorporated by George H. Bissell; it was later renamed the Seneca Oil Company.

In 1930, the first photograph showing the curvature of the earth was exhibited in Cleveland, Ohio.

In 1953, the first color TVs were offered for sale. The RCA CT-100 and Admiral C1617A both had a 15-inch screen.

Births

Asa Griggs Candler, Sr., American business tycoon and politician who developed Coca-Cola into a major company after buying the recipe for $238.98, 1851

Simon Guggenheim, American businessman, politician, and philanthropist, 1867

Tiger Woods, American professional golfer, businessman, philanthropist, 1975

Kevin Systrom, American entrepreneur, computer programmer, and investor; cofounder of Instagram, 1983

Deaths

Arthur Davidson, American businessman, cofounder of the Harley-Davidson Motor Company, 1950

Thought for the day

"It is possible to fly without motors, but not without knowledge and skill."
— *Wilbur Wright*

I pray that I use my blessings to glorify God

Read:
Proverbs, Chapter 30

December 31

Don't be afraid, for I am with you! Don't be frightened, for I am your God! I strengthen you—yes, I help you—yes, I uphold you with my victorious right hand! *(Isaiah 41:10, NET)*

Keeping your resolutions

These tips will help you keep your resolutions, whether you're making them at New Year's or any other time during the year:

Begin with a grateful and positive attitude. So many resolutions are sparked by negatives—you feel as though you don't have enough of something (money, friends, time), there's something wrong with you physically, your relationships aren't going well, or whatever. Before you make a resolution, put it in the context of gratitude for what's good in your life.

Write it down. Like any goal, a resolution you write down is harder to ignore than one that just gets made in your head.

Be specific and define what you want by the end result. What will keeping your resolution accomplish?

Give your resolution the same priority as other essentials in your life. Don't let your resolution slide because you're tired or busy.

Make your resolutions realistic. Set the bar high—but not so high that you're doomed to fail.

Finally, reward yourself when you succeed. Celebrate even the smallest of accomplishments. And don't beat yourself up over your failures—forgive yourself and try again.

Thought for the day

"The secret of change is to focus all your energy, not on fighting the old, but on building the new."

Socrates

I pray for new perspectives.

Today we observe

New Year's Eve
First Night
Freedom's Eve / Watch Night
Make Up Your Mind Day
Seventh Day of Christmas

On this day in history

Notable events

- In 1938, the Drunkometer, the first successful machine for testing human blood alcohol content by breath analysis invented by Rolla Neil Harger, was put into use by police in Indianapolis, Indiana.
- In 1997, Microsoft acquired Hotmail.com for $500 million and integrated Hotmail into its MSN group of services.

Births

- Charles A. Coffin, American businessman, cofounder and first president of General Electric Company, 1844
- Joseph S. Cullinan, American oil industrialist, founder of The Texas Company, which would eventually be known as Texaco, Inc., 1860
- Elizabeth Arden, Canadian-American businesswoman, founder of the cosmetics empire now known as Elizabeth Arden, Inc., 1881
- Diane von Fürstenberg, Belgian-American fashion designer, entrepreneur, and philanthropist, 1946
- Donald Trump, Jr., American businessman, political activist, and author, 1977

Deaths

- John Bevins Moisant, American aviator, flight instructor, and businessman; cofounder of Moisant International Aviators, a flying circus, 1910
- Thomas J. Watson, Jr., American businessman (president of IBM, 1952-1971) and politician, 1993

Read:
Proverbs, Chapter 31

About the Creators of
Christian Business Almanac

Jacquelyn Lynn and Jerry D. Clement manage Tuscawilla Creative Services, LLC, a boutique publishing and consulting firm that God owns in Central Florida.

Jacquelyn is an inspirational author, business writer/ghostwriter, and publishing consultant. She has written and ghostwritten more than 45 books plus thousands of articles, blogs, ebooks, newsletters, white papers, and more.

Jerry is an award-winning photographer, videographer, and designer. His work includes business and fine art photography, book covers, stock and custom videos, and the design elements in books published by Tuscawilla Creative Services.

As a team, they write and produce their own books and assist their clients through all aspects of creating and publishing books and other materials.

God brought them together first as friends, then as husband and wife, and eventually as business partners. When God is first, everything else falls into place as it should be.

Learn more and connect with Jacquelyn Lynn and Jerry D. Clement at CreateTeachInspire.com.

Download all the memes featured in *Christian Business Almanac* here:

CreateTeachInspire.com/CBAmemes

Let us continue to support you with our Shareable Saturday messages. Receive a scripture and inspirational thought delivered to your inbox every Saturday morning.
Sign up at:

CreateTeachInspire.com/sscba

www.ingramcontent.com/pod-product-compliance
Lightning Source LLC
Chambersburg PA
CBHW081427070526
44586CB00020B/2510